ACCOUNTABILITY IN
RESTORATIVE JUSTICE

CLARENDON STUDIES IN CRIMINOLOGY

Published under the auspices of the Institute of Criminology,
University of Cambridge, the Mannheim Centre, London School
of Economics, and the Centre for Criminological Research, University
of Oxford.

GENERAL EDITOR: PER-OLOF WIKSTRÖM (*University of Cambridge*)

EDITORS: ALISON LIEBLING AND MANUEL EISNER
(*University of Cambridge*)

DAVID DOWNES, PAUL ROCK, AND JILL PEAY
(*London School of Economics*)

ROGER HOOD, LUCIA ZEDNER, AND RICHARD YOUNG
(*University of Oxford*)

Recent titles in this series:

Crime and Markets: Essays in Anti-criminology
Ruggiero

**Parliamentary Imprisonment in Northern Ireland:
Resistance, Management, and Release**
McEvoy

Repair or Revenge: Victims and Restorative Justice
Strang

**Policing World Society:
Historical Foundations of International Police Cooperation**
Deflem

**Investigating Murder:
Detective Work and the Police Response to Criminal Homicide**
Innes

Forthcoming title:

Bouncers: Violence and Governance in the Night-time Economy
Hobbs, Hadfield, Lister, and Winlow

Accountability in Restorative Justice

DECLAN ROCHE

OXFORD
UNIVERSITY PRESS

OXFORD

UNIVERSITY PRESS

Great Clarendon Street, Oxford OX2 6DP

Oxford University Press is a department of the University of Oxford.
It furthers the University's objective of excellence in research, scholarship,
and education by publishing worldwide in

Oxford New York

Auckland Bangkok Buenos Aires Cape Town Chennai
Dar es Salaam Delhi Hong Kong Istanbul Karachi Kolkata
Kuala Lumpur Madrid Melbourne Mexico City Mumbai Nairobi
São Paulo Shanghai Taipei Tokyo Toronto

Oxford is a registered trade mark of Oxford University Press
in the UK and in certain other countries

Published in the United States
by Oxford University Press Inc., New York

© Declan Roche 2003

The moral rights of the author have been asserted
Database right Oxford University Press (maker)

First published 2003

British Library Cataloguing in Publication Data

Data available

Library of Congress Cataloging in Publication Data

Data available

ISBN 0-19-925935-6

3 5 7 9 10 8 6 4 2

Typeset by Kolam Information Service Pvt Ltd
Printed in Great Britain
on acid-free paper by
T.J. International Ltd, Padstow, Cornwall

For my parents, Michael and Katherine

For my parents, Michael and Katherine

General Editor's Introduction

The *Clarendon Studies in Criminology* was inaugurated in 1994 under the auspices of the centres of criminology at the Universities of Cambridge and Oxford and the London School of Economics. It was the successor to *Cambridge Studies in Criminology*, founded by Sir Leon Radzinowicz and J.W.C. Turner almost sixty years ago.

Criminology is a field of study that covers everything from research into the causes of crime to the politics of the operations of the criminal justice system. Researchers in different social and behavioural sciences, criminal justice and law, all make important contributions to our understanding of the phenomena of crime. The *Clarendon Studies in Criminology* aim at reflecting this diversity by publishing high-quality theory and research monographs by established scholars as well as by young scholars of great promise from all different kinds of academic backgrounds.

The idea of restorative justice challenges the operations of the traditional criminal justice system. Its pros and cons have been intensely debated. It is therefore of the utmost importance that the problems and prospects of restorative justice are carefully scrutinized. In her recent book in the *Clarendon Studies in Criminology*, Heather Strang (2002) discussed the role of victims within restorative justice. In this book Declan Roche takes another look at restorative justice, this time from the perspective of accountability. The book includes in-depth discussion of theory and mechanisms relating to accountability in restorative justice, drawing upon the findings of several case studies of restorative justice in action in many different English-speaking countries, and argues for a rethinking of the relationship between formal and informal justice. The author maintains that 'restorative justice offers a possible route for restoring not just victims and offenders, but also for restoring citizens' faith in governments perceived to be unresponsive to their concerns'. In Roche's book *Accountability in Restorative Justice* we have yet another important contribution to the debate on the future of our criminal justice system.

Per-Olof H Wikström,
University of Cambridge &
Centre for Advanced Studies in the Social
and Behavioral Sciences, Stanford (2002–3)
December 2002

Preface

Judges do not have a monopoly on the administration of justice; it can also be administered by ordinary citizens in everyday locations such as homes, neighbourhoods, and workplaces. Outside the formal rules and procedures of a courtroom justice can be done quickly and cheaply, and can provide an opportunity for people to display valuable qualities such as compassion and understanding. But processes of informal justice lack what is generally recognized as accountability; all too often, freed from the requirement to justify their actions, people use informal processes to bully and berate others, typically those who are already emotionally vulnerable and economically and socially disadvantaged. This is a persistent problem of informal justice in all its different manifestations, and it must be asked whether it is also true of the latest and most topical form, restorative justice, or whether or not restorative justice programmes have devised new ways of holding decision-makers accountable.

I became interested in restorative justice in 1996 after reading an article describing New Zealand's innovative restorative justice approach to juvenile justice. My interest in accountability developed while working for a judge the following year: watching judges toil over judgments in anticipation of their scrutiny by the public, lawyers, the media and—most of all—appeal court judges, I learned how they were accountable for their decisions. A restorative justice conference in Canberra around the same time—at which an offender agreed to wear a T-shirt with 'I am a thief' written across his front— had many people (myself included) wondering whether the same could be said for decision-makers in restorative justice meetings. To answer that question I visited twenty-five restorative justice programmes in Australia, Canada, England, New Zealand, South Africa and the United States, and drew on my own experience of convening conferences for young offenders in Queanbeyan, New South Wales. What I discovered was an inchoate system of accountability which, if properly developed, may be flexible enough to let people show their best sides, yet tough enough to guard against their showing their worst. Here I describe and develop that system in which participants in meetings are deliberatively accountable to one another, and where the state plays a key role in assisting—rather than hindering—citizens' deliberations.

As any author knows, behind every book is a willing band of helpers, and this is certainly true in my case. At the end of the book there is a long list of restorative justice practitioners and other people who kindly agreed to give up their valuable time to be interviewed. Gale Burford in Vermont and Annie Roberts in Minneapolis/St Paul helped by introducing me to many of the American practitioners whom I later interviewed. I was fortunate to begin this book as a doctoral student in the Law Program at the Research School of Social Sciences at Australian National University in Canberra where John Braithwaite, the chair of my supervisory panel, and Peter Cane, the head of the Law Program, were both generous with their time, always being ready to discuss ideas, read drafts of my work, and offer insightful comments and morale-boosting encouragement. Many other ANU colleagues helped make my time there enjoyable and productive, including Tony Connolly, Christos Mantziaris, Leighton McDonald, Patrick Power, Rick Bigwood, Val Braithwaite, Simon Bronitt, Richard Mulgan, Jane Stapleton, Heather Strang, John Uhr, and Leslie Zines. In subsequently turning my thesis into a book I was helped greatly by the thoughtful comments and suggestions of Arie Freiberg, Christine Parker, Philip Stenning, and Lucia Zedner. Since arriving at the LSE in September 2001 I have been grateful for the helpfulness and kindness of many new colleagues, none more so than Damian Chalmers, Christos Hadjiemmanuil, Coretta Phillips, Mike Redmayne, and Gerry Simpson. Niki Lacey volunteered to read a complete draft and made many suggestions which improved the final version considerably. I also appreciated the assistance of David Downes and Paul Rock, general editors of the Clarendon Studies in Criminology, and of John Louth and Geraldine Mangley at Oxford University Press.

The encouragement of friends including Robin and Ross Gengos, Dan Mulino, Damien O'Donovan, Tim Scanlan, Mark Williams, and Richard Windeyer, my brother Brendan and his partner Natalie McEwan was more important than they probably realize. I am especially indebted to Robin and Ross who carefully read and edited a draft of the entire manuscript and then tolerated countless emails and phone calls as I tested out rewordings (and rewordings of rewordings!). Finally, my parents Mick and Katherine have given me a lifetime of support, and it is with love and gratitude that I dedicate this book to them.

Contents

List of Figures and Table   xv

1. The Rise and Risks of Restorative Justice   1

2. The Meaning of Restorative Justice and Accountability   25

3. Methods and Overview of Programmes   60

4. Deliberative Accountability in Restorative Meetings   79

5. Multiple Uses of Deliberative Accountability   123

6. Supporting Deliberative Accountability:
   Neglected Accountability Mechanisms   160

7. Supporting Deliberative Accountability:
   The Role of Traditional Accountability   188

8. Semi-Formal Justice: Combining Informal
   and Formal Justice   226

Appendices

A. Case Studies   240

B. Observations   280

C. Interviewees   281

References   287

Index   309

Lists of Figures and Table

Table 3.1   Overview of programmes   70

Figure 6.1   Pyramid showing modes of accountability
for outcome compliance   176

Figure 7.1   Pyramid showing access to justice options   222

1

The Rise and Risks of Restorative Justice

In the summer of 2002 hundreds of fierce bushfires raged for weeks across New South Wales, Australia, forcing the evacuation of thousands of people, destroying over one hundred homes, and burning out huge expanses of bush land. When a number of children caught lighting fires were referred to restorative justice conferences, the New South Wales Premier Bob Carr proclaimed on national television: 'I think sending them to a juvenile prison is in some respects too good for them. What is better is to rub their noses in the ashes they've caused, by making them clean up the mess, work with the victims and go into a burns ward and talk to people who've suffered from fire' (ABC 2002). A few years earlier in Canberra, Australia, a restorative justice conference was convened for a 12-year-old boy caught shoplifting, who agreed to the proposal by his mother and the store manager that he should wear outside the shop a T-shirt emblazoned with the words 'I am a thief' (Braithwaite 2001: 160). Elsewhere, in Milwaukee, USA, a restorative justice programme was inundated with community volunteers when flyers were distributed with the heading 'It's payback time!' (Walsh 2000).

For all its promise of promoting healing and harmony, restorative justice can deliver a justice as cruel and vengeful as any. In just a few years, restorative justice has breathed new life into the age-old concept of informal justice, and in so doing, has provided both a rallying slogan and a theoretical basis for informal justice practices in a number of countries around the world. While most of the activity has occurred within the criminal justice field, where the restorative justice movement has become the most concerted and significant attempt to informalize modern criminal justice systems, the movement has spread beyond this field, influencing the treatment of bullying in schools and the handling of child welfare cases (Burford and Pennell 1994).

The best known element and centrepiece of restorative justice is the meeting, which brings together those people affected by a particular offence to decide on a consensual basis how to deal with the aftermath of that offence. As well as the offender and the victim (when there is one, and he or she accepts an invitation to attend), such meetings may also be extended to involve family and friends, community volunteers and various professionals such as judges, police, teachers and social workers. Meetings give to victims the opportunity to express in their own words the harm they have suffered, and to offenders the opportunity to explain their actions and begin to make amends, and perhaps assuage their feelings of guilt.

Advocates of restorative justice claim that such meetings serve as a forum which naturally promotes 'repair, reconciliation and reassurance' (Zehr 1990: 181). Meetings break down preconceived and fixed notions: victims discover that offenders are almost certainly less fearsome than they had imagined; and, brought face-to-face with their victims, offenders can no longer avoid responsibility by denying to themselves the harm they have caused.[1] In meetings, victims' and offenders' supporters play a key role, with victims' supporters helping to articulate the harm a victim has suffered, and those of the offender helping to provide a context for an offender's actions. In explaining the dynamics of a meeting, advocates often draw analogies with the way conflicts are resolved in a loving family, or a small town, or in ancient forms of indigenous justice where people strive to repair and maintain the relationships in which they are enmeshed, in all of which condemnation is directed at the sin and not the sinner.

Meetings do indeed provide an opportunity for ordinary people to resolve conflict in ways that display some of the best human qualities: the ability to empathize, to reconcile, to apologize and to forgive. The problem, however, is that the very informality which allows people to show their best side provides them with an opportunity to show their worst. Just as people can empathize, reconcile, repair, reintegrate, and forgive, so too can they scold and stigmatize, hector, and humiliate, dominate and demoralize. As E. P. Thompson (1988: 530) observed, 'Because law belongs to people, and is not alienated, or delegated, it is not thereby made necessarily more

---

[1] On the ways in which offenders neutralize responsibility see Sykes and Matza (1957).

"nice" and tolerant, more cosy and folksy. It is only as nice and as tolerant as the prejudices and norms of the folk allow.' Restorative justice can just as easily provide an opportunity for people to indulge their impulses for highly punitive and stigmatizing treatment. The rhetoric of restorative justice may be reconciliatory, but the reality can be pure vengeance.

Unfortunately, however, many restorative justice proponents take it for granted that restorative justice meetings will always bring out people's better selves, and that victims' anger and offenders' indifference will magically give way to compassion and empathy. It appears that proponents confuse their aspirations about the way people ought to respond to conflict with reality (Allen 1999). There is a grave risk in designing a system of justice around idealistic aspirations: American theologian Reinhold Neibuhr (1967) famously warned that love, when substituted for justice, may become 'an accomplice of tyranny', and scant attention has been paid to the tyranny which may emerge in restorative justice programmes. Not enough thought has been given to ways of closing the gap between what we hope people will do to each other and what they actually do, the gap between the warm and fuzzy rhetoric of restorative justice on the one hand and its sometimes ugly practice on the other. Accountability is vital to narrowing the gap between promise and performance in restorative justice.

Accountability is essential, for the simplest of reasons: it is one of the most important checks on the exercise of power. Many familiar principles and practices—such as the practice of democratic elections, the doctrine of ministerial responsibility, the principle of open justice, the practice of auditing—are based on the important supposition that decision-makers are less likely to abuse their discretion when they know that at some stage they will have to explain and justify their decisions. This need to ensure that decision-makers are accountable has become one of society's central preoccupations (Stenning 1995: 3). One of the reasons that many people are uneasy about the rise of restorative justice is the perception that such programmes lack the sort of public accountability we expect from criminal justice institutions, even if we do not always receive it.

The more widespread restorative justice programmes become, the more pressing it becomes to consider whether they contain any public accountability, and if not, what needs to be done to ensure it. This pressing concern is the subject of this book.

To answer questions about the existence, nature, and function of accountability in restorative justice, this study considers twenty-five programmes in six countries. What will emerge is that in many programmes there is already in place a number of overlapping modes of accountability. Those critics of restorative justice whose definitions refer only to the formal modes, neglect the informal but no less central modes of accountability already existing, including those built into deliberations between offenders, victims, and their supporters. This deliberative accountability provides a vital and inclusive structure which works to check decision-makers, without however extinguishing those feelings of trust and goodwill which motivate them to do the right thing. However, problems illustrated by the T-shirt shaming episode clearly point to the fact that existing informal deliberative accounting mechanisms are currently inadequate.

In a number of programmes there also exist more formal, traditional modes of accountability, such as systems for reviewing agreements reached in meetings. Their existence supplements, rather than supplants, informal accountability. Both judges and restorative justice administrators review agreements reached in meetings, the main difference being that when a restorative justice practitioner alters an agreement it is invariably to make its terms less onerous, whereas when judges intervene it is to increase the severity of outcomes.

Judges have an important role to play in monitoring restorative justice programmes, but should approach this role in a new way. If restorative justice is to achieve its stated goals of empowering citizens and promoting reparation and reintegration, offenders should be entitled to pay more compensation or do more work than a judge would otherwise order, and victims should be allowed to decline compensation if they wish, or otherwise accept less than they would have received had the case gone to court. An agreement's ultimate acceptability should not turn on its severity or consistency with other agreements and sentences, but on the quality of the decision-making process. Because restorative justice is premised upon deliberations between those affected by a crime, those reviewing the procedures should satisfy themselves that meetings honour this ideal, that people invited to a restorative justice meeting are able to participate effectively, and that their deliberations reflect the range of affected interests. Although agreements under this approach need not conform to traditional sentencing principles such as consistency and proportionality, they must comply not just with upper limits based on human rights but with lower ones based on public safety. When a judge finds that an agreement breaches these limits or else is the product of a faulty decision-making process, that agreement should be quashed and participants invited to make the decision afresh, perhaps with some input from the judge. Only when this invitation is declined would a judge be entitled to substitute his or her own decision for that of the restorative justice meeting.

The rise of restorative justice, and the emergence of informal modes of accountability, has the potential to broaden and deepen our understanding both of accountability and deliberative democracy. Restorative justice encourages us to see accountability in less rigid, formal terms than it is often seen. The process of giving and scrutinizing accounts need not wait to take place until after a decision has been made—as is often assumed in the accountability literature—but can also inhere in the decision-making process, when that process is a deliberative one. Findings here build on research in other fields which suggest the emergence of new forms of accountability in the regulatory state.[2]

One of the most significant recent trends in political science is a wave of support for deliberative theories of democracy (Dryzek 2000). Deliberative democrats argue decisions affecting citizens should not be decided just by the aggregation of votes, but through a process of deliberation, discussion, and debate. However, much of the study of deliberative practices by political scientists has been confined to processes such as citizens' juries and deliberative polls, ad-hoc processes used to make non-binding recommendations. The perennial problems of 'time, numbers and distance' are thought to be an almost insurmountable impediment to establishing small-scale deliberative democratic practices on a more permanent footing. The novelty of restorative justice, from a political science perspective, is the creation of a deliberative democratic process to make enforceable sentencing agreements.

[2] Colin Scott (2000: 60) argues that 'Close observation of the structures of accountability in the regulatory state suggests that the public lawyer's concerns, premised upon an over-formal conception of accountability, if not unfounded are then neglectful of the complex webs of extended accountability which spring up in practice'.

Before going any further, however, a little more should be said about the rise of restorative justice, and the aspirations and anxieties surroundings its growth.

The rise of restorative justice

Criminologists have described the 'bewildering' and often 'contradictory' range of recent developments in the field of criminal justice.[3] Developments such as mandatory sentencing and zero-tolerance policing are the most conspicuous of these, but not far behind them in prominence is the rise of restorative justice. During the 1990s restorative justice became a unifying banner 'sweeping up' a number of informal traditions of justice and capturing the imagination of many of those interested in reforming the criminal justice system. While it can take many forms, it is those processes that bring together victims, offenders, and their communities that have attracted most attention. Programmes using such meetings have been established across the world, from remote Aboriginal communities in Australia to inner city neighbourhoods in the largest American cities. It is difficult to estimate the number of restorative justice programmes worldwide, partly because there is disagreement over the definition of restorative justice (everything from chain gangs to memorials honouring victims of violence have been described as restorative justice!), and partly because there are so many small programmes which have not been properly documented or evaluated. As a rough guide, recent estimates from various countries and regions give some indication of growth in the area. In the United States it is estimated that there are around 770 restorative justice programmes for juvenile offenders (Schiff, Bazemore *et al.* 2001), in Europe in excess of 500 programmes (Umbreit 1999), and in Canada more than 400 (Braithwaite 2001). Well-established programmes also operate in countries such as New Zealand and Australia, and a long and growing list of other countries are now also establishing them, including Argentina, Papua New Guinea, Singapore, and South Africa.

The growth of restorative justice is also manifest in other ways. In a number of countries, parliaments have adopted legislation acknowledging and regulating restorative justice, and appeal courts in Canada, the United States, and New Zealand have delivered deci-

---

[3] See, for example, Lucia Zedner (2002) and David Garland (2001).

sions addressing the concept. Lord Justice Auld's recent review of English and Welsh criminal courts recommended the 'development and implementation of a national strategy to ensure consistent, appropriate and effective use of restorative justice techniques across England and Wales' (Auld 2001: Ch. 9, paras. 58–69). In 2001 a United Nations Expert Group developed a set of basic principles on the use of restorative justice in criminal matters which the United Nations Economic and Social Council recommends countries use in developing their own restorative justice programmes (Van Ness 2002). One of the prominent features of restorative justice is its ability to command political support from a wide range of political camps.[4]

It is this sort of growth and support which leads John Braithwaite (1996), one of the leading restorative justice scholars, to label restorative justice a 'profoundly influential social movement'. There is a difference, however, between restorative talk and action, especially when that talk comes up against the inertia of a highly punitive criminal justice system such as that which imprisons 2 million people in the United States alone (Walmsley 2002). David Garland (2001: 169), while noting the 'remarkable upsurge of interest' in restorative justice on the part of academics, reformers, and government ministers, says that 'at present these restorative justice initiatives play only a tiny role at the shallow end' of a criminal justice system characterized by its punitive, exclusionary, and retributive responses to crime.[5] This note of caution is important for at least two reasons: first, it reminds us to avoid exaggerating the impact of restorative justice; secondly, and perhaps more pertinently, it reinforces the need for safeguards such as accountability to ensure that restorative justice is not swept away by the punitive tide it attempts to swim against.

The appeal of restorative justice

Restorative justice owes part of its popularity to the widely acknowledged shortcomings of the modern criminal justice system, a defining characteristic of which is the marginal role played by

[4] The same is true for the ADR movement in civil law, with Cyril Glasser and Simon Roberts (1993: 452) remarking that 'ADR enjoys the support of almost everyone from conservative fundamentalists to liberal utopian reformers and the modern left'.

[5] For a different view, see Lucia Zedner's (2002) review of David Garland's most recent book.

those people most immediately affected by a crime. As Doreen McBarnet (1988: 300) puts it, in relation to victims: 'The state is not just the arbiter in a trial between victims and offender, the state is the victim... If victims feel that nobody cares about their suffering, it is in part because institutionally nobody does.' On those occasions where victims are called upon as witnesses, they are expected to provide a 'calm, deadpan recitation of "facts"', in a way that is unlikely to 'lead victims to believe that they have been able to express their suffering and find understanding and sympathy for their experiences' (Llewellyn and Howse 1999: 364). Offenders fare only slightly better: they are at least present in the courtroom and at some point are usually given the opportunity to speak. However, in many senses, they are also excluded, with the courtroom's rules, norms, and indeed its very architecture—with an offender isolated in the dock—conspiring to silence them (Rock 1993).

Modern criminal justice processes have not gone without reform. In a number of countries, governments now fund victim support services (which keep victims notified of the progress of their case). Moreover, in some jurisdictions victims are allowed to submit victim impact statements to court before a sentencing judge makes his decision.[6] Again, in some jurisdictions courtroom procedures have been informalized to make them less threatening to offenders. Such reforms, however, only tinker with the existing system. They do not fundamentally alter the balance of power in the criminal justice process. Victims and offenders remain observers—albeit better-informed ones—in a process run by professionals.[7] Restorative justice—in the form of meetings between victims, offenders, and their communities—constitutes a much more fundamental reform of the

---

[6] For an overview of developments in relation to victims in the criminal justice system see Lucia Zedner (2002).

[7] Practice directions on the use of victim impact statements recently issued by Lord Woolf (2001), the Lord Chief Justice of England and Wales, make the point well. A victim's statement can be taken into account—'so far as the court considered it appropriate'—in determining the consequences of a crime, but the victim's views as to the appropriate sentence are not relevant, and 'if despite the advice, opinions as to sentence were included in a statement, the court should pay no attention to them'. Indeed, it could be argued that receiving victim impact statements and then disregarding them in this way actually make things worse for victims, by raising and then dashing their hopes that their views will be considered and taken into account. Such a practice may only increase a victim's feelings of helplessness and powerlessness.

criminal justice system.[8] Restorative justice turns those traditional observers of the criminal justice system—victims, offenders, and their families and friends—into participants. In Nils Christie's (1977) terms, it returns conflicts to their rightful owners—the ordinary people most affected by them; victims and offenders are given the responsibility of deciding how to respond to the aftermath of an offence. In a meeting (called a conference, circle, mediation, reparative board, or panel) convened by a third party (called a convenor, circle keeper, or mediator) victims, offenders, and their respective supporters meet face-to-face, to discuss the circumstances, causes, consequences, and responses to crimes.

Virtually all such meetings require an offender to make an admission beforehand, and then begin with the convenor asking the offender to tell the other participants what it was he or she did, and then reflect on the consequences for the victims and his or her family. Victims are then given the opportunity to speak; to seek answers to their questions: 'Why did you want to steal?' 'Why did you choose to mug me?' 'What were you thinking?' 'Are you going to attack me again?', as well as to describe—in their own terms—the impact of an offender's actions.

This communicative encounter is designed to achieve a number of things. Through the recognition they receive from the offender and other participants, victims' situations may be improved. When an offender expresses remorse for his or her actions, and apologizes, this can help to ease a victim's suffering. In describing the consequences of a sequence of apology and forgiveness, writers are at their most effusive and unrestrained, some even describing the process in terms of the supernatural. Nicholas Tavuchis (1991: 6) refers to 'the almost miraculous qualities of a satisfying apology', while Heather Strang (2001: 186) says that 'the magic of apology is that, while it cannot undo the past, somehow this is precisely what is achieved'. Slightly more practically, a meeting allows the victim to also seek recompense from the offender. In addition to the apology, this can range from financial compensation to a promise to refrain from the

---

[8] For a different view, namely that informal justice is more of the same, see the critical literature on informal justice (e.g. Abel 1982; Cohen 1984; Pavlich 1996). George Pavlich (1996: 729), for example, argues that 'so long as community mediation is enlisted in the service of individual dispute settlement, the self-identities it tries to fashion are likely to perpetuate—rather than eradicate—the liberal, governmental power formations that nurture particular conflicts in the first place'.

offending behaviour in the future, or else to commit to performing some tasks for the victim or the community. Victims can also begin to see the offender as a person rather than just a criminal, gaining an understanding of the circumstances that can help explain—if not excuse—his or her actions. Offenders, for their part, may begin to better understand the harm that crime can cause. Listening to victims' stories, offenders begin to realize that the material or financial loss suffered by victims is often incidental compared with the emotional and psychological damage inflicted by crime. In the course of meetings offenders also discover the ripple effect crime can trigger, when the harmful consequences of their actions spread from the immediate victims to their partners and children, their friends and their neighbours as well as on to offenders' own families and supporters. They are offered the opportunity to express remorse, and an opportunity to discharge the shame they feel. John Braithwaite (1989) argues that the key to preventing reoffending is reintegrative shaming, that is, shaming of an offender's actions accompanied by expressions of support and validation for that person. Restorative justice meetings offer a forum in which a range of people—including, crucially, those whose opinion an offender values—can express both their disappointment and continued faith in an offender.[9]

Evaluations of various restorative justice programmes in Australia, Canada, England, New Zealand, and the United States provide

---

[9] The mention of reintegrative shaming—which draws on, and revises, labelling theory (Braithwaite 1989: 16–21)—might be a suitable moment to discuss my own use of labels. Throughout the book I refer to victims and offenders. In a number of respects these labels are inappropriate in this context. 'Offender' is inappropriate because the label usually refers to people who have been found guilty of committing a criminal offence, whereas many restorative justice programmes operate without an offender going to trial (Johnstone 2002: 31). It is also unfortunate because it threatens to define people by their actions, a person's deviancy becomes his or her master status. This is particularly inapt in the context of restorative justice, which seeks to put a person's actions into context. From a similar viewpoint the label 'victim' is unhelpful. In many contexts—especially that of domestic violence—people object to the label 'victim' with its downtrodden and helpless connotations, and prefer the label 'survivor'. 'Offender' (and to a lesser extent 'victim') also represent and reinforce the law's tendency to oversimplify the causes of crime, where fault is attributed to an individual on an all-or-nothing basis. The role of other individuals or the underlying social and economic conditions are not considered. Notwithstanding these shortcomings, I have chosen to use the expressions 'victim' and 'offender' throughout, purely on the basis of simplicity and conciseness.

evidence to support these claims.[10] A large majority of victims and offenders record high levels of satisfaction with restorative justice meetings, usually significantly higher than the satisfaction of victims and offenders processed through a court. Research findings also show that victims leave restorative justice meetings fearing revictimization less than do those victims whose cases are processed by a court,[11] and that when an offender makes an agreement in a restorative justice meeting (for instance to pay compensation or perform community service) he or she is much more likely to honour that agreement than offenders subject to court orders. Other evaluations also show that restorative justice programmes can reduce re-offending rates for some types of crime, notably those where there is a direct victim who has suffered serious harm.[12] These results must be treated with some caution, however, as most of them suffer from significant selection bias. Most studies evaluate only the experience of offenders (and victims) whom police or other gatekeepers consider suitable for a restorative justice programme and who agree to co-operate: few evaluations randomly assign offenders to restorative justice programmes.[13]

To many proponents, however, this sort of overview takes second place to the testimony of those who witness actual restorative justice meetings, either as observers or as participants. Advocates tell moving stories about meetings in which victims and offenders show amazing capacities to change. The vengeful victim becomes forgiving, while the hardened offender becomes remorseful, promising to

---

[10] For a recent meta-evaluation of separate restorative justice evaluations in a number of countries see Latimer *et al.* (2001).

[11] See results from the *Reintegrative Shaming Experiments (RISE)* in Canberra, Australia, which involved a large-scale comparison between court and restorative justice conferences, with offenders randomly assigned between each (Strang *et al.* 1999: Tables 7.15–7.16).

[12] This was the finding of the RISE research. When conferences were tested for re-offending they produced mixed results. Conferences for shop theft had no effect. Conferences for drink-driving offences led to a slight increase in reoffending rates, but conferences for violent offences committed by young people had a substantial effect on re-offending, reducing re-offending by 38% (Sherman *et al.* 2000).

[13] The exceptions include the evaluation of conferencing in Bethlehem, PA (McCold and Wachtel 1998) (although see John Braithwaite's (2001: 56) discussion of the assignment problems in this programme), the Indianapolis Restorative Justice Experiment (McGarrell *et al.* 2000), and the RISE diversionary conferencing experiment in Canberra (Sherman *et al.* 1997).

make amends and never reoffend. The most popular stories are those where there is some dramatic and unmistakable manifestation of personal transformation, for example, where the victim and offender embrace, or the victim offers the offender a job.

Limitations of restorative justice

Far fewer stories are told about the cases where restorative justice meetings achieve much more modest success. Yet, based on my experience of observing and convening meetings, there are many more of these.[14] Perhaps because they are less striking and more equivocal, these stories do not make it into practitioners' newsletters, reports, and speeches about restorative justice. Fewer still are told about those meetings where something goes badly wrong. Some cases, such as the agreement requiring the offender to wear an 'I am a thief' T-shirt, do come to light, but only because the agreement involves some activity that takes place in public.

In the absence of many of these stories, considering restorative justice in its historical context can help sensitize us to its risks. Restorative justice scholars often claim that its growth represents the revival of a long tradition which has been suppressed by the modern nation state. John Braithwaite (2001: 5), for example, claims that 'Restorative justice has been the dominant model of criminal justice throughout most of human history for perhaps all the world's peoples'. The sub-text—and sometimes the plain text— of such claims is that the important elements of restorative justice— in particular, the participation of victims, offenders, and their local communities, and the search for ways to right wrongs—are in fact part of an original, authentic, and natural approach to justice. Retributive justice, on the other hand, is a modern-day, state-led phenomenon.

In one sense the sentiments behind such statements can be understood. If we look beyond the criminal justice system, 'negotiation

---

[14] One conference I convened illustrates this point well. The case concerned a car theft by a young offender. The offender spoke about his actions, the victims described the impact of the theft of their only car, and all participants expressed their disappointment at the offender's action but also their faith in him for the future. The offender showed remorse, and then in crescendo, the victim expressed his forgiveness. By way of conclusion the victim asked the offender 'So, do you think you'll ever steal a car again?' 'Well', he said, 'I'm definitely not going to steal *your* car again.'

represents the primary, universal route to decision and action in the social world' (Palmer and Roberts 1998: 63):

The core features of negotiation are to be found in widely different contexts, ranging from the unselfconscious routines of everyday life to the formalized, set-piece exchanges of an international conference. These fundamental features remain constant whether the issue is uncontentious or a focus of extreme conflict. Thus, negotiation as a mode of decision-making spans everyday interaction and the more complex, stressful exchanges encountered in the context of disagreement and dispute.

In addition, albeit to a limited extent, claims about the historical pedigree of restorative justice are supported by both historians and anthropologists, who have uncovered numerous traditions of justice where affected parties and their communities meet to find ways to repair the harm caused by conflict. In this respect, the emergence of restorative justice has continuities with a long and widespread tradition of negotiated, participatory, and even compassionate, justice. However, it is absurd to suggest that restorative justice, or any other form of justice for that matter, is a 'natural' response to conflict. Systems of justice, like any social phenomenon, are the product of a wide range of economic, institutional, historical, political, and cultural factors. And reparative, negotiated traditions of informal justice are only one edge of a double-edged sword, the other of which is, one where the poor who cannot access the formal justice of the wealthy are forced to face swift, oppressive, humiliating, brutal, and often barbarous justice. However, this side of informal justice is almost completely neglected in the restorative justice literature, which endlessly valorizes, and rhapsodizes about, all forms of informal justice. But it is worth remembering some of the risks posed by informal justice, as the history of punishment practices in places without a properly functioning state system of justice illuminates many of the risks inherent in restorative justice.

In their emphasis on the significant role played by victims in restorative justice, proponents draw a parallel with the significant responsibility accorded to victims before the modern nation state 'stole' their conflicts. While it is true that prior to the establishment of state prosecutors victims played a much more significant role in the criminal justice system, such accounts often gloss over the intolerable burden this system imposed on many victims. They were not just responsible for prosecuting, they had to gather witnesses, attend preliminary examinations in front of magistrates and pay the expenses of the constables and the various officers of the courts. It was this burden which 'was one of the major reasons for the formation of police forces and the establishment of an official prosecuting system' (Shapland *et al.* 1985: 174).[15] Restorative justice risks heaping new burdens on victims, who may be pressured into attending meetings. This pressure is itself a considerable burden, especially when many victims are victimized by more than one person, and often more than once. As one victim put it 'it's like being hit by a car and having to get out and help the other driver when all you were doing was minding your own business' (Brown 1994: 281). Even practitioners in programmes only a few years old find themselves asking victims to attend meetings who have already attended other meetings, sometimes even for the same offender (in relation to an earlier, separate crime). For many victims the responsibility of having a say in determining an offender's sanction is a most unwelcome one.[16]

From an offender's perspective, the history of informal justice is also far from happy. While anthropologists observe the reconciliatory nature of some informal justice practices, they also find that the aim of reconciliation is not pursued consistently in all conflicts. For example, in many forms of indigenous law, reconciliation was sought primarily where parties shared a continuing, valuable relationship (e.g. through marriage, kinship, or economic exchange), but where no such relationship existed, parties were much more likely to have recourse to violent self-help (Palmer and Roberts 1998: 15–21). Even in cases where parties sought to defuse hostilities, their attempts to do so could often take a form that we may not recognize as reparative (for example, the banishment or spearing of an offender (Reynolds 1995: 72, Finnane 2001)).

Early village life is another popular wellspring of rhetorical images for advocates of restorative justice. This nostalgia is misplaced, however, as early village life was often the scene of miserable and severe prosecution of those considered 'deviant'. According to Lawrence Stone (1977: 115), early modern village life in England was a place 'filled with malice and hatred, its only unifying bond

---

[15] Further see Bruce Lenman and Geoffrey Parker (Lenman and Parker 1980: 19) and David Philips (1980: 179).
[16] This point is taken up by Richard Delgado (2000: 762).

being the occasional episode of mass hysteria, which temporarily bound together the majority in order to harry and persecute the local witch'. It is also difficult to discern the reparative elements in the charivari or 'rough music', the ritualised forms of mockery, harassment and humiliation that were popular throughout Europe from the end of the seventeenth century to the nineteenth century (Thompson 1988). Directed at individuals who offended against community norms, these informal sanctions could last for days, and took a variety of forms. Community members would make a commotion outside the front of a wrongdoer's home, playing music or games or parading, and sometimes burning an effigy of the person. Sometimes individuals were forced to undergo humiliating rituals such as riding an ass backwards around town, or being pelted with mud or excrement. The authorities' attitude was one of toleration, 'partly because they saw its advantages and partly because they were too weak to suppress it' (Posner 2000: 76). But perhaps the single most haunting reminder of the dangers of unchecked community justice is the practice of lynching that was part of the American tradition of vigilantism, a tradition which emerged in colonial times and survived, in parts of the South, into the first half of the twentieth century (Brundage 1993; Dray 2002; Walker 1980).

At first glance, these traditions seem a world away from modern restorative justice programmes but then when we think of calls to participate in 'payback' or to 'rub an offender's nose in it' (even metaphorically), the continuities begin to emerge.[17] 'I am a thief' T-shirts have an obvious historical precedent in the shaming practices of earlier centuries—from branding through to scarlet letters—but more typical restorative outcomes also raise doubts about whether the impulses which sustained 'rough music' have completely disappeared. Even an apology—the most common outcome in a restorative meeting—can quickly become a form of

---

[17] Despite the punitive rhetoric of the New South Wales Premier's announcements mentioned at the start of this book, many voters remained concerned that restorative justice was too soft. One letter to the editor of the *Sydney Morning Herald* (8 January 2002) read: 'So, juvenile arsonists will not be sent to prison but will only have to engage in conferencing with their victims. Tea and biscuits, anyone? Let the punishment fit the crime. They should be made to not only hear about the loss and pain they have inflicted but to experience it, too. All their possessions: CDs, computer games, toys, skateboards, clothes, photo albums—right down to the posters on their bedroom walls—should be piled up in the street in front of their house and covered in petrol. They should then be given a box of matches and forced to light the bonfire.'

self-abasement, especially when it is prolonged and public.[18] Indeed, the 'democratic' rhetoric used by vigilante groups in America, such as the South Carolina Regulator Movement, to defend the swift and brutal form of community justice they administered (Walker 1980: 123), suggests that we should not necessarily be reassured by the democratic rhetoric surrounding restorative justice.

Restorative justice programmes also retain elements of the idea of justice as a form of popular theatre, especially those in the United States where meetings can last for many hours and involve over one hundred people. The widespread use of community representatives raises similar concerns. Many volunteers appear to be motivated by a genuine desire to make a contribution to their local community, but some, such as the woman who told me 'I've been to 150 of these things, and I just love them!', arouse the suspicion that participation is part good citizenship, part voyeurism.

Even when informal justice did manage to be reparative and reintegrative, rather than punitive and stigmatizing, problems still arose. In early modern Europe informal justice was part of a two-tier system of justice, in which compensatory justice was only available to those who could afford to pay compensation. For those who could not, there was no option but the harsher justice of the court, as Bruce Lenman and Geoffrey Parker (1980: 27) explain:

Most societies, like the Anglo-Saxons, strictly forbade money compensation for any crimes committed by certain social groups: those who were unfree or otherwise economically dependent on the law-givers. There were two standards of justice, even in Germanic law, and the distinction was preserved throughout the middle ages and beyond. In the medieval towns of the Netherlands, the 'peace-makers' offered their services only to full citizens who had paid to be enrolled as members of the community. The poor were excluded and their crimes were dealt with by summary law-courts

Some critics express a similar concern about new forms of restorative justice. Jennifer Brown (1994: 1285), for example, claims that some victim–offender mediation programmes in North America

---

[18] During the course of my research administrators told me of apologies in one case involving a young person, who had sprayed graffiti on a school wall, agreeing to apologize to the whole school at an assembly. In another case, a young person who stole a lap top agreed to send a letter of apology once every year, for six years, to the lap top's owner.

'allow offenders to participate only if they are likely to be able to make restitution payments to the victim'.[19] This is but one instance of a more general concern about access to restorative justice programmes.

There remain many modern forms of informal justice that vividly illustrate the risks of unchecked community power, from South Africa (Roche 2002: 519–21) to Northern Ireland (Mika and McEvoy 2001), that can wreak the sort of violence, oppression, and terror they were designed to control. In Northern Ireland under the system of informal justice administered by Republican and Loyalist paramilitaries 'Thousands of individuals were shot in the knees, thighs, elbows or ankles, beaten with iron bars, baseball bats or hurling sticks, or forcibly excluded from their communities' (McEvoy and Mika 2002: 536).

An implicit (and sometimes explicit) theme of restorative justice scholarship is that retributive and punitive responses to crime only arrived with the modern state.[20] Even if such a view were true, it neglects the fact that the retributive practices of the state are embedded in, and sustained by, people's own punitive and stigmatizing attitudes.[21] It was these attitudes that made 'rough music' so popular and drew people to the spectacle of public executions. As Michael Ignatieff (1981: 145) observes:

The state, moreover, shared the punitive function with civil society, in the double sense that its public rituals (execution, pillory, whipping and branding) required completion by the opprobrium of the crowd if they were to have full symbolic effect, and in the sense that the household heads, masters and employers punished directly without invoking the state's power.[22]

[19] Although I found no evidence of such eligibility criteria in any of the twenty-five programmes I studied.

[20] See, for example, James Zion (1998: 141) who argues that 'restorative justice is in fact the original, pre-state form of law'.

[21] This is one of the reasons why within the restorative justice movement there is considerable opposition to state involvement (the title of a recent American Society of Criminology session expresses the sentiment well: 'Transformative Justice: What'll Save Restorative Justice From the Jaws of the State').

[22] Michel Foucault's *Discipline and Punish* (1977: 58–61) illustrates well people's ambivalence in relation to punishment, describing the way in which the gathered crowds would cheer in support of a prisoner, and on occasions, revolt against the execution (where, for example, they felt that the prisoner would have received a lighter penalty had he been born better or richer).

Notwithstanding the humane ideals of restorative justice, the unpalatable but inescapable fact is that restorative justice programmes are embedded in a contemporary cultural and political context where punitive and exclusionary punishment is dominant (Garland 2001). One pertinent manifestation of this dominance is the widespread resurgence of shaming penalties (Kahan 1996; Posner 2000). The precise form of these penalties varies—from punishing people who urinate in public by requiring them to scrub a street with a toothbrush (Kahan 1996: 633) to newspapers 'naming and shaming' convicted paedophiles[23]—but the basic goal is the same: to subject an offender to extreme shame and humiliation. Though such penalties are grossly offensive to the overwhelming majority of restorative justice practitioners, to many citizens they are not. Moreover, shaming only deters an offender when it is also accompanied by acts to reintegrate him or her. As the T-shirt case illustrates, in the shame-laden atmosphere of a conference the importance of ensuring an offender's reintegration can be easily swept aside and forgotten.

Proponents' silence about these risks suggests that their critical capacities have been blunted by the exigencies of promoting restorative justice. When so much of practitioners' time is spent selling restorative justice—to potential participants, to gatekeepers in the criminal justice system (such as judges and police), to victims' advocacy groups, politicians and policy makers—there is little strategic benefit in talking about those cases where something has gone wrong. More worryingly, it might be that practitioners do not actually foresee all the ways in which things can go wrong, mainly because the vengeful, punitive instincts that threaten restorative justice are so far removed from reformers' own instincts, and the values of the restorative justice movement to which they belong. Unfortunately, however, reformers' good intentions by themselves do not guarantee progressive reform: modern penal history yields many examples of reformers' benign ideals resulting in repressive controls (Ashworth 2002: 590). Even the modern prison was after all, the creation of humane reformers in the latter part of the eighteenth and early nineteenth century (Ignatieff 1981: 148; Morgan 2002: 1119–20).

---

[23] In the United Kingdom the *News of the World's* tactic of inciting vigilantism had particularly tragic consequences, leading to a number of deaths (Herbert 2002). The campaign took on tragicomic proportions when a paediatrician was attacked after her occupation was confused for paedophile (Lister 2002)

The accountability critique

Perhaps, then, as a result of almost blind faith in restorative justice, its proponents appear to have neglected the importance of ensuring that programmes possess sufficient procedural safeguards, including the point that programmes should themselves be accountable. Much restorative justice literature focuses on the ways in which offenders are held accountable in meetings; much less attention is paid to those institutional restraints that ensure that meetings and programmes are also held accountable. It is one thing to have a process where offenders can be forced to explain their conduct, but where are the mechanisms for ensuring that the participants in these processes are required to explain themselves? [24]

Many researchers have expressed concern about the adequacy of accountability mechanisms in programmes. Richard Young (2001: 211), who with Carolyn Hoyle has conducted a comprehensive evaluation of police-run conferencing in Thames Valley, England, says concerns about conferences 'highlight the need for stronger accountability mechanisms than are inherent in the semi-public nature of the process and its systematic setting in the shadow of the court'. Kate Warner (1993: 151) warns that problems may arise in a conferencing scheme that 'lacks public scrutiny and accountability'. Analysing restorative justice from the often-overlooked perspective of young female offenders, Christine Alder (2000: 117) refers to the need for some level of 'decision-making accountability'. Jennifer Brown (1994: 1252), in her critique of one form of restorative justice—victim–offender mediation—argues that such programmes have numerous procedural deficiencies, including a lack of public accountability.[25]

---

[24] That restorative justice thinking is dominated by the former much more than the latter was brought home to me when I attempted to explain my research project to practitioners. As one practitioner exclaimed when I explained I wanted to discuss the way in which his programme was accountable 'Oh, we'll show you offender accountability!' Even though I tried to be clear that I was talking about institutional accountability and the way programmes themselves were accountable, confusion was common.

[25] See also other critiques by Murray Griffin (1996: 4), Julie Stubbs (1995), Gabrielle Maxwell (1999), John Braithwaite, Kathy Daly, and Christine Parker (Braithwaite and Daly 1994: 206; Braithwaite 1998: 96; Braithwaite and Parker 1999: 108).

These criticisms of restorative justice build on those made about informal justice in the 1970s and 1980s. Among those levelled at the various kinds of informal justice then (including negotiation, mediation, arbitration, and neighbourhood justice centres), was the assertion that they lacked the procedural safeguards offered by formal justice (Abel 1981; Fiss 1984; Bottomley 1985: 184; Delgado *et al.* 1985). This was regarded as particularly problematic in the context of some crimes—such as domestic violence—where a serious power imbalance often exists between the parties (Lerman 1984: 72).

Concerns about the specific accountability of restorative justice programmes are better understood against the backdrop of the more general interest in accountability. In recent times, investigation of the concept has intensified, with a large and growing body of scholarship devoted to its analysis. In his introduction to a book of essays on the accountability of the criminal justice system, Philip Stenning (1995: 3) goes so far as to argue that accountability has become one of modern society's central preoccupations.

Notwithstanding the specific concerns voiced about the accountability of restorative justice programmes and the more general preoccupation with accountability, there has been no structured examination of the accountability of restorative justice programmes. As I have suggested, blind faith in the intrinsic goodness of restorative justice may be at least part of the reason. Another possible factor is that there is thought to be conflict between the principles of restorative justice and those of accountability: restorative justice, after all, aims to make the formal criminal justice system more informal, whereas accountability appears to be centrally concerned with the very opposite, that is, formalizing that which is informal. With few exceptions, writers have not attempted to bridge these two concepts. It appears that the underlying assumption is that one can choose restorative justice or accountability, but not both. This apparent incommensurability partly explains the absence of a sustained accountability analysis of restorative justice. I believe that this absence represents a serious gap in the study of the phenomenon of restorative justice, and this gap is the starting point for this book, the aim of which is to identify and assess the types of accountability in restorative justice programmes.

But first I must define terms.

Outline of the book

In the next chapter I clarify the meaning of the two capacious concepts of restorative justice and accountability. Four key values characterize restorative justice: personalism, participation, reparation and reintegration. The chapter examines the different senses in which accountability is used, and isolates the sense in which critics express concern about the accountability of restorative justice programmes. Accountability is defined as a procedural safeguard, whereby decision makers are required to explain or justify their actions or decisions, with the aim of improving the quality and legitimacy of decisions in restorative meetings.

Chapter Two also identifies some of the problems in restorative justice programmes which institutional accountability may address. These problems include the unfair exclusion of some offenders from programmes, traumatic meetings, inappropriate outcomes, and lack of follow-through on agreements. Given that accountability is usually just one of many means for promoting better decision making, it is difficult to isolate an accountability mechanism's contribution to good decision making. To address this problem, seven criteria are developed that can be used to assess the quality of an accountability mechanism: simplicity, timeliness, inclusiveness, motivational sensitivity, publicity, independence, and iterative accountability.

Chapter Three introduces the empirical component of the book, which is the basis of the later assessment of programmes' accountability. Using the definition of restorative justice articulated in Chapter Two, I explain the process of choosing restorative justice programmes to survey for the research, and then provide an overview of the twenty-five programmes which are the case studies for this book. These case studies come from several countries (Australia, England, New Zealand, South Africa, United States, and Canada), are run by a number of different institutions (community groups, justice departments, police, schools) and perform a variety of functions (some operating as an alternative to formal sentencing, some as part of formal sentencing, and others in addition to formal sentencing).

Chapter Four considers whether there is a form of accountability built into the deliberative process of a restorative meeting. This chapter considers whether participants are required to be accountable to each other, and makes a distinction between formal and informal obligations. As victims, offenders and other participants attempt to reach consensual decisions, they have to provide each other with reasons, claims, and explanations for their demands and decisions. Such a form of deliberative accountability has a number of potential strengths. As it occurs as part of the decision-making process in a restorative meeting, deliberative accountability may serve as a timely form of regulation. This chapter considers whether deliberative accountability avoids the problem from which many accountability mechanisms suffer, i.e. that requiring people to account for their actions can erode the feelings of goodwill and trustworthiness that may otherwise motivate them (Power 1997). It also explores the possibility that the informality of restorative meetings provides a form of accountability that accommodates a wider range of styles of expression than is generally permitted in more formal accountability mechanisms (such as a court). As well as exploring the potential of deliberative accountability, Chapter Four carefully elaborates the obstacles to its effective functioning. In particular, it analyses the way in which accountability collapses when participants can dominate each other, and proposes strategies for minimizing non-domination, such as inviting supporters and advocates to meetings, supplying free legal advice to offenders, scheduling breaks in meetings, and providing alternative forums for participants wishing to opt out of restorative justice meetings.

In Chapter Five I consider the extended uses of the accountability described in Chapter Four. I attempt to make a contribution to debates about police accountability, examining whether restorative meetings can, as some advocates claim, provide a forum where police and other state agents can be held informally accountable for their actions. Also considered are such obstacles as the practice of holding meetings in police stations, and of allowing police to convene conferences. A further accountability use of meetings is monitoring offenders' progress in completing restorative outcomes. The most exciting—but also most time consuming—model of the way this can occur comes from a programme for young African American offenders in inner-city Minneapolis where offenders participate in multiple meetings while benefiting in between meetings from mentoring provided by community volunteers. This chapter suggests a pyramid of responses for monitoring offenders' completion of the agreements reached in restorative meetings.

Chapter Six identifies a number of additional accountability mechanisms that are often overlooked in discussions of accountability of restorative justice programmes (and indeed, in accountability discussions generally). These include the role of restorative justice practitioners in selecting cases for a restorative programme, reviewing the outcomes agreed in meetings, and monitoring offenders' completion of those outcomes. Chapter Six also identifies and assesses a number of other forms of accountability present in the programmes surveyed (including, principally, the oversight provided by directors' boards and the scrutiny of researchers).

After the non-standard forms of accountability that were considered in Chapters Four, Five, and Six, Chapter Seven turns to consider the important role of more standard forms of accountability. Accountability critiques of restorative justice often focus only on the accountability provided by observers and judicial monitoring of outcomes. Chapter Seven reveals that programmes take one of three approaches to the question of whether observers can attend meetings: observers are allowed only where participants consent in the majority of programmes; other programmes are closed to all observers, while others still are open to observers on an unconditional basis. Wherever access is restricted, it will be argued that programmes could benefit from greater openness, and Chapter Seven considers strategies for minimizing the risks associated with this recommendation. In relation to review mechanisms, I examine the tendency of internal review to enforce upper limits on outcomes and external review to enforce lower limits and I propose that legislation should be adopted requiring judges to gauge the legitimacy of restorative justice agreements principally by the quality of the deliberative process used to decide them. In this respect, formal legal accountability reinforces deliberative accountability, building up a procedural conception of justice.

Restorative justice can be viewed as another instance of the widespread privatization of government. Chapter Eight concludes by arguing that it is wrong to assume—as many writers do—a straightforward relationship between privatization and accountability, whereby the former reduces the latter. Consistent with scholarship in other fields of regulation, empirical work across a range of restorative justice programmes has uncovered the emergence of new forms of accountability. These forms of accountability, particularly the deliberative accountability in a restorative meeting, have the potential to provide a more inclusive, dynamic form of accountability than many formal modes of accountability. The other important conclusion is that the potential exists for restorative justice and state justice to enjoy a mutually beneficial relationship. The model of accountability developed here envisages an important role for the state in acting to minimize domination in restorative meetings (while avoiding becoming a source of domination itself). Just as restorative justice requires the oversight of the state, the state requires restorative justice, with restorative justice offering the potential to reinvigorate democratic governments and their laws.

2
The Meaning of Restorative Justice and Accountability

Four values are suggested as the key to understanding restorative justice—personalism, participation, reparation, and reintegration. Because there is a tendency in restorative justice writing to see these key values as present in all informal modes of justice (and absent from all formal ones), advocates may have been led to underestimate the importance of ensuring that programmes are accountable. In particular, the popular notion that restorative justice is not a form of punishment but rather the revival of a universal, pre-state tradition of compassionate justice can encourage a false sense of security about the nature of informal justice.

Accountability is understood in the most general sense as explaining or answering for decisions made, and when people express concern about the accountability of restorative justice programmes they are referring to suspicions about the absence, or at least the inadequacy of mechanisms requiring decision-makers to explain their conduct.

While such mechanisms are designed to improve both the quality and legitimacy of decision-makers' actions, there is no guarantee that they will do so. On the other hand, it is highly likely that the imposition of unduly onerous and cumbersome forms of accountability will frustrate the goals of that design. We can only be confident that accountability mechanisms will serve these goals when they possess certain characteristics: simplicity, timeliness, inclusiveness, motivational sensitivity, publicity, independence, and iteration. These provide the criteria by means of which the accountability mechanisms in restorative justice programmes are assessed.

Restorative justice has become the dominant informal justice movement within the field of criminal justice and, increasingly, is making an impression beyond it. Until very recently, however, restorative justice was just one of a number of similar theories and practices including relational or reparative justice, reconciliation, making amends, and transformative justice.[1] Now, a bewilderingly diverse range of practices and programmes is labelled 'restorative justice'. Meetings between victims and offenders, healing lodges, victim impact statements, and court-ordered community service are just some of the practices that have been described as examples of restorative justice. It sometimes seems, as Paul McCold (2000: 358) says, that 'restorative justice has come to mean all things to all people'. It may help to clear up this confusion by thinking of restorative justice in terms of four key values mentioned earlier: personalism, participation, reparation, and reintegration.

Restorative values

Personalism

The starting point for restorative justice is that crime is first and foremost a violation of people and their relationships, rather than merely a violation of law. As leading restorative justice writer Howard Zehr (1990: 181) puts it, crime should be understood not as an abstract concept, but as an 'injury and as a violation of people and relationships'.[2] This 'injury and violence' extends beyond the victim's suffering; it also impacts on the offender, on the victim's and offender's families, and on the wider community. Restorative justice encompasses all these. The personal nature of restorative justice can be contrasted with the impersonal nature of the modern criminal justice system: at every stage, the response of the criminal justice system to crime is shaped by the law and the professionals who administer it; an offender is charged not with injuring a victim, but with committing an offence under the *Crimes Act*; prosecutions are brought not by victims, but by police or prosecutors, and then in the name of the state, rather than that of the victim; if the offender

---

[1] The newness of restorative justice's pre-eminence is illustrated by the fact that John Braithwaite and Stephen Mugford's 1994 *British Journal of Criminology* article 'Conditions of Successful Reintegration Ceremonies', one of the most cited writings on restorative justice, mentions restorative justice only once, in a list of theories and practices similar to reintegrative shaming (Braithwaite and Mugford 1994: 139).

[2] A smaller number of restorative justice writers would go further down this path and take a position similar to the abolitionist critique of punishment, that 'we should not think of "crimes"—actions prohibited by an authoritative law and inviting (if not entailing) a punitive response—but of "conflicts" or "troubles"' (Duff 2001: 33).

is convicted, a sentence is determined not by what the victim (or for that matter, the offender) wants but by a precedent laid down in earlier similar cases; and appeals are made not on the basis of how a victim feels about a sentence, but on an error of law. One of the consequences of this approach is that the physical and emotional damage crime does is suppressed, if not completely disregarded.

Reparation

The goal of any restorative response to crime is to repair the harm that has been caused. When a crime is committed, restorative justice asks 'How can things be put right?' and 'What can be done to make amends?', i.e. the process of reparation begins with acknowledging the harm a victim has suffered. Precisely what does need to be repaired will depend on the circumstances surrounding a specific crime, and in particular, the nature of the victim's loss or injury. To the limited extent that formal sentencing hearings are concerned with a victim's loss, they are mainly interested in that victim's material or physical losses, but for many victims the most serious losses are emotional and psychological, including the loss of dignity, happiness, confidence, security, personal power, and sense of self-worth.

Most restorative justice writers regard the ideal of reparation as an alternative to punishment. A contrast is drawn between retributive justice, which writers regard as the defining ideal of the modern criminal justice system, and reparation (e.g. Zehr 1990: 181; SATRC 1998: 1(5), para. 54; Consedine 1999). Martha Minow (1998: 92), for example, writes: 'Restorative justice emphasizes the humanity of both offenders and victims. It seeks repair of social connections and peace rather than retribution against the offenders.'

Furthermore, proponents link the ideal of reparation to indigenous and religious traditions of justice. Archbishop Desmond Tutu (1999: 51), for example, regards restorative justice as 'the characteristic of traditional African jurisprudence', in which the 'the central concern is not retribution or punishment but, in the spirit of ubuntu, the healing of breaches, the redressing of imbalances, the restoration of broken relationships'. Similar analogies are drawn with indigenous traditions in countries and regions as diverse as Canada, New Zealand, Hawaii, and the Navajo Nation in the United States. Chief Justice of the Navajo Court in Arizona, Robert Yazzie (1998: 129), says that whenever he and his colleagues go overseas to promote peacemaking 'other aboriginal leaders nod their heads with approval and tell us that it is the same as their traditional justice methods'. Indeed, some writers go so far as to identify a common restorative justice thread running through *all* indigenous societies (e.g. Bazemore and Schiff 2001: 22).[3] Writers also draw on the religious ideal of restoration, arguing that restorative justice is consistent with Christian biblical traditions of justice as well as the Talmudic teachings of the Jewish faith. The Bible, especially the Old Testament, is more commonly associated with retributive ideas of justice, but restorative justice writers claim that this is 'a perversion of biblical teachings' (Zehr 1990: 129). To make this point Howard Zehr (1990: 146) reconsiders the biblical saying 'an eye for eye', usually thought to exemplify the retributive nature of biblical law: ' "An eye for an eye" was a law of proportion intended to limit rather than encourage revenge. It limited destructive vengeance. In fact, this legal principle laid the basis for restitution, providing a principle of proportionality in response to wrongdoing.'

From a feminist perspective, a concern with the reparation of personal relationships, rather than punishment for breaching rules, is claimed to resonate with the ethics of care articulated by Carol Gilligan (1993) and others (Tronto 1993), that says the maintenance of relationships is more important than adherence to abstract rules (Masters and Smith 1998; Barton and Broek 1999. Cf. Daly 2002: 64).

Reintegration

In responding to wrongdoing, restorative justice aims to repair a victim's loss in ways that will also facilitate an offender's reintegration. Like victim reparation, reintegration is said to be an important ideal of pre-modern approaches to conflict. Supporters of restorative justice argue that the criminal justice system hinders, rather than

---

[3] These claims are often bound up with claims about the personalism of indigenous approaches to law. The United Nations Commission on Crime Prevention and Criminal Justice has recently adopted a resolution encouraging countries to draw from *Basic Principles on the Use of Restorative Justice Programmes in Criminal Matters* in developing and implementing restorative justice. The preamble to these principles includes the statement 'recognising that these (restorative justice) initiatives often draw from traditional and indigenous forms of justice which fundamentally view crime as harm to people' (principles posted at http://www.restorativejustice.org/, 21 May 2002).

helps, an offender's reintegration. Prison is most obviously the antithesis of reintegrative strategies, isolating and alienating the offender from society, but even alternatives which are not as utterly punitive and confining give little consideration to rebuilding an offender's ties with his or her community.

An offender can perform community service, pay a fine or attend probation, but is offered few opportunities to convey his or her repentance, and the community largely is denied the chance to demonstrate its acceptance of, or understanding towards, the offender. As John Braithwaite and Stephen Mugford (1994: 155) put it: 'When restitution is reduced to "the cheque is in the mail" (likely put there by the clerk of the court) matters of deep moral concern have been reduced to mere money, to the ubiquitous question "how much?"'

By contrast, restorative justice emphasizes the importance of strengthening an offender's ties with the local community. This starts with an offender acknowledging his or her wrongdoing, thus demonstrating that he or she remains part of the law-abiding community and recognizes its norms of acceptable behaviour (Johnstone 2002: 102, 117). By making amends, an offender can also assist his reintegration, taking the sting out of the victims' anger and earning the respect of the wider community. But the burden of reintegration does not fall just on the offender's shoulders—restorative justice emphasizes the responsibility of the wider community to ensure offenders are accepted and included. Restorative justice writers claim that this reintegrative approach is along the lines of the indigenous ideal of re-establishing community harmony which encompasses the need to assist the offender as much as the victim.[4]

More recently, the concept of reintegration has become prominently associated with John Braithwaite's theory of reintegrative shaming. Braithwaite believes that shaming delivers superior crime

---

[4] In restorative justice the ideal of reintegration is often subsumed under the goal of reparation or restoration, broadly defined to include the restoration of victims, offenders, and the wider community. Arguably, however, it is preferable to separate out these goals, especially as reparation is most commonly associated with repairing a victim's losses. The use of the term 'reintegration' makes it clear that restorative justice is equally directed towards assisting an offender. Such is the commitment of some restorative justice programmes to reintegrating offenders that some writers query whether restorative justice is really victim-friendly at all (e.g. Zedner 2002: 445–6). Another difference between reparation and reintegration is that the former is more backward-looking than the latter. Reintegration is done primarily with an eye to prevent future offending, while reparation is concerned with repairing losses.

control when it is combined with acts or gestures of reintegration, when 'expressions of community disapproval, which may range from mild rebuke to degradation ceremonies, are followed by gestures of reacceptance into the community of law-abiding citizens' (Braithwaite 1989: 55).

These gestures of reacceptance can take many forms, either very simple, involving a handshake, a compliment, or a smile, or quite elaborate, such as a meeting specifically to celebrate an offender's completion of his or her restorative conference agreement. The key to securing reintegration, according to Braithwaite (1989: 101), is to separate an offender's actions from his or her identity, signifying "evil deeds rather than evil persons in the Christian tradition of 'hate the sin and love the sinner' ".

Participation

Finally, restorative justice encourages the participation of the people most directly affected by crime—victims, offenders, and their communities—in the resolution of that crime: the ideal of participation is absolutely critical to restorative justice. The most cited definition of restorative justice uses terms almost exclusively concerned with this ideal: 'Restorative justice is a process whereby all the parties with a stake in a particular offence come together to resolve collectively how to deal with the aftermath of the offence and its implications for the future' (Marshall 1996: 37).[5]

Collective decision-making can take a number of forms, although in all but one of the twenty-five restorative justice programmes surveyed, decision-making works on a consensual basis. This suggests the need to refine Tony Marshall's definition: defined in participatory terms, restorative justice brings together all the parties affected by an incident of wrongdoing, to decide collectively on a consensual basis how to deal with the aftermath of an incident.

---

[5] This definition emerged when 'Paul McCold convened a Delphi process on behalf of the Working Party on Restorative Justice of the Alliance of NGOs on Crime Prevention and Criminal Justice to see if these disparate strands of the emerging alternative might settle on a consensual conception of restorative justice. A Delphi process iteratively seeks expert opinion, in this case on the best way to define restorative justice' (Braithwaite 1999: 5). The process did not produce consensus on a definition but it was agreed that Tony Marshall offered the most acceptable working definition.

Within these general parameters the restora'
considerably in its precise nature. Some of its r
include conferences, victim-offender mediatio'
cing panels. What all of these programmes have in cc
of some sort of deliberative process between offenders anu
the wider community or both. These processes are described in i.
detail in Chapter Three. Proponents refer to Nils Christie's (1977)
work to articulate and justify the ideal of participation. Christie
argued that conflicts belong to the people affected by them—victims,
offenders, and their local communities—and that criminal justice
professionals and institutions have 'stolen' these conflicts. To many
of us, the state's responsibility for investigating, prosecuting, and
sentencing crime is so much the usual course as to be beyond question. As Andrew Ashworth (1998: 302) observes, 'It has become
implicit in much modern Anglo-American legal doctrine that a
criminal offence is a crime against the state'. Such a view is only as
old or as strong as the state itself, and accordingly varies both
historically and culturally. In some indigenous cultures and weak
states it remains a quite alien concept and, historically, private
individuals have played a significant role in the policing, prosecution, and punishment of offenders (Volpe 1991: 198; Bronitt and
McSherry 2001: 108; Garland 2001: 29–30). Restorative processes
follow Christie's (1977: 14) urging to 're-establish the credibility
of encounters between critical human beings: low-paid, highly
regarded, but with no extra power—outside the weight of their
good ideas'.

Advocates of restorative justice argue that such a process
promotes the values of reparation and reintegration.[6] Restorative
meetings acknowledge a victim's suffering and provide an opportunity for victims to ask questions. As Zehr (1990: 28) explains, victims
typically want answers to many questions, such as 'Why did
this happen to me?', 'Did this person have something against me?',

---

[6] Restorative processes such as these are not the only way to pursue restorative
values. The means for pursuing restorative values are almost innumerable. Victim
support groups, art, music, and memorials to honour victims of violence and a court
order to pay compensation can all also be considered as examples of restorative
justice in the sense that they promote a victim's reparation. So too can drug treatment programmes for offenders, as can the Minnesota Program that finances
laser treatment to remove gang tattoos, on the basis that they assist an offender's
reintegration.

nd 'Is he or she coming back?' Meetings also provide an opportunity for victims to detail their victimization. Storytelling is often 'an important bridge... between the mute experience of being wronged and political arguments about justice' (Young 2000: 72).[7] Last, but by no means least, meetings can be an opportunity for victims to seek material reparation, which may take a variety of forms.

In so far as it is easier for an offender to deny responsibility where the victim is 'physically absent, unknown or a vague abstraction' (Sykes and Matza 1957: 668), meetings should offer the possibility of forcing offenders to accept responsibility for their actions. Restorative processes may also assist in the reintegration of offenders. Offenders are no longer spectators while others determine their fate, but participants in discussions about how to put things right. By respecting their ability to make choices, such a process may help restore offenders' dignity. The restorative process also presents an opportunity for an offender to apologize and seek forgiveness. Further, after meeting offenders and their families, victims and community members may rethink their preconceptions about the offender. As one offender later reflected on his treatment in a London conference: 'I was treated like a normal human being, not a crackhead.' Face-to-face meetings may also, it is claimed, help restore communities by dispelling the anxiety many community members feel about offenders and crime.

Providing a forum in which victims and offenders can exchange stories can be seen as an attempt to institutionalize what Richard Rorty (1998: 167–85) calls 'sentimental education'. Rorty contends that moral education which appeals to people's sentiment is most likely to change people's thoughts and habits. This sentimental education, according to Rorty (1998: 185), consists of telling 'long, sad stories' that begin, 'you should care about this person because this is what it is like to be in her situation ...'.

---

[7] A similar claim is made in relation to rights-based discourses. Hilary Charlesworth (1994: 49), for example, writes that 'The assertion of rights can have great symbolic force for oppressed groups within a society offering a significant vocabulary to formulate political and social grievances which is recognized by the powerful'. Storytelling, however, may be a more accessible language than that of rights, which presupposes some level of formal education.

Limitations of restorative justice

Presenting restorative justice as the universal form of pre-state justice sacrifices accuracy for simplicity. The complexity and diversity in indigenous laws are grossly oversimplified, in much the same way as their more inhumane manifestations are glossed over in order to present these laws as embodying restorative values (Blagg 1997, 1998; Cunneen 2000). Even though anthropological and historical work cautions against making such sweeping generalizations,[8] the champions of restorative justice continue to make sweeping claims about the history of punishment. It appears that these advocates' intentions are not so much to write authoritative histories of justice as a rhetorical one which can be used to build support for their cause. As Kathy Daly (2002: 63) puts it, 'Advocates are trying to move an idea into the political and policy arena, and this may necessitate having to utilize a simple contrast of the good and the bad justice, along with an origin myth of how it all came to be'.[9]

Personalism, reparation, reintegration, and participation all involve normative claims about how crime should be dealt with; unfortunately, the normative dimension of restorative justice is obscured by the myth that restorative justice is 'authentic' justice. The many historical, spiritual, and philosophical associations made by advocates have the effect—if not the intention—of suggesting that people are genetically programmed to respond restoratively to conflict. The aspirations of restorative justice champions about how people *should* respond are confused with the reality of how people

[8] In relation to customary African law, for example, Max Gluckman (1973: 55) cautions against attributing to the value of reconciliation an 'ultimate, almost mystical' status. Reconciliation was not sought, for example, in disputes between two people who were comparative strangers to each other (1973: 55). Olawale Elias (1956: 131) also notes that to characterize African customary law as restorative is to fail to acknowledge its punitive side (see also (Thompson 1995: 26)). Notwithstanding these qualifications, however, and the considerable variations in laws and customs both within and across African tribes, anthropological studies suggest that reconciliation and reparation are indeed prominent characteristics of customary African law (Bohannan 1957; Gluckman 1965; Gluckman 1973). Sinclair Dinnen (2002) makes similar observations in relation to customary law in Papua New Guinea.

[9] Such selective histories of indigenous justice also perpetuate an ethnocentrism their authors would wish to avoid (see Jackson 1992: 8; Said 1995; Blagg 1997, 1998; Perrett 1999: 17; Daly 2002).

do respond (Allen 1999). Restorative caricatures of the history of justice may be an effective means of building political support for restorative justice, but they risk blotting out important historical lessons about the dangers of informal processes. Restorative justice reopens the door to the kinds of private vengeance and vendettas which the development of the 'impersonal' modern criminal justice system was designed precisely to restrain and repress. If the humane origins of 'eye for an eye' could be so completely corrupted, surely there is a risk that exactly the same thing could happen to the benevolent ideals of restorative justice?

Equally problematic is the assertion that reparation is an alternative to punishment. In fact, there are good reasons to regard reparation not as an alternative to punishment, but as an alternative punishment. Taking the simplest view of punishment—a sanction imposed with the intention of expressing censure—reparation can be thought to fulfil both criteria (Daly 2000, 2002; Duff 2001). Separation of restorative justice from punishment can serve to justify a lack of attention to procedural safeguards. After all, if people are not at risk of unfair punishment, and all we are doing is helping them, why do they need protection? As one practitioner I interviewed put it, 'Once you take punishment away, you don't need lawyers, their [offenders'] liberty is not at threat. Lawyers just get in the way and justice delayed is justice denied.'

However, restorative justice meetings lacking adequate accountability can depart from the ideals, and without accountability there is also the potential for abuse of power both before and after meetings. These problems, critics argue, have been neglected in the promotion of restorative justice; accountability mechanisms may address them.

Potential problems in restorative justice meetings

Time and circumstance limit what can be achieved in meetings between victims and offenders. Even the most reintegrative of meetings cannot 'magically undo the years of social marginalization and exclusion experienced by so many offenders', nor can it repair all of a victim's harm (Morris 2002: 596). These concerns do not so much raise the need for programme accountability as the need for other initiatives to provide long-term support and counselling, and to address alcohol and other drug abuse, lack of education, lack of job skills, and so on. In addition, it is worth bearing in mind that, from a victim's perspective, meetings offer nothing to the overwhelming majority of victims whose offenders have not been caught (Johnstone 2002: 78).

Accountability mechanisms are better suited to addressing concerns not to do with the inherent limits of restorative justice, but with stopping meetings from going badly wrong. Far from helping reintegrate offenders and repair victims' harm, meetings may make things worse, traumatizing victims and offenders alike. From their observation of a number of Australian restorative justice conferences, Suzanne Retzinger and Thomas Scheff (1996: 13), express their worries about the damaging effects of participants intentionally shaming offenders, particularly through the use of sarcasm, moral superiority, and lecturing. One of the unfortunate aspects of concentrating on the personal dimension of crime and attempting to repair the emotional harm suffered by a victim is that offenders may be put under considerable pressure to respond in a grovelling, self-abasing fashion. Many victims may not be interested in either reintegration or reparation, or even if they are, that which helps repair their harm may hinder an offender's reintegration.[10]

Meetings may also be traumatizing for victims. In separate evaluations of conferencing in New Zealand and Australia, a significant minority of victims reported that they felt worse after a conference (Maxwell and Morris 1993: 119; Strang 2000). This is particularly problematical in cases involving domestic violence and sexual assault, where offenders may attempt to minimize the extent of their responsibility or seek to blame victims for their victimization, or both. One of the achievements of the women's movement in the 1970s and 1980s was to change public opinion so that violence against women and children is now more widely seen as a crime, and critics are concerned that restorative justice does not serve to

---

[10] This point is illustrated by one conference I convened in Queanbeyan, a small town near Canberra, Australia. The case involved a boy who had fallen off his bike trying to avoid a rock thrown at him by another boy, in the process injuring himself and damaging his bike. In the course of preparing the conference I met with the victim's father who asked what outcome he could seek in the conference. 'What did he have in mind?' I asked him. 'I'd like him to have to stand naked on the roof of his house for a few hours.' I explained the idea was to come up with ideas that would help repair the harm suffered. 'Well, seeing him stand there would bloody well make me feel better', the father replied.

jeopardize these hard-won achievements. It is also important to be realistic about the potential ability to repair the harm caused by crime: in the most serious crimes—such as murder—the loss is plainly irreparable. All that can be done is to make a gesture or acknowledgement of the victim's and their family's losses.

Another problem can be the expectation of forgiveness in order to aid reconciliation and an offender's reintegration. Writing in the context of South Africa's Truth and Reconciliation Commission— characterized by many as reflecting restorative justice—Martha Minow (1998: 17) explains why the pressure to forgive is objectionable:

> Observers of South Africa's Truth and Reconciliation Commission note that although many who were victimized are prepared to forgive or reconcile with police officers and government officials from the apartheid regime, the survivors recoil when perpetrators greet victims with open arms and handshakes. In these cases, forgiveness is assumed, rather than granted. A survivor may think, 'Should you not wait for me to stretch out my hand to you, when I'm ready, when I've established what is right?' Forgiveness is a power held by the victimized, not a right to be claimed. The ability to dispense, but also to withhold, forgiveness is an ennobling capacity and part of the dignity to be reclaimed by those who survive the wrongdoing. Even an individual survivor who chooses to forgive cannot, properly, forgive in the name of other victims. To expect survivors to forgive is to heap yet another burden on them.

The goal should be to create institutional spaces where victims can forgive and offenders apologize, but where neither is obliged, or even expected, to do so (Braithwaite 2001: 15); there is a worry, though, that in many programmes, apology, forgiveness, and reconciliation are regarded as crucial to the success of meetings (Johnstone 2002: 132–3).

Even though restorative justice stresses the personal dimension of crime, in many programmes criminal justice professionals play a significant role in meetings. The role of convenors is often central to worries about restorative processes. Critics observe the part convenors may play in pressuring both victims and offenders. Trina Grillo (1991: 1585) puts this objection: 'The mediator also can set the rules regarding who talks, when they may speak, and what may be said. The power of the mediator is not always openly acknowledged but is hidden beneath protestations that the process belongs to the parties.'

Problems are gravest in cases such as domestic violence, where there is suspicion that convenors will display 'minimizing, trivializing and victim-blaming attitudes towards battered women which are so commonly found' elsewhere, and that other participants' lack of familiarity with restorative justice processes will mean that convenors' attitudes dominate (Hooper and Busch 1996: 108; Braithwaite and Daly 1994: 207).

Evaluations of New Zealand family group conferences raise the problem that professionals tend to overtake, distort, and undermine proceedings. When parents of young offenders were asked who they thought had made the decisions in family group conferences, 19 per cent of responses identified professionals alone as the decision-makers (Maxwell and Morris 1993: 113). These worries become particularly acute when restorative meetings are convened by police officers: Harry Blagg (1997: 483) argues that police-run restorative justice programmes give 'police a very direct and overt (as opposed to simply indirect and covert) role in the deployment of punishments'.

A significant part of most restorative justice meetings is the negotiation of an agreement between participants which sets out what offenders intend to do to make amends for their actions. This agreement or outcome can prove problematical. First, there is the problem previously discussed, that outcomes will inappropriately shame offenders, such as the notorious 'I am a thief' T-shirt case mentioned at the beginning of Chapter One (Hepworth 1998). There is also the possibility that victims will demand outcomes which are too onerous; and insist on excessive amounts of compensation or community service, for example (Levrant et al. 1999: 8).[11] It is this risk that leads Jenny Bargen (1995: 3) to call for the monitoring of outcomes to ensure that they are 'no worse for young people than the court might have imposed'.

At the other end of the spectrum is the possibility that restorative justice programmes will produce outcomes that fail to reflect the gravity of some offences. An outcome may be acceptable to the parties involved in its negotiation, yet fail to address some community concern such as the likelihood of further dangerous offences

---

[11] This concern was well illustrated by one restorative meeting I attended in the United States where community volunteers sought a commitment from a young person who had admitted a charge of handling stolen goods that he would re-enrol at school, change friends, attend a prison education programme, and then look into establishing his own welding business!

being committed. The New Zealand Ministry of Justice (NZMJ 1995: 61) argues that 'judicial consideration of outcomes would provide a means through which the public interest could be weighed against the private interests involved'.

Further reservations exist about culturally specific outcomes that may be alien to Western liberal conceptions of human rights, such as traditional Australian Aboriginal practices of spearing and banishment. In addition to these worries, the outcomes of restorative justice meetings may not accord with mainstream sentencing principles such as consistency and proportionality. In court, sentences are imposed according to a tariff designed to ensure that a sentence is proportional to the gravity of offence and the offender's degree of responsibility, and consistent with sentences imposed on similar offenders for like offences committed in like circumstances. According to critics, monitoring is needed here to ensure that the individualized outcomes of restorative meetings reflect the principles of proportionality or consistency (Sarre 1994: 4; NSWLRC 1996: 368; Roberts and LaPrairie 1997: 82).

Many restorative justice advocates agree that outcomes should be monitored, but argue participant satisfaction and not proportionality or consistency should be the appropriate measure (McEvoy *et al.* 2002: 469), as proportionality and consistency belong to a punishment paradigm that restorative justice disavows.[12] Agreements are incomparable both with other agreements and traditional court-imposed sentences as they represent the result of the negotiations of a unique combination of people affected by a unique crime. Braithwaite (1999: 105) argues that restorative processes give priority to both victims and offenders in a way that the offender-centred notion of consistency does not. Instead of aiming to ensure the consistency and proportionality of outcomes, he advocates monitoring outcomes to ensure that they do not exceed defined upper limits (Braithwaite 1999: 105).

Pre-meeting concerns

There are two kinds of problem with decisions made prior to a restorative justice meeting: one relates to the question of who is

---

[12] Although see Kathy Daly's (2000: 35) argument that restorative justice incorporates punishment. See also Heather Strang and John Braithwaite's (2000: 207) response.

given access to a restorative justice programme, the second relates to other aspects of the handling of a case.

Unfairly excluding offenders from restorative justice programmes

Some writers believe that some types of offenders—particularly members of minority groups—will be unfairly denied access to programmes. Ethnic minorities are less likely to benefit in the exercise of police discretion than other ethnic groups. Chris Cunneen (1997: 297) argues that this 'central feature in the relationship between Indigenous young people and juvenile justice systems' is pertinent to restorative justice programmes, pointing to low referral rates of Aborigines to programmes in Western and South Australia. Perhaps less obviously, offenders may be discriminated against on the basis of poverty. Jennifer Brown (1994: 1285) tells us that some victim–offender mediation programmes in the United States 'allow offenders to participate only if they are likely to be able to make to restitution payments to the victim'. In Canada, Carol LaPrairie (1999: 146) believes that the 'reality may be that people already well-known to the system and who are most vulnerable to imprisonment because of criminal records, may be systematically excluded from participation in these alternative approaches'.

Making decision-makers accountable for any exercise of their discretion is one way to minimize the possibility of partial access to restorative justice programmes. Another way is to restrict the decision-maker's discretion. This is the approach taken in New Zealand where for most crimes it is mandatory to refer to a conference young offenders who do not deny committing an offence.[13]

Net-widening

Further to these is the possibility that access to programmes may be too inclusive rather than not inclusive enough, i.e. that they can potentially widen nets of social control, drawing into them those people who previously may have remained outside and subjecting others to more intensive treatment than they would have otherwise received. The expressed fear is that restorative justice ends up supplementing, rather than, as promised, replacing traditional methods

---

[13] For a discussion of this feature of the New Zealand legislation see Harry Blagg (1997: 485) and Patrick Power (2000). This feature of New Zealand conferencing is discussed in more detail in Chapter Six.

of criminal justice intervention (Cohen 1985: 44, 54; Levrant *et al.* 1999; Johnstone 2002: 32). This is not just an accountability problem. At a conceptual level, the view that social control is inherently objectionable deserves questioning. Instead of generally condemning social control, we should identify the precise consequences of impugned interventions (Seymour1988: 233). Furthermore for some undetected crimes—such as some types of white-collar crime, domestic violence, and schoolyard bullying—there is even a good argument for restorative justice programmes to expand the net of social control (Braithwaite 1999: 91). Where a legitimate fear of net-widening does exist, a variety of different strategies may be adopted, including such measures as limiting the types of offences referred to restorative justice programmes, as well as making gatekeepers accountable for their decision to refer cases to a restorative justice meeting.

Access to a restorative justice programme can mean that the decision to refer a case to a programme hands someone (often, as I will show, a police officer) additional discretion. The second type of pre-meeting concern is of a slightly different nature: namely, by taking cases out of court where judges can scrutinize police conduct, programmes remove a source of accountability over existing police discretion (Delgado 2000: 769). While judges or magistrates may exclude evidence and criticize police where scrutiny of their actions shows that they have acted unlawfully or improperly, in practice this offers only a weak form of accountability, particularly when many (and in some countries, most) defendants end up pleading guilty. Nevertheless, critics are concerned that any illegalities and improprieties are even less apparent when cases are dealt with by a restorative justice meeting (Warner 1993: 142).

Post meeting concerns

Most disquiet about what takes place after a restorative meeting revolves around the outcome negotiated in the course of the meeting. Problems can arise after a restorative process when one or more of the participants decide they are dissatisfied with the negotiated outcome. In court, parties in such a position may be able to appeal, and in so doing, hold the sentencing judge accountable. We need to look at what accountability mechanisms exist in restorative justice programmes.

The question of accountability again arises at the point of completion of outcomes. A common fear is that programmes lack the accountability mechanisms to monitor an offender's completion of an outcome plan, and ensure its completion (Pennell and Burford 1997). Reintegration must be a key value of restorative justice, but it is naïve to think that genuine reintegration will be achieved by any one-off meeting, particularly in cases linked to other behaviour such as substance abuse (Latimer et al. 2001: 18). There is doubt about the adequacy of mechanisms to hold other people accountable for assisting offenders to discharge their obligations (such as attending drug treatment, or giving blood, which was a popular outcome in Canberra conferences for drink-drivers) (Levrant et al. 1999: 16). It also seems that too much of the burden for assisting offenders falls on women, who already share a disproportionate burden of unpaid caring anyway, especially in troubled communities (Braithwaite 2001: 154).

The meaning of accountability

Like the term 'restorative justice', accountability is another concept in danger of coming to mean all things to all people. In his article entitled ' "Accountability": an Ever-Expanding Concept?', Richard Mulgan (2000: 2) observes that accountability, a 'word which a few decades or so ago was used only rarely and with relatively restricted meaning... now crops up everywhere performing all manner of analytical and rhetorical tasks'.

Accountability in one sense suggests a person's or an institution's compliance with external standards, or with his or her own conscience or moral values (Bardach and Kagan 1982; Harmon and Mayer 1986: 47; Heimer 1998: 18). A person is said to be accountable when his or her conduct complies with these standards.[14] The term is also used to refer to the consequences that should follow when a person's behaviour fails to meet those standards. In this sense it refers to the 'political, moral, or legal liability (or in all or some of these senses) for the results, mostly harmful, of a given form of

[14] Richard Mulgan (2000: 558) makes the observation that the expansion of accountability has been accompanied by a corresponding contraction in responsibility. Mulgan argues that accountability used to be seen as the external aspect of the broader concept of responsibility, whereas now responsibility is seen as the internal aspect of the broader concept of accountability.

behaviour or event' (Bovens 1998: 25). This is the meaning people have in mind when they remark that a person 'should be held accountable' for his or her actions (for example, a director should be held accountable for his or her mismanagement of a company, or a dictator for his or her abuses of power). A person is said to have been 'held accountable' when he or she experiences consequences (usually in the form of some sort of penalty) considered appropriate in the estimation of the person using the expression. The restorative justice literature is replete with references to accountability in the sense of the consequences that should follow a person's commission of a criminal offence.[15]

In a different sense, accountability commonly refers to the various mechanisms used to control the actions of individuals and institutions. In this sense, as Mulgan (2000: 556) observes, accountability comprises the 'various institutional checks and balances by which democracies seek to control the actions of the governments'. This is a popular use of the term (for examples see Bayley 1985: 160; Goldring and Blazey 1994: 147; Goldsmith 1995: 112). The trouble with these definitions is that, defined this way, accountability 'threatens to extend its reach over the entire field of institutional design' (Mulgan 2000: 563). Under such an extended definition, any rule or procedure could conceivably be described as a form of accountability.

The classic sense of accountability

The term 'accountability' is used by critics of restorative justice to limit its sense to a particular type of control or restraint. They refer to accountability in the sense of those processes for giving an account

---

[15] One of the reasons the American Bar Association (ABA 1994) supports victim–offender mediation is because it can 'hold offenders accountable for the harm caused by their behaviour' Frequently, accountability is framed in terms of a response based on restorative values or processes. Mark Umbreit (1997: 22), for example, argues that 'Restorative justice emphasizes the importance of increasing the role of crime victims and communities in the process of holding offenders accountable for their behaviour'. Gabrielle Maxwell and Allison Morris (1993: xvi) refer to accountability as one of the goals behind conferencing in New Zealand: 'emphasizing the importance of young people paying an appropriate penalty for their crime and making good the wrong they have done to others.' The Balanced and Restorative Justice Model promoted by the US Department of Justice and developed by Gordon Bazemore, Mara Schiff, and Mark Umbreit (1998: 9), defines accountability 'as taking responsibility for your behaviour and taking action to repair the harm'.

of events or answering for a person's or institution's performance (Mulgan 1997; Mulgan 2000: 555). Richard Mulgan and John Uhr (2000: 1) describe the nature of this type of accountability:

When public agencies or officials are 'called to account', we expect them to be required to report on their activities and to provide the reasons behind their decisions. The original, and still important, sense of being called 'to account' is the financial 'account' in which revenue and expenditure decisions are reported to the authorising body, typically Parliament. Beyond financial accounts, accountability covers a wide range of reports, written and oral, formal and informal, in which agencies and officials are subjected to scrutiny, obliged to provide information to members of the public and to explain their actions.

It is in this classic sense, with 'the longest pedigree' (Mulgan 2000: 555), that accountability is usually perceived to be an essential part of formal justice systems.[16] For all their faults, courts are open institutions which monitor other parts of the criminal justice system, and can themselves be monitored (Cappelletti 1983; Gleeson 1995; Doyle 1998; Lloyd 1998). The apparent lack of accountability and of formal processes for scrutinizing the performance of restorative justice programmes has been the subject of much criticism, but even if the term is restricted to its classic sense, it quickly becomes apparent how much accountability mechanisms vary. There are, however, three main dimensions to this variation—the nature of the obligation to be accountable, the powers of the person receiving and scrutinizing the account, and the timing of the process.

Formal and informal accountability

Accountability in the classic sense, then is the obligation to explain or justify behaviour or decisions. If someone is not under the pressure of such an obligation to give an account of events, he or she is not really accountable. That said, it is nonetheless important to bear in mind that there are many different kinds of obligation. Some writers hold that an obligation only exists when it can be formally enforced (e.g. Stenning 1995: 48), and it is certainly true that many modes of accountability rely on formal enforcement mechanisms:

---

[16] The origins of this type of political accountability can be traced back at least as far as ancient Athens, when administrative officials were required to account for their conduct to the Assembly of Citizens ten times a year, as well submit a review of their performance at the end of their term of office (Day and Klein 1987: 6).

for instance, if a company fails to keep proper accounting records, its officers face possible fines or imprisonment.[17] But to suggest that accountability mechanisms must possess formal enforcement mechanisms is to take an unduly restrictive view, and ignore those modes of accountability where obligations are informally enforced. For example, the requirement that judges explain their decisions is regarded as an important form of accountability, yet judges are under no legally enforceable obligation to give reasons for their rulings. Similarly, we might understand that a person is accountable to his family for his behaviour, even though there is no formal enforcement mechanism. In these informal accountability mechanisms, a combination of informal incentives and sanctions are used to persuade a person to account for his or her actions. Praise and censure, as well as appeals to common morality, are substituted for formal sanctions.

From a legal standpoint we might be tempted to conclude that forms of accountability with formal enforcement mechanisms will always be more effective than those with informal ones. However, the vast body of criminological and regulatory literature on the relative effectiveness of informal versus formal sanctions should make us pause before drawing such a conclusion (Braithwaite 1989; Ayres and Braithwaite 1992; Ellickson 1991). Strong obligations to give accounts may arise through both informal and formal enforcement mechanisms, or some combination of the two.

Restorative justice meetings, I shall argue, can possess just such an informal mode of accountability, inherent in the deliberative process of a meeting. Because this accountability is inbuilt, it gives outcomes of deliberation their legitimacy. As Anne Phillips (1995: 164) explains: 'The outcomes of deliberation are more often said to derive their legitimacy from having followed the appropriate procedures; thus, people have to give reasons for whatever they propose, and they have to accept the results of the more powerful argument.'

Persuasive and directive accountability

A second dimension in which mechanisms vary is the power held by the person responsible for scrutinizing the decision-maker's account. There is a view that in addition to seeking accounts, accountability always connotes a power on the part of the scrutinizer to then punish

---

[17] e.g. in the United Kingdom see s 2 Companies Act 1989.

a decision-maker's transgressions or, at the very least, correct them (Schedler 1999: 16; Mulgan 2000: 570). This is true for many forms of accountability, such as that of an employee to an employer, or that of a defendant to a court. In such mechanisms, if scrutinizers are not satisfied with someone's account, they can take further action (such as changing the decision or sacking the decision-maker). However, not all scrutinizers have such power.[18] In some mechanisms—such as many ombudsmen—the scrutinizer's formal powers are limited to demanding an account, and once the decision-maker has discharged this obligation by providing reasons for his or her decision, he or she is under no formal obligation to do anything more (Chan 1999: 252; Schedler 1999: 17). If a scrutinizer wishes a decision-maker to take further action, for example, to take a second look at the decision, he or she must persuade—rather than direct—the decision-maker to do so.[19]

What emerges from this study of restorative justice programmes is that in some accountability mechanisms scrutinizers possess the power to direct decision-makers to take further actions ('directive accountability') while in others scrutinizers who are unhappy with decision-makers' accounts must persuade those decision-makers of their viewpoint ('persuasive accountability').[20]

Retrospective and ongoing accountability

A third dimension within which accountability mechanisms vary is in the timing of the accounting process. Controls on decision-making

[18] It is also often thought that accountability takes place within a relationship of superior and subordinate, where the person in a subordinate position is accountable to the person in a superior one. But this is also inaccurate, as in some situations a person we would consider to be in a superior position is required to give accounts to subordinates (such as management to workers).

[19] This will usually be the case where the scrutinizer is in a subordinate position to the account-giver, but it may also be true in some situations where the scrutinizer is in a superior position to the account giver. For example, police ministers are entitled to seek accounts from police officers for investigative decisions, but cannot direct police to change them.

[20] What I describe as persuasive accountability, Geoffrey Marshall (1978) calls 'explanatory and co-operative', and what I term directive accountability, 'subordinate and obedient'. I prefer not to use Marshall's terms for their tendency to conflate the nature of accountability with the nature of parties' overall relationship, wrongly implying 1) that superiors are never accountable to subordinates, and 2) that the sort of accountability owed by subordinates to superiors is always directive. (These points are discussed in footnotes 18 and 19 above.)

processes can be divided into *ex post facto* (or 'retrospective') controls, and those which regulate decision-making in advance (or 'prospectively') (Cane 1996: 134). Accountability is usually classed as a retrospective control, although in practice the distinction between retrospective and prospective controls is often blurred. Retrospective controls can give prospective guidance to decision-makers by clarifying goals, objectives and standards of performance, by forcing decision-makers to organize themselves to report on their work and by conditioning the values and expectations of decision-makers to correspond with those of the prevailing authorities (Cane 1996: 134; Thomas 1998: 353). Moreover, accountability can also occur on an ongoing basis as part of a decision-making process. Ongoing accountability occurs when decision-makers are required to obtain approval before deciding or acting (for example, when police are required to obtain approval before commencing undercover operations) or when decision-makers are required to keep others informed about the course of their conduct (for example, a boss gives an employee a task, and asks to be updated regularly on the employee's progress).

The purpose of accountability

Accountability is valuable for the way it promotes transparency. It is not clear, however, that this alone justifies the considerable time, money, and effort that accountability mechanisms can consume. The much stronger justification for accountability lies in its instrumental value, and it is in these terms that most people seek to defend it.

Improving the quality of performance

When people are expected to account for their actions, this may improve the quality of their performance in a number of ways. The process of giving an account, and probably more importantly, anticipating doing so, can help prevent the abuse of power (Thomas 1998: 348). Moreover, the prospect of being exposed to scrutiny can deter those tempted to abuse their powers, and where it does not deter, it may nevertheless allow that abuse to be identified and, depending on the type of accountability mechanism, corrected and punished. For these reasons John Braithwaite and Philip Pettit (1994: 767) regard accountability as an essential element of any criminal justice system:

The system should equally implement a pattern of checking every form of power that it bestows on its agents; such checking may be realized by any of a variety of measures—review procedures, credible professional self-regulation, appeal mechanisms, etc.—and is essential for the reduction of people's exposure to arbitrary power.

Accountability may also improve the quality of performance by more generally improving the quality of decision-making. Decisions may not involve any abuse of discretion (that is, intentional misuse) but nevertheless be sub-optimal. The prospect of accounting for a decision may provide an incentive for a decision-maker to make better decisions. Accountability reminds decision-makers of the views that they should take into consideration when deciding on a course of action (Uhr 2001: 4). Australian High Court Chief Justice Murray Gleeson (1995: 122) argues that the principle of open justice, which imposes on judges the obligation to expose and explain their reasoning in public, has this effect on judges. Judges strive to make good decisions knowing that they may be subjected to comment from a range of perspectives (see also Spigelman 1999, 2000).

Andrew Gordon and John Heinz (1979: xiv) describe this is as a 'prophylactic effect', arguing that public scrutiny increases the range of positions that must be considered and in this way increases the constraints on decision-making. Mindful of possible scrutiny, a decision-maker may abandon an indefensible position, and consider adopting alternative arguments. One could argue that accountability mechanisms take their justification from the philosophical rule of publicity, expressed by Immanuel Kant (1795): 'all actions affecting the rights of other human beings are wrong if their maxim is not compatible with their being made public.'[21]

So long as the smallest possibility exists that scrutiny may occur, accountability mechanisms can be effective, even if no scrutiny ultimately takes place (Uhr 2001: 9). Furthermore, if a decision is subsequently scrutinized and judged to be sub-optimal, the accountability mechanism may allow it to be corrected. Whether this correction is a matter of choice or obligation for the decision-maker will depend on whether the model of accountability is directive or persuasive. So, for example, an appeal court judge can simply

---

[21] On the publicity principle see Robert Goodin (1992: 124–46) and David Luban (1996).

vary a trial judge's decision, but an ombudsman will need to persuade a government agency to take remedial action.

Many argue accountability is only necessary because decision-makers cannot be trusted to do the right thing, endorsing James Madison's view (1961: 290) in *The Federalist Papers*, 'If angels were to govern men, neither external nor internal controls on government would be necessary'. This is based on the understanding that the only function of controls is to detect abuses by decision-makers, but as I have pointed out, this is only one of the functions of accounting. No assumption of untrustworthiness underlies the other function of assisting decision-makers by informing or reminding them of the views they should take into account when making decisions. In the task of governing, even angels would benefit from exposure to the full range of interests they should consider as governors.

Enhancing legitimacy

In addition to improving the quality of performance, accountability may also enhance the legitimacy of a decision-making process. Australian High Court Chief Justice Gleeson (1995: 122) argues that, in addition to improving the quality of decision-making, the general acceptability of judicial decisions is promoted by the obligation to explain them. This is important for legal institutions whose effective functioning depends on the voluntary compliance of most citizens (Tyler 1990). American Supreme Court Judge Warren Burger explains how public accountability enhances courts' legitimacy: 'People in an open society do not demand infallibility from their institutions, but it is difficult for them to accept what they are prohibited from observing. When a criminal trial is conducted in the open, there is at least an opportunity both for understanding the system in general and its workings in a particular case.'[22]

Many people assume that the legitimacy of their legal system is unshakeable. However, there are numerous instances even in stable democratic societies, where the legitimacy of a legal institution has been challenged. One such instance lies in the early history of the Australian Family Court. Under legislation establishing the court, proceedings were held in closed courtrooms and a blanket ban was

---

[22] *Richmond Newspapers Inc v Virginia* 448 US 555 at 572 (1980).

imposed on reporting proceedings.[23] Parliament's rationale for closing the court to public access was that no public good was served by exposing the domestic conflicts of individuals to the public gaze (Sackville 1994: 348). However, the early history of the Family Court was a troubled one, with a number of violent attacks by dissatisfied litigants against judges and their families. Subsequent inquiries into the operation of the Family Court attributed the problems partly to the closed nature of proceedings, which 'led to accusations of the Court being akin to a "Star Chamber"' (JSC 1992: 348). As the Chief Justice of the Family Court, Alastair Nicholson (JSC 1992: 348) explains:

> Litigants who complained that they had been denied justice could make allegations concerning the Court and the conduct of Judges and those involved in the proceedings without these allegations being capable of rebuttal. The administration of justice in the Family Court was open to criticism by slur and innuendo and thus, from the outset, the administration of justice in the Court was capable of being portrayed as being of a different category to that of other courts.

Consequently, in 1983 the Act was amended to permit proceedings to be held in open court. The blanket prohibition on publication was also relaxed to allow reporting provided that parties were not identified.[24] The subsequent cessation of violence directed at judges suggests that public confidence was restored.

Complementary means of pursuing accountability ends

The important ends which it is designed to serve suggest that 'High hopes indeed rest on the shoulders of accountability'

---

[23] See the *Family Law Act* (1975) (Commonwealth), sections 97 and 121.

[24] A recent judgment of the English Court of Appeal also touches on this issue. The British government established an inquiry in the wake of the conviction of Harold Shipman for the murder of fifteen of his patients. In *Regina v Secretary of State for Health, Ex parte Wagstaff and Others, Regina v Same, Ex parte Associated Newspapers Ltd and Others* (2000), the government's decision to take evidence in private at the inquiry was appealed against by the victim's support group and the media. In allowing the appeal, Lord Justice Kennedy held that: 'The fact that the deaths occurred over a long period without detection was suggestive of a breakdown in those checks and controls which should operate to prevent such a tragedy; as a result there was likely to be a widespread loss of confidence in a critical part of the National Health Service which needed to be addressed.' Lord Justice Kennedy held that one of the benefits of a public inquiry was that it created a 'perception of open dealing which helped to restore confidence'.

(Diamond *et al.* 1999: 2). But accountability is just one way of improving the quality and legitimacy of decision-making. In addition, many prospective controls are directed towards the same goal. To improve the quality and legitimacy of decisions, a decision-maker's discretion may be confined, or its exercise structured through the adoption of flexible standards or procedural rules (on controlling discretion, see Davis 1969). Beyond control mechanisms many other means exist for pursuing accountability ends, most of which can be used in tandem with accountability mechanisms. Better training for decision-makers, and carefully specifying tasks to be performed can also improve decision-making. Just as requiring judges to give reasons for their decisions is designed to encourage better decision-making, judicial education may serve the same purpose.

Any discussion of compliance would be incomplete without a discussion of the importance of trust in promoting good decision-making. A growing body of empirical and philosophical research examines how trust can promote good decision-making and minimize the abuse of discretion (Putnam 1993; Pettit 1995; Braithwaite 1998; LaFree 1998; Scholz 1998). Robert Putnam's (1993) famous study of Italian regional government concluded that the interpersonal trust in Northern Italy—nurtured by civil associations from choral societies to soccer clubs—partly explained the better economic and institutional performance in that region. A similar finding emerges from a study of Australian nursing homes by John Braithwaite and Toni Makkai (1994). In their study of 410 Australian nursing homes they found that when 'chief executives of nursing homes believed that they were treated as trustworthy by inspectors, their nursing homes experienced a significant improvement in compliance with the law during the two years following that inspection' (Braithwaite 1998: 346). Accountability has to work in tandem with these other means of generating good decisions, something considered in the following discussion of accountability principles.

Guiding principles of accountability

I use the definition of accountability articulated earlier to identify those accountability mechanisms in restorative programmes which may address the sort of concerns outlined above. However, we also need some basis for assessing the modes of accountability uncovered. If we accept that a large part of the value of accountability lies in its instrumental value, then it follows that our assessment of a particular type of accountability will depend on the extent to which that type of accountability helps improve the quality and legitimacy of a programme's performance.

For a number of reasons, it is not possible to be sure about the exact contribution a single accountability mechanism makes towards these goals. For a start, there is no consensus about what constitutes good performance in a restorative justice programme. Moreover, even if consensus could be reached and it were possible to quantify how well a programme performed in the agreed sense, it would be difficult to determine to what extent this was the result of accountability. For one thing a great many factors combine to produce a certain level of performance, be it good or bad. Moreover, even in those cases where accountability does have an effect on a decision-maker's performance, it will often be subtle. Before doing or saying anything, decision-makers may alter their planned course of action in anticipation of being held accountable. In short, knowledge about how an accountability mechanism affects a particular case will not necessarily be available to us.

What is possible, however, is to argue that accountability processes are more likely to achieve their ends when they possess some core properties. Based on these properties, there are seven principles: simplicity, timeliness, inclusiveness, motivational sensitivity, independence, publicity, and iterative accountability.

Simplicity

Accountability processes should be simple: in a choice between two accountability processes, all other things being equal, we should prefer the simpler of the two. Any accountability process that is unnecessarily time-consuming, expensive and labour-intensive will ultimately be counter-productive, as decision-makers' accountability obligations will serve to distract them from their task. Moreover, more onerous obligations will employ scarce resources which could otherwise be put to substantive uses, like advancing justice. Put simply, everyone will be accounting and no one will be doing. Ultimately, complex processes can cripple an institution's productivity. Michael Power (1997: 2) observes that:

some societies have tried to institutionalize checking on a grand scale. These systems have slowly crumpled because of the weight of their information demands, the senseless allocation of scarce resources to surveillance activities and the sheer human exhaustion of existing under such conditions, both for those who check and those who are checked.

The importance of simplicity is especially critical for programmes in poor communities which rely on limited funding and volunteer labour. Many of these programmes simply do not have the resources to establish or maintain complex processes. Even where no trade-off has to be made between accountability and production, simplicity is still a virtue because citizens can readily understand, and therefore, use simple checks and balances.

Timeliness

The process of giving an account should occur in a timely fashion. When accounting does not follow quite soon after the making of a decision, it becomes less likely that this prospect will provide an incentive for the decision-maker to make a good decision. This is partly because people respond better to incentives which exist in the short run than in the long run. Decision-makers may also calculate that when events are no longer fresh in people's memories it will be easier to account for their actions in a way which precludes effective scrutiny. Not only is there less incentive to improve the quality of performance, but delayed accountability processes also make it harder to correct mistakes and abuses: the passage of time makes it more difficult to scrutinize a decision-maker's performance, to detect mistakes and abuses, and to correct them.

Inclusiveness

When people are obliged to account for their actions, those affected by those actions should be represented in the process of scrutinizing any accounts.[25] Inclusion can be justified on an intrinsic as well as an instrumental basis. Intrinsically, of course, inclusion is preferable to exclusion. It also promotes better decisions because it 'allows for maximum expression of interests, opinions, and perspectives relevant to the problems or issues for which a public seeks solutions' (Young 2000: 23). Inclusion may be achieved directly (as in the case

[25] For a good discussion of the principle of affected interests see Richard Mulgan (1984: 115)

of shareholders' entitlements to scrutinize the performance of directors at a shareholder's meeting) or indirectly (as in the case of an ombudsman who takes up the case of a person aggrieved by a government decision). Inclusion means in practice that processes of accountability should not exclude people by unreasonably restricting the way in which they participate in the process. As Young (2000: 6) argues 'to the extent that norms of deliberation implicitly value certain styles of expression as dispassionate, orderly, or articulate, they can have exclusionary implications'. This principle may run up against other principles. In particular, there may have to be a trade-off between the need for simplicity and the need for inclusiveness.

Motivational sensitivity

Decision-makers are motivated by a diverse and complex range of motives. They may be motivated to exercise their discretion responsibly, or to abuse it, or they may be indifferent as to how they exercise it (Goodin 1996: 41). The design of institutions should be sensitive to this fact, i.e. design should be sensitive to the reality of motivational complexity. In situations where many people respond positively to trust, it is unnecessary to treat everyone as untrustworthy. Unnecessary and counterproductive, because when decision-makers feel that they are not trusted they may lose the incentive to behave in a trustworthy manner (Pettit 1995; Braithwaite 1998).

Of all the aspects of institutional design, it is particularly important that processes of accountability should be sensitive to the principle of motivational complexity. Because while accountability may strengthen trust in decision-makers by confirming their competence and integrity (Uhr 2001: 4), decision-makers will often interpret the obligation to give an account of their actions as expressing a lack of trust in them. Accountability mechanisms backfire when this distrust is communicated. By assuming, as David Hume and Thomas Hobbes do, that 'men are knaves', they can make knaves of potentially more honourable actors (for examples see Bayley 1995: 98; Anechiarico and Jacobs 1996: 207). At the same time accountability mechanisms need to be capable of deterring and detecting the real knaves. Sensitivity to motivational complexity means that processes of accountability should aim to both deter and catch those decision-makers who deliberately flout rules and abuse their discretion, while avoiding alienating those people who aim to do the right thing.

Publicity

Publicity is important for several reasons. First, quite apart from any instrumental effect, the public claims an interest in the resolution of criminal matters. By interfering with—or threatening—a person's freedom, crime affects the public's interest in a most fundamental way. The public's interest is also financial: many restorative programmes are funded by public money. Secondly, on an instrumental basis, publicity may help curb the abuse of power. Conversely, there is considerable scepticism about the value of accountability mechanisms which are not public. Andreas Schedler (1999: 21), for example, says: 'As a rule, only public accountability can achieve its aim of curbing power, while confidential accountability, exercised behind closed doors, tends to be perceived as a farce, a caricature of accountability.' Thirdly, accountability may enhance not only the quality, but also the legitimacy, of a decision-maker's decisions. This is particularly important in the context of a legal system, because its effective functioning depends on the voluntary compliance of most citizens; this compliance in turn depends on a range of factors, including citizens' perception of the legitimacy of that system, and when citizens know that decision-makers are accountable they are more likely to respect the legitimacy of their decisions. Effective functioning requires not only the existence of an accountability mechanism, but the publicizing of its existence.

Accountability mechanisms may satisfy this requirement when the mechanism itself is a public one, as elections are. According to Richard Mulgan and John Uhr (2000: 1) the term 'public accountability' refers to accountability 'acted out in public with the aim of generating a public record of performance open to community examination and debate'. Accountability mechanisms which are not themselves public may nevertheless satisfy the requirement of publicity when they are part of a chain of accountability, at the end of which is some form of public accountability, such as the accountability of public servants to government ministers, who are accountable to Parliament, whose members are in turn accountable to the public through the ballot box.

It goes without saying that the legitimacy effect of a type of accountability does not depend solely on its publicity. Publicizing a poor form of accountability will not necessarily serve to enhance the legitimacy of the account-giver. An example of this is the televising of question time in the Australian Parliament in which parliamentarians routinely abuse and harangue one another. This can—and probably does—decrease the government's legitimacy in the eyes of its citizens. Concerns about the effects of negative publicity underlie the practice of keeping jury and cabinet deliberations secret. The justification offered is that if disagreements were to become public, confidence in the institutions and their decisions would be undermined.

The principle of publicity illustrates clearly the interplay between principles in that it is likely to work in the same direction as the requirement of inclusiveness: that is, the more public a form of accountability the more inclusive it is likely to be. But satisfying the principle of publicity (and that of inclusiveness) may require more elaborate, expensive, and time-consuming forms of accountability, thus conflicting with the principles of simplicity and timeliness.

Independence

This principle means that the reviewer should be independent of the decision-maker. That is, for an accountability mechanism to function effectively, the person to whom the account is given should be independent of the person providing the account. Accountability will only prompt better performance when a decision-maker anticipates scrutiny. A lack of independence makes the prospect of such scrutiny less likely: where a reviewer's interests are tied too closely to the decision-maker's, that reviewer has less incentive to properly scrutinize an account, as to do so may adversely affect his or her own interests.

Advocates of external accountability will see no problem with this requirement, since one of the main reasons for external accountability is the independence it is thought to provide. It may cause problems for those who argue that internal forms of accountability can also be effective, but it is not suggested that all internal forms lack independence. Rather, the implication is that internal forms can have varying degrees of independence, and that the better form of internal accountability, all other things being equal, is that in which the person scrutinizing the account is more independent from the person providing the account. Further, while internal forms of accountability lack independence compared with external forms, they may have advantages in terms of simplicity, timeliness, and motivational sensitivity.

Notwithstanding the importance of independence, it is questionable whether complete independence is either possible or desirable. Even institutions whose independence is prized—such as the judiciary in countries where the rule of law is respected—remain susceptible to a variety of influences, and desirably so. While it is important that the judiciary has the power to hold the government to account, it is equally important that there be some mechanism for removing a judge found to be unfit for office. Similarly, the notion of peer review (embodied in mechanisms such as the disciplinary boards operated by the medical and legal professions) is built upon the idea that the 'people best suited to judge the performance of others are those who work most closely with them' (Peiperl 2001: 48). John Braithwaite's (1997b: 312) work attempts to take these empirical and normative qualifications into account. In the context of the separation of powers, he argues that the ideal is not of complete independence but of 'enough independence' or 'semi-autonomous power' so that one branch of power is not overwhelmed or dominated by another. In the context of accountability, the principle of independence should be understood in a similar way. People to whom others account must have sufficient independence that they can properly scrutinize an account, but they may still be in some ways subject to their influence.

Iterative accountability

Finally, effective accountability requires that a person to whom an account is given is himself or herself also accountable: this requirement is called iterative accountability. Accountability processes, by subjecting decision-makers to scrutiny, are designed to reduce the risk of poor decision-making, but when a decision-maker is required to account to someone who is not themselves accountable, this has the effect of simply transferring, rather than reducing, the risk of poor decision-making. Instead of worrying about how the original decision-maker exercises discretion, we now have to worry about how the person who receives the account uses his or her's. This problem is present most obviously in directive models of accountability, in which the person receiving the account exercises power over decision-makers beyond the power to demand an account. In persuasive accountability, where the accountability agency is only entitled to insist that a decision-maker provide an account, there is less discretion to abuse or misuse.

The standard obstacle to achieving iterative accountability is that of infinite regress. As Andreas Schedler (1999: 26) puts it, 'Since any second layer of institutional accountability is susceptible to the same kind of failures as the first layer, we face the possibility of infinite regress' (see also Braithwaite 1997b: 348). Schedler identifies two ways to avoid this problem: 'We may establish *reciprocal* accountability: two agents, A and B, "check and balance" each other. Or we may establish *recursive* accountability: A is accountable to B, who is accountable to C, who is accountable to A again.'

Juggling principles

Across a range of regulatory settings these principles are indicia of good accountability; when an accountability mechanism reflects them, we can have some confidence that it is of a means likely to promote the best accountability ends. Although a number of these principles can be assumed to be essential, it cannot be presumed that all readers would choose the same guiding principles, nor is it suggested that this is an exhaustive list. They do, however, provide a clear basis for assessing the forms of accountability identified in restorative justice programmes.

A number of these principles push accountability in different directions. No attempt is made, however, to rank them. To a large extent, the relative importance of these principles is context-specific. So, for example, it could be expected that inclusiveness would be particularly important in the context of a community with a history of exclusion and discrimination. Ideally, under the philosophy developed here, finding the right balance among these principles in a specific policy context is something accomplished through dialogue between practitioners, community groups, policy makers, and academics.

Competing concepts

Designing or assessing any type of accountability is not simply a matter of ensuring it reflects these principles in some combination or other. Even well-designed accountability processes (that is, accountability reflecting these seven principles) will also need to consider specific arguments against accountability itself. These arguments will vary from one policy context to another, but all are used to justify closing, rather than opening, decision-making processes to the scrutiny of others. In a political context, the interests of national security may be used to resist demands for accountability. In a business context, the interest may be a commercial one. In the context of institutions of justice dealing primarily with the attribution of individual responsibility, those individuals' privacy is the most common source of arguments against accountability. In Chapter Seven I consider privacy arguments in the context in which they usually arise in restorative justice programmes; namely, whether meetings should be open to the public.

Conclusion

Restorative justice can be thought of as a set of normative claims about how societies should respond to conflict. A response is restorative when it acknowledges the personal dimension of crime, allows for the participation of the people affected, and seeks to repair a victims' harm and reintegrate offenders. It is often assumed that when victims, offenders, and their supporters meet, reparation and reintegration will naturally follow. In many cases they may, but a participatory process that gives rein to the personal dimension of crime can equally become an occasion for oppressive, traumatizing encounters between victims and offenders. By presenting restorative justice as the authentic pre-state form of justice and as an alternative punishment, advocates risk losing sight of these destructive possibilities. There are many risks inherent in restorative justice, present during restorative justice meetings themselves, as well as before and after meetings.

Accountability mechanisms aim to close the gap between promise and performance, between the ideals of restorative justice and its sometimes ugly practice. In this context, accountability refers to procedural safeguards with the following elements:

- People with decision-making responsibilities are obliged to explain and justify themselves;
- Other people scrutinize that account, or have the right to scrutinize that account. (Accountability does not necessarily require actual scrutiny, but there must be some realistic possibility of scrutiny);

- The obligation to give accounts may be enforced formally or informally;
- A person's obligation to be accountable may be the limit of a person's obligation (persuasive accountability), or the obligation may also entail an obligation to take directions from the person scrutinizing the account (directive accountability);
- The process of accounting may occur after a decision has been made (retrospective) or on an ongoing basis throughout the decision-making process (ongoing).

Given that accountability is usually just one of a number of means of promoting the quality and legitimacy of decision-making, it is difficult to isolate any particular accountability mechanism's contribution to good decision-making. To address this problem, seven criteria have been developed which can be used to assess the quality of an accountability mechanism: simplicity, timeliness, inclusiveness, motivational sensitivity, publicity, independence, and iterative accountability. These principles are used subsequently to identify the modes of accountability found in the programmes surveyed. Of course, being restorative and being accountable are not the only criteria for evaluating restorative justice programmes, but the argument here is that they will be potentially revealing dimensions.

3
Methods and Overview of Programmes

Restorative justice programmes are now to be found in a number of countries. In order to investigate the range of these, twenty-five were selected as case studies. The term 'restorative justice' covers a wide range of practices. Although this range illustrates confusion about the meaning and application of restorative justice, there remain four fundamental ideals: personalism, reparation, reintegration, and participation. Once they are unravelled, we can begin to see why such a diverse—and sometimes contradictory—range of practices fall within the limits of the same defined term. Many of the practices labelled as 'restorative justice' reflect at least one of the basic elements: for example, both victim support services and government compensation schemes aim to assist victims and repair some of the harm they have suffered; more symbolically, a memorial to honour the victims of violence can also be regarded as a reparative gesture; alternatives to incarceration—such as probation and community service—attempt to reintegrate offenders. In other words, once we realize 'restorative justice' possesses a number of different strands, we can see how a long list of practices can be properly considered to be restorative, at least in some sense.

A smaller number of programmes attempting to combine all four basic elements—personalism, reparation, reintegration, and participation—are the driving force of restorative justice and the focus of this study. Of interest here are those programmes which acknowledge the personal dimension of a crime through creating opportunities for all of those most affected by it to come together in an attempt to find ways of ameliorating or repairing the harm created, and to reintegrate the offender and his or her family.

To illustrate the diversity of these particular restorative justice programmes, it was necessary to select multiple case studies, eventually reduced to twenty-five of the most representative. There were five distinct types: conference programmes, circle programmes, sentencing panels, mediation programmes, and multi-form programmes (i.e. programmes using a combination of some or all of the above methods). They were from six different countries (Australia, England, New Zealand, South Africa, United States, and Canada); were run by a variety of different institutions (community groups, justice departments, police and schools) and performed a variety of functions (some operating as an alternative to formal sentencing, others as part of formal sentencing, and yet others as an adjunct to formal sentencing).

Research method

Three main research methods were employed in this empirical study: document analysis, participant observation, and interviews with restorative justice practitioners. The use of multiple methods means that data from one source could be used to illuminate data from the others, thus enhancing reliability and validity.

Analysing documents provided a valuable starting point for identifying restorative justice programmes. They were also in themselves a valuable source of data. Some documents took the form of evaluations of programmes, conducted either by programme staff themselves or by independent researchers. Other documents were more descriptive, designed to be given to people seeking information about a programme, such as potential participants. Not all programmes, however, were so well documented, and what documentation there is often makes little mention of accountability. An additional source of (electronic) documentary material came from a number of e-mail lists devoted to restorative justice, in which both practitioners and researchers shared ideas and materials and answered each other's queries.[1]

'Participant observation' is a loose term describing a range of research methods in which the researcher unobtrusively collects data in the course of social interaction with the researcher's subject, in the subject's environment. The extent of participation

---

[1] As it seems with many such e-mail lists, the life of these lists was sometimes limited. Lists broke down through technical problems (such as server difficulties), disuse, and in one case, through an altercation between the manager of the list and some of the regular contributors.

and observation involved can be placed on a continuum. At one extreme, the researcher becomes a total participant, joining in the research subjects' activities and engaging them in conversation in addition to watching their behaviour. At the other, he or she becomes a total observer, restricting him or herself to observing research subjects' activities. In many cases, a researcher adopts a position somewhere in between.[2]

The style of participant observation used in this study moved backwards and forwards along this continuum. Some data was gathered as a total participant, convening conferences for young offenders in New South Wales, Australia,[3] when my role as a convenor took priority over my role as an observer. In other restorative justice meetings I was a total observer, watching meetings from the back of the room, or a participant-researcher in those programmes where the practice was for observers to also participate in the meeting. Freed from the demands of organizing and convening meetings, on these occasions I was able to turn my attention much more towards observing.

While participant observation methods are popular because they allow researchers to gain rich, detailed information about research subjects and their settings, any interaction between researchers and their subjects is likely to give rise to problems. In particular, the presence of a researcher—whether as participant, observer, or participant-observer—may well affect behaviour within the meeting. Social research is not carried out in an 'autonomous realm' insulated from the wider society and biography of the researcher, but is a reflexive process in which the researcher influences his or her research environment, and vice versa (Hammersley and Atkinson 1995). Possible distortion is particularly relevant when one is simultaneously acting in a combination of roles: as a researcher (observing conferences) and a practitioner (convening them). Such

---

[2] Herbert Gans (1982) distinguishes between total participants, total researchers, and researcher participants. The category 'researcher participant' is further divided into sub-categories of 'participant as observer' and 'observer as participant' (Burgess 1982:5–6), but whether this distinction is of any value is a moot point (Hammersley and Atkinson 1995: 108).

[3] Under the *Young Offenders Act* (NSW), community members are employed on a part-time basis to organize and convene restorative justice conferences after undergoing an initial selection process, approximately three days of training and then finally, a second selection process.

problems reinforce the more general requirement not to accept at face value the validity of knowledge, whatever its form or origin, as well as to recognize the importance of using multiple research methods to enhance the reliability and validity of the research.

Participant observation can also be unpredictable, as proved by this empirical study. In particular, it was difficult to organize visits to programmes so that they coincided with restorative justice meetings. Even when visits were scheduled around planned meetings, meetings sometimes were cancelled for a variety of reasons. As a result, it was not possible to observe meetings in all programmes (Appendix B lists the meetings observed or convened). In all but three cases I attended the restorative meeting,[4] and all but two of the meetings observed were from case-study programmes.[5]

Some fifty interviews, the third research method, ranging in length from thirty minutes to three hours were conducted.[6] Mainly with practitioners, interviews were usually conducted on a one-on-one basis, except on one occasion when practitioners asked to be interviewed together. In order to encourage a free flow of conversation and facilitate expression of the interviewee's thoughts about accountability, interviews were not approached with a rigid order

---

[4] The exceptions were mediation sessions run by the Texas Victim/Offender Mediation/Dialogue Program where observers are not allowed to attend sessions but, where participants consent, can later view a videotape of the meeting.

[5] Of the two meetings, one was a mediation session in Minneapolis which I was invited to by the mediator. The other was an offender's healing circle from a healing lodge in Quebec, Canada. Originally my intention was to include non-meeting based forms of restorative justice, so as to achieve the maximum possible diversity. With this in mind, I included in my first fieldwork trip visits to two programmes in Canada (Waseskun House in Quebec, and the Canim Lake Family Violence Programme in British Columbia), both of which draw on restorative justice principles but do not centre around meetings between victims and offenders. Subsequently, however, it became clear to me how vast an array of programmes could legitimately be considered examples of restorative justice and that consequently it would be arbitrary to include only these two programmes. If these programmes were included, why not also victim support groups, and if victim support groups, why not victim impact statements? Although not wanting to suggest that these practices cannot be differentiated, eventually I decided, for the reasons outlined above, to exclude all programmes not based primarily on restorative processes. For a description of the Canim Lake Family Violence Programme see Barry Warhaft, Ted Payls, and Wilma Boyce (1999: 168).

[6] I refer to these interviews throughout the following chapters. Unless otherwise indicated, quotations come from these interviews.

of questions, but instead with a list of issues to be covered in whatever order seemed appropriate at the time. This semi-structured approach helped put practitioners at ease, as did allowing interviewees to choose the time and setting for the interviews.

Most interviewees appeared comfortable answering questions about the general nature of their programmes. Many have spent considerable time providing such information to criminal justice system professionals, potential funding bodies, researchers, and others. By contrast, however, conversation flowed less readily on the topic of accountability. To draw out practitioners' own perceptions of accountability, an effort was made to avoid leading questions; however, it was sometimes necessary to spend some time clarifying the particular sense of accountability in which I was interested, namely, the forms of institutional accountability.

How an interviewer presents him or herself can have an important influence on the responses he or she obtains. In some situations it was helpful for me to emphasize experience as a practitioner, a useful strategy when meeting any practitioner who appeared wary; some interviewees volunteered that they enjoyed the opportunity to talk about their work with a fellow practitioner. In some other situations, however, it was useful to adopt the role of learner, especially where it was otherwise difficult to encourage interviewees to speak in sufficient detail. A combination of contemporaneous and subsequent note-taking was used to record interviewees' responses.[7]

Sample of programmes

An initial sample of programmes was selected from available literature as suitable sites for research: Canada and the United States both offered a diverse range of programmes. Within the United States, the twin cities of Minneapolis/St Paul were a particularly rich microcosm of restorative justice activity. Indeed, the twin cities can claim to be the site of the greatest diversity of restorative justice programmes anywhere in the world. Interviews with practitioners in the initial sample revealed other programmes that had not been discovered by reviewing the literature. This snowball method subsequently

---

[7] Appendix C lists the names of the interviewees.

proved an effective method of generating a diverse sample of pro-grammes.[8]

The Australian data were collected steadily from 1999 to 2001, while data from programmes elsewhere were collected in two separate periods of fieldwork, the first in late 1999, the second in late 2000. Although the survey includes a diverse range of programmes, it nevertheless suffers from the limitations imposed by the heavy bias in favour of programmes from English-speaking countries, neglecting the numerous restorative justice programmes elsewhere.

Within the sample, there is a strong emphasis on conferencing programmes (twelve of the twenty-five case studies are conferencing programmes). This proportion partly reflects the fact that conferencing appears to be the fastest growing form of restorative justice, but a more representative survey should perhaps include more victim–offender mediation programmes. This is not just because by the year 2000 more than 300 victim–offender mediation programmes were operating in the United States alone (Umbreit *et al.* 2001), but also because victim–offender mediation pre-dates almost all other types. Indeed, as Tony Marshall (1999: 7) suggests, the term 'restorative justice' is generally attributed to Randy Barnett (1977) in referring to certain principles emerging out of early mediation projects in the United States. In mitigation of the shortcoming produced by this emphasis, however, is the fact that the distinction between victim–offender mediation and conferencing in practice is becoming increasingly blurred, as mediators routinely use what they call 'multi-party mediation', in which both victims and offenders are encouraged to bring supporters.

Although this survey encompasses a large proportion of the diversity of programmes in a criminal justice or educational setting, the survey does not extend to programmes established to address other types of harm, such as the South African Truth and Reconciliation Commission (established to address political crimes) and the many conferencing programmes used in child welfare cases.[9] However,

---

[8] This approach is similar to Christine Parker's (1999: 230) 'difference discovery method', a variation on the snowballing technique which is consciously 'oriented towards the pursuit of diversity in views and experiences'.

[9] For a restorative justice perspective on the South African Truth and Reconciliation Commission see Kader Asmal (2000), Martha Minow (1998), Jennifer Llewellyn and Robert Howse (1999), and Archbishop Desmond Tutu (1999).

these programmes are referred to in later chapters, and it is hoped that the discussion of accountability will also have relevance to these programmes.

Overview of surveyed programmes

Conference programmes

Conferences, a common form of restorative justice process, have their modern origins in New Zealand. They aim to involve the victim and offender and a number of their families or supporters. Many run as alternatives to formal conviction and sentencing by the criminal justice system; others run in conjunction with it. This survey includes both types of programmes. It includes programmes run by police departments, agencies such as other government departments, and community groups and schools.[10]

Circle programmes

There are substantial similarities between conference and circles. Both bring together the people immediately affected by an incident, and use a deliberative, consensus-based approach in which the emphasis is on attempting to repair the harm created by an offence. However, circles (with their origins in Native American communities) tend to involve wider community participation than either conferencing or mediation programmes, and are distinctive for their emphasis on ritual. Such a ritual might include beginning and ending with a prayer and the use of a talking piece (an object such as an eagle feather) which is passed around the circle from one participant to

[10] The following conference programmes were included in the survey:
- Family Group Conferencing, New Zealand;
- Police Conferencing, Wagga Wagga, NSW, Australia;
- Australian Federal Police Diversionary Conferencing, Canberra, ACT, Australia;
- Woodbury Police Conferencing, MN, United States;
- Thames Valley Police Restorative Justice Programme, UK;
- Youth Justice Conferencing, NSW, Australia;
- Community Conferencing, QLD, Australia;
- Community Conferencing, Central City Neighbourhoods Partnership, MN, United States;
- Waitakere District Court Restorative Justice Pilot, Auckland, New Zealand;
- School Conferencing, Sunshine Coast, QLD, Australia;
- Fredrick H. Tuttle Middle School, South Burlington, VT, United States.

another, entitling the holder to speak without interruption. Another quite significant difference is the practice of holding multiple meetings for an offender (rather than just a single meeting as is the case in other types of programmes). Here we consider six different circle programmes, ranging from ancient Navajo peacemaking to very recently established programmes. These programmes exist in a wide range of settings from remote, non-urban settings such as the Yukon Territory in Canada and the Navajo Nation in Arizona to urban settings in very poor South African townships, as well as three programmes in the American twin cities, Minneapolis/St Paul.[11]

Sentencing panels

Typically, meetings in sentencing panels involve a group of volunteers and the offender and in some cases, an offender's supporters. Like all restorative justice programmes, victim participation in sentencing panels varies from one programme to another, but sentencing panels consistently appear to have little direct victim input, with community volunteers instead representing direct victims. While there are variations within and between these programmes, their form often mirrors courtroom practices. The offender appears before a panel, similar to the way an offender appears before a judge. In one programme—the Toronto Community Council—the panel even asks the offender to retire while the panel makes its decision in private, in the same way that a judge or jury does.[12]

Mediation programmes

Modern victim–offender mediation has its origins in North America (Umbreit *et al.* 2001: 122). Many small mediation

---

[11] The circle programmes surveyed are:

- Navajo Peacemaking, Navajo Nation, AZ, United States;
- Carcross Circle Programme, Yukon Territory, Canada;
- Northside Community Justice Committee, MN, United States;
- South St Paul Restorative Justice Council, St Paul, MN, United States;
- Zwelethemba Peacemaker Committee, Western Cape, South Africa.

[12] The following programmes can all loosely be described as sentencing panels:

- Reparative Boards, Vermont Department of Corrections, Burlington, VT, United States;
- Toronto Community Council, Ontario, Canada;
- Vancouver Restorative Justice Programme, BC, Canada;
- Youth Offender Panels, England and Wales.

programmes operated in both Europe and North America well before the emergence of the restorative justice movement (Marshall 1996). Indeed, the modern development of restorative justice 'probably began in response to the first victim–offender mediation programmes developed in the mid-1970s in Canada', also known as VORPs (Victim–Offender Reconciliation Programmes) (Ness *et al.* 2001).[13] Early programmes limited participation to the offender and directly affected victims, but increasingly, mediation programmes encourage supporters to accompany victims and offenders (in what practitioners call 'multi-party mediation'). However, some do continue to run mediation solely for victims and offenders. As a general rule mediation programmes remain less prescriptive about the attendance of supporters, instead varying the number of participants according to the nature of the dispute and the wishes of the victim and the offender. Again, mediation programmes sometimes use shuttle negotiation between the parties, whereas conference and circle programmes prefer to run face-to-face meetings between participants.[14]

Multi-form programmes

These programmes use a combination of the processes described above. That is, depending on the circumstances, a programme may use mediation (either direct or indirect), a conference, or a circle, as well as a range of other interventions.[15]

Size, authority, and function of programmes

The programmes surveyed vary in size from nationwide (in the case of New Zealand) and statewide (in the case of New South

---

[13] For a brief history of victim–offender mediation see Mark Umbreit, Robert Coates, and Betty Vos (2001: 122).

[14] The following victim–offender mediation programme was included in this survey:
- Victim/Offender Mediation/Dialogue Program, TX, United States.

[15] The following multi-form programmes were included in the survey:
- 'Just Youth' Project, Spectrum Youth and Family Services, Burlington, VT, United States;
- Washington County Community Justice, MN, United States;
- Prince William County Restorative Justice Program, VA, United States;
- Connections Program, Minnesota Correctional Facility, MN, United States.

Wales, Australia), through to small programmes which serve a part of a town or city. The larger programmes tend to be located in Australia, New Zealand, England, and Wales, and the smaller ones in Canada, the United States, and South Africa.

Legal authority for these programmes comes from a variety of sources: larger programmes tend to be established expressly by a statute,[16] while in some smaller ones there is general legislation authorizing the creation of restorative programmes. Many programmes have become established under the discretion of police, prosecutors, school principals, and prison authorities.

Generally, meetings which are run as an alternative to formal sentencing deal with less serious offences,[17] while those which are part of the formal sentencing process deal with more serious crime.[18] This is only a rough rule, however. On occasions, some of the programmes running as an alternative to formal conviction and sentencing also deal with serious crimes (notably the Zwelethemba Peacemaker Committee and the Toronto Community Council).

Table 3.1 (see p. 70) collates some of the key features of the programmes surveyed, following which is a summary of the main variations at different stages of the process: pre-meeting, meeting, and post-meeting.

Pre-meeting

Most programmes rely for referrals on institutions within the criminal justice system.[19] In most cases, professionals within these institutions have considerable discretion about which cases they will refer to a restorative justice programme. As a result, many practitioners are forced to spend considerable time and effort explaining to

---

[16] New Zealand Family Group Conferencing, New South Wales Juvenile Justice Conferencing, Queensland Community Conferencing, and the English and Welsh Young Offender Panels.

[17] Such as property offences, and minor assaults. Some programmes also deal with 'victimless' crimes such as under-age drinking (Woodbury Police), drug related offences (NSW Youth Justice Conferencing), and drink-driving (Australian Federal Police Diversionary Conferencing, and Vermont Reparative Boards).

[18] Such as violent assault, including sexual assault, and in one programme, homicide.

[19] Among the programmes surveyed, the exceptions to this are the school programmes, and the Zwelethemba Peacemaker Committee in South Africa, which receives requests for assistance directly from victims and offenders.

TABLE 3.1. Overview of programmes

	Family Group Conference, NZ	RISE, Wagga Wagga, NSW	Australian Federal Police, ACT	Woodbury Police, MN	Thames Valley Police, UK	Youth Justice conferencing, NSW	Community conferencing, QLD	CCNP Community Conferencing, MN	Waikato pilot, NZ	Queensland Schools	Frederick Middle School, VT	Navajo Peacemaking	Gacaca Circles	Northside Justice Committee, Territory	Sparwood St Paul, MN	Zwelethemba Peacemaker	Reparative Boards, VT	Toronto Community Council	Vancouver RJ program	Youth panels, Erie & Niagara	Just Youth / Victim Offender mediation, TX	Washington County, VT	Community Justice Program, MN	Red Wing, MN
Referral Source: Community (C), Teacher (T), Police (P) Prosecutor (PR), Judge (J)	P J	P	P	P PR J	P J	P J	J	J	T J	T	C PR J	C PR J	C PR J	T PR J	C	C PR J	C PR J	J	J	C	C T P PR	J PR	P PR J	C
Admission required	√	√	√	√	√	√	√	√	√	√	√	√	√	√	√	√	√	√	√	√	√	√	√	
Function of Meeting: Part of Sentence (S) or Diversion (D)	S D	D	D	D	S D	S D	S D	S	D	D	S D	S D	S D	S D	D	S	S	D	S	S	S D	S S	D	
Types of Offenders: Juvenile (J), Adult (A)	J	J	J	J	J A	A	A	A	J	J	A	J A	J A	J	A	J A	A	J	A	A	J A	J	A	J
Offender Participation: Voluntary(V),or Mandatory(M)	M	V	V	V	V	V	V	V	V	V	V	V	V	V	V	V	V	M	M	V	V	V	V	V
Victim participation: Voluntary (V) or Mandatory (M)	V	V	V	V	V	V	V	V	V	V	V	V	V	V	V	V	V	V	V	V	V	V	V	V
Victim Veto Over Offender Participation	√	√					√			√														
Supporters Participate	√	√				√	√	√	√	√	√	√	√	√	√	√	√	√	√	√	√	√	√	
Additional Community Representatives Participate	√	√											√					√	√	√	√	√		
Investigating Officer Invited	√	√	√	√	√	√	√	NA	√	√	√	√	√	NA	NA	√	√	√	√	√		√	NA	
Convenor: Professional (P), Community (C); Co-convenors (2)	P	2P	2P	P	P	C	C	2C	P	P	2C	2C	C	2C	P	C	C	C	2C	2C	2C	C	P	P
Decision Making By Consensus	√	√	√	√	√	√	√	√	√	√	√	√	√	√	√	√	√	√	√	√	√	√	√	√
Meetings: Closed (C),Open (O) or Authority required (A) for Media (M) Public (P) Researchers(R)	CM CP AR	CM CP AR	AM AP AR	CM CP AR	CM CP AR	AM AP AR	AM AP AR	CM AP AR	CM OP OR	AM OP OR	AM OP OR	OM OP OR	AM AP AR	CM OP OR	OM OP OR	CM CP CR	CM CP CR	CM CP CR	AM AP CR	AM AP AR	CM AP CR	CM AP AR	OM OP OR	AM AP AR
Further Action Taken Where No Agreement Reached	√	√	√	√	√	√	√	√	√	√	√	√	√	√	√	√	√	√	√	√	√	√	√	
Single Meeting (S) or Multiple Meetings (M)	S	S	S	S	S	S	S	M	S	S	S	M	M	M	M	S	S	M	S	S	S	M	S	M
Monitoring Outcomes: Internal (I), Judge (J)	I J				I J	I J	I J	I	I J	I J	I J		I	I	I	I J	I J	I J	I J	I J	I J	I		I J
Formal Enforcement of Outcome Compliance	√	√	√	√	√	√	√	√	√	√	√	√	√	√	√	√	√	√	√	√	√	√	√	

them the benefits of restorative justice. An exception to this picture is New Zealand, where conferences have been made mandatory for most offences.

Even though all programmes have some sort of screening process for referrals, both the nature of this process and the criteria by means of which the screening takes place vary enormously. In the majority of programmes a single person is responsible for screening referrals; however, in one programme screening is done by a panel.[20]

Once a programme accepts a referral, the offender and the victim are asked if they wish to participate in a meeting.[21] If the offender declines, the meeting does not go ahead and he or she is instead referred to an alternative forum (in most programmes, court). A feature unique to New South Wales conferencing is that offenders are encouraged to seek legal advice before agreeing to participate in a conference, and are given the phone number for a government-funded toll-free legal advice hotline. In most programmes, if the victim declines to participate, the meeting goes ahead in his or her absence. In a minority of programmes (as Table 3.1 shows) the victim is given the additional power to decide whether the offender should be offered a meeting at all.[22]

In about half the programmes surveyed, convenors are community volunteers. In the other half, convenors are people from the community who are employed on a part-time basis, or people employed in positions such as police officers or teachers, whose responsibilities include organizing and convening meetings. Training for convenors varies from a couple of hours in some programmes to almost one hundred hours in the Texas Victim/Offender Mediation/Dialogue Program.

---

[20] Wagga Wagga, NSW, Australia; and in the Woodbury Police Program, St Paul, USA, Dave Hines has plans to establish a panel for screening serious cases.

[21] Nearly all of the programmes surveyed share the assumption that restorative values are best pursued through a meeting. However, a small number of programmes do not start with this assumption, instead speaking separately to the victim and the offender to discover what would repair the harm caused by the offence and help reintegrate an offender. These programmes offer a range of options, only one of which is a meeting. The best example of such a programme is the Spectrum Youth and Family Services 'Just Youth' Project in Burlington, Vermont.

[22] Within the sample of programmes, there are five programmes which give victims this extra responsibility. These are Queensland Community Conferencing, Minneapolis Central City Neighbourhoods Partnership, South St Paul Restorative Justice Council, and the Victim/Offender Mediation/Dialogue Program in Texas.

The time between the decision to hold a meeting and the meeting itself varies from a matter of days (in the case of the Zwelethemba Peace Committee) to eighteen months (in the case of the Texas Victim/Offender Mediation/Dialogue Program); in most programmes, however, meetings are usually held within a matter of weeks rather than months. In some, deadlines are set for the organization of meetings, but where this is the case, these deadlines are exceeded more often than they are met.

Meeting

Where police run restorative programmes, meetings are held in police stations, and when they are school-run, they usually take place on school grounds. Elsewhere, meetings typically are held in venues such as community halls, since they are thought to provide a neutral setting. Yet others are held in venues with some cultural significance for the offender and his family (such as a New Zealand marae, a Maori meeting place).

The programmes vary enormously in terms of the number and identity of participants in a meeting, but as a minimum all meetings involve an offender and a convenor. Table 3.1 shows that a number of programmes use two convenors. In some programmes, such as Texas Victim/Offender Mediation/Dialogue Program, and the Zwelethemba Peacemaker Committee, victims always attend. These programmes are in a minority, however. In the great majority of programmes, victims attend with a frequency somewhere between rarely and regularly.

Conferencing, circle, and sentencing programmes encourage offenders and victims to bring supporters with them to meetings. These supporters may be family, friends, or, quite often in the case of young offenders, schoolteachers. The practice of mediation programmes is more varied. In multi-party mediation, victims and offenders are encouraged to bring supporters with them, but in strict mediation, only the offender, victim, and mediator participate.

A small number of programmes make provision for formal advocates for victims and offenders to attend meetings. This may be an offender's lawyer (as is sometimes the case in some of the circle programmes), or it may be an advocate provided by the government (as is the case in both of the New Zealand programmes surveyed).

A number of programmes make provision for the participation of community members, sometimes, as mentioned, as a convenor. Table 3.1 shows that other programmes, mainly circles and sentencing panels, make provision for community members to participate not as convenors, but as community representatives.

In relation to the role of community members, a number of programmes make provision for the involvement of community elders. In the case of the Navajo Peacemaking Program this is as a convenor. In other programmes elders participate in, but do not convene, meetings, usually at the invitation of the convenor or the offender.[23]

The attendance of state officials is another variable across and within programmes. In police-run programmes, police convene meetings, and in some other circle and conferencing programmes, state representatives participate in other ways. In some, police officers participate not as convenors but as the investigating officers. For example, in the New Zealand Family Group Model, a police officer attends nearly all cases (Maxwell and Morris 1993: 75), and in Queensland, Australia, the investigating officer attends nearly every conference. More commonly, however, there is some level of resistance to police attending, both on the part of the programme staff and of the police. The most extreme form of this occurs in the English and Welsh Young Offender Panels where police officers are prohibited from attending. Other state officials who might attend meetings include social workers,[24] victim and offender advocates, and in the case of sentencing circles, a prosecutor and a judge.

Restorative meetings are designed to serve a number of purposes: to seek explanations from offenders for their actions, to allow victims to describe the harm they have suffered, and to reach agreement about how offenders can repair that harm. The way they attempt to achieve these goals varies considerably. In some programmes there is an emphasis on convenors saying as little as possible; in other programmes convenors are encouraged to make a much greater contribution. The most striking example of the latter is the Navajo Peacemaking Program, where convenors (called 'peacemakers') tell Navajo stories which carry

[23] For example, under s 47 of the *Young Offenders Act* (1997) (NSW), convenors can invite respected members of the community, including Aboriginal elders.

[24] Gabrielle Maxwell and Allison Morris (1993: 75) report that in nearly two-thirds of all family group conferences, a social worker attends.

some moral for participants. In some conferencing programmes, convenors convene meetings by asking participants a number of prepared questions in a pre-determined sequence. This 'scripted' version of conferencing is promoted by REAL Justice, an American NGO.

Through a process of deliberation and negotiation, participants collectively decide what an offender should do. In all but one of the programmes decisions are made by consensus.[25]

Some programmes provide for a short break to be taken during a meeting, to allow the offender's family to confer and devise possible outcomes, which are then presented to the other participants for further discussion.

Restorative justice advocates often stress that the exact nature of an agreement is 'limited only by the imagination of the parties' (Maxwell and Morris 1993: 10). Typically, however, agreements usually involve an offender agreeing to apologize to the victim of an offence, and often to paying some form of financial or other material reparation. Participants cannot agree to send an offender to prison, but in a small number of programmes there is provision to make such a recommendation to a judge who may attend the meeting,[26] or who may subsequently review the meeting's recommendations, before handing down his or her sentence.[27]

Table 3.1 shows that, in all but five programmes, if an agreement cannot be reached about a suitable outcome the matter is referred to court (or in the case of school programmes, some alternative forum), although in practice interviewees report that it is rare for parties not to reach agreement. An offender's failing to turn up to a meeting is

---

[25] The exception is Youth Offender Panels in England and Wales where an outcome does not require a victim's approval. In some programmes there is not a strict requirement of consensus, but as a matter of practice convenors aim to reach consensus. For example, victim approval is not strictly required in the Thames Valley model, but in practice, where a victim attends a conference, the convenor seeks to ensure that the victim approves of any proposed outcome. The Youth Offender Panels, which were in the process of being established at the time of writing, may in practice end up operating in the same way.

[26] As in the case of the Carcross Circle Program in the Yukon Territory, Canada.

[27] This is the case in the Waitakere District Court Programme, where conferences are held prior to sentencing. It can also occur in the New Zealand Family Group Conferencing, and Washington County Community Justice (Minneapolis) programmes in pre-sentence meetings about serious crimes.

also in most programmes grounds for referring a case to court though again, this is reported to be a rare event.

The survey of programmes reveals three broad approaches to the question of whether or not observers may attend. The great majority of restorative justice programmes place some restriction on observers in order to protect the privacy of participants, or to prevent participants from being distracted. The most common approach is to allow observers to attend only when other participants consent. A second, less common, approach is that the meeting is generally closed to all observers, including the media (although a number allow researchers to attend with the permission of participants). In contrast to these two approaches which restrict attendance in differing degrees, a third approach, practised by a small number of circle programmes, is to open meetings to anyone wishing to attend (see Table 3.1).

As Table 3.1 shows, in most programmes outcomes are reviewed internally by programme managers, and in some by a court as well (either routinely or on appeal). Most programmes impose a requirement that the outcome be oriented towards repairing the harm created by the offence. In some, there is the additional requirement that an outcome not be more severe than a judgment which might have been imposed in court proceedings for the same offence. In others, where outcomes involve community service or the payment of compensation, outcomes must not exceed certain specified limits.

Post-meeting

A further point of variation is whether or not a programme's intervention consists of single or multiple meetings. In some programmes, a series of further meetings is scheduled to monitor an offender's progress towards completing his or her agreement, as well as to mark the completion of that agreement. However, in nineteen of the twenty-five programmes, the intervention consists of but a single meeting. In most cases a further meeting is a contingency only held if a problem arises (for example, an outcome becomes unworkable). In programmes monitoring an offender's completion of the agreement, this is usually done by one or more participants from the original meeting, or else perhaps the manager of the restorative justice programme. Where the monitor is someone other than an employee of a restorative programme, he or she informs the programme staff when an agreement has been fulfilled.[28]

If an offender fails to complete his or her agreement, he or she is referred to an alternative forum in most, but not in all, programmes.

Overall performance/reviewing performance

In nearly all programmes there is some sort of obligation to report periodically on the programme's activity,[29] usually a requirement to report to funding bodies, whether they be government agencies, private foundations or both.

A number of programmes hold regular meetings between convenors and arrange for other forms of peer review among them. In New South Wales, regional managers attend conferences to provide feedback to convenors on their performance. Three of the programmes have established a board to oversee the operation of the programme, and in a fourth programme, plans are afoot to do the same.

Practitioners' view of accountability

To some extent, practitioners' views about accountability reflect views discussed in Chapter Two. Asked to think about accountability, most practitioners described the ways in which their programmes hold offenders (rather than them) accountable. When asked to consider how the programmes themselves, rather than the offender, are held accountable, participants generally did not identify accountability mechanisms in the classic sense. More commonly, practitioners referred to accountability in the broader, more general sense of controls or restraints on the exercise of power. In particular, practitioners emphasized that attendance was voluntary, and that outcomes could not be imposed without the agreement of all participants. Some also mentioned specific additional safeguards. For example, in the New South Wales Youth Justice Conferencing programme it was emphasized that young offenders are encouraged to

[28] In Wagga Wagga this was done by providing victims with a form, which they asked were to complete and mail to police (using the stamped, addressed envelope provided by police) once an offender had completed his or her agreement.

[29] The only exception is some of the school programmes where meetings are just one of a number of disciplinary techniques, rather than a separate programme.

receive legal advice before they decide whether to admit an offence, participate in a conference, or agree to an outcome.

However, this was not the end of the story. When asked to think specifically in terms of processes for giving and scrutinizing accounts, a number of practitioners argued that the deliberative decision-making process in a restorative meeting implies an important degree of accountability; participants in a meeting are required to explain and justify themselves to each other.

Moreover, in the course of interviews while it became clear that programmes possess a number of additional modes of accountability (such as review by courts, or opening up meetings to observers), although generally, practitioners did not nominate these features when asked to describe the ways in which their programme was accountable. Nor in many cases was it even suggested that these mechanisms served any accountability purposes. Rather, these mechanisms were regarded as necessary for other purposes including—most commonly—ensuring a programme's survival. Most practitioners considered that if their programme were to continue to receive referrals and other forms of support from various parts of the criminal justice system, they must allow the system to retain some control over the process. So, in the words of one practitioner, judicial monitoring of outcomes is necessary to 'keep judges on side'.

Conclusion

These twenty-five restorative justice programmes were surveyed using a combination of documentary analysis, participant observation, and interviews. They are examples from six countries at the forefront of restorative justice developments (Australia, Canada, England, New Zealand, South Africa, and the United States), are run by a number of different institutions (community groups, justice departments, police and schools), and perform a variety of different functions (some operating as an alternative to formal sentencing, some as part of formal sentencing, and others in addition to formal sentencing). In terms of their size, programmes vary widely from neighbourhood-based to nationwide.

In accountability mechanisms, there is considerable variation. Before meetings, all programmes have some sort of screening mechanism, but both the nature of this mechanism and the criteria for screening vary enormously. In terms of the process, programmes display the whole gamut of restorative justice programmes, with conferencing, circle, sentencing panel, and mediation programmes, as well as multi-form programmes which select one of these processes to suit the particular circumstances. Some interviewees, in response to questions about their programmes' accountability, suggested that the deliberative process between victims, offenders, and their supporters implies an important degree of accountability. The presence of observers strengthens accountability, but in most programmes, observers are allowed to attend only with the consent of participants. A smaller number of programmes adopt a strict policy irrespective of the participants' consent, some allowing no observers, while others allowing all or any observers. In most programmes, the outcomes reached in meetings are reviewed internally by managers and in some also by a court (either routinely or on appeal). This and other types of involvement by the criminal justice system were generally seen as an unwelcome intrusion necessary to keep the criminal justice system on side, rather than as constructive accountability mechanisms.

In a minority of programmes, a series of further meetings is held after the initial meeting in order to monitor an offender's progress towards completing his or her agreement, and to mark the eventual completion of that agreement. The more common approach, however, is to hold additional meetings after the first only if a problem should arise: in these programmes an offender's completion is usually overseen by one of the participants from the original meeting, or by staff from the restorative justice programme.

4

Deliberative Accountability in Restorative Meetings

'We would like you to pay compensation' the young woman said to the teenager who, looking for money to buy drugs, had broken into her business. Asked how much, the woman replied, '$1000—that's $200 for the excess we had to pay on our insurance policy, and $800 for the increase in our premium.' The 17 year-old offender said that that was 'a lot of money', but that he would repay it. Two of his supporters, a family friend and his grandmother (an elder of the local Aboriginal community) also considered it a large sum, but neither objected. The family friend had already offered the young man a job, and said that she would deduct $50 a week from his wages for five months to repay the debt. Then the young man's case-worker spoke up: 'I think $1000 is too much—this will be Tony's[1] first job, and he isn't used to saving or budgeting'. Tony looked relieved that his case-worker had voiced his concern. The victim said that she was prepared to accept a smaller amount of compensation, and suggested instead $20 a week for five months. When the convenor asked the other participants for their reactions to the new proposal, everyone agreed that $400 was a more manageable amount.

Introduction

Proponents claim that restorative justice meetings can achieve a number of things: help repair the harm a victim has suffered, teach offenders about the consequences of their actions, reintegrate offenders, and—more ambitiously—strengthen communities. This chapter explores a different sort of claim, namely that there is a type of accountability inherent in the sort of deliberative process described above: a type of mutual accountability is built into meetings where participants provide verbal accounts which are scrutinized

---

[1] Tony is not the offender's real name. Descriptions of meetings throughout the book do not use the real names of victims or offenders.

and assessed by other participants, whose own accounts are in turn scrutinized.[2] However, for this deliberative accountability to provide a rigorous and sensitive check on restorative justice, practitioners must give careful attention to the identity of participants and the conditions of deliberation, as well as to the need for formal modes of accountability, such as judicial review, to support deliberative accountability.

The sources and direction of accounts

The requirement to give accounts?

During the course of this research, respondents were given the opportunity to explain and evaluate in their own terms their programme's accountability. A number of practitioners claimed that a form of accountability inheres in restorative justice meetings,[3] with one of the pioneers of conferencing in schools, Marg Thorsborne, going so far as to nominate this accountability as one of the 'most exciting features of conferencing'. The question is whether practitioners' claims can be supported by the definition of accountability previously advanced, and if so, whether the process reflects the indicia of effective accountability.

While it is clear that participants in a restorative justice meeting provide reciprocal accounts, what is less clear is whether this reciprocity amounts to accountability. Giving an account does not necessarily constitute accountability; account giving only becomes a mode of accountability when the person giving the account is actually required to do so (Stenning 1995: 48). This requirement is crucial if accountability is to enhance the quality and legitimacy of decision-making. If decision-makers know they can elect not to provide an

---

[2] The example above illustrates how this works. The victim puts to the group her request for compensation, which she substantiates and explains. The offender's case worker objects to the amount, justifying his objection in such a way as to persuade the victim, who revises her claim, allowing parties to reach an agreement.

[3] A small number of interviewees described the deliberative process in a restorative meeting as providing a source of accountability: John Cartwright, Community Peace Programme, Western Cape South Africa; Terry O'Connell, Wagga Wagga Conferencing, NSW, Australia; John Perry, Vermont Reparative Boards, VT, USA; Patrick Power, Youth Justice Conferencing, NSW, Australia; Marg Thorsborne, School Conferencing, Sunshine Coast, QLD, Australia; Diane Reid, Waseskun Lodge, Quebec, Canada; Jonathan Rudin, Toronto Community Council, Ontario, Canada.

account, or can juggle the time at which time an account is given to suit their convenience, the prospect of accounting ceases to be a spur to improve performance. Similarly, explanations provided purely at the discretion of the decision-maker is unlikely to enhance the decision-maker's legitimacy in the eyes of those receiving them. When information is distributed in such a whimsical or arbitrary fashion, it may be more appropriate to describe the process as a form of public relations than as a mode of accountability (Stenning 1995: 48).

Requirements to act depend on the existence of enforcement mechanisms which can be formal or informal, yet discussions of accountability have a tendency to concentrate on the formal. Lawyers especially have a tendency to assume that obligations cannot exist in the absence of a formal enforcement mechanism. By contrast, sociologists and political theorists highlight the important role that informal sanctions play in holding people accountable. For example, the political convention of ministerial responsibility to parliaments depends for its effectiveness not so much on formal legal sanctions but on the 'fear of disrepute and its political implications' (Smith and Brazier 1998: 38). Certainly, empirical research suggests that informal sanctions are much more effective than formal legal ones, particularly on deviance:[4] the obligation children feel to parents is often more profound than their obligation to the law.

In restorative justice programmes, formal and informal mechanisms are combined. In the first place, meetings rely on participants to informally enforce against each other the requirement to give accounts. A participant's concern about what other participants think of him or her in itself makes him or her accountable to them. In other words, participants' ability to grant or withhold approval and censure is an immediate enforcement mechanism of deliberative accountability. But why should the approval of fellow participants matter?

It matters partly because of the nature of the decision-making process used in restorative justice meetings. One of the findings to emerge from the overview of these twenty-five particular restorative justice programmes is that meetings make decisions on a consensual

---

[4] John Braithwaite (1989: 69; 1997b: 314) reviews some of the vast literature on this point. On the role of informal sanctions see also Robert Ellickson (1991).

basis.[5] In such a process, participants must seek to justify and explain their wishes to other participants if they hope to persuade them. For example, in the conference reported at the beginning of this chapter, participants are seen to account to one another in the course of deciding how much compensation the offender should pay. It is the very ability of each participant to withhold consent from any proposal which makes other participants' approval important, and which ultimately makes participants mutually accountable.[6]

In most programmes, this informal enforcement mechanism is strengthened by the presence of a more formal accountability mechanism. All but five of the programmes surveyed operate against the backdrop of some alternative intervention (Table 3.1), most commonly, formal conviction and sentencing, or in school programmes, suspension or expulsion. Even in those programmes where there is no immediate alternative some degree of coercion may exist. In the Zwelethemba Peacemaker Committee Programme, committee members sometimes warn offenders that they will help a victim go to the police if the offender does not co-operate.[7] Providing an alternative forum can certainly guard against the threat of non-cooperation, but also carries its own risks.

Coercion and domination

Restorative justice meetings must strike an importance balance. While participants should be able to exert pressure on each other to account for their opinions and claims, no participant should be able to dominate any other as excessive pressure destroys deliberative accountability. Participants who do dominate others circumvent the necessity to explain or justify themselves: rather than having to engage in a process of negotiation they can simply assume the agreement of others. When this occurs, accountability is no longer mutual, but

[5] Tony Marshall's (1996. 37) popular definition of restorative justice refers simply to collective decision-making, but as Table 3.1 shows, in all but one of the twenty-five programmes surveyed the collective mode of decision-making is consensus-based.

[6] A participant's identity, and relationship to other participants, may also be important in making participants feel accountable. Restorative justice assembles a victim and offender and their supporters to deliberate. The relationships between these parties may make participants feel obliged to account for their positions. So, for example, an offender may feel obliged to account for his actions or views because he desires the good opinion of his mother or sports coach.

[7] Under the heading 'Providing an alternative forum'.

instead travels in only one direction, from the dominated to the dominator. It cannot be sufficiently stressed that participants be able to exercise the right to negotiate.[8]

If restorative justice meetings are to provide a working mode of accountability, that accountability must be persuasive rather than directive, because in directive forms the reviewer of a decision-maker's account has the power to impose sanctions or, at the very least, issue directions. This requires a relationship in which one party has authority over another, inconsistent with the notion of mutual accountability during meetings. People may well end up changing their positions as a result of the comments of others. For example, when a person makes a request, but the accompanying reasons or explanation are not sufficiently persuasive, the original request must be amended if agreement is to be reached. (Thus, to obtain compensation, the victim mentioned at beginning of this chapter must do more than simply justify why she wants $1000; she also must be prepared to reduce the compensation she is seeking.) The difference, however, between this process and directive forms is that parties change their positions through a process of deliberation, justification, and persuasion, not a process of direction.

Sources of domination

Covering people to participate in meetings destroys deliberative accountability. In all programmes surveyed, the victim's attendance is voluntary, and in all but two of the programmes, so is the offender's.[9] This is not done for accountability reasons, but rather, because restorative justice practitioners argue that coercion is unlikely to be conducive to the process of reparation and reintegration when they depend on sincerity and sentiment. However, although restorative justice programmes describe their meetings as voluntary

---

[8] When one person effectively stands above other participants we are left with the classic accountability dilemma facing all hierarchical forms of accountability: 'Who watches the watchmen?' The only way out of this dilemma is to establish a system of mutual accountability, what John Braithwaite (1997b: 348–9) calls 'arranging guardianship in a circle'. In the context of restorative justice meetings, this means ensuring participants are not able to dominate each other.

[9] See Table 3.1. The exceptions are New Zealand Family Group Conferencing and the English and Welsh Youth Offender Panels. In New Zealand, if an offender refuses to attend, a social work report is called for and the judge can sentence the offender or order the conference be reconvened.

and non-coercive, the threat of initiating or reviving some alternative less desirable treatment puts pressure on offenders to agree to any demands made of them by other participants.[10]

Apart from the threat of formal prosecution and sentencing, there are numerous other potential sources of domination. For a start, any communicative process favours smooth talkers over the tongue-tied (Brown 1994: 1285–6). In the United States, Richard Delgado (2000: 768) argues that victim–offender mediation 'sets up a relatively coercive encounter in many cases between an inarticulate, uneducated, socially alienated youth with few social skills and a hurt, vengeful victim'. Results from the large-scale evaluation of conferencing versus court in Canberra, Australia (the Re-integrative Shaming Experiments (RISE)), confirm that some offenders do indeed feel intimidated. For example, in conferences for juvenile property cases (such as theft, shoplifting, and property damage) approximately 30 per cent of offenders reported feeling too intimidated to speak.[11] A smaller but still sizeable percentage of offenders in youth violence cases (19.2 per cent) and drink-driving cases (13.6 per cent) also reported feeling this way (Strang et al. 1999: tables 5.13–5.16).

In many cases, communication difficulties reflect some underlying form of inequality and domination. In an abusive relationship, power imbalances may well prevent a victim of abuse speaking up and negotiating with her abuser (Hooper and Busch 1996: 105). A long history of oppression can work to affect the communicative ability of whole groups and communities. Australian linguists and anthropologists observe 'the very common Aboriginal conversational pattern of agreeing with whatever is being asked, even if the speaker does not understand the question' (Eades 1994: 244). This pattern has been described as a

---

[10] Richard Abel (1981:258) makes this point about informal justice programmes more generally.

[11] Juvenile property cases in the RISE results consist of juvenile personal property offences (31.3%) and juvenile property (security) offences (29.6%). Note that these results do not mean that these offenders did not actually speak. RISE results (Strang et al. 1999: tables 4.21–4.24) show that offenders in conferences spend a higher percentage of time speaking than offenders in court (for youth violence offences, 18.8% versus 7.7%; for juvenile personal property offences, 19% versus 11.1%; for juvenile property (security) offences, 20.2% versus 16.6%; for drink-driving offences, 25.8% versus 20.4%).

strategy of accommodation [that Aboriginal people have developed] to protect themselves in their interaction with Anglo-Australians. Aborigines have found that the easiest method to deal with white people is to agree with whatever it is that the Anglo-Australians want and then to continue on with their own business (Liberman 1981: 248–9).

Preventing domination

Restorative programmes can, and sometimes do, use a number of techniques to prevent domination in meetings. Some of the most important ones are providing alternative forums for resolving the aftermath of the crime, inviting supporters and professional advocates to restorative meetings, assisting participants to prepare for meetings, and providing participants with access to free legal advice.

Providing an alternative forum

Domination must be identified and counteracted if meetings are to properly provide deliberative accountability. Of fundamental importance is that an offender not be punished for electing not to attend a restorative justice meeting.[12] If restorative justice is to be justified on participatory grounds, offenders must not be dragooned into attending—either by the threat of more serious punishment or any other means.[13] Furthermore, when a participant feels unhappy with the direction a meeting is taking, he or she must not be forced into going along with it. A participant must be able to refuse a proposal, and instead elect to have the case heard by a court (or in the case of programmes outside the justice setting, some other forum). If both victims and offenders know that failure to resolve it means that the case will be referred to an alternative forum, the

---

[12] It might initially strike readers as odd, or even contradictory, that an obligation to account could arise from a voluntary choice but this is often the case. People volunteer to enter a process, institution, or relationship and in doing so bind themselves to the obligations of the process, including the obligation to account. Employees become accountable to employers only once they choose to work for them, and people become accountable to the electorate only if they choose to stand for Parliament. This is equally true for participants in a restorative justice meeting. Of course, institutions vary in the degree of voluntarism they enjoy and meetings are not free of tacit coercion to participate. The arguments here recommend the maximum voluntarism consistent with the unacceptability of the state doing nothing at all when confronted with a serious criminal offence.

[13] One practitioner interviewed says that he encourages the prosecutor's office to 'prosecute very aggressively' those offenders who decline to participate in restorative justice meetings.

availability of the alternative forum provides both an additional incentive to provide an account ('If I don't explain myself, the victim/offender will walk away and the case will end up in court, where I lose my say'), and an escape route where the parties feel under too much pressure ('What the victim/offender is demanding/offering is unreasonable; I'd prefer to take my chances in court').

If courts are to play this role in counteracting domination, however, they must be capable of enquiring into the reasons why a meeting broke down, and be able to discern a justifiable refusal to reach agreement from one without foundation. If courts simply adopt the approach that defaults to court should count as a black mark against the offender's name, negotiations in a meeting straightaway become loaded in the victim's favour. In this respect courts can be assisted by receiving reports from convenors, and if necessary calling victims and offenders to court.[14]

Inviting Supporters

A further strategy for ensuring the non-domination of participants is ensuring the presence of victim and offender supporters. While all but one of the programmes make provision for victims and offenders to invite supporters,[15] the degree to which they may be effective varies. In a Reparative Board hearing in Vermont I attended, a teenager named Paul had agreed to plead guilty to a charge of handling stolen goods for his role in a hold-up of a corner store. One of the community volunteers expressed her wish that Paul attend an education programme run by a former offender because she thought it would reinforce his commitment not to re-offend. Paul himself voiced no objection to the proposal, but as it happened the volunteer was accountable to his father who said that such a commitment would clash with the young boy's part-time job at a local fast-food restaurant and that Paul's part-time job should take priority.

Restorative justice advocates regard this plurality of voices as one of the most important improvements upon earlier experiments with informal justice. Advocates claim that it can help address even the most serious forms of domination, such as those characteristic in domestic violence. One case I observed in the South African township of Zwelethemba illustrates how this might work. A young

---

[14] The role courts should play is discussed in more detail in Chapter Seven.

[15] The exception is the Victim–Offender Mediation/Dialogue Program in Texas.

woman came to the peace committee complaining that her boyfriend had beaten her after finding her in a shebeen (an illegal township bar) late one evening. A peace gathering was convened to which the young woman brought along her sister and another female friend, and the young man a male friend. Five peace committee members, four women and one man, also attended. Once the meeting got underway, the young man readily admitted to beating his girlfriend and apologized for his behaviour; just as quickly the victim accepted his apology and expressed her forgiveness. The swiftness of both the apology and forgiveness suggested that these were familiar roles, and observers may well have been left with serious doubts about the woman's safety. Fortunately, however, this was not the end of the meeting. One of the peace committee members then asked each of the other participants in turn if they were satisfied with the young man's apology and when it came to the victim's sister, she strongly expressed her dissatisfaction, explaining to the group that the offender had apologized for beating her sister on previous occasions only to resume the beatings shortly thereafter.[16] 'What is different about this time?' she demanded. The sister's protest prompted the group to reconsider the young man's behaviour, with the peace committee members ultimately warning him that if he did continue to beat his girlfriend, the committee would assist her to go to the police to bring charges against him, and illustrated how supporters may help alter the power dynamic between the victim and offender.[17]

Is it not unrealistic, though, to assume that every offender and victim will have supporters they can ask to attend a restorative meeting? After all, one of the factors which puts young people at risk of offending is the absence of stable supportive relationships (Farrington 1996). Even so, advocates claim that even the most marginalized members of our communities do have such relationships, and there is some empirical evidence to support this claim. Ethnographic studies point to the existence of networks of friendship and support even among homeless people who are usually considered society's

[16] This was, however, the first time the victim had taken the problem to the peace committee.

[17] It also illustrated the danger of relying on community norms. While there was consensus among the participants about the unacceptability of the young man's actions, much of this disapproval was expressed with admonitions such as 'this woman is not your wife, you are not entitled to discipline her', suggesting that had the couple been married condemnation may not have been as forthcoming.

most ostracized and marginalized members.[18] In John Hagan and Bill McCarthy's (1997: 163) research on homeless youth in Toronto and Vancouver, youth speak of their 'street families' who look out for them: 'you really learn what friendship is...If I need them, they're there for me.' Gwendolyn Dordick (1997: 45) shows how homeless people in New York City form into stable groups in which members boast a willingness to help others in times of need, urging one man to go to hospital to get a wound treated, helping another with bad eyes move around, visiting as a group a man in hospital, and encouraging another to stay 'on the wagon' after his return from detox.

But even if it is true that everyone has at least some supportive relationships, can these networks be deployed to provide support in restorative justice meetings? It requires considerable effort from a convenor to find these people and secure their attendance, especially when they may not have a telephone, private transport, or even a permanent address. These difficulties are often so acute, and are confronted by practitioners so often, that even the most patient, tireless, and dedicated practitioner can become exhausted. There are also limits to the degree of support members of these networks can, or are willing to, provide.[19] Such difficulties force us to question seriously the simplicity of deliberative accountability. While incorporating accountability into the initial decision-making process is simple in the sense that it often avoids the need for time-consuming and expensive reviews, ensuring that the crucial people will participate can be anything but simple.

Even if supporters can be found and organized to attend, their contributions will not necessarily be accepted by other participants, who may question their right to speak. In the case I previously mentioned, where the father expressed reservations that a proposed offender programme clashed with his son's part-time job, the volunteer replied, 'We want to hear this from Paul'. Such problems can probably be minimized by emphasizing to all participants before a

---

[18] Thanks to John Braithwaite for first drawing this to my attention. Braithwaite (2001: 142) argues that the view that such groups 'are somehow asocial, non-communal' is part of our stigmatization of them.

[19] This point is alluded to by Dordick (1997: 48): 'Ron and Donald's friendship is predicated on the fact that both trust one another to help in times of need and such times are relatively infrequent. Constant need and dependency make matters more difficult.'

meeting the participatory ideal of restorative justice whereby the offender's (and victim's) supporters are given the opportunity to participate.

In most cases, people invited as supporters do play a supportive role.[20] But cases such as the 'I am a thief' T-shirt case, where the offender's mother played a role in devising the offender's penalty, show that supporters do not always act in the interests of those who have invited them. When programmes foreshadow this possibility during the preparation phase, they generally do one of two things: exclude the affected supporters or recruit a wider range, attempting to offset any perceived bias. Exclusion is the approach of the Toronto Community Council and the Vancouver Restorative Justice Programme. Programme co-ordinator Jonathan Rudin says that while offenders are encouraged to bring a supporter with them, that person is not always invited to be present during the meeting. Rudin explains that an offender's putative supporter 'may be part of the problem', and offers the example of an offender who appeared before the Council for the second time on a charge of shoplifting. This woman came to the hearing with her husband, who regularly beat her, stole money from her, and prevented her from leaving the marriage. The Council decided that the husband should not be in the room because he was clearly part of the problem, and the Council needed to discuss with the offender how she could end her relationship with him. In one sense this approach is very understandable; excluding the abusive partner may make it easier for the offender to speak. The problem is that it leaves the victim on her own at the end of the meeting to face her violent husband, who is likely to have been angered by his exclusion.

The second, more common, approach to unsupportive 'supporters' is to invite an even wider range of supporters in the hope that someone in this wider group will counteract their lack of support. The rationale is that it is better to include an unsupportive 'supporter', especially if their relationship with an offender is a close one, as they are part of the social context in which the offender committed the crime. In addition, the presence of unsupportive family

---

[20] RISE results (Strang *et al.* 1999: Tables 5.41–5.44), for example, reveal that a high proportion of offenders agree with the proposition that 'others spoke up on my behalf at the conference'. By category of offence the percentages are drink-driving (87.1%), juvenile personal property (85.4%), juvenile property (security) (65.9%), and youth violence (76.9%).

members may also encourage empathy on the part of other participants. For instance, in one conference I convened, an offender's
mother was asked for her opinion about her son's criminal actions.
'He's always been hopeless' she said. Immediately the victim's
parents leapt to the young offender's defence, saying 'We can't
believe that!'

A different risk in inviting supporters to counteract domination is
that they may themselves become a source of domination. In Canberra, Australia, a young man who had viciously attacked a young
boy he mistakenly thought had thrown a rock at his car invited a
number of like-minded young male friends to attend the conference
for his assault. These friends turned out to be more concerned about
the damage to their friend's car than about the boy's extensive
injuries, and proceeded to dominate the meeting, sermonizing to
the victim and his mother about the preciousness of their friend's
car, and how their friend's fury, albeit misdirected, was readily
understandable.[21] The conference proved a harrowing ordeal for
both the victim and his mother, who afterwards expressed their
frustration and anger at their inability to change the offender's
unrepentant attitude. Such problems can be avoided principally by
ensuring that an offender's supporters constitute a diverse group,
and are not just clones of the offender. In practical terms, this means
ensuring that a male offender does not just bring along his drinking
mates, but also brings along his girlfriend, his teacher, and perhaps
his grandmother. (Part of the problem in this case was the police
practice of simply asking offenders to bring supporters without
enquiring just who the offender intended to bring.)

Solutions to possible domination are not as straightforward as
may first appear, though, because, in the same way that allowing an
offender or a victim to nominate their own supporters might be a
recipe for domination, so too might any other criterion of invitation.
It could indeed be argued that the convenor of a meeting is exercising
a form of domination over participants by specifying particular
offender supporters, whether they are siblings, grandparents, sports
coaches, or employers. In many cases offenders and their immediate
families feel a deep shame which makes them want to hide the crime
from others. A possible solution here is for a convenor to suggest a

---

[21] Heather Strang (2003) discusses this conference further as one of the cases in her
study that provided the highest victim dissatisfaction.

wide range of people who might attend a meeting, without being too restrictive. So, for example, when an offender wants to bring half his football team, a convenor might say 'well, how about you invite one mate from your football team, and then someone else that you respect from a different part of your life?' Similarly, faced with an embarrassed father who wants to 'keep things in the family', a convenor could suggest a compromise such as 'What about one of Tony's relations then? Maybe a relative who already knows that Tony is in trouble, and would like to help, someone that Tony gets on well with?' In most cases, my own experience of convening suggests that the ensuing discussions will unearth someone who can provide a different perspective, and whom the offender and family are happy to have present. That the offender or his or her family do not originally suggest such a person might be not because they were opposed to inviting that person, but often simply because it did not occur to them.

Professional advocates can also play a role in minimizing domination. In the Australian conference described at the start of this chapter, it was a case-worker from the Department of Youth Justice who spoke up on the offender's behalf. In New Zealand there is provision for a young offender to attend a conference with a government-funded youth advocate, although originally there was no equivalent provision for victim advocates to attend conferences, which some victims regarded as unfair. As one victim interviewed by Gabrielle Maxwell and Allison Morris (1993: 119) put it: 'He (the offender) had a free lawyer. We had no help.' Since then a legislative amendment has been passed to allow a representative from 'Victim Support', a government-funded office established for the advocacy and assistance of victims, to attend juvenile conferences.[22] Staff are located in police stations and provide support to victims from the moment police are notified about a crime. Victim Support helps victims through the criminal justice process, including helping them prepare for a conference and, if the victim requests, attending

---

[22] Originally no provision existed for a victim or victims to bring supporters to a conference (under s 251(f) *Children, Young Persons and Their Families Act* (1989)). This was amended by s 37(2) *Children, Young Persons, and Their Families Amendment* (1994), which states that victims 'may be accompanied by any reasonable number of persons (being members of his or her family, whanau [extended family], or family group or any other persons) who attend the conference for the purpose of providing support to that victim'.

it as well. In addition, Victim Support staff attended conferences run as part of the (now concluded) Waitakere District Court Restorative Justice Pilot in Auckland.[23] However, we need to keep in mind that just as is the case with supporters drawn from the ranks of a victim or offender's family and friends, professional supporters can become a source of domination themselves. This is a particular risk in the case of lawyers and advocacy groups, whose professional images are of loyal partisans (Palmer and Roberts 1998: 307): many restorative justice practitioners fear that these self-images are too entrenched to break. Training professionals in restorative justice may address this concern, especially where such training includes observing a number of meetings before being allowed to participate in one.

Preparation and free legal advice

Inviting additional supporters is not the only way to ensure parties are not dominated. Another technique is to provide additional support and assistance to participants in the preparation phase leading up to a meeting. This is the approach taken by the Victim/Offender Mediation/Dialogue Program run by the Victim Services Division of the Texas Department of Criminal Justice. This is the only programme surveyed that does not allow supporters to participate, regardless of their disposition. They can certainly attend, but they must sit at the back of the room or wait outside. The programme seeks to ensure that parties are not dominated by carefully screening and preparing them over a period between six months and two years.

In New South Wales, Australia, convenors help offenders before conferences by giving them the telephone number of a government-funded toll-free legal advice hotline which they are encouraged to ring to obtain legal advice before agreeing to participate in a conference. Some NSW practitioners interviewed describe this as a form of accountability in itself; however, it does not constitute a classic form of accountability as neither programme managers nor meeting participants are required to account to the lawyers. The better view is that it is a device for strengthening deliberative accountability: lawyers can in fact help offenders decide whether they wish to participate. They can also give some indication of the range of penalties a magistrate might impose for such an offence, which

---

[23] In conferences run by the Fredrick H. Tuttle Middle School in Burlington, VT, school counsellors are asked to attend as supporters where victims or offenders do not bring their own.

offenders can keep in mind when negotiating with victims and other participants. While the cost of such a service may be beyond the resources of small programmes, in a large jurisdiction like NSW its cost has proven surprisingly modest as a percentage of the entire programme costs. Richard Funston, Senior Solicitor for the NSW Children's Legal Service, says that the service—which is open seven days a week from nine in the morning to midnight—receives four to five hundred calls a month. Not all relate to conferencing; the service is designed to give advice to children about any criminal proceedings or dealings with police (the hotline number is advertised on posters in every NSW police station). Funston says that this service costs approximately $100,000 (Australian) a year. Lawyers are expensive in the context of litigation, but not in the context of very basic advice of this sort. The bulk of this expense is the cost of the toll-free line, as well as overtime paid to solicitors rostered on to answer calls.[24] The NSW experience suggests that where such a service is provided it will be used.[25]

Structure of the meeting

The structure of the meeting itself may also help minimize domination. In New Zealand, conference convenors always schedule a short break during a meeting which allows an offender to discuss a proposed outcome privately with his family. This 'family time' can provide the opportunity for a young person to voice worries that they may not have felt comfortable expressing in the larger group.[26] Some restorative justice practitioners in Australia, where the idea of a break has been introduced in some programmes, argue that it is unnecessary to always schedule 'family time'. In some circumstances it may assist the deliberative process,[27] but in others nothing will be

---

[24] To fully maximize the benefit of this service, Funston says that when young people call from a police station it is important that they are able to make their calls in private so that they can speak candidly to the solicitor at the other end of the line.

[25] Other studies show that where legal advice is available free of charge the proportion of people taking it increases (Reiner 1997: 1027)

[26] For further discussion see Power (2000).

[27] For example, in NSW there is provision for a break in the meeting to allow the young offender to discuss matters with his or her supporters or seek legal advice on the toll-free hotline (see s 50(3) *Young Offenders Act* (1997): a conference may be adjourned at any time for the purpose of allowing a child to obtain legal advice or representation by a legal practitioner).

gained by adjourning that process. Indeed, to do so may, in the words of one convenor, 'interrupt the flow of a meeting'. Terry O'Connell, one of the pioneers of conferencing in Australia, goes further, arguing that it is wrong to adjourn meetings for family time, as it is in this family time that the offer of repair tends to be worked out. 'Victims,' O'Connell argues, 'should not be excluded from this process.'

Revising opinions and non-domination

Non-domination, which includes inviting supporters to attend with victims and offenders, and helping them prepare for a meeting, is absolutely vital to deliberative accountability. Non-domination is not just a prerequisite for accountability, but is also important in ensuring the independence of this form of accountability.

Typically, victims and offenders will have separate, independent interests; however, it is not suggested that these independent interests will remain fixed. Implicit in the justification of restorative processes is the claim that the process of deliberation will transform the preferences, interests, beliefs, and judgments of participants. In the light of information and arguments provided by others, it is hoped that participants will modify their opinions. Proponents of deliberative democracy express the same hope: that deliberation will not just express and register people's beliefs and preferences but transform them in the light of the arguments and information presented (Campbell 1998: 82; Young 2000: 26). Practitioners frequently describe how, in the process of discussing an offence, victims and offenders converge, victims growing compassionate and offenders remorseful. Some practitioners even describe meetings where offenders end up seeking a stiffer punishment while the victim insists on a less severe outcome. This phenomenon is entirely consistent with the model of accountability developed here, provided that any such transformation is the product of non-dominated choice.

Ensuring an equal voice in meetings arises most usefully from a variety of perspectives. Cass Sunstein (2000) suggests that this variety of perspectives is also needed if deliberative processes are to modify participants' opinions. Sunstein believes that deliberative processes often do not transform participants' beliefs, as deliberative democracy advocates assume, but instead merely confirm and reinforce their original positions. People predisposed to racism, for example, will become more racist after discussions with people of the same persuasion. Sunstein (2000: 105) argues that the way to counteract this is to ensure deliberation occurs with the help of a diverse range of viewpoints. When this occurs, people are exposed not to just louder and softer echoes of their own voices, but also to differing viewpoints challenging their opinions. An example of this is the practice of 'deliberative polling', in which randomly selected groups of diverse individuals are invited to come together to deliberate about various issues. When such a poll was held in England on law and order, deliberation produced some shifts in individual views, such as reducing support for imprisonment and increasing support for procedural safeguards (Fishkin 1995: 168).[28] It follows from this that if the deliberative process of a restorative meeting is to 'check our partiality and widen our perspective',[29] a variety of people should be invited.

For all these reasons the wider community has a role to play in meetings, a situation which has a significant bearing on the inclusiveness and publicity of deliberative accountability in meetings.

The role of the community

There is no question about the entitlement of either victim or offender to attend meetings, and there is also general acceptance that the community should play some role in restorative justice meetings. An invitation extended to members of the wider community recognizes the fact that crime affects the wider community as well as the victim; the hope also is that community members can assist in a victim's reparation and an offender's reintegration, strengthening local communities in the process (e.g. Latimer et al. 2001: 2).[30] However, there seems to be no consensus about just who should represent the community (McCold and Wachtel 1998: 77), or the precise role representatives should play. Even I, a foreigner visiting only briefly, was invited to participate in meetings in a number of programmes, as a member of the 'community'.

From an accountability perspective, community participation enhances the inclusiveness of deliberative accountability. When a meeting is attended only by a victim, offender and supporters'

[28] Deliberation failed to change people's views on other subjects, however, such as support for the death penalty (Fishkin 1995: 168).

[29] John Rawls' (1972: 358) description of the benefits of deliberative processes.

[30] See Adam Crawford's (1997: 312–13) caution against constructing communities around crime prevention.

deliberations may focus solely on repairing the victim's harm and so may ignore other issues such as the wider harm an offender has caused, or the risk the offender continues to pose to the public. Community participation also enhances the publicity of deliberative accountability in meetings: the more people involved in a meeting, the more widely publicized is the accountability in that meeting.

However, at the same time as acknowledging that community representatives may serve a variety of purposes, it is also important to recognize the limits of their usefulness. Although restorative justice meetings are said to provide a forum for the communication of shame to an offender, Nathan Harris' (1999) research, based on diversionary conferences in Canberra, Australia, shows that the participation of strangers in a conference does not usually induce shame or remorse in an offender, because it is only the participation of people who are themselves highly respected by the offender that induces these feelings.

Community volunteers

A number of programmes make provision for community members to act either as convenors or participants in restorative meetings (Table 3.1), and in many such programmes community members participate on an unpaid, voluntary basis. Among restorative justice practitioners, it is usually assumed that unpaid volunteers are more representative than paid ones (e.g. Walther and Perry 1997: 23), but this assumption is highly questionable. At their very best, volunteers represent other similar community members with the time and inclination to volunteer themselves.

A more representative (and inclusive) basis on which to choose community participants might be by random selection from electoral rolls, in a way similar to that in which juries are selected. Such an approach would access a wider cross-section of the population and may also perform an educative role, providing a valuable opportunity for people to meet others from different backgrounds. One problem with this suggestion, however, is that even though they were obliged to attend meetings these people may not be committed to reaching agreement, which is such an important prerequisite for deliberative accountability.

A further way to achieve more representative community participation is to pay people. It is often said that unpaid community volunteers have a greater impact, because when the victim and offender know that the community representatives are there only because they really want to be there, the victim and the offender will 'feel more worthy' (RCAP 1996: 151; Pranis in Braithwaite 2001: 4). It is unproven whether in fact a community member's volunteer status make victims and offenders feel more worthy; it seems clear, however, that it makes some volunteers feel more worthy. In one meeting I observed a community volunteer introduced himself by saying 'I'm a volunteer—a v-o-l-u-n-t-e-e-r—do you know what means? I don't get paid.' But even if volunteers do make victims and offenders feel more worthy, unpaid volunteerism excludes those people who cannot afford the time it takes to undergo training, and then organize and convene meetings. Recent surveys of community Youth Offender Panel members in England confirm that volunteers were most likely to be female, white, middle class, and middle aged (Crawford and Newburn 2002: 483). On the one hand, programmes should nurture the participation of these community members, but they should also consider strategies for tapping into those parts of the population less likely to volunteer, and offering to pay them is one way of doing this.[31] Yet another problem is the way in which the involvement of volunteers affects the participation of victims, in that the more involved are community volunteers ('indirect victims' as they are sometimes called), the less involved are the direct victims.

The value of representation

Two of the programmes using community representatives—the Toronto Community Council and the Vancouver Restorative Justice Programme—select only people of the same cultural and racial background as the offender. Behind such an approach is the view that community participants must be able to understand an offender's needs and interests and they cannot do this simply by trying to imagine what it would be like to be in the offender's shoes, but only by sharing with the offender certain experiences or characteristics. As Anne Phillips (1994: 76) puts it, 'no amount of thought of sympathy, how careful or honest, can jump the barriers

---

[31] This is the practice of New South Wales juvenile justice conferencing and the Zwelethemba Peace Committee. A number of the other programmes provide reimbursement for expenses.

of experience'.[32] This justification can be criticized on its own terms. If the underlying justification is that no amount of sympathy can jump the barriers of experience, how can a Cree Nation community member understand a Métis or Algonquin offender? And how can a female Métis community member understand the experiences of a male Métis offender? And so on. This objection is not necessarily fatal, when while it could be argued that although no two Aboriginal offenders share the exact same experience, they nevertheless share certain fundamental experiences of exclusion and powerlessness. However, once their common experiences are expressed in these more general terms, as they must be, the door should be opened to allowing people from other groups with similar experiences. For example, migrants and other groups with experiences of exclusion and alienation could and should be invited to participate in programmes such as those for Aboriginal offenders.

This is not the only problem with the idea of group representation. Even where offenders come from the same group, they may be estranged from—and dominated by—that group. Choosing the community around an offender's identity may also create the perception that the process is centred more around the offender's interests than the victim's, especially where the victim comes from a different cultural group. Additionally, it may create the perception that it is only an offender's cultural group which is affected by his or her crime and so may serve to alienate the victim. In some instances the victim and the offender will be from the same cultural group, but in urban, multi-cultural environments this will often not be the case. Programmes, however, wishing to defend this approach may concede that the wider community has an interest, but respond that their interest should be assigned to the community of the same cultural background as the offender.

A perhaps even more disconcerting problem is that, by attempting to create segregated systems of justice, programmes resign themselves to a world where people from different cultures cannot relate to each other. Will Kymlicka (1995: 141) argues that 'To renounce the possibility of cross-group representation is to renounce the possibility of a society in which citizens are committed to addressing

---

[32] This is also the standard justification for group representation in political processes (Kymlicka 1995: 138–9), such as dedicated Maori seats in the New Zealand Parliament (Mulgan 1989).

each other's needs and sharing each other's fate.' Marginalized communities may be better served by creating opportunities for people from other cultures to learn about their needs and interests. Even though it might be argued that restorative meetings are too sensitive and personal an occasion to be used for this purpose, it could equally be argued that such an occasion provides the very best opportunity to confront prejudice and nurture empathy and understanding. First-hand stories of discrimination may change other people's attitudes much more than general, abstract exhortations to love one's neighbours.

The approach taken by many programmes is both to encourage the participation of community volunteers from a wide variety of backgrounds, as well as to invite the victim and offender to bring their own supporters (explaining to them the virtues of having supporters from different parts of their lives). This practice meets a number of goals. By opening up participation to people from a variety of backgrounds, programmes increase the opportunities for people to learn about others from different circumstances (as well as enhance heterogeneity of perspectives, which Sunstein (2000) argues is necessary for people to change their opinions). By encouraging victims and offenders to bring supporters of their choosing, programmes also maximize the possibility that there will be present those people who might best understand their needs and interests. In accountability terms, open community access enhances the inclusiveness and publicity of restorative meetings, while supporters help ensure meetings consider victims' and offenders' interests in an empathetic way (which is important for both the inclusiveness and motivational sensitivity of meetings).

The role of indigenous elders in meetings

A number of programmes[33] make provision for the involvement of indigenous elders. Typically, this is done in the hope that some form of symbiosis will occur, that elders will make a contribution to restorative justice meetings while, at the same time, meetings will provide a forum for re-establishing the authority of elders and the

---

[33] NSW Youth Justice Conferencing, Navajo Peacemaking, Toronto Community Council, Vancouver Restorative Justice Programmes. John Braithwaite (1999: 25–6) discusses other programmes not included in this survey.

traditional cultural values of which they are custodians.[34] Here one of the most important and controversial questions is the degree of authority or control elders should have over meetings. Some people argue that Aboriginal elders must be given final authority over proceedings, in the same way that judges preside over some sentencing circles. But this is problematic in indigenous communities where the question of 'Who has authority, over which matters, and in which contexts, may itself be contested' (Mantziaris and Martin 2000: 40), and is also problematic in communities where the havoc wreaked by colonialism has resulted in abuse and exploitation by elders themselves (LaPrairie 1992; Braithwaite 1997: 505; ACPU 2000: 33).

One alternative seems to be to invite elders to participate as part of the deliberative process, to which they can contribute while themselves being held to account. Jeremy Webber (1993: 147) argues that Aboriginal institutions should be reinvented so that they draw upon indigenous traditions and insights in a manner appropriate to the new situation.[35] Webber argues that this reinvention may involve 'inventing checks to prevent abuse that were unnecessary two hundred years ago, or which existed in a very different form'. The deliberative accountability in a restorative justice meeting offers one such check that Aboriginal communities could consider adopting. Community-wide deliberations among Aboriginal communities will unearth other appropriate roles for elders in restorative justice programmes. Marcia Ella Duncan, Chair of the Aboriginal Justice Advisory Council in New South Wales, tells us how commu-

---

[34] Donna Coker (1999: 99) considers the possible contradictions within this, in the context of Navajo peacemaking.

[35] Moreover, in some contexts it is argued that hierarchical authority structures are not an intrinsic part of indigenous cultural traditions. In the context of Australian Aboriginal communities, Christos Mantziaris and David Martin (2000: 302–3) make the following observations. 'In most areas of Aboriginal Australia now, and particularly in areas with long histories of contact with the dominant society, those individuals with authority to make decisions about matters pertaining to the indigenous domain are referred to as "elders" ... However, the category of "elder" is not simply a phenomenon of the indigenous societies themselves; it has been created in part through the interactions between indigenous and non-indigenous societies. "Elders" have become the individuals with whom governments, agencies and resource developers consult to ascertain the views of indigenous groups about issues ranging from the protection of heritage and sites to the welfare of indigenous children.'

nity convenors use elders as mentors when organizing conferences for young Aboriginal offenders, seeking their advice to ensure conferences are run in a culturally sensitive fashion.

Some opposition to the idea that communities reassess and re-design community elders' roles can be expected. In an interim evaluation report of conflict resolution training among the Toaripi of the Gulf Province in Papua New Guinea, villagers were asked why only a small percentage of village leaders had attended the training. A common response was that restorative justice, with its democratic principles, conflicts with traditional 'Bigman' systems in which power is exercised by leaders over other villagers, and 'many traditional leaders may see this as a threat to their status and power' (Howley 1999: 8). This suggests that the challenge for local communities will be to hold elders to account, while showing respect for their wisdom and experience.

Community representation and preserving accountability

Community participation may well contribute to enhance the inclusiveness and publicity of the accountability occurring in restorative meetings. However, there may well be a trade-off between enhancing publicity and including wider interests on the one hand, and ensuring that this does not happen at the expense of victims and offenders' interests on the other. Programmes tackle this problem in a number of ways. Most expect community members to participate in a way consistent with restorative values. Community volunteers in some programmes are explicitly told that a meeting is not a forum for punishment, but one for seeking ways to repair harm caused by an offence. The influence of these values is manifest in a variety of ways including training, and in the case of Zwelethemba Peacemaker Committee, requiring community volunteers to comply with a code of conduct (Roche 2002). In some programmes community members are expected to ensure outcomes fit other parameters as well, so convenors in New South Wales are expected to ensure that outcomes are not more onerous than penalties imposed by a court and that they do not exceed set upper limits in terms of financial compensation and hours of community service.[36]

It goes without saying that not all citizens have restorative attitudes. Nor do all programmes promote themselves in restorative

---

[36] In practice the only constraint which is an effective one is the upper limit, as it is difficult to compare conference outcomes with court outcomes.

terms. A striking example of this is the Milwaukee restorative programme inundated with community volunteers when it distributed
flyers that read, 'It's payback time' (Walsh 2000). During the early
stages of the diversionary conferencing programme in Canberra,
Australia, some police—when faced with drink-driving conferences
stacked with offenders' drinking mates—favoured those community
representatives with punitive attitudes. In a post to a conferencing
e-mail list, Stephen Mugford, who helped establish the programme,
shared these observations:

we find the role of community reps also to be interesting. If a conference
has a choir of supporters all singing the same tune ('X is a fine person, X is
really sorry, X needs no further punishment') then some community reps
will get sucked into singing along too. The police find this very annoying
and do not like to use such reps again. Others, however, move towards an
opposed pole, becoming very demanding and punitive. The police often
like this and ask such reps to come to other conferences. But of course the
offenders and supporters can be quite hostile to this (usually covertly so). In
interviews, we occasionally get very negative comments about the reps
along these lines ('...that bitch the cops brought along...').[37]

Another possible problem in increasing community participation
is that restorative meetings can become too long, too large, or both. In
the United States, some meetings involve up to one hundred people,
most of them community participants, and last up to seven or eight
hours.[38] It is often argued that these mass meetings are needed
because so many people are affected by the original crime. In other
cases, it is argued that the complexity of issues arising from the
offence requires the sustained, combined efforts of a large number
of people. This is often the case in care and protection conferences.

---

[37] Talking to researchers involved in evaluating conferencing in Canberra, it seems
these problems were largely corrected. However, in 1999 one regular community
representative did proudly boast to me that he is called in 'whenever there is a hard
nut to crack'.

[38] For example, the Vermont Department of Corrections posted on its website a
description of a conference attended by ninety-one participants (Dinnan undated).
The conference was convened after a group of high-school footballers beat up two
junior players on a bus trip home from a game as part of 'hazing' or initiation process.
Ted Wachtel from REAL Justice refers to five-hour conferences involving up to
seventy-five people (Braithwaite 2001: 74). The meetings I observed and convened,
however, were all between one and two hours in duration, except for the meetings in
the victim–offender mediation/dialogue programme in Texas where the three meetings
I observed (on videotape) lasted between five and eight hours. Between one and two

Practitioners insist that large conferences do not produce chaos and that, in fact, conferences with more participants unfold more easily and naturally (Braithwaite and Strang 2000: 205).

The risk in such circumstances, however, is that participants may become intimidated or plain exhausted. We should be particularly concerned about the risk of this happening to an offender in mass meetings, where anecdotal evidence suggests the bulk of the crowd see themselves as indirect victims. If the offender does become over-whelmed, he cannot hold other participants accountable, with the result that his interests may not be properly reflected in the decision-making process. This would suggest that the inclusion of community participants must be kept within reasonable limits, both in terms of the number of participants and the length of time they are allowed to speak in a meeting. My own experience as a convenor is that meet-ings become difficult to convene with more than 15–20 people.

But what to do about those cases affecting a large number of people? A variety of practical strategies might be used here. The affected group might consider informally electing a smaller number of representatives who can attend the meeting on their behalf and then report back. So in an arson case where a lawn bowling club was destroyed (O'Shea 2001) the distressed bowling club members could have held a meeting before the conference to consider their views and elect a member to convey them to the conference. In particular, where the severity or complexity of a matter demands a long meeting, it may be preferable to schedule multiple meetings, or at least to have regular breaks in the one meeting. In one care-and-protection con-ference in Hawaii which I attended, this seemed to be done to good effect by having a dinner break halfway through the conference.

The role of the state in meetings

In a number of programmes, the state through its various agencies plays a large role. Police convene meetings in four of the subject conferencing programmes, and attend regularly in a number of others. In a number of circle programmes prosecutors attend,[39]

hours is similar to the average duration of Canberra conferences observed by RISE researchers, where drink-driving cases took on average 87 minutes, juvenile personal property 85 minutes, juvenile property (security) 70 minutes, and youth violence 93 minutes (Strang *et al.* 1999: Tables 4.1–4.8).

[39] Prosecutors attend in the following programmes for those cases referred by court: Community Conferencing, Queensland, Carcross Circle Programme, Yukon Territory, and South St Paul Restorative Justice Council, St Paul.

and in two of the programmes judges also attend.[40] In addition, state employees from other departments (such as corrections departments) play a role in other programmes. Although there is general agreement among restorative justice practitioners and theorists that the community is a legitimate stakeholder in meetings, there is considerable disagreement about the appropriate role of the state, some even arguing that state bodies should have no role at all. Many practitioners and theorists fear the involvement of the state on the grounds that it will engulf informal justice,[41] a concern expressed most strongly in indigenous communities where formal state justice has failed so miserably and where new restorative justice programmes are seen as expressions of the right to self-government (Palys 1999: 2).

Practitioners try to circumscribe the role of the state in various ways, arguing that 'The role of government officials, such as police, should be limited to that of facilitators and information providers, not key contributors to the decision-making process' (McCold and Wachtel 1998: 82). Another approach is that of the South St Paul Restorative Justice Council, where Restorative Justice Planner Michael Stanefski requests that judges and district attorneys attend in a private, rather than a professional, capacity. Similarly, Philmer Bluehouse, chief Navajo peacemaker, says that lawyers can attend with offenders provided they 'do not attend in attorney mode'. Bluehouse says that he prefers lawyers to use their skills in a peacemaking circle in other ways, for example in helping the parties write up agreements.

It is a fact that many programmes wish to exclude or restrict the role played by state agencies because they consider the state will ruin restorative justice. The danger of state involvement is particularly pertinent from a deliberative accountability perspective: if state players dominate other participants then the accountability described in this chapter collapses, as police, prosecutors, and judges

---

[40] Carcross Circle Program, Yukon Territory, and, where a circle is held as part of the sentencing process, the South St Paul Restorative Justice Council, St Paul.

[41] The title of one of the sessions at the 2001 American Society of Criminology Meeting in Atlanta, GA, catches the sentiment well: 'Transformative justice: What'll save restorative justice from the jaws of the state.' Seminars in this session included 'IMAGINE: From the restorative state to no state'. Larry Sherman (2001) argues that underpinning restorative justice is a Protestant ethic which, unchecked, can lead to a hatred of all government.

become unaccountable; however, at the same time we must recognize that state agencies can play a big part in strengthening deliberative accountability, since government-funded advocacy groups can act as supporters for victims and offenders in meetings. The state may also assist in other ways, in circumstances where a victim may forgive an assailant who continues to pose a risk to other members of the community.[42] Here a prosecutor can play a constructive role and represent the interests of the wider community by requesting that, notwithstanding the victim's forgiveness, the offender report for supervision and treatment on a regular basis. Similarly, in a conference for a repeat drink-driver a prosecutor can represent the interests of other road users who are put at risk by that driver's behaviour.

Prosecutors and judges have the advantage over community citizens in that they are themselves accountable in a variety of ways outside the meeting for their participation, in a way that community volunteers usually are not.[43] Restorative justice advocates tend simultaneously to overlook both the arbitrary, coercive nature of community justice and the egalitarian side of state justice. It may be unrealistic to expect state representatives to participate in a personal capacity when it is their professional capacity that brings them to the meeting in the first place. Rather than excluding state representatives, or asking them to attend in a personal capacity, it may be preferable in some circumstances to include them but to encourage them to discharge their professional duty in an open-minded and flexible way. Training in restorative justice can help in this aim.

If restorative justice programmes are serious about encouraging free expression and deliberations, then criminal justice professionals should not convene restorative justice meetings. When a judge or police officer convenes a meeting, whether they like it or not, they enjoy an authority which has little to do with the ideal role of a

---

[42] Some victims are amazingly forgiving. In one case I convened which dealt with the theft of a car, I asked the victim to describe the impact of the offence. He admitted it was mildly inconvenient 'but life has its ups and downs, doesn't it?' He then mentioned that the car was returned in excellent condition, and said that he wanted to thank the young person for driving the car so carefully. He did not even complain about the 300 km round trip to retrieve the car saying it was 'it was nice to get out of town and go on a bit of a trip'.

[43] But indigenous advocates sometimes retort that judges are accountable not to the community but to the rule of law that has oppressed indigenous groups, and to which indigenous justice seeks to provide an alternative.

convenor, and everything to do with their professional role and authority. As Michael Palmer and Simon Roberts (1998: 131) point out, 'Courts are places where other people tell us what to do... This in itself is going to colour the way in which mediatory intervention by registrars and judges is perceived by disputants, whether the specialists themselves want this or not.'

One question for restorative justice programmes is whether to incorporate the state in the deliberative accountability described here, or instead leave formal justice in the background as an option for those dissatisfied with the informal justice of a restorative justice meeting. From a perspective of accountability there is no easy answer. Where state involvement is needed, it is simpler and more timely to include that perspective in the original decision-making process. However, it is difficult to predict in which particular cases that involvement is necessary, and it would be unnecessarily complex for the state to attend every case. One option, by way of compromise, is to do as some programmes do and reserve state involvement for meetings dealing with more serious offences. Here when a programme manager reviews a referral to a programme she may decide to invite the prosecutor to attend if the file shows the offender to be a serial drink-driver, but decide that it is not necessary in the case of a young first-time offender vandalizing a bus stop. This tentative conclusion again reinforces the importance of careful, thoughtful preparation prior to any restorative meeting.

The timing of accounts

It is on the question of when accounts are given that deliberative accountability differs most obviously from more familiar types. Generally speaking, accountability is thought to operate as an *ex post*, or retrospective control, in that the process of accounting normally occurs after a decision has been made: a board of directors must account to shareholders for their performance during the previous financial year, judges give reasons for their decisions once they have made them, and parliamentary elections hold governments to account for their performance in office.

However, it is important to remember that accountability can also operate on an ongoing basis throughout a decision-making process. This happens when decision-makers come under an obligation to seek approval for their planned actions or be monitored in the course of their decision-making.[44] The deliberative accountability in restorative meetings, where the obligation to be called to account is built into the decision-making process, is just such a type. Most importantly, accountability which inheres in the decision-making process has the advantage of timeliness: the closer the obligation for accountability is to the decision-making, the more likely it is to provide an incentive to make good decisions, and the easier it is to detect and correct poor ones. On this criterion, accountability in restorative meetings rates highly. Not only are participants subject to immediate scrutiny by others, but also where mistakes or problems are detected (such as the quantum of compensation) adjustments can be made immediately. While the whole process has the appearance of simplicity, by reducing the need for expensive and time-consuming review processes, this simplicity belies the time and effort required to organize and participate in meetings.

A perhaps less obvious quality of this timely accountability is its motivational sensitivity. When accountability occurs as part of the original decision-making process it is less likely than an *ex post* checking process to engender distrust among those held accountable. Decision-makers often feel that accountability mechanisms only exist to guard against the risk that they lack competence or trustworthiness, and that but for the suspicion that they are doing the wrong thing, accountability would not be necessary. In such circumstances, they can easily become unhappy, resentful, and even defiant. On the other hand, when the obligation arises as part of a decision-making process which places responsibility (and implicitly expresses trust) in participants such problems are largely avoided. This advantage applies even more obviously to the medieval accountability institution of the jury, since it is much easier to bribe a judge than the twelve jurors who have to give accounts to each other; even so this accountability seems to jurors a natural part of the process of getting to the right decision and considering all the arguments. It does appear to have been designed to check corruption, and so they do not feel distrusted. In fact, it is profoundly democratic in its design and workings. Meeting-based accountability is less of an affront to the decision-making process than *ex post* types in that it is simply

---

[44] Parliamentary elections can also be interpreted in this way, with victory giving a mandate to parties to implement their election manifesto.

one aspect of a larger process (which gives victims a chance to question an offender, and offenders a chance to make amends).

It is arguably the hierarchical or directive nature of many forms of accountability which is prone to communicate a lack of trust. A structure in which one person stands in a relationship of superior authority to another implies that we can trust the person on top but not the one on the bottom.[45] As a result of the relationship, the person on the bottom can easily become disheartened and defiant. Deliberative accountability between participants carries no such implication (and also satisfies the requirement of iterative accountability).

The subjects of accounts

Deliberations in a restorative meeting can roam across a wide range of topics, but the starting point for any meeting is generally to consider the actions of the offender which have led to the meeting being held.[46] In this sense offenders are accountable to other participants, and required to give a verbal account of how and possibly why the offence took place. Some meetings may also scrutinize a victim's account as well whenever relevant. In one conference I observed, participants quizzed a victim about his actions where it was revealed he had mocked the offender with racial taunts immediately prior to being assaulted.[47]

These sorts of accounts are outside the scope of this book, which is more concerned with the way accountability works within a programme, and that programme's response to an offence, than accountablity for the commission of an offence. The response largely depends on the conduct of participants and on their accountability within the programme. The form of accountability identified here works most obviously in negotiating outcomes in those meetings in which participants' ability to withhold agreement places the obligation on

[45] John Braithwaite (1997b: 348–9) argues that this assumption is the very problem with hierarchical models of power: 'If the guardian at the top of the hierarchy is corrupt, then all assurance against abuse of power by the system collapses.'

[46] Although not always. In Zwelethemba, meetings can be convened to discuss a problem more generally.

[47] It should also be noted that restorative meetings create the risk of unwarranted and unacceptable victim-blaming (such as the victim of a sexual assault who is blamed for wearing a short skirt) (Braithwaite and Roche 2001).

participants to justify their claims. Deliberative accountability may in this way address some of the worries about outcomes.

But what of those concerns not immediately related to outcomes? The situation can arise when one participant may abuse another in the course of a meeting. In these circumstances it may be argued that participants are under no obligation to account for such behaviour because, unlike demands for compensation or reparation, they do not depend upon the agreement of other parties. However, participants may nevertheless be required to account for their comments if they wish other participants to continue with the meeting, and to look favourably on any claims that they subsequently may make. In other words, participants in a restorative justice meeting may be capable of holding others accountable not only for requests, but also for other types of behaviour during meetings.

Modes of accounting

The most obvious way accountability can fail is by excluding people altogether, a denial of the inclusiveness which is such an important principle of accountability mechanisms. A less obvious, though perhaps more insidious, way to exclude people is to allow them to participate but to structure the rules and norms governing their participation in such a way that they are effectively excluded. Patricia Day and Rudolf Klein (1987: 5) argue that 'accountability, even at its simplest in the relationship between individuals, presupposes agreement both about what constitutes an acceptable performance and about the language of justification to be used by actors in defending their conduct'.

More specifically, most accountability mechanisms expect decision-makers to give accounts in a formal, logical, and dispassionate manner. Perhaps nowhere is this more so than in the courtroom, where the dominant mode of communication is technical, dispassionate, reasoned, and logical (see e.g. Gibbons 1994: 197). It should not be assumed, though, that restorative justice is necessarily more inclusive than this. Deliberation is also often thought to require, or at least favour, expression that is formal, deductive, and unemotional (Cohen and Sabel 1997: 329). As Iris Young (1997: 64–5) explains:

Speech that is assertive and confrontational is here more valued than speech that is tentative, exploratory, or conciliatory...Norms of assertiveness, combativeness, and speaking by the contest rules are powerful silencers or evaluators of speech in many actual speaking situations where culturally differentiated and socially unequal groups live together... The norms of deliberation also privilege speech that is formal and general. Speech that proceeds from premise to conclusion in an orderly fashion that clearly lays out its inference structure is better than other speech... These norms of 'articulateness', however, must be learned; they are culturally specific, and in actual speaking situations in our society exhibiting such speaking styles is a sign of social privilege. *Deliberation thus does not open itself equally to all ways of making claims and giving reasons...* [48]

Young (2000: 39) goes on to say that the favouring of certain speech styles often correlates with other differences of social privilege; that is, that the dispassionate speech culture of white middle-class men tends to be favoured over others.[49] For deliberative processes to be more inclusive, Young (1997: 69; 2000) argues that three elements must be accommodated in addition to critical argument: greeting or public address, rhetoric, and storytelling. These elements are considered in turn.

Greeting

Young (1997: 70) uses the expression 'greeting' in a very loose sense to refer to any communication that 'makes no assertion and has no specific content', the absence of which is felt as 'coldness, indifference (and) insult'. As well as expressions of greeting and farewell, Young (1997: 70) also means the non-linguistic gestures 'that bring people together warmly, setting conditions for amicability: smiles, handshakes, hugs, the giving and taking of food and drink'. Interviews with practitioners and observations of meetings reveal the importance to restorative justice of these various forms of greeting. Meetings begin with the introduction of participants (in most programmes by participants themselves, in some by the convenor).[50] In many programmes, serving food and drink is an essential part of the process, whether it is in providing refreshments at the

---

[48] Emphasis added.

[49] While it is uncontroversial to suggest that there are variations in communication styles both across and within groups, drawing differences too strictly along gender and racial lines essentializes and stereotypes these groups.

[50] Real Justice, the company responsible for training convenors in some of the conference programmes, recommends that the facilitator introduce participants by saying their names and stating their relationships to the offender or victim (O'Connell *et al.* 1999: 55). It is arguably more inclusive, however, to allow participants to

end of the meeting (which is the most common practice) or serving a full meal during a break (which happened during an 'ohana' (family) child welfare conference I observed in Hawaii). These informal moments provide an opportunity for what John Braithwaite and Stephen Mugford (1994: 156) describe as 'backstage intimacy' to occur, where actors remove the masks they 'feel impelled to sustain during the conference proper'. In one conference I convened, a coffee break provided the occasion for an offender to approach the victim away from the view of other participants, and offer him a private apology. Among the programmes surveyed, the circle programmes perhaps emphasize the importance of 'greetings' more than any other type of programme. It was typical in the circles that I attended that meetings began and ended in prayer, and on one occasion, in song.

Another dimension of greeting is the use of physical gestures. From their observation of conferences in New Zealand and Wagga Wagga, John Braithwaite and Stephen Mugford (1994: 150–1) note the importance of other gestures:

The verbal apology can be accompanied by physical acts. The most common physical accompaniment to apology is the handshake. Female victims sometimes hug young offenders, an especially moving gesture when it reaches across a racial divide. In Maori conferences, kissing on the cheek, nose pressing and hugging occur among various of the participants...[51]

Some readers might readily agree that such acts should be accommodated yet query their relevance to accountability. Young (2000: 60) herself acknowledges that 'such gestures do not offer information or further arguments directly by giving reasons or criticisms'. But genuinely inclusive accountability requires the accommodation of those gestures surrounding the 'real business' of giving accounts. As Christine Parker (1999: 224) argues, such acts are 'necessary for reaching first understanding of each other and then

introduce themselves. Lily Trimboli's (2000: 43) evaluation of NSW conferencing notes that some participants complained that 'there should have been an opportunity to introduce ourselves'.

[51] Braithwaite and Mugford (1994: 155) argue that these physical acts help encourage healing in a way that more mechanical forms of interactions do not. For the frequency of such acts in Canberra conferences see Heather Strang *et al.* (1999: Tables 4.57–4.64).

agreement'. Moreover, these gestures can help keep commitment to discussion at times of anger and tension (Young 1997: 70).

The hearings of the South African Truth and Reconciliation Commission provide a vivid illustration of the importance of accommodating different modes of expression. Between 1996 and 1998 the Commission received twenty thousand statements from victims, two thousand of these in public hearings conducted in cities and smaller towns throughout South Africa (Krog 1999: ix).[52] Antjie Krog (1999: 207) describes one of these witnesses, Chief Anderson Joyi, opening his testimony before the Commission:

Chief Anderson Joyi punctuates the names of every one of his nineteen generations of forbears with his knobkerrie on the floor:
King Thembu begat Bomoyi; And Bomoyi begat Ceduma And Ceduma begat Mngutu;
And Mngutu begat Ndande; And Ndande begat Nxego;
And Nxego begat Dlomo;
And Dlomo begat Hala;
And Hala begat Madiba;
And Madiba begat Thato;
And Thato begat Zondwa;
And Zondwa begat Ndaba;
And Ndaba begat Ngubenuca;
And Ngubenuca begat Mtikara
(this is the house where Matanzima comes from, the right-hand house);
And Mtikara begat Gangeliswe;
And Gangeliswe begat Dalindyebo;
And Dalindyebo begat Jongiliswe;
And Jongiliswe begat Sabata;
And Sabata begat Buyelekaya;
And this is where I begin.

The Commission's Xhosa interpreters used King James' English to give an impression of the 'deep, deep Xhosa' the Chief was using. Chief Joyi's explanation for opening his testimony with the names of his forbears eloquently illustrates the importance of 'greetings': 'Their names organise the flow of time . . . Their names give my story a shadow. Their names put what has happened to me in perspective. Their names say I am a chief with many colours. Their

[52] These statements were received by the Human Rights Violations Committee, one of the Commission's three committees (the other two being the Amnesty Committee, and the Reparation and Rehabilitation Committee).

names say we have the ability to endure the past . . . and the present'
(Krog 1999: 207).[53]

The accommodation of greetings can make a process more inclusive, but greetings themselves can become a source of oppression. Before every match, the All Blacks, the New Zealand national rugby team, line up on the halfway line facing their opposition and perform a *haka*, a traditional Maori greeting ceremony. They do not use this form of greeting to put their opponents at ease, or set the conditions for amicability, or bring the teams together warmly. On the contrary, they use it to intimidate their opponents.[54] One can imagine greetings in a restorative justice meeting having a similar effect, even where it is unintended.

There is also a risk that forms of greetings will be used in a tokenistic way. For example, some New Zealand conferences begin with prayers or Maori welcome and blessing. Gabrielle Maxwell and Alison Morris (1993: 87, 106) say: 'In terms of process it is important to go beyond the tokenism of including greetings and prayers in a different language. Cultural appropriateness cannot be achieved without handing the management of the process over to those who fully understand the culture.'

Rhetoric

In addition to greetings, Young (2000: 65) argues that we should pay attention to the importance of rhetoric, which refers to aspects of communication such as the emotional tone of communication. Participants in restorative justice meetings are quite free to express emotion, but convenors will also often encourage participants to stay calm.

Restorative justice programmes must be careful to ensure that rhetoric, like greetings, does not become its own source of exclusion and oppression. Participants in restorative meetings are still expected to master a language—not the formal, dispassionate language of the courtroom—but the nuanced and complex language of

[53] Other cases also illustrate the importance of non-communicative gestures. Take for example a New Zealand conference for a young offender charged with dangerous driving causing death. At the conclusion of the conference the boy's Korean parents asked the deceased's family for permission to establish a traditional altar as a sign of respect for the deceased. After participants had laid flowers at the altar, the victim's father read a poem in memory of his son.

[54] Thanks to John Dryzek (2000: 69) for this example.

the emotions. Some will be highly proficient at expressing their feelings, able to communicate convincingly remorse and sorrow, forgiveness and empathy. Some will master it so well they can abuse it—using rhetoric to deceive, manipulate, and flatter.[55] Others, however, will find the language of emotions in restorative justice occasions as foreign and inaccessible as the formal language of the courtroom. Many young people, for instance, may feel absolutely genuine remorse for the harm they have caused, yet simply be unable to find the words to express it.[56]

Storytelling

According to Iris Young (2000: 70), inclusive processes should accommodate storytelling. When allowed to fully relate a story, many people may be able to more easily express themselves than they otherwise might, particularly those people from cultures with an oral tradition. One of the limitations of formal court processes is their traditional reliance on interrogation to elicit information (see ALRC 1987: para. 15(d), para. 111–12).

Storytelling is fundamental to restorative justice, particularly as it allows a victim to detail the harm he or she has suffered. As Young (2000: 72) points out, 'those who experience . . . wrong, and perhaps some others who sense it, may have no language for expressing the suffering as an injustice, but nevertheless they can tell stories that relate a sense of wrong' (see also Bandes 1996: 364). Storytelling is not used by victims only. An offender's family may share a story that places his actions in context. Navajo peacemaking emphasizes the importance of peacemakers telling Navajo creation and journey narratives to assist in the resolution of crimes. Based on her research into the use of peacemaking in domestic violence cases, Donna Coker (1999: 59) notes that such stories may play a

[55] As Dryzek (2000: 67) points out, some contemporary deliberative democrats want to 'purge rhetoric from deliberation on the grounds that rhetoric can open the door to demagogues, manipulators, deceivers and flatterers'.

[56] One case I observed dealt with a charge of handling stolen goods. This offence had been committed in the context of a young male keeping watch for his friends while they robbed a storekeeper of cigarettes. There were no customers in the store during these events, and the offender was outside at all times. During the meeting, the young person was asked to comment on the impact his offence would have had on customers if there had been any in the store. Participants allowed a full two minute silence to elapse while they waited for the offender to answer.

valuable role in peacemaking processes as they 'underscore the importance of harmony, particularly gender harmony, and may support a gender-egalitarian view'.

That said, restorative meetings do not rely solely on informal, narrative forms of communication. Some participants use more formal, structured forms of communication, and an individual may choose to use a variety of styles, switching from formal to informal and back again. A conference in New South Wales illustrates this point. The conference was convened after a young teenager threw a stone at another teenager riding past on a bicycle, causing him to lose his balance and fall off his bike, sustaining minor injuries. At the conference, the young offender sought to downplay the significance of his actions. After all, he argued, the stone had not struck the boy; the boy caused his own injuries by falling off his bike. The investigating police officer attending the conference explained why the young offender's actions were considered in law to have constituted an offence. The police officer then switched tack, following his dispassionate account of the law with a story about a case he had investigated some years earlier in which a young person's seemingly minor reckless act resulted in the death of another person. In that earlier incident the young person's actions resulted in the offender being sent to jail bearing a deep sense of guilt for the tragic consequences of his actions. This personal story, which would not be admitted in a courtroom, appeared to powerfully reinforce the police officer's legalistic explanation as to why the offender had been referred to the conference.

Storytelling is sometimes objected to on the basis that it is a subjective process that is inconsistent with the goal of finding the objective truth. This was one of the criticisms of the emphasis on narrative in the South African Truth and Reconciliation Commission (SATRC 1998: vol. 1(5), para. 35; Jeffery 1999: 69–70). Underlying such objections is the popular belief, questioned by restorative justice, that there is a discoverable truth about events which exists independently of people's subjective opinions. This belief is partly sustained by the adversarial formal justice system, where truth is won, in Paul Rock's (1991: 267) words, 'dialectically and agonistically'. Trials work by reducing and reconstructing 'the indeterminacy and muddle of everyday life' into bleak choices between innocence or guilt, truth or falsehood, this or that account (Rock

1993: 36).[57] In such a contest, it is usually the narratives of the least powerful which are rejected in favour of those of the dominant. Restorative justice aims to do something quite different, attempting to create a multi-layered truth reflecting people's different, and sometimes conflicting, perspectives.

While it is inclusive to accommodate these types of communication in a restorative meeting, it is not inclusive to force them on participants. Not all participants wish to hold hands[58] or begin a meeting with a prayer, maybe because it is not part of their culture or it is not a cultural tradition that they wish to respect. Many Navajo peacemakers describe the alienation of Navajo people from their culture and see 'their role [as peacemakers] as trying to help people understand the relevance of traditional teaching'. Coker (1999: 98–9) refers to the opinion of battered women's advocates who 'point to the fact that significant numbers of Navajo are not fluent in the Navajo language, and thus stories and teaching in Navajo do not carry either the literal meaning or the cultural resonance that peacemakers presume'.

Restorative meetings provide an inclusive form of accountability when they offer participants the opportunity of using these forms of communication. Offenders who come before the Toronto Community Council are invited to participate in a smudging ceremony[59] at the start of a meeting, and Jonathan Rudin says that some offenders accept the opportunity, while others decline.

It is particularly important in multicultural communities not to impose practices on participants where citizens may be used to quite different forms of expression. As Gabrielle Maxwell and Allison Morris (1993: 127) observe in a New Zealand context: 'Real difficulties can arise, however, when offenders are of one ethnic group and victims are of another. Pakeha (white) victims on occasions

---

[57] This is particularly the case at the conviction stage, which is an all or nothing process. However, as Joanna Shapland, Jon Willmore and Peter Duff (1985: 189) point out, 'in sentencing, the nature of the offence and the offender is able to be considered in much finer detail. Large numbers of different mitigating and aggravating factors are allowed...'

[58] This is the practice in two of the circle programmes I observed: Northside Community Justice Committee, Minneapolis, and South St Paul Restorative Justice Council, St Paul.

[59] In smudging ceremonies participants take it in turns to wave the smoke from lit tobacco leaves over their body, in order to cleanse themselves spiritually.

claimed not only that they felt intimidated by the large number of whanau (extended family) but also that they resented discussions in Maori and felt alienated in a Maori environment.'

These kinds of problems may be resolved by negotiation between the parties. It may also be possible to alter the structure of meetings so that they are able to accommodate cultural practices in a way which does not alienate other participants. For instance, meetings may begin with a short period of silence, providing participants with an opportunity to pray, or if they prefer, simply to sit in quiet contemplation.

Although restorative meetings have the potential to be more inclusive of different styles of communication, it is just as important to recognize that the form and venue of a restorative meeting can stymie communication between the parties; for example, in a number of programmes meetings take place in a police station.[60] In the context of the history of the relationship between Australian Aborigines and police Harry Blagg (1997: 492) questions whether a police station can ever be neutral territory that favours neither victim nor offender:

The use of the police station for holding victim/offender meetings may, indeed, 'lend a certain gravity to the proceedings' but the formal symbolism here may... [signify] 'white-fella law' rather than neutrality. The idea of police stations being neutral territory flies in the face of the historical and contemporary reality of police/Aboriginal relations... and the role played by police cells and lock-ups in the capture, enclosure and genocide of Aboriginal people.[61]

Meetings should take place in a venue which is comfortable and non-threatening. Moreover, in some situations there may be a more culturally appropriate venue. Blagg (1997: 486) contrasts police-run conferencing programmes in Australia with the New Zealand programme, where he argues that the use of the marae as the site for many conferences reflects the prominence given to Maori forms of conflict resolution.[62]

---

[60] Wagga Wagga Police; Australian Federal Police, Canberra; Woodbury Police, St Paul; Thames Valley Police.

[61] References omitted.

[62] Although note Maxwell and Morris' finding that marae were 'rarely used' as a venue: only 5% of Maori family group conferences during the sample period were held on a marae. They report that Department of Social Work facilities were the most

The role of convenors

No single image of the ideal convenor emerged from this study. In fact, quite conflicting ideal images emerged. At one extreme is the traditional western stereotype of a mediator or convenor as someone impartial, even neutral, 'an intervener carefully distanced from the interests of either party' (Palmer and Roberts 1998: 107); as one practitioner puts it, 'invisible and uninvolved as possible'. At the other extreme, another image emerges: in some programmes, such as Navajo Peacemaking, convenors (or peacemakers, as they are called) are encouraged to play a very active role, leading discussions and telling stories with moral lessons.

What can be said about this range of images from the perspective of ensuring inclusive deliberative accountability? Both extremes carry their own dangers. If convenors are too involved, they may overwhelm, and effectively exclude, participants. For this reason, a hesitancy to intervene can be a 'healthy guard against overdirective practice' (Bush and Folger 1994: 210). Equally, however, if a convenor does not intervene at all, he or she may miss the chance of assisting parties to deliberate more freely. Michael Palmer and Simon Roberts (1998: 123) describe some of the ways in which convenors can help participants' deliberations: 'Arguments can become so diffuse that concentration and perspective may have been lost. In any case, where the variety of issues, or the range of particular issues, is wide, the mediator's careful questioning and suggestions may produce some acceptable and useful focal point around which further exchange can concentrate.'

One practice on which programmes divide is whether to separate participants in the course of their deliberations. I have already considered the practice adopted by some programmes of taking an adjournment during deliberations. A variation on this is the practice of the Zwelethemba Programme outside Cape Town where peace gatherings begin with the committee separating the disputants and taking written statements from them. Peace committee members

common venue (66% of cases), followed by the offender's home (25% of cases) (Maxwell and Morris 1993: 73).

Blagg (1998: 7–8) himself now considers that he may have 'overstated' the extent to which conferences represented a genuine empowerment process, and now claims that 'Many Maori now believe that their cultural ideals and practices have been co-opted as an 'add on' to an essentially unreformed system'.

then present these statements to the gathering of disputants and their supporters. Clifford Shearing argues that this process allows basic facts to be established without unnecessary disagreement and emotional stress, and provides a non-intimidating environment in which victims can make allegations that peace committee members can then articulate to the group.

This practice can be queried, however, on the basis that attempting to streamline the process of dialogue deprives victims of the full opportunity to describe their victimization and receive acknowledgement. Relying in the first instance on peace committee members to describe a victim's harm may have less impact on an offender than when a victim and his or her supporters describes that harm in their own words. Such an approach also risks creating the perception in the minds of both peace committee members and disputants that the peace committee members are elevated from the other participants in the way that a judge is in a courtroom. Sally Engle Merry and Neal Milner (1993: 5) observe that it is common for forms of popular justice to mimic state law, noting that, 'Even tribunals ideologically opposed to state law and founded on a critique of its failures still borrow its forms'. This is particularly worrisome in the context of South African townships which have a history of informal bodies replicating the worst aspects of formal justice systems and thereafter turning increasingly authoritarian and punitive. Community Peace Programme staff records reveal worries that peace committee members intervened excessively in initial meetings. A process in which participants rely to some extent on peace committee members to communicate between them may encourage this tendency. It may be preferable to seek to allow participants to speak by widening the circle so that there are people present who can support those participants who may otherwise be intimidated.[63]

In a number of programmes, convenors convene meetings using a series of scripted questions. This approach, pioneered by Terry O'Connell, and then developed by REAL Justice, is carefully designed to ensure that a process of emotional transformation

---

[63] It should be remembered that in the Zwelethemba Programme there is not always an admission by one party which can provide the starting point for dialogue, nor is there effective access to police investigation, both of which points may partly justify the unusual process.

takes place in a conference (O'Connell *et al.* 1999: 25). The questions are designed to encourage participants to express disapproval about an offender's actions but also to emphasize the offender's intrinsic worth as an individual, 'separating the deed from the doer' (O'Connell *et al.* 1999: 26). There is concern in this case that some facilitators slavishly follow the script, 'attempting to mould the comments and interactions of the participants to conform to an ideal envisaged by the "cautioning script" rather than allowing them to express themselves freely or communicate directly with one another' (Young and Goold 1999: 133–4). Because of this, one of the programmes surveyed has abandoned the script, and two others have modified it.[64]

Truly skilful convening requires a subtlety and deftness which cannot be reduced to simple rules such as 'Never interrupt participants', or 'Always stick to the script'. Mostly convenors should let people speak, but there will be occasions where convenors should intervene (for example, to ask a boorish or abusive speaker to give others an opportunity to be heard, or, to remind participants of an earlier comment or request that has been overlooked) and similarly, following a script may sometimes stilt—rather than assist—proceedings. What convenors really need is a well-developed sense of when they should intervene, and when they should stay quiet. Of course, this is easier said than done, but there are a number of ways training can help develop these skills. First and foremost, training should stress the importance of undominated deliberation in restorative justice meetings. It is a mistake for restorative justice practitioners to become preoccupied with trying to achieve reparation or forgiveness or reconciliation, as these things should not—and cannot—be forced by convenors. Instead, training should stress that convenors should focus on the more modest objective of ensuring that participants are able to participate effectively. By concentrating more on procedure rather than on results, convenors not only safeguard deliberative accountability but, ironically, are more likely to produce the desired results. When a convenor ensures a victim is able to speak and be heard, that victim will be more inclined to forgive than one pressured to do so. As well as explaining these principles, training should give convenors numerous opportunities to develop these

---

[64] REAL Justice cautions against this, arguing that 'Facilitators take an unnecessary risk when they abandon or change the script' (O'Connell *et al.* 1999: 30).

skills, through convening mock meetings, observing other convenors convening meetings, and then sharing their successes and failures with fellow convenors and researchers.

Conclusion

Those critics who come to the conclusion that restorative justice lacks accountability do so on the basis that some programmes lack formal mechanisms such as public access and appeal rights. In focusing solely on these more traditional modes, they seem to have overlooked the potential meetings have to provide their own inbuilt informal deliberative mode. The main advantage of this form of accountability is that it has the potential to provide a timely, inclusive, motivationally sensitive, public, independent, and iterative mode of accountability. Its main disadvantage is that it is not simple: in order to be all these things, careful thought must be given to who attends, their preparation, the conditions of deliberation, and the availability of more formal modes of accountability. Accordingly, the key recommendations for strengthening deliberative accountability are that:

- Attendance should be voluntary, and offenders should be advised of the availability of an alternative forum which will impose a penalty without prejudicing the offender's right to decline to participate in a restorative justice meeting;
- Decision-making in meetings should be on a consensus basis, with participants advised that an alternative forum will decide the matter if they cannot. That alternative forum should investigate the reasons why agreement broke down, and should not punish an offender for any failure to reach agreement when negotiations were carried on in good faith;
- Meetings should include a diverse range of participants. Care in the preparation phase is crucial to the quality of deliberative accountability in the subsequent meeting. In particular, the quality of deliberation between the convenor and the immediately affected parties depends on assembling a diverse group of participants;
- Meetings should not be too big or too long. If meetings are to be justified on the basis that they allow the free negotiation of affected parties, they should be structured in such a way as to allow this. This may also mean scheduling regular breaks;

- The state has a key role to play in ensuring the diversity of participants, who should represent the broader community's interests and ensure that immediate participants are represented. This can be done by provision of advocates and free legal advice;
- Meetings should allow parties to express themselves in terms that they find comfortable and other participants find unthreatening.

These recommendations caution against making the common assumption that restorative justice is a simple form of justice which can be easily organized. Organizing and running restorative justice meetings properly is a great deal more time-consuming than processing cases through court. Only a thorough examination of the comparative costs and benefits, across a range of dimensions (including participant satisfaction, reoffending, and respect for human rights), will tell whether the effort is worth the trouble.

5

Multiple Uses of Deliberative Accountability

Susan listened to her son attempt to describe the harm he had suffered as a result of the attack six months earlier. His facial injuries had been so serious that he had required plastic surgery. When he had finished speaking, Susan took over: 'And the harm we suffered was made worse by the failure of the police to treat this matter seriously. You (looking at the investigating officer) never returned our calls, and as far as we could tell, didn't care about our case. It's taken six months for this case to be dealt with—Why?' All eyes turned to the investigating officer. 'I'm sorry—sitting here, hearing what you're both saying—I must admit I had no idea that Adam's injuries were so serious. You see, I thought this was just a schoolyard scuffle, and I was sort of snowed under with other work at the time, but I should have given it more attention. I'm sorry I didn't'.

Introduction

Up to this point we have seen how deliberative accountability can govern the behaviour of participants and the decisions they make in restorative justice meetings. Proponents claim that in fact these are just two of the multiple uses for deliberative accountability. A number of writers advocate the reform of police complaints procedures (and more generally, police management) along the lines of restorative justice principles (e.g. Dobry 2001; McLaughlin and Johansen 2002), building on earlier recommendations to handle complaints against police by using—wherever appropriate—informal mediation between complainants and police officers (e.g. Scarman 1981: 7.24). Proponents claim that complaints against police may also be dealt with as part of the proceedings in restorative justice meetings between victims and offenders. However, meetings can provide this particular type of accountability only when they are not convened by police officers themselves, and only where the common knowledge exists among participants that aggrieved citizens can pursue their complaints in an alternative forum should they not find satisfaction in the informal one. In addition to serving as an informal forum for state accountability, meetings may also be useful mechanisms for re-examining agreements and then monitoring their compliance.

Policing police

Achieving police accountability is made difficult by the 'practical autonomy of street-level policing, the low visibility and high discretion of rank-and-file officers' (Reiner 1995: 91). As Robert Reiner observes, there are two main mechanisms for holding individual police accountable: courts and complaints processes (Reiner 1997: 1025). When a court hears an offender's case, it can to some extent hold the state accountable by insisting that the police comply with procedural rules related to the treatment of a suspect, and also by scrutinizing the manner in which evidence is obtained. One of the possible problems with restorative justice programmes, and informal justice more generally, is that when a case is processed through such a programme, police can evade this sort of legal accountability.[1]

Among restorative justice writers, opinion is strongly divided as to whether restorative justice meetings do, in fact, provide an alternative type of accountability. On the one hand, some proponents suggest that an informal type of state accountability can occur during the course of meetings. David Moore (1994: 44), for example, argues that in meetings, police 'are under a very effective form of scrutiny...the literal direct scrutiny of the community affected'. Similarly, John Braithwaite and Christine Parker (Braithwaite 1997: 504; Braithwaite and Parker 1999: 114) argue that the fact that conference participants are able to criticize police in meetings makes the police more, rather than less, accountable.[2] Others, however, are highly sceptical. Harry Blagg (1998: 12), for example, says:

---

[1] While acknowledging the shortcomings of this type of accountability, writers such as Richard Delgado (2000: 769) and Kate Warner (1993: 142) worry that in restorative justice programmes police do not face the prospect of this sort of scrutiny.

[2] John Braithwaite provides some examples in support of this claim, which are considered later in this chapter.

I do not share John Braithwaite's optimism that communitarian conferencing, as currently practised, can open up in a way that allows for criticism of powerful agencies such as the police. They have, to borrow a phrase of David Garland's (used in relation to correctional system)?, N[sic] a heavily inscribed sense of their own naturalness and appropriateness as the 'real' agents for the dispensation of justice.

Richard Young (2001: 213), drawing on his research with Carolyn Hoyle on the Thames Valley Police Conferencing Programme, is similarly doubtful, concluding: 'As for Braithwaite's suggestion that inappropriate police behaviour will be challenged in the conference setting, the Thames Valley research found much evidence to the contrary.'

What emerges from this study is that a variety of state actions prior to a restorative justice meeting can potentially come under consideration in that meeting, but that programmes are often structured in such a way as to block such scrutiny.

The subjects of accounts

Offenders' treatment

For the very reason that the primary purpose of a restorative justice meeting is to consider an offender's actions and the consequences of those actions, details of his or her treatment at the hands of police may well emerge in the course of an offender's narrative. This treatment includes the manner in which police speak to offenders as well as apparently more serious questions such as whether or not police have respected their rights (such as the right to consult a lawyer). In one conference I convened in New South Wales, Australia, a young offender was asked to describe events leading up to the conference. After describing how he committed the offence, the offender then told the conference what had happened when the police officer visited his house. The officer arrived and immediately threatened him, saying 'I'm going to send you to jail'. This revelation visibly alarmed the other conference participants, because for one thing, the relatively minor assault he had committed did not seem to warrant a term of imprisonment and, moreover, it was obviously not the police officer's responsibility to send anyone to jail. Sensing others' alarm about the inappropriateness of his remark, the police officer hastily explained that he had only intended to warn the young person that if he continued to commit offences, a judge may eventually have no choice but to send him to jail.

As meetings are not constrained by laws of evidence, any aspect of police treatment of an offender might come under participants' scrutiny. This may include situations where police do not interact with an offender directly, although an officer's actions nevertheless might have an impact. This is best illustrated by a conference for a young offender who had admitted to stealing.[3] The young boy's parents had contacted police upon discovering that their son had stolen money from them. According to the boy, the investigating police officer had said to the parents that in disciplining their child they could 'do anything except break his legs'. Prior to the conference, the offender asked the convenor whether he could question the police officer in the meeting about why he had said that. The convenor advised him that he could, provided that he asked in a respectful fashion. When the offender put the question to the officer in the presence of the other participants (who included a representative from a social services government department, and a school counsellor), the officer looked most uncomfortable and embarrassed at the question. According to the convenor, the boy's question also caused his mother (who was present at the conference) to begin to reassess her approach to her son, apparently previously unaware that he had thought his parents were too tough on him. It is possible to imagine many other kinds of experiences similar to this one, which would fall outside legal standards of relevance in a courtroom but become the subject of scrutiny in a restorative justice meeting.

It is not only the laws of evidence constraining scrutiny of an offender's treatment in the courtroom. Lawyers advise offenders (and their parents) against complaining against police in court on the basis that any complaints are likely to backfire and lead to a longer sentence (Braithwaite 1999: 55). Richard Funston, Senior Solicitor with the Children's Legal Service in the New South Wales Legal Aid office, said that although such issues are regularly raised in trials (where they may have some bearing on the prosecution's ability to prove an offence) they are rarely raised in sentencing hearings:

---

[3] The administrator of this programme requested that the programme not be identified.

Issues of impropriety are canvassed regularly in hearings. Police informants are cross-examined about such matters going to their credit [credibility as witnesses], but in sentencing it would be rare for a defendant to raise such an issue, and indeed to do so, would be to risk inflaming the court.

Victims' treatment

In addition to considering the treatment of offenders, meetings may also consider police treatment of victims. Research shows that initially, victim satisfaction with police is generally high, but then tends to decline steadily as the case progresses: 'failure to keep victims informed, perceived inefficiency, unhelpfulness, or unfairness' are the key factors for this decline (Zedner 1997: 599). In a courtroom these matters are not addressed, but in a restorative justice meeting the way a victim has been treated by police can emerge in the course of the victim's description of the impact of the offence (as it did in the conference described at the beginning of this chapter).[4]

The manner of police action

In many cases it is the manner of police action rather than its official outcome, which is objectionable. What people really want is for police to speak respectfully to them, a fact very often overlooked by police (Bayley 1995: 106). This is well illustrated by Jenny Brockie's Australian documentary, *Cop it Sweet* (1991), which followed New South Wales police officers around Redfern, a predominantly poor, inner suburb of Sydney with a large Aboriginal population. This particular documentary generated extensive publicity, mainly for the racist way in which some police officers were shown speaking to, and about, local Aborigines. As Janet Chan explains, the conduct of the police officers was unexceptional: 'As a real-life exposé of police deviance it paled against the brutal beating of Rodney King... (but) what was most disturbing of all, in the words of a viewer, was that the police were "on their best behaviour for the cameras".' Jenny Brockie's (1994: 178) subsequent observations point to the role of police culture in shaping ideas about what constitutes 'best behaviour':

---

[4] This conference was described to me by Peter Brock, a conference administrator with New South Wales Juvenile Justice Conferencing, responsible for conferencing in Blacktown, one of the outer areas of Sydney.

As we were filming *Cop It Sweet,*...some police seemed more worried about whether or not they were wearing their hats when the cameras were rolling, than about the way they spoke of Aborigines. There was a message here, a significant pointer to the priorities communicated to police by their own bureaucracy. A primary emphasis on discipline, formality, procedure: being seen to be 'proper' in the most limited sense, even if it meant losing sight of the big picture.

As we have seen, meetings provide a corrective to this sort of bureaucratic distortion, by allowing participants to remind police of the importance of virtues such as respect and civility.

One further advantage of using restorative justice meetings to hold police accountable is that police themselves can discuss the context in which an incident occurred. In the case described at the beginning of this chapter, a police officer explains quite honestly—as he certainly needs to—some of the difficulties in conducting an investigation. A common failing of police accountability mechanisms is that they focus on the individual incident while ignoring the larger framework in which these incidents occur (Bayley 1995; Goldsmith 1995: 116). Paying attention to an incident's context enhances the motivational sensitivity of this form of accountability. When police are provided with an opportunity to discuss the background to a set of actions they are less likely to feel their integrity is being questioned, or alternatively, if they feel that it is, that they have an opportunity to defend themselves.

One of the obvious shortcomings of this form of accountability is that it only catches those instances of police dysfunction which do not prevent a restorative meeting from taking place. Accountability will not work in cases where police treatment results in either the victim or the offender not attending a meeting.

Generally speaking, there are worries that some offenders will be unfairly excluded from restorative justice programmes, and in particular that offenders from poor minority backgrounds with prior offences will be excluded in favour of middle-class first-time offenders from good homes.[5] For various reasons, some victims are also excluded from meetings. In New Zealand, only half of all conferences are attended by a victim, while victims' reasons for non-

---

[5] This concern is shared by Jennifer Brown (1994: 1285), Chris Cunneen (1997: 297), and Carol LaPrairie (1999: 146). This concern is common to many informal, diversionary procedures (Seymour 1988: 232; Cunneen 1997: 292).

attendance included the simple fact that they were not invited, or that the time for the conference was unsuitable, or that inadequate notice was given (Maxwell and Morris 1993: 79). The very nature of these sorts of bureaucratic failings puts them beyond the scrutiny provided by these victims and offenders. Alternative types of accountability and control that can be used to prevent these problems are suggested in Chapter Six.

Wider state accountability

It is not just police actions which may be raised for consideration at a restorative justice meeting. School restorative justice practitioners who were interviewed describe how meetings can be used to hold accountable key figures such as schoolteachers and school managers. Marg Thorsborne (1999), who led school conferencing in Queensland, says that, 'By practising a restorative approach to problem-solving, schools are made accountable for those aspects of structure, policy, organisation, curriculum, and pedagogy which have contributed to the harm and injury'. In one Queensland conference it emerged that there had been insufficient playground supervision in one part of the school, which had contributed to the problem discussed at the conference. The school principal, who was present, promised to rectify this situation. Similarly, John Braithwaite and Christine Parker (1999: 114) report observing conferences where 'even without the support of youth advocacy groups, citizens from both the victim and offender sides have decided to join together to confront a school on the destructiveness of its policy of suspending the young offender involved in the case'. There are numerous other examples of state officials having been held accountable. Kay Pranis (1999: 293) reports on a circle convened by the Northside Community Justice Committee in Minneapolis where participants 'respectfully, but firmly' confronted a judge over an aspect of his decision-making. And John Braithwaite (personal communication, 26 July 2001) reports that in some English care-and-protection conferences for children, it is a common practice to make a list of the often numerous government agencies which a family is dealing with, and for the family to make recommendations about which of them are 'useless' and therefore should be taken off their case. One can imagine that the conduct of other professionals, such as probation officers and juvenile justice staff, could also come under the scrutiny of participants in restorative meetings (for example, offenders might challenge prison staff about those management practices that allow assaults within prisons to occur).[6]

The sources and direction of accounts

We have seen how at least some matters of state responsibility may be considered in restorative justice meetings, and considered the advantage of using a restorative meeting as a forum for state accountability when it involves those people whose interests have been affected. The principle of inclusiveness demands that decision-makers should account to those affected by their decision, but in policing accountability mechanisms. Police do not usually have to account to those who have complained (Goldsmith 1995: 124–5).

Holding police accountable to those affected by their actions is not just inclusive; it can also be simple. The nature of this form of accountability, with both the complainant and the police officer present, can promote the swift resolution of many matters. David Bayley (1995: 107) observes that

Many complaints (about police) are matters of misunderstanding rather than real misconduct. They can be cleared up through frank discussions between police and citizens. Often citizens only want to express their point of view, to vent their sense of grievance, while officers want citizens to know why they really had no choice and had to do what they did. A great deal of anger and hostility can be dissipated when people say, 'Oh, I didn't know that', or 'I guess I overreacted, I'm sorry'.

Whether restorative meetings do in fact provide a forum for state accountability depends on the obligation of state officials

---

[6] When meetings allow wide-ranging discussions, this opens up the possibility of canvassing state responsibility for historical wrongs. So, for example, in one Australian conference when a young Aborigine's aunt was asked for her reaction to her nephew's actions she expressed her disapproval, but then also spoke about her community's treatment at the hands of 'white-fella' governments. Similarly, in welfare conferences, there are reports of Native American grandmothers describing to Department of Social Services officials the impact of American government policies separating Native American children from their families (personal communication, 21 July 1999). Clearly these actions are beyond the personal responsibility of any single state official present at a meeting, but the offices they represent have an ongoing responsibility for these policies, just as the consequences of these policies have ongoing consequences for indigenous communities. Meetings provide an opportunity to pursue an informal sort of accountability that many of these disempowered citizens would otherwise not have.

to account for their actions, which in its turn depends on their attendance.

Requiring state officials to attend meetings

An accountability mechanism cannot begin to work if the person required to give accounts does not take part. This is problematic in the context of using restorative justice meetings to pursue state accountability, as in many programmes it is uncommon for state representatives to attend. Only one of the programmes surveyed requires the investigating officer to actually attend a meeting,[7] and in fact, in the Youth Offender Panels in England and Wales, the investigating officer is prohibited from attending (presumably for fear he or she will dominate proceedings). Moreover, even in those programmes where state officials are invited to attend (see Table 3.1) they do not always do so.[8]

Practitioners' general wariness of criminal justice professionals partly explains the poor attendance rate of investigating officers. Practitioners regard the presence of those professionals to be inimical to the personal, participatory ideals of informal justice. Restorative justice transfers responsibility for resolving crimes from the state to its citizens, and practitioners want to ensure that the state does not wrest back responsibility by taking over restorative justice meetings.[9]

These are absolutely legitimate concerns. Against them, however, is the thought that if community participants are to be properly

[7] Community Conferencing, Queensland. This is not a legal requirement. If a matter is referred to conference by police, s 18D *Juvenile Justice Act* (1992) requires that a police officer attend the conference, but it does not stipulate that this be the investigating officer. However, as a matter of practice, Gail Pollard, Project Officer for Queensland Community Conferencing, says that the investigating officer always attends.

[8] For example, data collected from the RISE experiment in Canberra show that the investigating officer attends in a minority of cases, and, mostly, less frequently than in court. The informant police officer was in attendance in: 9.4 % of drink-driving conferences (compared with 4.8 % of court cases); 21.4 % of juvenile personal property conferences (compared with 33.3 % of court cases); 11.5 % of juvenile property (security) conferences (compared with 35.5 % of court cases); 35.3 % of youth violence conferences (compared with 44.4 % of court cases) (Strang *et al.* 1999: 126–7).

[9] Gabrielle Maxwell and Allison Morris' (1993: 113) evaluation of New Zealand Family Group conferencing suggests that there are grounds for this concern. They found that in 19 % of conferences, parents of young offenders considered that the professionals present (most typically police) were the sole decision-makers.

empowered, they need to be able to question state representatives whose actions have a bearing on the case: there is quite a lot of evidence that participants do want to question investigating officers. In a number of restorative meetings I witnessed participants quizzing police. In addition, a survey of 969 participants in New South Wales Juvenile Justice Conferences found that there was support among victims, offenders, and their friends and families for the investigating officer to attend, rather than delegating the responsibility to some other police officer (Trimboli 2000: 67). If people wanted a police officer to attend solely to guarantee their safety, presumably they would be indifferent about which police officer attended. One possible explanation of the reason participants want the investigating officer present is that they want to question him or her personally.[10]

Moreover, the involvement of the state in restorative justice processes is not inherently inconsistent with the principles of restorative justice. On the contrary, the state can help ensure that all parties affected by a crime are able to decide collectively how to deal with its aftermath. Not only can state officials help prevent the domination of either victims or offenders, they also can represent the perspective of the wider community. Furthermore, they can also assist by accepting scrutiny of their conduct. The goal should not be to exclude the state but to seek to ensure that its participation assists, rather than hinders, the deliberative process in a restorative justice meeting.

Not just wariness on the part of restorative justice practitioners explains professionals' poor attendance rates, since the latter often find it difficult to combine attending meetings with other work commitments. In Minnesota I interviewed a prosecutor and a judge who attend restorative meetings conducted by the South St Paul Restorative Justice Council.[11] Both of them commented on how time-consuming this practice was. As one of them put it: 'These

---

[10] In the context of the Thames Valley Police Restorative Justice Programme, Richard Young (2001: 209) suggests another explanation, namely that participants wanted police with a good knowledge of the case because 'participants sought a authoritative disposition of the matter and/or because they saw such knowledge as important if the process was not to founder on arguments about factual details, such as who had done what to whom'.

[11] Judge Leslie Metzen and Assistant County Attorney Mary Theisen.

things are valuable, but they do take up a lot of my time, and my office's time.'[12]

Frequently there are institutional obstacles to state officials attending. To begin with, many restorative meetings are held out of work hours. Bob Sobey, a police officer and conference convenor with the Australian Federal Police, explains that the Canberra Conferencing Programme suffers from the disadvantage that police officers are entitled to collect overtime for attending court but not for attending conferences. Consequently, for police officers to attend meetings they must do so off-duty, or attempt to squeeze in attendance with their other duties, placing a burden on colleagues forced to cover for them. Attending meetings in their own time imposes a considerable burden on police officers and teachers, particularly when (as is often the case) they are asked to attend numerous meetings.

Of programmes surveyed, it was the two school programmes which appeared to have the greatest success in encouraging authority figures to attend.[13] In this respect, schools have the advantage of running fewer meetings, and then at times which can be scheduled around teachers' availability. In a school setting it also appears that there is less hostility to the inclusion of people other than the offender, the victim, their supporters, and the convenor.

Without more institutional support (such as providing overtime or extra staff to cover for staff attending meetings) it is unlikely that many state officials will attend meetings. One way of juggling state accountability with scarce state resources is to offer participants the option of inviting state officials to attend. In the preparation phase, participants should be advised that the meeting is also an important opportunity to raise concerns about police conduct; this advice could be incorporated in brochures distributed to participants ahead of the meeting. This way, in cases where an offender was unhappy about his or treatment by police, he or she could request that the police officer attend. Advocacy groups could assist victims and offenders by advising them when to exercise this option and also by accompanying them to meetings. Such a policy could in itself

---

[12] Both also suggested that they could envisage a time in the future where they trusted the programme sufficiently to make it unnecessary for them to attend every meeting. In other words, they primarily saw themselves as holding other participants accountable (and not vice versa).

[13] Queensland Schools Conferencing and Totell Middle School, Burlington.

achieve some measure of accountability, while at the same time avoiding the trouble and expense of state attendance (and the risk of state domination) in cases where other participants do not consider it necessary to call state officials.[14] In order for such a system to work, however, it would need to receive the support of senior police, who could command police officers to attend and control work conditions to make this possible.

However, in spite of careful preparation, there will still be occasions when the fact that someone is aggrieved about some aspect of police conduct will only become apparent in the meeting itself. This gives rise to an argument for videotaping meetings; when there is a videotape of a meeting, this tape (with the participant's permission) can later be shown to the officer who is the subject of complaint and possibly to his or her superiors.

State officials' obligations to account for their actions

Difficulties in organizing the attendance of its officials are only one of the problems in using restorative justice to hold the state accountable. Not merely attendance, but an obligation to provide an account is required for police to be held accountable for their actions. Otherwise, when their conduct is questioned by other participants, police may well respond 'Why should I answer your questions? I'm not the one on trial here.'

In some cases, the general human desire to enjoy the favourable opinion of others (see Pettit 1990: 745) may ground an obligation to be held to account. State officials may justify their actions in order to avoid other participants' disapproval and censure, but in many cases this informal sanction may be insufficient to compel police to justify their actions. After all, if a police officer did mistreat an offender in the first place it suggests that he or she was not greatly concerned about the offender's opinion, and if not valuing that opinion then, why later just because of the meeting? The idea that police will ever value the esteem of ordinary citizens also seems less likely in the light of what we know about police perceptions of civilian review boards. Civilian review of police has become increasingly commonplace in countries such as the United States (Skolnick

---

[14] Such a system may have a preventive effect: knowing participants have this option, police and other state officials would have an incentive to be thoughtful in their dealings with participants.

1994: 108; Walker and Wright 1994), Canada, Britain, and Australia (Lewis and Prenzler 1999) but there is a common perception that police resent this form of accountability, regarding review boards as 'kangaroo courts filled with ethnic biases, hidden agendas, and lay people who neither understand nor appreciate the nuances and pressures of policing' (Skolnick 1994: 109; see also Bayley 1995: 103).

In restorative justice meetings, however, there are design features which make it more likely that police will value the opinion of citizens. In a meeting, citizens talk about how they feel about their own experiences with police; they do not just relay other people's hearsay (as many civilian review boards do). Just as restorative justice meetings endeavour to get through to offenders by bringing them face-to-face with the consequences of their deeds, so they may also get through to state officials. The police may challenge the veracity of these stories, but they cannot simply dismiss them as second-hand or inconsequential.[15]

Moreover, it is not just the offender—or for that matter the victim—whom the state official must face in a meeting, but potentially a circle of people which includes parents and family friends, teachers and social workers. So while a police officer may not value the esteem of a single individual, he or she may value that of at least one member of the larger group, especially if those participants come from a variety of backgrounds. The larger and more diverse the group, the greater the chance that there is someone in that group whose esteem a state officer will value.

However, to be confident that police will feel required to be accountable, it is crucial that when they do not get satisfaction in a restorative justice meeting, participants have access to alternative forums for resolving their complaint. Both the aggrieved citizens and

---

[15] Another advantage of these sorts of stories is that they do not challenge the self-image of police as skilled professionals. As David Bayley (1995: 98) says 'concerned with being viewed as the manual labourers of the criminal justice system, police have sought to enhance their status by stressing the scientific nature of their work, the subtleties of making decisions on the spur of the moment in dangerous and complex situations, the legal expertise required, and the stressful and dangerous nature of their work'. One of the reasons civilian review boards backfire is that they suggest not only that police cannot be trusted but 'that inexperienced outsiders can evaluate the propriety of operational decisions as well or better than they can'. Meetings do not question the stressful, dangerous, and technical aspects of police work, but provide feedback about the effects of that work on ordinary citizens.

the police must be aware that such forums exist. These alternative forums perform two functions: first, they provide a mild threat, useful in persuading reticent state officials to participate in meetings; secondly, they can provide alternative access to justice in cases where participants are unlikely to obtain satisfaction from the restorative meeting. Interestingly, none of the programmes surveyed advertised the existence of alternative forums.

Police accountability in a restorative justice meeting is a persuasive, rather than directive, form of accountability. Participants have no power to command state officials to do anything, and have no formal power to impose sanctions on them. Nor is it realistic to expect that police officers would experience any obligation beyond the obligation to explain and discuss their actions with participants.[16] Some readers might be tempted to regard this form of accountability as a toothless tiger, particularly when dealing with instances of egregious conduct. But directive models of accountability rely upon deterrence models of compliance which we know empirically often backfire (Braithwaite 1997*b*: 314). Non-deterrence based approaches such as restorative meetings may in some circumstances do a better job. From a police officer's perspective, because there is little to lose (unlike a police disciplinary hearing in which a police officer's career could be on the line), he or she may be less inclined to be obstructive or deny any wrongdoing. At the very least, restorative justice meetings offer a simple type of accountability to try before escalating to more formal ones.

Police-convened conferences

In the four police-run programmes surveyed,[17] police convene restorative justice meetings, while in the two school programmes, teachers convene meetings.[18] In all, the officer or teacher responsible for investigating a case is not permitted to convene the meeting, on the grounds that personal involvement may impair the ability to do so in

[16] Because it is a persuasive model of accountability it is less important whether participants are themselves accountable. As I pointed out in Chapter Two, iterative accountability is most important in those forms of accountability where the person scrutinizing an account exercises considerable power over the people providing them with accounts. That is unlikely to be the case here.

[17] Wagga Wagga Police, New South Wales; Australian Federal Police, Canberra; Woodbury Police, St Paul; Thames Valley Police Restorative Justice Programme.

[18] School Conferencing, Sunshine Coast, QLD, Australia and Frederick H. Tuttle Middle School, South Burlington, Vermont, US.

an objective manner. But this sensible rule does not go far enough: if programmes are to use meetings as a forum for state accountability, no colleague of either the investigating officer or teacher concerned should not be able to act as convenor. When colleagues convene a meeting there is a very real risk that they will dismiss any complaints which may arise against the officer or teacher concerned.[19] If state accountability is to be nurtured, the convenor must be independent as much as possible. Two of the police-run programmes have started to do this using community volunteers instead of police officers to convene conferences.[20] This was done not so much to promote state accountability, as because police officers could not cope with the volume of cases. Regardless of the reason, though such practice enhances the convenor's independence; even in those cases where a police officer attempts to be scrupulously impartial, the alternative presence of a community volunteer would enhance the equally important *appearance* of independence.

To make it possible for state officials to be held accountable, it is better that meetings do not begin with the attending police officer giving his or her version of events (as happens in the two New Zealand programmes surveyed).[21] Although these two programmes both make a point of giving offenders an opportunity to disagree with the police officer's version, such a practice immediately serves to put offenders at a disadvantage.[22] It is also important to convene meetings in a venue other than a police station. Some writers argue that a police station is neutral territory which at the same time lends an appropriate atmosphere of seriousness to the proceedings (Moore 1994), while others claim that holding meetings in police stations makes victims feel safer (particularly when they are convened by a police officer) (McCold 1998: 12). One might well ask how a police station can be simultaneously both a neutral venue and one that reassures victims. Police stations may be more victim-friendly than

[19] Based on his and Carolyn Hoyle's research in the Thames Valley, Richard Young (2001: 214) concludes that police-convened conferences stymie criticisms of police: the 'typical reaction of the facilitator was defensive'.

[20] Woodbury Police, St Paul; Thames Valley Police Restorative Justice Programme.

[21] New Zealand Family Group Conferencing, and Waitakere District Court Restorative Justice Pilot, Auckland.

[22] There are other reasons, unrelated to state accountability, why it may be preferable for the offender to describe the offence, including that it allows the victim to hear the offender describe things in his or her own words. Police versions may also include details about a victim that the victim would not have chosen to raise his or herself.

offender-friendly, but often they will be neither. This uncertainty carries consequences for making restorative meetings a mechanism for state accountability. As Harry Blagg (1997: 492) points out, a police station—a powerful symbol of colonial oppression—is the most unlikely of places for Australian Aborigines to attempt to challenge state authority. If meetings are to provide an inclusive form of state accountability and allow some prospect that marginalized communities can question state practices, then these requirements underscore the need to hold meetings in genuinely neutral venues. The best way to ensure that a venue is neutral is to ask participants beforehand to suggest venues, or suggest venues to them, and find one that satisfies both the victim and the offender.

It is possible to select a venue and personnel such that neither detracts from the seriousness of the event or compromises the safety of victims. Often, however, there will be other factors that may militate against using community volunteers, and neutral venues. Certainly it will often be simpler and more timely for an institution to convene a conference using internal convenors and venues. However, if an institution is serious about promoting a restorative justice programme as an independent and inclusive form of state accountability, then it should spend the extra effort and time required to find neutral convenors and venues.

Expanding the circle of participants

Any restorative justice meeting requires a circle of participating people if police are to value their opinions. There are other reasons in favour of inviting supporters to join in. Victims and offenders by themselves may be reluctant to challenge state officials; it is especially unrealistic to imagine young offenders doing so. However, if victims and offenders can also bring family and friends to a meeting, they may be able to encourage victims and offenders to challenge police conduct or make that challenge on their behalf (for example, the victim's mother complaining about police delay). Similarly, John Braithwaite (1997: 504) says that he has 'seen mothers criticize the police for excessive force or victimization of their child in a way that they would never be allowed to do in court'.

One of the conclusions I reached in Chapter Four is that there are substantial benefits in having people other than just the victim, the offender, and the convenor present in a restorative meeting. That opinion was offered in the context of participants holding each other accountable for the decisions made in a restorative meeting, but it also holds true in keeping state officials accountable for what happens outside a restorative meeting.

Expanding the circle of participants may also enhance the inclusiveness and publicity of this form of accountability, and that publicity could be further enhanced by allowing people to observe meetings.[23] This may partly answer the concerns of writers such as Owen Fiss (1984) and Richard Delgado (2000: 759) who worry that informal justice 'forfeits the public dimension of adjudication'.

Exposing state officials to a wide range of people may have another incidental benefit. David Bayley (1995: 105) urges police chiefs to begin training on multiculturalism 'so as to enhance the ability of officers to empathize with people different from themselves'. He suggests officers be sent on placements with community organizations in minority neighbourhoods on the basis that such proposals:

offer a more meaningful way of expanding the intellectual and emotional horizons of young recruits than the usual canned lectures on 'multiculturalism'. Police readily admit that there is no substitute for on-the-job training in learning about policing. Can this be less true of learning about the diverse people whom police deal with?

Restorative justice meetings, where police officers can hear about the lives of the people they police, constitute a further promising alternative to 'canned lectures'. As we have seen previously, it will not always be easy to find supporters, and furthermore those supporters may fail to support an offender or a victim. A striking example of this is described by Heather Strang (2000: 168; also described in Braithwaite 2001: 48) reporting on a Canberra conference convened after a bouncer violently assaulted a young man. When the offender arrived at the conference, the victim said that he did not look anything like his assailant. The investigating officer was not present at the conference, and the young man's employer and workmates insisted that he was the assailant (though his family did not appear to believe that he had been involved). It turned out that his workmates wanted him to take the fall because, unlike the other bouncers, he had no prior convictions. In the light of the victim's insistence that the police had the wrong man, the police

---

[23] See discussion of this in Chapter Seven.

officer convenor eventually abandoned the conference, and no further action was ever taken.

In some respects, this particular conference represents a failure of state accountability: the combination of a police-convened conference and the complicity of the offender's workmates in the bungled police investigation meant that the conduct of the investigating police escaped scrutiny. Partly as a result, the victim left the conference highly dissatisfied. It is worth remembering, however, that had this been a court case no one would have known, since victims rarely attend sentencing hearings. Notwithstanding the victim's dissatisfaction, the process at least prevented the injustice of an innocent person being punished, but the case demonstrates that in order to hold the state accountable for its incompetent investigation a great deal more needs to be done. In particular, such cases emphasize the need for non-police convenors and the availability of alternative avenues of complaint. In this, professional advocates for victims and offenders may also have helped, as they would have been less likely to collude in the state's bad practice in the way the hotel staff did, and overall may have provided more assertive support.

The importance of timing in state accountability

When meetings hold state officials accountable for their actions prior to a meeting, they provide a standard *ex post* form of accountability. With this in mind, it becomes clearer that restorative meetings can exhibit a multi-focus type of accountability that operates on an ongoing basis (regulating participants' conduct during restorative justice meetings) and *ex post* basis (reviewing the pre-meeting conduct of offenders, victims, police officers, and others). Like all *ex post* forms of accountability, in this latter function deliberative accountability is susceptible to the criticism that it is not timely: as Bayley (1995: 94) puts it, 'it catches people after the damage is done'. In some cases, the conduct in question might have occurred a very long time before the meeting (for example, where people hold state officials accountable for the policies of previous governments). In other cases, however, the conduct will be much more recent and it may be possible to swiftly repair the damage, for although some meetings will reveal systemic issues which cannot be easily resolved, in others it may be possible to resolve a matter simply by bringing together the affected parties: in the case of the victim who feels neglected, the police officer can try to repair any damage by apologizing on the spot.

Modes of accounting

One of the benefits of a restorative justice meeting is its flexibility in the way people are able to choose to communicate with each other. Because formal accountability mechanisms often favour certain styles of communication over others, they work to exclude people who cannot express themselves in ways in line with the dominant modes. Although police are practised at conforming to these modes, they too may also benefit from the opportunity to express themselves more freely. For instance, when an offender alleges that a police officer has used excessive force, the officer is able to give his side of the story straight away, in a way that explains the pressures on police (of which the public is often unaware). Police are called upon to act only when problems which other people and institutions have failed to address became acute. David Bayley (1995: 101) argues that police:

are undoubtedly more restrained most of the time than members of the public would be in similar circumstances. Most of the time they ignore what would be regarded as 'fighting words' by most of us. Indeed, given the frequency with which police encounter anger and aggression, the wonder is that brutality does not occur more often.

These stories should not excuse unsatisfactory conduct, but can better help place a police officer's behaviour in context in the same way that restorative justice meetings attempt to place an offender's actions in context. Police accountability can help build empathy and understanding between them and citizens in a way that may be difficult to achieve otherwise. Offenders can learn about the pressures police work under and also how:

police often shape their actions according to the demeanour of citizens towards themselves—rude or polite, aggressive or acquiescent, sassy or restrained, demanding or passive, foul-mouthed or refined...Police talk quite openly about people who 'flunk the Big A', meaning the attitude test. People with a 'bad attitude' are seen not only as threatening to police individually, but as constituting a symbolic attack on the law itself (Bayley 1995: 101).

Equally, the police can learn about how their own attitude and demeanour influences people's behaviour. Terry O'Connell, a former police officer who pioneered the Wagga Wagga Programme in New South Wales, Australia, says that he has often seen young offenders, when accused by police of being unco-operative respond, 'I didn't think you were treating me right'. No matter what their alleged crimes or situations, offenders expect to be shown the same respect police officers themselves demand. Ray McDonald, a young Aborigine from the town of Taree, in NSW, Australia, puts it simply: 'If you treat me like a human, I'll react like a human: treat me like an animal and I'll react like an animal' (Stevenson 2000). Tom Tyler's (1990) research shows systematically that this is true: single procedurally unjust encounters with authority can have a direct effect on a future career in law-breaking.

The flexibility of restorative justice meetings also allows police to make understood the impact on them of witnessing people ruin their lives and the lives of others. In the earlier case in which the police officer had made an inappropriate threat to send an offender to jail, the officer talked to participants about his frustration at constantly witnessing good kids mess up their lives. This frustration, he said, led him to make the inappropriate threat to try and 'jolt' the young boy out of the possibility of future offending. In more formal accountability situations, such an account may never be aired, but restorative justice meetings are able to accommodate these more personal, complex, and perhaps more meaningful, accounts of police action.

Juggling state accountability with individual accountability

In spite of the very real benefits which may be thus achieved, there is a real risk that using restorative justice meetings as a forum for holding police accountable will get in the way of holding offenders accountable, the primary focus of a meeting. However, for a number of reasons, it is nevertheless desirable to juggle state accountability with offender accountability. Foremost among these refers back to the way restorative justice seeks to deal with events in a manner acknowledging their ambiguity and complexity. Furthermore, dealing with state accountability as an incidental aspect of offender accountability may also allow for police to be praised for their conduct when appropriate, as well as reduce the tendency of offenders to unjustifiably blame others.

Criminal law—and law generally—works by individualizing responsibility and ignoring the social context in which individuals commit crime. Informal justice, critics argue, shares the same characteristic, concentrating on individual disputes while blocking out the larger picture (Abel 1982: 7; Pavlich 1996: 714). In fact, it is argued that informal justice may do even less to address social justice because it works to pacify the community unrest which may otherwise force social change. Richard Abel (1982: 280) argues that 'Informal institutions neutralize conflict by responding to grievances in ways that inhibit their transformation into serious challenges to the domination of state and capital'.[24]

Restorative justice is susceptible to the same criticism. However, by allowing issues such as police behaviour and school policy to be discussed in meetings, restorative justice programmes slightly broaden the traditional, individual focus of the law. It remains important, however, not to exaggerate the effects of the phenomenon described here. While restorative meetings often have a broader focus than court cases, the offender's liability remains the event around which meetings are convened and deliberations concentrate. Moreover, meetings usually do not deal with the underlying structural causes of an offender's behaviour, such as unemployment, poverty, and family breakdown.[25] Indeed, a cynical critic could argue that it is this false appearance of its capacity to address these causes that makes restorative justice so attractive to governments.

When state accountability is incidental to offender accountability, meetings can also provide a forum for recognizing commendable state conduct. Examples here have all dealt with cases where participants have complained about police conduct, but it is also possible to imagine others where state officials are acknowledged as having done well. In such a case, an offender may report that police were polite, or a victim may mention that trauma was eased by the care and concern shown by police. This positive feedback is important for

[24] See also Jerold Auerbach (1983: 144) who argues that, 'Alternatives are designed to provide a safety valve, to siphon discontent from courts. With the danger of political confrontation reduced the ruling power of legal institutions is preserved, and the stability of the social system reinforced.'

[25] The partial exception among the programmes surveyed is the Zwelethemba Peacemaking Programme, which directs money earned from peacemaking activities to a peace-building fund supporting the building of community facilities and the financing of micro-enterprises (Roche 2002).

nurturing motivational sensitivity. It is important that accountability mechanisms do not, presumptively, treat people as untrustworthy, as this can breed long-term resentment and poor conduct but instead respond sensitively to people's varying motivations and dispositions. One way to achieve motivational sensitivity is to ensure that mechanisms do not serve solely to detect suspect conduct, but also to praise and reward good conduct. There is evidence from regulatory research that regulators' use of praise is more effective in improving compliance than the use of negative sanctions for poor compliance (Makkai and Braithwaite 1993). This insight is important in all contexts, but especially so in the context of policing, where there is a conspicuous lack of opportunities for police to receive positive feedback. Jerome Skolnick and James Fyfe (1993: 236) argue that: 'Cops need to know how well they are doing and to be rewarded for doing well. When they are not told how they are doing, they get the idea that nobody cares, that nobody is watching. When this happens, they become understandably cynical and sometimes even brutal.'

There is a third possible advantage in combining state accountability with offender accountability, when we consider that one of the standard techniques used by offenders to neutralize responsibility is to condemn their condemners. By attacking others, the offender shifts or suppresses the wrongfulness of his behaviour:

The delinquent shifts the focus of attention from his own deviant acts to the motives and behaviour of those who disapprove of his violations. His condemners, he may claim, are hypocrites, deviants in disguise, or impelled by personal spite. This orientation toward the conforming world may be of particular importance when it hardens into a bitter cynicism directed against those assigned the task of enforcing or expressing the norms of the dominant society. Police, it may be said, are corrupt, stupid and brutal. Teachers always show favouritism and parents always 'take it out' on their children (Sykes and Matza 1957: 668).

When state officials are absent from meetings and an offender alleges that he was treated badly by the police officer, participants have no way of knowing whether an allegation is legitimate or is simply a convenient means of shifting blame. When investigating officials are present, meetings provide a forum where such allegations can be raised and tested.

There may be some circumstances in which allegations about police behaviour cast doubt on an offender's guilt, for example, when that offender alleges he was entrapped.[26] When the improper police behaviour does bear on an offender's responsibility, the offender may elect not to participate in the conference, instead pleading not guilty, and attempt to hold the police accountable for their behaviour in court (e.g. by relying on the defence of entrapment, or seeking to have the tainted evidence excluded). Alternatively, he could agree to participate, on the basis that the meeting consider the harm caused by both himself and the police. In standard criminal justice processes, shame or embarrassment may deter offenders from complaining about such police impropriety, but in a restorative justice process, there is a greater likelihood of state accountability. Restorative justice meetings are capable of accommodating real-life situations where responsibility for an incident is shared among participants. A meeting may well consider how the victim of an assault provoked that assault by making racist insults (as happened in one of the televised Thames Valley conferences), while still not condoning an offender's actions. Similarly, in a solicitation case, a meeting could consider how the police went too far in encouraging an offender to commit the offence, while still condemning the offender's actions. Carefully managed meetings may be capable of juggling multiple, shared responsibilities in a way that courts or other adversarial approaches cannot.

Some meetings may raise issues which are too large or too difficult to discuss in a single restorative meeting; in others an offender's crime might be such that the focus should solely be on it. One possible solution is to identify any concerns about state conduct in the offender's meeting, and then schedule a later meeting to specifically address the investigating official's conduct and any other related issues. A range of people could be invited to the subsequent meeting including state officials with the power to make systemic changes. When meetings have been videotaped, the later meeting could watch a tape of the earlier one with the participants' permission. The initial restorative meeting is thus used as an accountability device to reveal more systemic, organizational problems which can be subsequently addressed.

---

[26] For example, in the Community Conferencing Program run by Central City Neighbourhoods Partnership in Minneapolis, a conference was held after an offender had solicited sex from an undercover police officer posing as a prostitute (Gerard and Nelson 1998: 6).

Community policing by restorative justice

Restorative justice meetings, used in the way described here, could theoretically form an important part of a community policing strategy, the essence of which is that 'the police are able to carry out their tasks satisfactorily only through constructive co-operation with the public' (Skolnick and Fyfe 1993: 253). Unfortunately in practice, community policing often has amounted to little more than token gestures, such as putting a few police officers on bicycles, or merely re-branding conventional policing practices.[27] Genuine attempts to form constructive partnerships between police and the community are all too rare, but restorative justice could help community policing move beyond mere tokenism.

Meetings provide forums for the 'grass-roots feedback' that David Bayley (1984: 29) says is necessary: 'If the police are going to do community policing they have got to open themselves up for commentary on their performance from the community.' Jerome Skolnick and James Fyfe (1993: 253) argue that 'community policing involves not only the sympathetic listening but the creation of opportunities to listen'. Until now, this has often taken the form of Neighbourhood Watch programmes and door-knocking campaigns in which police in a proactive manner discuss general concerns with members of the public. The rationale underlying such activities is that the mutual distrust between police and the public is caused by the fact that they usually interact only in situations of conflict (Mukherjee and Wilson 1987: 6), and that the path to building more constructive relationships is to create different types of opportunities in which police and the public can interact. Restorative justice, on the other hand, offers the possibility that relationships can be forged around the interactive discussion in meetings of specific incidents. For one thing, meetings will not always involve only conflict: they also provide an occasion when police can be thanked and praised; but when they do involve conflict, that conflict should not be avoided, but rather used as an important learning opportunity.

---

[27] The definition of community policing offered by British comedian Alexi Sayle (quoted in Bayley 1994b: 105) captures this problem nicely: 'I'll tell you how you know when you've got community policing. It's when you are walking along a street and a police van pulls up, several coppers leap out, pin you to the ground, and tell you what time it is.'

Feedback built into the processing of individual offences is also important because it ensures that police get it from the communities most directly affected by police. One problem with Neighbourhood Watch programmes is that they bring together police and those members of the community with whom they have the least likelihood of contact (Bennett 1990: 84). If police are serious about getting feedback from the populations they police most intensively—such as the young and poor minority populations—then they must look to forums where those citizens are likely to be present; restorative meetings provide such a forum.

The model of informal accountability described in this chapter may partially re-create in a modern urban context some of the accountability dynamics in smaller communities. Australian Federal Police officer, Bob Sobey, says that one of the problems with modern policing is that police are allowed to escape the consequences of their actions. Sobey contrasts this with his experience policing in the small community of Norfolk Island, an Australian territory in the Pacific Ocean. There, he said, if police did the wrong thing by someone, they had to face that person and his or her friends when they went to buy their meat at the butcher the next day. As David Bayley (1994*b*: 139) puts it: 'Small-town police deal with familiar people; city police deal with offenders.' Restorative justice meetings may re-create some of the informal accountability dynamics at work in small communities, and consequently give some much-needed starch to the concept of community policing.[28]

Revising agreements

All but one of the programmes surveyed provide for a meeting to be reconvened (Table 3.1) for any one of a variety of reasons. Participants may decide shortly afterwards that the outcome of the meeting is likely to be unsatisfactory. Alternatively, an offender may discover that the outcome is unworkable. In one such case, a Canberra conference was reconvened after police discovered that a victim had grossly inflated her claim for compensation in the original meeting. Some programmes provide for an automatic review

---

[28] For further critiques of community policing see Neil Cameron and Warren Young (1986), Lorraine Beyer (1993), and Dennis Rosenbaum (1994).

meeting to consider these sorts of issues (Table 3.1), whereas some other programmes reconvene meetings only if the need arises.[29]

Reconvening a meeting is a less timely and simple form of accountability than that described up to this point. It may be an imposition on parties to have to reconvene a meeting, especially after having already spent between one and two hours in the original meeting plus any time consulting with the convenor prior to the meeting. The extent of any imposition will, of course, vary according to the nature of the case and the identity of the participants. For example, Michael Stanefski of the South St Paul Restorative Justice Council says that it is easier to reconvene cases involving school students, as the students are together at school each day. Whether the imposition is justified will depend on issues to be considered in the meeting. It would be difficult to demonstrate that there always is a need in programmes which conduct reviews as a matter of course; although it should be noted that in these programmes victims are not expected to attend more than one meeting, programmes relying instead on community volunteers in any subsequent meetings.

Where reviews do not happen as a matter of course, meetings can usually be reconvened at the programme's discretion, at the request of any of the parties. In South St Paul Restorative Justice Council participants are advised that a meeting can always be reconvened, and are told that should they wish this to happen, they should approach the convenor or another nominated person (should a participant's problem be with the convenor). In some instances parties may prefer the outcome to be reconsidered by some other body (such as a court).

Enforcement of agreements

Commitments made by offenders

As we have seen, restorative justice meetings aim to reach agreement about how to deal with the aftermath of an incident. This usually involves offenders agreeing to do something either for the victim or

---

[29] For example s 55(1) *Young Offenders Act* (1997) (NSW) states that 'A conference may be reconvened by the relevant conference administrator, on the conference administrator's initiative or at the request of more than one participant in the conference, for the purpose of reconsidering any aspect of the outcome plan or any recommendation at a conference'.

themselves or the wider community or for a mixture of all three. Apologies, financial restitution, and community service are typical commitments made towards victims and communities. Often meetings also end up with offenders making commitments for the benefit of themselves or their own families, such as to work harder at school, observe a curfew, or spend more time with their mothers. In many cases the distinction between what benefits the offender and what benefits the victim or the wider community is blurred, as often victims say that what will benefit them is for an offender to do something to benefit him or herself. A conference I convened in New South Wales, Australia, provides a good example of this. A middle-aged married couple came to the conference to meet the young person who had stolen and damaged beyond repair the car the husband had spent three years and thousands of dollars restoring. In the conference the man explained to the offender that he had done great damage to the car, probably without realizing it. After he finished speaking, his wife volunteered that her stoic husband had been privately shattered about the loss of a car which he had hoped to display at car shows and that he did not have the heart to start over. Moreover, their daughter was in the advanced stages of a difficult pregnancy, and the loss of the car had made it difficult for them to help her with tasks such as collecting grandchildren from school and doing the grocery shopping. Nonetheless, despite the harm, the couple declined offers of physical labour from the offender, insisting that the only outcome that would help them was one that helped him (in this case, taking small steps to resume his education) (Braithwaite and Roche 2001: 68–9).

Whatever the nature of the commitment, in most programmes offenders are held accountable for their completion, firstly to other participants in a meeting, and failing that, more formally, to some alternative forum (such as court). I consider the nature of these forms of accountability in more detail below.

Commitments made by other parties

While it is most common for the offender only to make commitments in a meeting, in some meetings other participants will also make them. Another meeting I convened illustrates this point. This was the meeting described in Chapter Four, held after a boy threw a rock at another boy riding past on his bicycle, causing the boy to crash, injuring himself and damaging the bicycle. In the course of the meeting it emerged that the incident was part of an ongoing dispute between two groups of students at the high school they both attended. This was reflected in the outcome plan:

1. Adam agrees to pay $10 to Steve for bicycle repairs;
2. Adam and Steve agree to invite the students listed below to a lunchtime meeting at school to report on what happened at the conference, and explain that Adam and Steve want any conflict or hostility between their friends to cease.

   Students to be invited: Roger, Dean, Jason, Bart.

   Meeting to be supervised by Mr Smith (a teacher present at the conference);
3. Adam and Steve to attend meeting with Mr Smith four weeks later to report on how they're getting on.

Victims sometimes, as in this case, make some sort of commitment reflecting both involvement in the offence and their capacity to prevent its recurrence. Coincidentally, from time to time, participants other than victims make commitments: in a burglary case in the Waitakere District Court Restorative Justice Pilot, a young man's parents and college course administrator agreed to stay in more regular contact with each other. One of the problems with restorative justice programmes is that these commitments, unlike offenders' commitments, are not enforceable. At best, programme staff simply urge parties to honour them.

The direction and timing of accounts

In restorative justice, offender accountability begins in a low-key way: an offender is required to report to other participants, either individually[30] or in a reconvened meeting. If those participants are not satisfied with his efforts, the offender is usually obliged to report to the people running the programme. If after this he still has not honoured the agreement, some more formal alternative is activated. In some programmes this will mean sending a case back to the original referral agency, which will consider whether or not to begin or resume a formal prosecution. In other programmes—such as school programmes—offenders will be dealt by a more traditional disciplinary approach.

---

[30] In many meetings, agreements will nominate one of the participants to monitor the offender's completion of his or her commitments.

This process can be more appropriately likened to a directive form of accountability. Offenders must account to those who have power not just to seek an explanation or an account of their progress towards honouring any commitment, but when that account is unsatisfactory, to direct them to complete the outcome or else refer them to an alternative forum. Though this is the case for the majority of programmes surveyed, in a small number there is no threat of enforcement hanging over the offender's head; programmes instead hope feelings of moral obligation alone will motivate the offender to honour his or her agreement.[31] The difficulty with such programmes is that they are then powerless in the face of recalcitrants, who go on posing a risk to public safety. For this reason, it remains appropriate that programmes have the ability to move offenders to more formal kinds of justice when the informal ones do not work.

In most programmes offenders report in the first instance to other participants either individually or in a meeting. Here the role of community members as participants in monitoring reflects the restorative justice philosophy that criminal processes should encourage active participation by victims, offenders, and their communities (Ness 1996: 23). It is also consistent with broader trends in criminal justice (Crawford 1997; Braithwaite 2000), and public policy more generally (Garland 1996: 452 (n. 10)). David Garland (2001: 124–5) characterizes this trend as a 'responsibilisation strategy':

Instead of addressing crime in a direct fashion by means of the police, the courts and the prisons, this approach promotes a new kind of individual action, in which state agencies activate action by non-state organizations and actors ... The primary objective is to spread responsibility for crime control onto agencies, organizations and individuals that operate outside the criminal justice state and to persuade them to act appropriately.

From the perspective of the state, relying on participants to monitor offenders' completion of outcomes is simpler and cheaper than placing primary responsibility on state agencies. Moreover, in nearly all cases it appears to be quite adequate to ensure that offenders do

---

[31] See Table 3.1. The programmes are the Wagga Wagga Police Programme; Thames Valley Police Restorative Justice Programme; Zwelethemba Peacemaker Committee; the Toronto Community Council; Victim/Offender Mediation/Dialogue, Texas; Connections Program, Red Wing. In the Zwelethemba Programme, peacemaker committee members may encourage a victim to take their original complaint to the police if an offender fails to honour his or her commitment.

honour their agreements. From a survey of thirteen separate evaluations of programmes, a number of which were multi-site studies, John Braithwaite (2001: 52) concludes that there is a high level of compliance with restorative justice agreements, higher than is the case with court orders. Meta-analysis of eight studies by Jeff Latimer, Craig Dowden, and Danielle Muise (2001: 17) also finds that 'offenders who participated in restorative justice programmes tended to have substantially higher compliance rates than offenders exposed to other arrangements'. These findings replicate those concerning American mediation programmes in the 1970s and 1980s (Palmer and Roberts 1998: 144).

Consistently high levels of compliance owe probably as much— if not more—to the form of the original restorative meeting as they do to the form of monitoring. A person who has actively participated in the negotiation of an agreement in a meeting is more likely to comply with its terms than a person upon whom a penalty is imposed. The fact that compliance is monitored by people known to and respected by the offender may also explain these high levels. Those in the meeting may be in a position to encourage or assist offenders to complete their agreement; additionally offenders may well feel a moral obligation to them, arising out of a desire to repay their faith or make amends. In other words, high compliance rates can be explained by a combination of both the inclusiveness of the initial decision-making and the motivational sensitivity of the monitoring technique.

An offender's accountability may be to just one participant, or all of them, or initially to one and then later on to all. In some programmes the offender reports to just one individual, such as a victim or a teacher, who is then responsible for notifying programme staff. An offender may be required to report only on completion of the agreement or, before then, also to provide progress reports. All except one programme surveyed allow programme managers to reconvene a meeting,[32] in most programmes only if a problem arises,

---

[32] The exception is Queensland Juvenile Justice Conferencing. In Queensland, a police officer has the legislative power to reconvene a conference. Section 18J(3)(c) *Juvenile Justice Act* (1992) states that where a child contravenes an agreement made at the community conference, a police officer may refer the offence to another community conference, with or without the same convenor. Other options open to the police officer are to take no action, administer a caution to the child, or start a proceeding against the child for the offence.

however, in some as a matter of course (see Table 3.1). Reconvening may happen on the completion of the outcome or, prior to that, to review progress. Generally, meetings in circle programmes and sentencing panels are more likely to be reconvened on a routine basis than meetings in conference and mediation programmes (where reconvened meetings are reserved for problems).

Individual-based accountability

A common practice in restorative meetings is for the group to nominate a person to be responsible for monitoring an offender's completion of the outcome. The independence of this form of accountability will depend on the identity of that person. Victims are likely to provide a more independent form of accountability than when responsibility for monitoring is left to a member of an offender's own family; according to James McDougall, Operations Co-ordinator, Youth Justice Conferences, New South Wales Department of Juvenile Justice, this is one of the reasons justice conference convenors in New South Wales are discouraged from allowing a member of an offender's family to take responsibility for monitoring an agreement. On the other hand, it may be more motivationally sensitive for an offender's mother, for instance, to be the one scrutinizing an offender's progress. A follow-up meeting may combine the motivational sensitivity of supporters with the independence provided by other citizens.

By itself, reporting to an individual is not a public or fully inclusive form of accountability, as a range of people who have an interest in the commitment may not know if it has been honoured. This is why a number of programmes have adopted the practice of keeping other meeting participants informed about progress. The programme going to the greatest effort in this way is the Community Conferencing Central City Neighbourhoods Partnership in Minneapolis. As is the case with many programmes, participants are informed whether an offender has actually completed an outcome, but in this particular case, participants are also provided with additional information such as any comments by community services organizations about the work an offender has done for them.

In order to make this individual-based accountability more timely, a number of programmes schedule reviews of an offender's progress prior to the final deadline. This is a move away from the usual *ex post* type of accountability towards an ongoing form, in the course of which an offender can raise any problems as they arise. Although this form of routine review is a bit more time-consuming to begin with, many programmes judge the initial effort to be worth it, on the basis that offenders may be less likely to ultimately default on their commitment, thus saving time in the long run.

Group-based accountability

Holding an offender accountable to a group of participants is usually much more complicated. Any additional meetings are time-consuming for convenors to organize and may be regarded as a burden by those asked to attend.[33] In particular victims of the original offence may resent additional demands on their time: though attendance is not compulsory, victims may still feel obliged to attend for the benefit of the offender and come to resent this obligation. Holding multiple meetings for an offender only increases the burden; even more so in those not uncommon cases in which a person has been victimized more than once, or has been victimized by co-offenders;[34] victims' diaries could be filled with an almost never-ending succession of meetings.

For such reasons many programmes schedule a second meeting only if they consider it absolutely essential.[35] In deciding whether or not to reconvene, the programmes surveyed duly consider the burden it will impose on the various parties (including the victim

---

[33] The difficulty of organizing additional meetings, and the burden on participants will depend on the location of a restorative programme. Where participants come from a small, relatively well-defined community (such as a school, or a small town like Carcross in the Yukon territory or the South African township of Zwelethemba) it may be easier to organize follow-up circles. This is the opinion of Michael Stanefski from the South St Paul Restorative Justice Circle Program, who says that when participants come from the same school, follow-up circles can be convened quite easily. In programmes where parties are separated by great distances, the difficulty, expense, and inconvenience of reconvening will often make it infeasible.

[34] Many programmes attempt to deal with co-offenders together in the same meeting (although not the Youth Offender Panels in England and Wales). In practice, however, it is can be difficult to do this—particularly where cases are processed through the criminal justice system before being referred back to a restorative programme.

[35] One of the most striking examples of this was in the Zwelethemba Peacemaker Committee. There a man failed to return a door belonging to a woman, after agreeing to do so in a peacemaking session. At the woman's request, the committee reconvened the meeting, asking the man to bring the door with him to the meeting!

and the offender). For example, in New South Wales conferences, administrators are required to keep in mind a number of principles in deciding whether to reconvene a meeting, including these:

- An offender should not be punished a second time by having to reconvene if the breakdown of the outcome plan arose because of the actions of other people;
- A victim should not be re-victimized by being expected to put further time and effort into a conference because of the failure of the offender to keep their agreement (NSWDJJ 2000: 64).

Despite the cost and difficulties of reconvening meetings, some programmes hold them routinely. One of the real benefits of this approach is that meetings become more than just forums for exploring harm and its consequence, but also forums for monitoring agreement compliance and 'championing reintegration' (Crawford and Newburn 2002: 479). From the perspective of the principle of motivational sensitivity it is important that accountability processes lavish praise and encouragement, not just attribute blame: unfortunately, the idea that good behaviour should be positively reinforced is reflected in too few accountability mechanisms. Completion of an agreement provides a good opportunity to congratulate an offender on his or her accomplishment. Even for hardened offenders praise is known to affect compliance, 'nurturing law-abiding identities, building cognitive commitments to try harder, encouraging individuals who face adversity not to give up in the face of that adversity and nurturing belief in oneself' (Makkai and Braithwaite 1993: 73; see also Braithwaite 2001: 41).

This positive feedback is part of the rationale of both the Northside Community Justice Committee in Minneapolis and the Connections Program in the Red Wing Correctional Facility in Minnesota. These programmes schedule a number of meetings which culminate in a circle where volunteers, the offender, family members, and victims (if they wish) meet to celebrate the completion of an offender's commitments. The process provides an occasion when offenders can enjoy the congratulations and respect of a group of people to many of whom they have previously only been known as offenders. While motivational sensitivity may be the principal benefit offered by this form of accountability, it also provides a level of independence, inclusiveness, and publicity. A number of other programmes[36] also schedule completion meetings, but the Northside Community Justice Committee and the Connections Program are the most explicit about their purpose by calling them 'celebratory circles'.

These particular programmes also usually schedule a meeting between the first and the final meeting to monitor an offender's progress. Like accountability to individual participants, this form of accountability attempts to deal with problems in a more preemptive, rather than reactive, manner. Moreover, there is an additional benefit in using a group of people in this form of review. A more inclusive kind of accountability, it incorporates perspectives of those people who may be able to assist in ensuring that an offender completes an undertaking.

This point was well illustrated by an 'Ohana conference which I observed in Hawaii.[37] In Honolulu 'Ohana conferences are used in some child welfare cases. The one I observed was a routine review conference, held to review an agreement made at a conference held four months previously. At that initial conference, a number of decisions had been made about a variety of matters including the parents' attendance at treatment centres for drug and alcohol addictions. In addition, arrangements had been made for the children's grandmother to care for the children while their parents were in full-time treatment. At the review circle, attended by twenty-five people, (including the extended family, three social workers, and two conference convenors) it was clear that the grandmother was exhausted by the daily wear and tear of caring almost full-time for her four grandchildren. The advantage of this form of review emerged when other members of the group volunteered to share in the care of the children while the parents continued in their intensive treatment course. After a short period of deliberation, a new arrangement

---

[36] Caraway Circle Programme, Yukon Territory (where they are called 'closing circles'); Northside Community Justice Committee, Minneapolis; Reparative Boards, Vermont; Youth Offender Panels, England and Wales.

[37] 'Ohana means 'family' in Hawaiian. The Hawaii Program was not included in the programme on the basis that it was of a different character than the other programmes, dealing with welfare cases. In practice the differences between this programme and other 'criminal programmes' in terms of the harms they address, and the underlying problems may be quite similar. For an evaluation of the programme see (SMSRMS 1999).

was arrived at under which various relatives agreed to take turns in relieving the grandmother.

It is highly unlikely in criminal cases that the same sense of shared responsibility would emerge as often as in welfare cases. In criminal cases, offenders are expected to bear primary responsibility for compliance. Nevertheless, the Hawaiian conference shows how more creative solutions, better tailored to individual needs, emerge when more voices can be heard. This form of accountability offers solutions that a single person would find difficult to devise.

Routine meetings provide a more public form of accountability for offenders' completion of agreements (although participants may be just as happy to be kept informed at a distance of their progress). Group-based accountability also is more iterative: offenders are accountable to individuals who are then accountable to each other for assessing an offender's progress towards completion.

One final benefit of multiple meetings is that participants may be able to hold others accountable for commitments they make in restorative meetings. One shortcoming of restorative programmes is that most have mechanisms for holding offenders accountable for their commitments but not other participants. It is possible to imagine subsequent meetings reviewing, for example, such matters as a teacher's promise to try and help get an offender back into school or perhaps into a reading programme. Equally, meetings could review a parent's or a social worker's promise to help get an offender into a drug treatment programme. Such reviews can most easily be imagined occurring in a fairly informal way, similar to that in which the state is held accountable for what happens prior to the original restorative meeting. The prospect of facing the others should provide an incentive for participants to deliver on the promises they make.

It is significant that the programmes regularly scheduling more than one meeting draw on community volunteers; in addition, they do not expect victims to come to more than one meeting (although they are welcome to do so if they wish). For those programmes interested in gaining the benefit of this repeating accountability it seems essential that community volunteers, rather than victims, be asked to assume the burden that accompanies this more demanding—but possibly also more rewarding—form of monitoring offenders' completion of their commitments. It is indeed true that straightforward cases scheduling multiple meetings would amount to overkill. However, in circumstances where an offender is at risk of reoffending, a more intensive intervention (such as that used by Northside Community Justice Committee in Minneapolis), may be a good use of volunteers' time as well as a wise investment in the future.

Conclusion

What emerges from this chapter is that meetings can provide a forum in which participants are held accountable for what they do outside the meeting itself. In particular, restorative meetings can hold state agencies such as police accountable for their conduct prior to meetings, as well as hold offenders (and possibly other participants) accountable for completion of the commitments they make in meetings.

A meeting is an appropriate occasion to consider the way that police treat not only offenders, but also victims who traditionally are forgotten when thinking about police accountability. Unlike a court, meetings are not constrained by the laws of evidence and so can consider any aspect of police conduct, including any background to the immediate complaint (such as a housing estate's history of problematic relations with police). In many cases it is the manner of police action—rather than the actual outcome of that action—which concerns people most and meetings provide a forum in which police can be reminded of the importance of virtues such as respect and civility. In the process, restorative justice can be a vehicle for implementing community policing in providing an opportunity for police to listen to the people they police. From a police perspective, meetings offer a forum where they too can be heard, about both the organizational constraints under which they work and the difficulties of their duties.

However, this accountability will only work under certain conditions:

- where a diverse group of participants attend meetings;
- where police do not convene meetings;
- where alternative forums for complaint exist, and where the common knowledge exists among participants that aggrieved citizens can pursue their complaints in an alternative forum if they do not find satisfaction in the informal one;

• where meetings do not take place in police stations, but in genuinely neutral venues agreed by the parties.

Even under optimum conditions there remain fundamental limits to the type of accountability described here. Clearly, meetings are incapable of revealing those cases where police discriminate against offenders by not offering them the opportunity to participate in a restorative justice programme. Other kinds of accountability are needed to catch such conduct. A further limitation is that even in cases where meetings involving police and other state officials are held, issues may well arise beyond the scope of the meeting. But meetings can act as catalysts for larger changes, especially when videotapes are made available to senior police officers and further meetings are able to be convened with appropriate officials.

Finally, I have considered how participants can hold one another accountable for their actions after a meeting. In some programmes this form of accountability happens when offenders report to other individual participants, while in others offenders will be held accountable through a reconvened meeting. Though more time-consuming, this second form of accountability has the advantages that other participants can be held accountable for their promises to help offenders and offenders can be praised for their accomplishments. This last benefit is evident most obviously in two programmes—the Northside Community Justice Committee in Minneapolis, and the Connections Program in Red Wing—where a celebration circle is held for offenders once they have successfully completed their commitments.

Whatever the precise form of participant-based accountability, the available evidence suggests that compliance with restorative outcomes is higher than it is with outcomes of traditional court-ordered reparation and community service. It may be that these high levels of compliance owe as much, if not more, to the nature of the original decision-making process as they do to the form of accountability; however, they do show that these informal modes of accountability, supported by formal modes, can be highly effective in securing offenders' compliance with restorative justice agreements.

6

Supporting Deliberative Accountability: Neglected Accountability Mechanisms

Introduction

Critics of restorative justice overlook not only deliberative accountability, in which participants are accountable to each other, but also a range of additional mechanisms by which decision-makers explain themselves to people outside of meetings, and in some mechanisms, outside of programmes. First, there are review mechanisms for scrutinizing conduct before a meeting (such as decisions about whether to refer offenders to restorative justice programmes and decisions made in preparing a meeting). Secondly, programme personnel review agreements reached in meetings; together with courts they also hold provide a form of accountability for monitoring offenders' compliance with agreements. Thirdly, a number of bodies—including funding bodies, advisory boards, and researchers—hold programmes accountable, not so much for individual cases as for the performance of the programme as a whole.

Accountability for events prior to a meeting

The referral decision

One of the most serious criticisms of restorative justice programmes is not about restorative justice *per se*, but resides in the question of access to programmes. The worry is that a gatekeeper's discretion may be exercised unfairly against certain specific kinds of offenders, particularly against repeat offenders from minority backgrounds.

The Zwelethemba Peacemaking Programme avoids these problems by bypassing the gatekeeper altogether. The peace committee receives the overwhelming majority of referrals not from police or teachers but directly from township residents: the policy is to help anyone seeking the assistance of the committee. A typical sequence of events is that a person aggrieved by someone else's actions approaches the committee, who then invite the parties involved in the matter to a meeting. Among the programmes surveyed, however, this approach is very unusual: typically the state is inextricably involved in the administration of criminal justice, and while some programmes say they will accept cases directly from the community, few referrals come via this route. It is only where a state does not or cannot police an area that programmes are likely to obtain many cases from communities directly.

One way to control the exercise of a gatekeeper's discretion is to limit it.[1] This is the approach adopted in the New Zealand juvenile justice system where police are legally required (under the *Children, Young Persons and Their Families Act* (1989)) to deal with juvenile offences by administering a warning or, for more serious offences, by referring young offenders to family group conferences.[2] By having police officers' discretion confined in this way, offenders can be assured they will not be denied access to family group conferencing. This decision, to make conferences mandatory in cases where warnings were insufficient, was critical to restorative justice becoming a central part of the juvenile justice system in New Zealand.

By contrast, in most programmes criminal justice gatekeepers have considerable discretion over whether or not they refer a case to a restorative justice programme. Consequently, programme personnel spend considerable time educating gatekeepers about restorative justice and persuading them to refer cases. Education in this field can take many forms, but in most programmes it involves—at the very least—approaching individual police officers, prosecutors, and judges, to explain the benefits of restorative justice. All practitioners interviewed said that this was an important aspect of their work (see

---

[1] K.C. Davis' classic text on the subject, *Discretionary Justice* (1969) identifies three main methods of controlling discretion: confining discretion by setting limits on a decision-maker's discretion; structuring discretion by controlling the way a decision-maker uses discretion, either by employing flexible standards or procedural rules; and checking discretion by means of a second look. For a critical view of Davis' work, see Robert Baldwin and Keith Hawkins (1984).

[2] The only exceptions are very serious offences. Cases involving homicide are automatically transferred from the Youth Court to the High Court, and other serious offences, such as arson and armed robbery, can be transferred to the High Court at the discretion of the Youth Court Judge.

also Hayes and Prenzler 1998), because they realized that their programme would receive very few referrals without the gatekeepers' cooperation. They reported that when they approached gatekeepers to explain how their programme worked, people's reactions varied considerably; some were highly sceptical, while others were immediately enthusiastic. Carolyn McLeod, the Co-ordinator of the Washington County Community Justice Program in Minneapolis, says that one judge, on learning of the availability and possible benefits of restorative justice, exclaimed 'Why didn't someone tell me before we could do it this way?' McLeod says that this comment is typical of the responses she receives from many state officials.

In larger programmes, such as Youth Justice Conferencing in New South Wales, Australia, training begins at a more institutional level, with all new police recruits receiving compulsory training in restorative justice. Michaela Wengert, Conference Administrator for Youth Justice Conferencing in southern New South Wales, says that 'the referrals are the fruits of this training', with many referrals coming from newly trained, often junior, officers, including some of the most serious cases to be referred to conferences (such as an arson case involving $1.8 million damage to a bowling club (O'Shea 2001)).

Internal review of referral decisions

All of these strategies, together or separately, which work to ensure that programmes receive appropriate cases, can be used in tandem with accountability mechanisms. The most common of these is screening of cases by restorative justice practitioners. Within each programme there is a person responsible for screening referrals, regardless of whether or not referrals come from internal sources (in the case of school-based, and police-based programmes) or external ones (in the case of the majority of programmes).

This screening process is a directive model of accountability. That is, a gatekeeper's referral to a restorative justice programme is reviewed by someone with the power to accept or reject it. However, in some programmes there was evidence that this formal, directive, *ex post* form of review was evolving into a more informal, persuasive, ongoing form of accountability, where police gatekeepers consult with programme staff before deciding whether to refer a case to a programme. Hillary Kramer and Mary Ellen Woods from the Spectrum Just Youth Restorative Justice Project in Burlington, Vermont, report that police often contact them before making a decision about how to deal with an offender, and vice versa. This finding is consistent with Nancy Hennessy's (1999:72) findings on the exercise of a gatekeeper's discretion in New South Wales Juvenile Justice Conferencing: 'A practice which has developed in some areas, and appears to have had positive results, is for YLOs (police youth liaison officers) to ring the conference administrator before referring a matter to check that the conference administrator agrees that it is appropriate.'

Without elaborating too much on minor variations between pro- grammes, some general points can be made about the effectiveness of this form of accountability. Its simplicity, timeliness, motivational sensitivity, and independence will vary according to whether the person screening referrals comes from the same institution as the people making them. A trade-off can be observed between simpli- city, timeliness, and motivational sensitivity on the one hand, and independence on the other. A police officer who reviews the referral decisions of fellow officers (as occurs in the Woodbury Police, St Paul) provides a simple and quick type of accountability which is likely to be accepted by other officers, if only because the reviewer is one of them. When referral decisions are reviewed by someone outside the police, the process is more independent, yet is likely to be more lengthy and perhaps incur the resentment of police officers. Regardless of whether screening is done by insiders or outsiders, this form of accountability falls short of being public.

Stan Cohen (1985) identifies the tendency for forms of community control—such as community service and weekend detention—to supplement, rather than replace, traditional methods of state con- trol.[3] Some critics have expressed disquiet that restorative justice may have a similar effect, ensnaring minor offenders who otherwise would have received no more than an informal caution. While potentially any review mechanism can address this problem by throwing out cases which are too trivial, internal review by restora- tive justice programme managers may be poorly suited to this task, as managers may have their own incentives to accept every case: many programmes really struggle to get referrals and every time they knock back one, they lose a valuable 'customer'. One practitioner told me they 'will accept whatever we can get our hands on', and

---

[3] See the discussion of net-widening in Chapter Two.

many others described their reluctance to reject cases because they found it so difficult to get any in the first place.

A related problem is the pressure on programmes to accept cases where the offender is below the age of criminal responsibility. Many programme managers suspect that police use meetings to ensure that those children who are too young for formal prosecution are not able to escape punishment altogether. The meeting I observed involving a seven-year-old boy who had slashed two car tyres seemed to illustrate vividly the rationale for a minimum age of criminal responsibility: the boy seemed unable to properly appreciate the nature of his wrongdoing or to participate in proceedings (spending most of the meeting running around the room making car noises and throwing paper clips).[4]

The temptation to accept anything and everything is greater when the funding of a programme depends on the number of cases it handles. For this reason it is important that a programme receives sufficient referrals so that there is less pressure to boost numbers by accepting unsuitable cases. It is also important to devise broader assessment criteria that do not assess programmes solely by the number of cases they run.[5] A number of interviewees mentioned that they were in the process of attempting to persuade their funding bodies to broaden the criteria for assessment of their programme.[6]

A far more fundamental problem with this form of accountability, however, is that programme managers can only review those cases which have been referred to them. They can screen out unsuitable or inappropriate referrals but cannot screen those which should have been referred, but were instead sent to court. This shortcoming reinforces the need for an internal review to be complemented by

---

[4] 'One of the most stirring conferences' John Braithwaite (2002: 68) knows of involved four Aboriginal children below the age of criminal responsibility (Real Justice Web site 'Outback Vandals' at http://www.restorativepractices.org/Pages/rjstory3.html). The children, aged five, six, seven, and eight years old, were referred to a conference by a local police officer after vandalizing a local community hall.

For discussion of the legal doctrine of *doli incapax*, the presumption that children below a certain age are incapable of criminal wrongdoing, see Andrew Ashworth (1999: 211) and Simon Bronitt and Bernadette McSherry (2000: 151–3).

[5] This may be one advantage to those programmes where running meetings is only part of an institution's function. Such programmes are usually criticized on the basis that restorative justice ends up taking second place to the institution's primary function (whether it be education, policing, etc.) (see, for example, Wright 2002: 658).

[6] Discussed further below under 'Accountability for Overall Performance'.

the sorts of controls and strategies considered above, such as rules requiring mandatory referral, providing gatekeepers with restorative justice training (see further Prenzler and Hayes 1999), and lastly provision of additional review mechanisms, to be considered below.

Referral agency and external reviews of referral decision

In addition to internal reviews, there are three main types of review for screening referrals to restorative justice programmes: internal review within the referral agency; review panels; and review by separate criminal justice agencies, such as courts and prosecutors.

Referral agency internal accountability

When someone from a referral agency decides not to refer a case to a restorative meeting, the decision may be reviewed by another person within that agency. The New South Wales Police Service has appointed Specialist Youth Officers (SYOs) to deal with juvenile offenders. Under Section 9(2) *Young Offenders Act* (1997), if investigating officers decide that it is not appropriate to issue a warning or a formal caution to an offender, they are required to refer the case to an SYO, who is responsible for determining whether the matter is suitable for a conference. This accountability mechanism was established with the intention of ensuring that appropriate matters were referred to conferences. The rationale was that specially trained officers, removed from the immediacy of investigation, would be more likely to follow Parliament's intention to divert young people away from court wherever appropriate to do so.

In practice, however, police often do not comply with these legislative requirements. Nancy Hennessy's (1999) evaluation of this aspect of conferencing in New South Wales finds some police 'making decisions to commence criminal proceedings without first referring the matter to an SYO'. The moral of the New South Wales experience seems to be that it is not always sufficient to adopt a rule requiring someone to be accountable; even legislative requirements can be circumvented. The same experience suggests the importance of ensuring that review officers have sufficient clout: SYOs are frequently marginalized because there are too few of them, and because they are inadequately resourced and are not ranked highly enough to command the attention of investigating officers (Hennessy 1999).

Panels

Two of the police-run programmes surveyed—Wagga Wagga in NSW, Australia and Woodbury in Minnesota, USA—have established panels which provide some accountability for referral decisions. Terry O'Connell says that the original motivation for establishing a Sergeants' Review Panel for the police-run conferencing programme in Wagga Wagga, Australia, was not to hold police officers accountable for dispositional decisions but to generate police interest in restorative justice; in his own words, 'to get cop buy-in'. Later, O'Connell and the other developers of the programme began to proclaim the panel's benefits in terms of accountability, arguing that the panel ensured that offenders were neither unfairly excluded nor inappropriately included in the conferencing programme (Moore and O'Connell 1993: 57), and partly attributed the fall in the number of young people charged with minor offences to the existence of the panel: 'general-duties police officers had to take account of the fact that a panel of sergeants would review any charge they might make, and would not take kindly to trivialities that involved the wounded pride of an officer on the beat or on patrol' (Moore and O'Connell 1993: 57). With the benefit of hindsight, Terry O'Connell, when interviewed for this study, says that the 'real value of the review panel was that it introduced some rigour into decision-making, particularly as there had not really been any great checks and balances in terms of policing the disposition of matters involving young offenders'.

Woodbury Police Force is in the process of establishing a panel to oversee the selection of cases to its conferencing programme. The difference between this panel and the one in Wagga Wagga is that the former will be comprised of community volunteers, who will not only be responsible for screening cases, but also for monitoring offenders' completion of outcomes. Again, the real motivation behind the establishment of this panel is not so much to provide accountability, as to ensure specifically that the programme survives Dave Hines, the officer who founded the programme. The programme currently runs a large number of conferences primarily because Hines, who is well-liked and respected by his colleagues, has persuaded them to always consider the option of conferencing young offenders.

One of the main advantages of using a panel over a single person to screen cases is that its members are accountable to one another.

This provides a level of iterative accountability. The logistical burden, however, of organizing meetings means that a panel rates poorly in terms of simplicity and timeliness: panel members must find time to meet on a regular basis and referral decisions must wait for the next panel meeting before they can be reviewed. The external form of accountability envisaged by Hines provides a greater level of independence and publicity than does an internal panel, but these benefits must be weighed against the cost and delay involved in running such a panel. Hines is mindful of these costs, and plans to minimize them by only involving the panel in more serious cases; this would allow panel members to meet only once every two weeks. However, if the panel is convened infrequently, there is a risk that officers wanting a quick resolution of matters will find the process too slow and inefficient and will instead send cases straight to court.

Separate criminal justice agencies

A number of programmes accept referrals from multiple points in the criminal justice system: from police, prosecutors, judges, and probation services (Table 3.1). These agencies act as accountability mechanisms, screening the dispositional decisions of agencies earlier on in the criminal justice process. If a police officer refers a case to a prosecutor rather than diverting it to a restorative justice programme, the prosecutor reviews the officer's decision, and if he or she disagrees with it refers the case back to the restorative programme. Similarly, a judge acts as a form of accountability, reviewing the decisions of police and prosecutors, and referring cases to restorative programmes wherever appropriate.[7]

In a number of programmes, this appears to be an important form of accountability. In the first twelve months of the operation of Juvenile Justice Conferencing in New South Wales, over 50 per cent of cases came from courts (Hennessy 1999: para. 171). Reviews by separate criminal justice agencies can provide a degree of independence and, when a judge reviews a decision in open court, publicity. Reviews by criminal justice agencies also provide some iterative accountability: a prosecutor who reviews a police officer's decision is accountable for that review to a judge, who is in turn publicly

---

[7] In many jurisdictions a prosecutor will make the decision to refer the case to court, in which case the court reviews both the prosecutor and the police officer's decision. In some jurisdictions for some types of crimes, however, the police prosecute cases themselves, so courts are only reviewing the decisions taken by police.

accountable for decisions. It should not be assumed, however, that judges will always provide an independent review. Despite making provision for magistrates to refer cases, the Juvenile Justice Conferencing Programme in Queensland, Australia, received no court referrals. From interviews with Queensland magistrates, Tim Prenzler and Hennessey Hayes (1999:17, 27) concluded that magistrates did not refer any cases 'partly because of magistrates' deference to police decisions': 'The magistrates interviewed were of the view that they and their colleagues generally defer to police and prosecution views, so that if police deem a matter unsuitable for conferencing the magistrates are unlikely to refer them from the bench.'[8]

The other great disadvantage of this form of accountability is the cost and delay of involving multiple criminal justice agencies in the process of deciding whether to refer cases. For those cases eventually sent back to restorative meetings, the delays may make convening meetings more difficult. In particular, it can be difficult to obtain the cooperation of participants, especially in cases where participants have already experienced the delays and frustrations involved in attending court.[9] In New South Wales in crimes involving young co-offenders, it is quite common for police to refer the less serious offender to a conference and the more serious one to a court. If the magistrate eventually refers the more serious offender back to the conference (as they often do), by the time this happens, the conference for the first offender has usually taken place, and the victim may understandably be reluctant to attend yet another conference. What makes this all the more frustrating for practitioners, as New South Wales Conference Administrator Michaela Wengert puts it, is that 'it is the more serious offender who stands to gain the most from a conference in the first place'.

These additional forms of review are absolutely essential for detecting cases which should most appropriately be referred to a restorative justice programme. At the same time, it is in everyone's

---

[8] Prenzler and Hayes (1999: 27) also identify other factors 'such as magistrates' doubts about the fulfilment of agreements, lack of awareness of the option, delays required to obtain victim consent, or outright philosophical opposition'.

[9] The delays and hidden costs of attending court (such as getting time off work), compared with the small penalties imposed by lower courts, led Malcolm Feeley (1979) to conclude that for offenders the process is the punishment. The process also punishes victims.

interests that if a case in all aspects is suitable for a restorative meeting it should be referred to the programme at the earliest possible opportunity. Not all victims will be in a position to attend a meeting immediately (some will, but others will need weeks or months, and some will be unable to talk about the effects of crime for years (Wright 2002: 658)), but if there is to be a delay it should be based on the parties' needs and not one forced on the parties by bureaucratic delays. One way to avoid unnecessary delays is to ensure that police are informed when judges or prosecutors refer to diversionary programmes, so that police will know to refer future similar cases directly to restorative programmes.[10]

The victim's role pre-meeting

One factor I have yet to consider is the role of the victim in deciding whether an offender is referred to a meeting. In most programmes the victim does not determine whether or not a meeting takes place. In these programmes, once a decision is made to refer an offender, both the victim and offender are asked if they wish to attend. If the offender declines, the meeting does not proceed, but if the victim declines, the meeting nevertheless goes ahead (his or her place being filled by community volunteers and/or victim representatives). While this is so for the majority of programmes, in a small number the victims are given considerably more power, being asked not only whether they wish to participate, but also whether they wish the offender to be offered access to a restorative programme at all.[11]

Some practitioners see this power of veto as a form of accountability. It certainly could be regarded as a type of directive accountability whereby practitioners account to victims who either accept or reject their proposal. The problem is that it rates poorly in terms of the ideal of inclusiveness, because victims are under no

---

[10] It should not be assumed that police are so informed. For example, investigating officers do not always attend court personally. See David Dixon (1997: 205) for a discussion of the factors which affect police reception of a judicial decision. He concludes that 'the result [of the various means by which decisions are communicated] is often rather like the apocryphal whispered message which changes in the telling'.

[11] See Table 3.1 The five programmes surveyed that give victims this choice are: Woodbury Police, St Paul; Community Conferencing, Queensland; Community Conferencing run by the Central City Neighbourhoods Partnership in Minneapolis; South St Paul Restorative Justice Council, St Paul, and the Victim/Offender Mediation/ Dialogue Program in Texas.

obligation to consider anyone's interests other than their own, and rates poorly in terms of iterative accountability, because victims are not answerable to anyone for their decisions. The positions of victim and offender are polar opposites. Like victims, offenders make decisions on the basis of self-interest; however, declining to participate in a restorative programme (effectively also denying the victim's opportunity to participate) will mean being held accountable to some alternative forum (usually a court). Some might argue that that this is all as it should be: that it would be unfair to allow an offender to decide whether a process should go ahead and not give victims the same right; furthermore, that it is perfectly appropriate that offenders should have to account for their decision while victims should not. This is a powerful argument, but on the other hand, it could also be argued that notwithstanding offenders' wrongdoing, eligibility for a restorative programme should not depend on a victim's whim; that while it is fundamental that victims should be allowed to decide about their own participation, they should not also be allowed to determine whether an offender is allowed to participate when an offender's freedom is at stake.

The organization of a restorative meeting

For several reasons the preparation phase of a meeting is crucial. Convenors must be absolutely scrupulous in the way they treat both victims and offenders. Treatment perceived as uncaring or disrespectful can exacerbate victims' feelings of powerlessness, anger, and resentment, and can further alienate and antagonize offenders and their families. Conversely, thoughtful and respectful preparation by a convenor sets the stage for a successful meeting. For one thing, preparation is the key to the quality of deliberative accountability. The requisite suitably diverse group of participants is best identified by the convenor through patient dialogue with the offender and his or her family, and the victim and his or hers. Unfortunately, practice often falls short of these ideals: on many occasions, victims are not even invited to attend.

The quality of preparation can be scrutinized after the resulting meeting. For example, when a review process discovers a victim did not attend a meeting, the reviewer should enquire whether that victim was even invited. In such cases, convenors can be held accountable for any failures in preparation. A convenor's preparation can also be monitored in the period leading up to the meeting. The level of pre-meeting monitoring of a convenor's preparation varies considerably: in some programmes there is little supervision, with reliance on individual convenors to ensure that meetings are properly organized; in others, however, internal accountability mechanisms hold convenors accountable for their preparation. The most common is an informal ongoing accountability, where convenors are expected to speak with programme managers prior to a meeting to discuss their preparation of a case. In New South Wales convenors are also required to submit to the Conference Administrator a written checklist confirming that they have made contact with all the principal parties, invited supporters and the investigating officer, booked a culturally appropriate venue, and enquired whether any participants have language difficulties requiring the assistance of an interpreter, as well as seen to a number of other matters. The meeting cannot go ahead until the conference administrator receives this list.

Given the importance of competent preparation, all programmes should have some such form of accountability for monitoring a convenor's preparation. The prospect of post-meeting review provides convenors with an incentive to organize a meeting properly; however, this form of review suffers from the shortcoming that it comes too late to stop poor preparation affecting the meeting. By contrast, when a convenor's preparation is reviewed before a meeting, errors and shortcomings can be corrected before the meeting suffers as a result. A light-handed, informal, ongoing form of accountability between convenor and manager (and possibly other convenors) seems best for this task, as this allows managers to ensure that convenors are not cutting corners, as well as allowing convenors to seek advice on dealing with problems as they arise. Provided that the process is presented as one designed to assist them, convenors are likely to appreciate the opportunity to account for their actions and proposed actions. Such an arrangement delivers superior accountability, especially in terms of those desirable principles of simplicity, timeliness, and motivational sensitivity.

Whatever the form of accountability mechanism, it is important that it not apply unrealistic standards. In England and Wales, an offender's first youth offender panel must be held within fifteen working days of the first court appearance, and in New South Wales, a convenor must convene a conference within twenty-one days of referral from a programme administrator. The very low rates of compliance with time limits for organizing meetings (8.1 per cent in NSW (Trimboli 2000: 68), and 31 per cent in England and Wales (Newburn *et al.* 2002: 23–4)) suggest that the modern obsessions with speed and efficiency have given way to an agreement in practice that good practice includes allowing sufficient time for convenors to uncover participants' relationships of care, and for victims and offenders to make decisions without being unduly pressured.

Internal review of agreements

Internal review, that is, review by programme staff, is the most common form of the *ex post* review of meetings. Usually it takes place when a convenor provides a programme manager with a copy of the outcome from a meeting. In some cases these managers will be police officers; in other cases they will be other public servants including teachers, and employees of justice departments and corrections departments.

Most interviewees indicated that if they discovered a problem they would not simply vary the outcome unilaterally, but rather would request that the parties reconsider it. In such cases, internal review is closer to a persuasive model of accountability than a directive one. Where the matter can be easily rectified, this is done by consulting with the parties individually or, if the problem is more serious, by reconvening a meeting.

While programme staff approach the task of reviewing outcomes in a variety of ways, all interviewees emphasized the importance of satisfying themselves that the outcome represented the result of group deliberation. To determine this, programme staff require a list of the people present at a meeting and some evidence of their participation and agreement (such as signatures at the bottom of the outcome). For this reason in some programmes staff attend meetings as observers, to satisfy themselves that the parties agree to any outcomes as well as to provide feedback to the convenor. In a minority of instances, programme staff said that as long as participants reached agreement, they would not intervene in an outcome, even if they personally considered the outcome to be excessive or inappropriate in some other way. As one put it, 'As long as people agree it, it's all good—who am I to say it's not?' For such advocates, to do anything else would be to compromise the restorative commit-ment to personalism and participation.

More commonly, however, deliberative agreement is regarded as a necessary but not sufficient condition for an outcome to be seen as acceptable. A number of interviewees said that outcomes must also be oriented towards repairing the harm caused by an offence. In the Community Conferencing Program run by the Central City Neigh-borhoods Partnership in Minneapolis, this requirement was intro-duced after Gena Gerard, the programme coordinator, found herself objecting to the outcomes from some early conferences but without any basis on which to reject them. Now she says she can intervene even when all parties have reached agreement if the outcome is not oriented towards repairing harm.

In addition to the requirement that agreements reflect restorative values, a number of programmes impose other restrictions. These include the requirement that outcomes be no more severe than those which may be imposed by a court, as well as specific limits on com-pensation and community service. When asked about how they approached the task of reviewing outcomes, none of the practition-ers interviewed expressed any concern about outcomes being too lenient and, additionally, there were no reports of programme man-agers asking participants to reconsider a case on the grounds that an offence warranted a stiffer penalty. I return to this empirical finding later in Chapter Seven when it is contrasted with the way external review operates.

As *ex post* forms go, internal review is relatively simple and timely, but questions remain about how inclusive or public or independent this kind of accountability might be. It is not always clear, looking at criteria like independence and inclusiveness, exactly whose interests managers represent—those of the victim, the offender, the commu-nity, or even managers themselves. Even if it is thought that these interests will often coincide, it is vital to develop and publicize standards against which internal review is undertaken. Without adequate standards, internal review may be subject to the perception that it is a whimsical form of accountability based on nothing more than a managers' own personal preferences, or else that it simply reinforces the dominant values of the manager's profession, such as those of the police, social workers, or teachers.

It is not clear, either, whether internal review reflects the principle of publicity. If review mechanisms are to ever promote the legitimacy of programmes, their existence must be well and truly publicized. Because this kind of accountability does not involve the public, nor does the public necessarily know of its existence, this can be a challenge. On the question of iterative accountability, internal review fares a little better: most managers are themselves accountable in some way to more senior managers or funding bodies, although we might well ask whether they are accountable for their actions in individual cases, rather than at a general policy level.

Accountability for completion of agreements

Honouring commitments

We have previously seen in Chapter Five how participants can hold offenders accountable for agreements made in meetings, either through offenders reporting to an individual participant from a restorative meeting, or reporting to a reconvened meeting, or both. This form of accountability is not the only one for ensuring that offenders do actually deliver on the promises they make; in the majority of programmes, participant-based accountability is backed up by a number of alternative forms.

First, however, I consider those programmes in which there is no back-up form of accountability when an offender does not complete an agreement. In four of the programmes, interviewees indicated that they were powerless to formally enforce agreements made in restorative meetings.[12] In one of these programmes, the Toronto Community Council, non-enforcement goes further: it is a deliberate choice. Programme co-ordinator Jonathan Rudin says that this is because the council is part of an attempt to establish a separate system of justice for indigenous people, and consequently, the programme should permanently divert indigenous offenders from the

---

[12] In conferencing programmes run by New South Wales in Wagga Wagga, and the Thames Valley Police in England, conferences are run as a form of police caution. Terry O'Connell from the Wagga Wagga Programme and Simon Beaton from the Thames Valley Programme indicated that an offender has completed his or her obligations once he or she attends a meeting (which is the caution). In the Connections Program in Redwing, Minnesota, Kelly Pribyl says that once an offender leaves the facility the facility has no authority to enforce any agreements made in a meeting. In the Texas Victim/Offender Mediation/Dialogue Program, David Doerfler says that the Department of Criminal Justice has no authority to enforce agreements made by prisoners.

criminal justice system, rather than do so on the condition that they will be returned if they fail to co-operate. The only coercive element in the programme is that if an offender fails to turn up or co-operate, or fails to complete an agreement, that offender will not be entitled to appear before the council in the event of any future offences. Similarly, in the Zwelethemba Peacemaking Programme, Clifford Shearing says that it is a matter of design that offenders are not held accountable to the formal criminal justice system when they fail to honour their commitments.[13]

In most programmes, an offender will have to face some alternative forum if he or she does not comply with the terms of an agreement. All practitioners stress that offenders are given every opportunity to honour commitments made in meetings, but eventually when an offender persists in not completing an agreement, practitioners refer the case back to the police or—if the case has come from court—to a judge, who will then consider whether to resume formal prosecution and sentencing. In most cases, the result is that an offender risks a far worse fate when he or she fails to complete an agreement.

The practice of exhausting any informal mechanisms of accountability before escalating to more formal, and usually more punitive, ones is consistent with Ian Ayres' and John Braithwaite's (1992; Braithwaite 2001) model of responsive regulation. Their model suggests that informal mechanisms should be employed first, because in many cases persuasion will be sufficient to induce compliance. One of the main reasons for this result is that informal methods provide an opportunity to motivate people by treating them as trustworthy. Only when these simpler, and in most cases more effective, methods fail should we resort to more demanding and punitive forms of enforcement. As Braithwaite (2001: 29) explains: 'The basic idea of responsive regulation is that governments should be more responsive to the conduct of those they seek to regulate in deciding whether a more or less interventionist response is needed.' This idea has long been the compliance strategy in dealing with

---

[13] Although in this programme—which sits outside the criminal justice system—victims retain the right to complain to police if they do not gain satisfaction from the peacemaking process. Indeed, in one of the peacemaker meetings I observed, peacemaker committee members said that they would assist the victim to go to the police if the offender failed to keep his promise not to assault her again (see Chapter Four and also Roche 2002: 526).

corporate crime, but governments have been slow to apply the insights to street crime.[14]

If persuasion by itself is to work, Ayres and Braithwaite (1992: 47; Braithwaite 2001) argue that stiffer forms of accountability must loom as a threat in the background. Programmes which do not provide for any alternative form of accountability can encounter problems when agreement cannot be reached in a meeting or when an agreement is not completed. Without an alternative, informal deliberative accountability risks collapsing.

A responsive regulatory pyramid for securing compliance with restorative outcomes would take the following form:

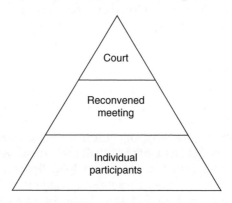

FIG. 6.1.   Pyramid showing modes of accountability for outcome compliance

According to this pyramid, programmes should move up and down between the first two levels according to the needs of the offender. The third level—at the apex of the pyramid—should remain in reserve in case all other methods fail.

There is a potential problem with this arrangement, however. Even when held in reserve, the availability of formal enforcement mechanisms threatens to undermine and even destroy informal ones. Because informal mechanisms work by appealing to an offender's sense of responsibility and trustworthiness, this appeal can easily fail to deliver any result when everyone knows that the possibility of formal enforcement looms in the background.

[14]   For a discussion of traditional compliance strategies for corporate crime see Neil Gunningham (1987).

However, as Ayres and Braithwaite (1992: 48) argue, threat and trust are not mutually exclusive. The trick, they say, is to keep threat in the background rather than the foreground: the difference is one of 'subtle social construction'. For restorative justice, this means the convenor thinking carefully about how to communicate the existence of alternative enforcement mechanisms. 'Subtle social construction' may require a convenor to say something along the following lines:

Tony, it sounds as if everyone here has no doubts that you will complete your agreement, especially Bob, who told us how important you are to the football team he coaches, and who's volunteered to supervise your work. However, one of my duties in every conference I convene is to tell people that I am required to refer your case to the police/court if for some reason you don't complete the outcome. To avoid this situation, if any problems come up, make sure you get in touch with Bob, or myself and we can work it out.

We have seen in Chapter Five that research demonstrates that compliance rates with restorative agreements are superior to those decisions ordered by courts. This finding suggests that it is not just the availability of formal enforcement which primarily motivates offenders to comply with restorative justice agreements. If it were so, you would expect court-ordered decisions relying exclusively on the threat of formal enforcement to deliver equivalent compliance levels. The higher relative compliance suggests that the bulk of that compliance is secured through a combination of the original participatory decision-making process and informal methods of enforcement.

Accountability for overall performance

The directions of accounts

In contrast to accountability for the conduct of individual cases, some of the principal varieties of accountability for assessing a programme's overall performance remain to be considered. Four of the most common sources of such accountability are funding bodies, advisory boards, researchers, and internal review (in the form of quality assurance and monitoring).

Funding bodies

Almost all programmes surveyed are obliged to submit regular reports to their funding bodies. Funding comes from a variety of sources: most programmes are wholly government funded, while a small number are funded through a combination of government and private foundations.[15] They receive regular financial reports to assess a service provider's performance in quantitative terms: how much work has been done, how quickly, and at what cost. According to David Garland (2001: 188) this approach has 'saturated' the whole crime control field; moreover, 'managerialism' has created incentives to neglect the quality of work in order to maximize its quantity. When courts are rated in terms of their caseloads, lawyers may not have sufficient time before a trial to review the evidence, interview witnesses, or prepare a proper defence. Justice delayed is justice denied, but as Carol Jones (1993: 195) points out 'Justice speeded up may also, therefore, be justice denied'.

Mark Umbreit (1999) expresses a similar worry about restorative justice programmes. Umbreit (1999: 227) cautions against judging programmes simply in terms of how many meetings they conduct. It is important that convenors not feel pressurized to rush their preparation of a meeting or cut short the meeting itself:

Allowing little time for the sharing of facts and feelings related to the crime, the mediation session could become 'agreement driven' rather than 'dialogue driven'. While this is not to say that such mediation is of no value, healing and true peace making require more time and patience. The temptation to focus the mediation process primarily upon securing a mutually satisfactory restitution agreement is great, and it is understandable. As ... mediation programmes seek to justify their existence with large numbers of case referrals, programme staff may be tempted to downplay the dialogue phase of the mediation encounter.

Notwithstanding widespread concern about the detrimental effects of managerialism (or 'McDonaldization' as Umbreit and others[16] call it), my survey reveals scant evidence of these effects in restorative justice programmes. Among the programme managers interviewed,

---

[15] Programmes funded by a combination of private and public sources are: Community Conferencing, Central City Neighbourhoods Partnership, Minneapolis; Zwelethemba Peacemaker Committee, Cape Province.

[16] In The McDonaldization of Society, George Ritzer (1996) provides examples of this tendency across a range of fields, from health care, to shopping, to higher education.

only two reported feeling direct pressure from their funding bodies to increase the volume of cases they process.[17] (The much more common view was that their regular reports generate little, if any, response.) However, even though currently there is little evidence that the philosophy of managerialism is having a detrimental effect on restorative justice, programmes would be wise to pre-emptively guard against it.

One way to do this is to ensure that a wider range of indicators is used to assess the overall performance of a programme. James McDougall from the Youth Justice Conferencing Programme in New South Wales says that one of the criteria by which programmes should be judged is the level of compliance with outcomes. McDougall says that compliance rates capture the quality of preparation for a conference: a thorough preparation is much more likely to produce a conference outcome with which an offender will comply. Other programmes also wish to be judged by broader considerations. For example, the Community Peace Programme which established the Zwelethemba Peacemaker Committee asserts that criteria such as female representation and participant satisfaction levels are relevant criteria by which to judge peace committees.

Advisory boards

Three of the restorative justice programmes surveyed have advisory boards, and two others have plans to establish one.[18] From the available evidence it seems that programme practitioners do not

---

[17] Jenny Bargen, Director of the Youth Conferencing Directorate within the New South Wales Department of Juvenile Justice, says that the Treasury Department is preoccupied with the number of conferences run. Bargen says that this is an aggregate figure that 'does not begin to acknowledge the complexity of the work involved in running a good conference'. Similarly, David Doerfler, the State Co-ordinator of the Texas Victim/Offender Mediation/Dialogue Program says that 'periodically we are questioned about the number of cases we do'. This particular programme is especially vulnerable to this criticism: the very lengthy preparation period prior to mediation means that the programme only handles a small number of cases. However, asked his reaction to this questioning, Doerfler says 'I don't worry about it—we just get on with our work'.

[18] The three programmes are: Australian Federal Police, Canberra; New South Wales Juvenile Justice Conferencing; Community Conferencing, and Central City Neighbourhoods Partnership, Minneapolis. Spectrum Just Youth Restorative Justice Project, Burlington and Woodbury Police in St Paul have plans to establish boards.

resent the involvement of these boards. On the contrary, in the two programmes where there are plans to establish boards, these plans have come about as a result of practitioners' requests. Mariellen Woods and Hillary Kramer, of the Spectrum Just Youth Restorative Justice Project in Burlington, Vermont, USA, would like an advisory board to be established because, as Woods says, 'we're feeling that we are charting un-chartered waters here'. Woods and Kramer envisage a Board which could answer their queries as they arise, and provide ongoing advice. Dave Hines of the Woodbury Police Restorative Justice Program in St Paul, Minnesota, USA, hopes that an Advisory Board could provide continuity to the programme when he himself retires.

Advisory boards are not in a good position to hold programmes accountable in individual cases, but they may be able to hold a programme accountable for its overall direction. The chief problem is the effort involved in running a board. Regular meetings of an advisory board are time-consuming to organize and to attend. Richard Funston, senior solicitor for the NSW Children's Legal Service in NSW and one of the members of the committee which oversees conferencing in New South Wales, stresses that for boards and committees to function as an accountability mechanism they must receive current, accurate data. For programmes run on a small budget, it may be infeasible on the grounds of expense alone to establish and maintain an advisory board. In one programme a board which had been established no longer meets, and in another, a number of key players no longer attend board meetings. Their failure to do so may be because they trust the programme, but it appears more likely to be the result of a lack of time or interest.[19]

Research and evaluation

Researchers can play an important role in evaluating a programme's performance, for the simple reason that they can help capture, pool, make sense of, and then publicize programmes' vast range of experiences. Keeping records and pooling knowledge is particularly im-

---

[19] In Canberra the Diversionary Conferencing Advisory Committee has not met since September 1998, and in the Community Conferencing Program run by the Central City Neighbourhoods Partnership in Minneapolis, Gena Gerad says that police and prosecutors have stopped attending meetings of the advisory board. Also, in a third programme that was eventually omitted from the survey, the Canim Lake Family Violence Program, the advisory board no longer meets.

portant when so many programmes are small and decentralized, and practitioners in separate programmes can face similar problems without realizing it. Precisely how to evaluate programmes raises questions about the relative merits of quantitative and qualitative evaluation, and just which method is more appropriate. In keeping with the restorative justice emphasis on storytelling, many programmes rely heavily on qualitative methods, while other advocates and practitioners—without belittling the importance of qualitative evaluation—urge programmes to also conduct more quantitative types of evaluation.

There is no doubt that quantitative research is very important to the assessment of restorative justice or, for that matter, of any policy initiative. It allows us to determine what works and what does not, and often also explains the reasons why. It also allows restorative justice interventions to be compared with existing interventions.[20] The problem with rigorous quantitative research is that it is a time-consuming, expensive, and technical task. Large-scale quantitative evaluations such as those conducted of conferencing in New Zealand (Maxwell and Morris 1993) and Canberra (Strang et al. 1999) and of mediation in the United States (Umbreit 1998) require large amounts of money and sophisticated social science skills.

For many programmes, this sort of systematic comprehensive evaluation is simply out of the question. As a more realistic alternative, restorative justice writer Paul McCold proposes minimum information be recorded by anyone developing a restorative justice

---

[20] One of the chief difficulties in making these sorts of comparisons is the self-selection bias involved in outcome studies of restorative justice programmes. Restorative justice meetings are only held when an offender and other participants choose to participate, while participants in a control group (e.g. court-processed offenders) are given no choice. This makes it difficult to know whether differences between the treatment and control groups are attributable to differences in the treatment or differences in the groups. The Reintegrative Shaming Experiment in Canberra, Australia, dealt with this problem by randomly assigning between conference and court those offenders who indicated a willingness to have their matter dealt with by conference (Sherman et al. 1997). The advantage of this approach is that the treatment and control groups are comparable; the disadvantage is that the research only studies the comparative effectiveness of restorative justice and court on motivated offenders. Jeff Latimer et al. (2001: 17) suggest a different approach. They recommend administering questionnaires designed to measure participants' motivation prior to participation, and then comparing the results of motivated, moderately motivated, and unmotivated individuals in each group.

programme. In a post to an Internet discussion group on family group conferencing McCold (2001) argues that at the individual level, programmes should record:

- the nature of a case (that is, whether it is for an adult or juvenile, where the referral comes from, and the type of crime);
- the length of time spent preparing the meeting;
- the length of the meeting;
- the number of participants;
- the nature of the agreement;
- and for cases where a meeting does not take place, the reason why.

At the programme level, McCold argues that programmes should record:

- the number of cases referred;
- the sources of referral;
- the number of cases where meetings are held;
- the number of agreements reached, and the number of agreements complied with.

Ideally, McCold says that programmes should also survey participants to ask them:

- whether they were satisfied with the way a case was handled;
- whether they regarded the processing of their case as fair, and whether they would recommend restorative justice to other people in their situation.

The advantage of this evaluation is that it is less technically demanding than a large-scale systematic one; the disadvantage is that such aggregate information tells us very little about how a programme actually works. It does not, for example, tell us whether Aboriginal offenders are being unfairly excluded from meetings, nor whether a convenor spoke too much or whether outcomes are too burdensome. When the limited usefulness of such information is assessed against the considerable amount of time spent collecting it, we are forced to question whether conducting such rudimentary quantitative evaluation is really worth the trouble.

An alternative strategy for restorative justice is to leave quantitative analysis to researchers who have the funding and expertise to undertake such research. A more fruitful path for other programmes may be to involve researchers in a more qualitative type of accountability, where researchers sit in on meetings. There is some opposition to their doing this, but usually the demands of research can be met in a way which does not interfere with the privacy of participants or the intimacy of a restorative meeting. Researchers can sit in the corner at meetings, and report meetings without revealing the identity of participants.[21] Their presence may provide some accountability in relation to what occurs in that particular meeting. Kathy Daly and Jan Kitcher (1998: 7) speculate in their evaluation of South Australian conferencing that 'the research project likely affected the *practitioners* (i.e. co-ordinators and police) more than it did the conference *participants* (e.g. offenders, victims and their supporters).... One co-ordinator felt "more accountable", another said that he "sat a little more on the edge of my chair".' To gain a more complete picture of how a programme works, researchers can complement these observations with interviews with programme staff, as well as reading materials such as training manuals.

Quality assurance and training

Earlier I considered how restorative justice programme managers review the outcomes of restorative meetings. Reviewing outcomes, however, is not the only form of internal review of what takes place: staff also monitor the performance of their programmes in other ways. An important part of this process involves managers observing convenors at work in meetings. In addition there are a number of other persuasive accountability devices, ranging from informal debrief interviews where managers ask convenors about their performance through to more formal processes where convenors are required to submit reports reflecting on their organization and running of a meeting.

In some programmes this relationship is not just between the convenor of a particular meeting and the manager, but also other convenors. Again, much of this activity occurs in the meeting itself. A number of programmes use co-convenors (Table 3.1). And in some programmes, such as the Vermont Reparative Boards, programme volunteers are encouraged to observe other volunteers' meetings. There is also a variety of mechanisms outside meetings. A number of people interviewed mentioned that regular meetings are held between convenors, and a number of programmes also

---

[21] This is discussed in more detail in Chapter Seven.

distribute regular newsletters (although these do tend to have a self-congratulatory tone).

It is not difficult to see how this sort of activity is helpful in terms of raising the quality of convening. People with experience of convening can make a strong claim that they are well-qualified to judge their peers' performance in that role. Moreover, much of this monitoring is not seen as a one-way process where observers simply rate convenors. Instead, it is intended that this sort of activity will assist the 'monitors' as well as the 'monitored'.

It is particularly important that peers and researchers be allowed to sit in on meetings. The problem with relying too much on other forms of accountability such as reports prepared by convenors is that these may be written to document what someone should have done rather than what really happened. Errors, or matters where there might be differences in interpretation, tend to be written about circumspectly (Heimer 1998). Similarly, in newsletters and discussion groups, programme staff may have an incentive to raise only their success stories, and not their failures.

By sitting in on meetings, and discussing someone's performance, it is hoped that people will learn things themselves as well as providing the convenor with constructive criticism and helpful suggestions. These strategies have the virtues of simplicity, timeliness, and, provided the practice is couched in terms of a mutual learning exercise, and praise is given where it is due, motivational sensitivity. This qualitative, deliberative form of monitoring within and between programmes is critical to raising the standards of convenor practice, as it allows convenors to learn from the successes and failures of other convenors' efforts.

Devising new forms of meta-monitoring

With the assistance of the Community Peace Programme, the South African government is in the process of devising an alternative regulatory framework for peace committees. The first proposal, recommended by the South African Law Commission (SALC 1999) was to establish Community Forums. These forums, completely separate from the courts, were to act as a second tier above peace committees. One of the functions envisaged for them was resolving complaints about meetings. This proposal gave way to a second, quite different, approach under which 'regulators' would monitor peace committees, with the power to suspend the operation of a peace committee where it was demonstrated that it was not acting according to its code of good practice. Under the draft bill the regulator would have been responsible for registering peace committees, auditing and monitoring their performance, providing training, drafting operating guidelines, and investigating complaints.[22] The regulator would be authorized to attend any gathering of a peace committee and to request committees to submit documentation, and would be entitled to suspend the operation of a peace committee not operating in accordance with its code of conduct.[23] Peacemaker committee members agree to be bound by a code of good conduct. Under the code of good conduct, committee members make the following commitments:

We help to create a safe and secure environment in our community;
We respect the South African constitution;
We work within the law;
We do not use force or violence;
We do not take sides in disputes;
We work in the community as a co-operative team, not as individuals;
We follow procedures which are open for the community to see;
We do not gossip about our work or about other people;
We are committed in what we do;
Our aim is to heal, not to hurt.

Currently, a third, simpler approach is under consideration which would make funding contingent upon informal programmes establishing a code of conduct. The latter two regulatory proposals are examples of what Peter Grabosky (1995: 543–4) calls 'meta-monitoring'. The challenge for modern governments, according to Grabosky, is not to implement and monitor their own programmes, but to oversee new forms of private and semi-private orderings, ensuring that that these new relational forms have effective internal systems for keeping their affairs in order.

The ongoing debate[24] about the most suitable form of accountability is an example of the government's ongoing struggle to devise affordable forms of governance for enhancing individual and social justice in post-apartheid South Africa.

---

[22] Section 5(1) *Draft Bill (unnamed)* (SA).
[23] Section 5(3) *Draft Bill*.
[24] At the time of writing (July 2002) no final decision has been made.

Conclusion

Beyond the deliberative accountability in restorative justice meetings there are other less obvious modes, in particular those internal mechanisms for screening referrals, checking the convenor's preparations, monitoring the offender's compliance with any agreement arising from the meeting, and looking generally at overall performance. In common with many forms of internal review, the principal advantages of these types of accountability lie in their simplicity, timeliness, and motivational sensitivity. Conversely, forms of internal review may lack inclusiveness, publicity, independence, and iterative accountability, suggesting the need for supplementary mechanisms which do possess these qualities.

Ideally external review should provide a back-up form of accountability for those cases which internal review misses, or where internal review fails. Moreover, accountability mechanisms—whether internal or external—must be complemented by other laws, practices, and policies also designed to enhance decision-making. For example, the most reliable technique for preventing gatekeepers from unfairly excluding offenders from restorative justice programmes is to confine their discretion through legislation (as happened in New Zealand).

In accountability terms, a well-run restorative justice programme will have a number of elements:

- a number of referral points from which cases are accepted. Prosecutors and judges play an important role reviewing dispositional decisions of police and referring appropriate cases back to restorative justice programmes;
- a form of ongoing, informal accountability between the convenor of a restorative justice meeting and the programme's manager, which monitors both a convenor's contact with victims and offenders and organization of a meeting. This accountability plays an important role in safeguarding the quality of the deliberative accountability in meetings;
- evaluative criteria which do not put pressure on programmes to accept any case and run meetings without allowing sufficient preparation time;

- internal review of the agreements concluded in meetings against clear well-publicized standards;[25]
- external mechanisms to enforce agreement compliance for cases where informal and internal mechanisms fail;
- ongoing informal accountability assessing the quality of a programme's performance. Such accountability may take the form of managers and practitioners sitting in on fellow practitioners' meetings, and visiting other restorative justice programmes; and
- openness to large-scale quantitative research conducted by separately funded researchers with appropriate expertise.

A number of programmes have devised more ambitious forms of accountability, such as panels to screen all referrals and boards to monitor a programme's performance. The high failure rate of these bodies suggests that practitioners and policy makers should carefully consider whether such resource-intensive forms of accountability can be maintained.

---

[25] Possible standards are discussed in the next chapter.

7
Supporting Deliberative Accountability: The Role of Traditional Accountability

Introduction

A number of accountability mechanisms regulate some restorative justice programmes and could, under the right conditions, regulate others. These mechanisms are overlooked by most critics because they generally have, at most, two types of accountability in mind: the openness of restorative justice meetings to observers; and judicial oversight of the agreements reached in restorative justice meetings. Their preoccupation with these types reflects the comparative nature of their critiques. Restorative justice (and any other form of informal justice) is compared with formal, courtroom justice, where open justice and appeal rights are two of the most important modes of accountability. This chapter examines the role these traditional types of accountability play in restorative justice programmes. The majority of programmes place varying forms of restriction on observing restorative justice meetings, the most common of which is that participants' consent is required to observe a meeting. Yet, meetings could be made more open to the public, while still respecting the privacy considerations underlying restrictions. A number of programmes already provide for some form of judicial oversight. When internal review intervenes, it does so to decrease the severity of agreements made in restorative justice meetings, whereas when judges intervene they do so to increase an agreement's severity. In other words, internal review tends to enforce upper limits, and external review, lower ones. This chapter then reconceptualizes the role of monitoring mechanisms. An agreement's acceptability should not turn simply on its severity or leniency. Offenders should be allowed to do more than is required of them, and victims to demand less than that to which they are entitled. Under the approach advocated here, legislation should require judges to gauge the legitimacy of agreements principally by the quality of the deliberative process used to decide them. Judges become public monitors of citizens' deliberations, and formal legal accountability reinforces deliberative accountability, building up a procedural conception of justice.

Observers at meetings

One of the most frequently mentioned sources of disquiet about restorative justice is the inability of the general public to attend restorative meetings (e.g. Zedner 1994: 242; Griffin 1996:4; NSWLRC 1996: 368; Braithwaite 1998: 96). This objection is an example of a more general tendency to identify the characteristics of courtroom justice absent from restorative justice (and other modes of informal justice).

The comparison is both useful and problematic. Problematic, firstly because not all programmes operate as an alternative to court, and some (such as the school programmes in Vermont, USA, and Queensland, Australia and the community-based programme in Zwelethemba, in South Africa) operate completely outside the criminal justice system. Furthermore, even among those programmes which do operate within the criminal justice system, a number deal with offenders who would never have reached court (as they would be dealt with by police administering a caution) or those offenders who are already in prison. Consequently, if one were interested to compare a restorative justice programme with its alternative, court is not always the appropriate comparison. Restorative justice programmes replace, and supplement, a range of institutions within and outside the criminal justice system, many of which are not open to the public. Indeed, most parts of the traditional criminal justice system remain largely closed to public scrutiny. As Philip Stenning (1995: 3) explains: 'In the first place, despite the expectation that "justice must be seen to be done", many of the most critically important institutions of criminal justice (especially police, security, and correctional agencies) have long been noted for their "low visibility" and for claims that at least some (and in some cases, a great deal of) secrecy is vital to their effectiveness.'

A comparison is nevertheless necessary, because in many programmes, meetings perform a task that would otherwise be undertaken by a sentencing judge, and even where they do not, courts provide a useful case study for exploring the question of accountability provided by observers.

The principle of open justice

Openness is the natural enemy of arbitrariness and the natural ally in the fight against injustice (Davis 1969: 98).

The principle of open justice, which encapsulates the public's right to attend court, is considered 'one of the most pervasive axioms of the administration of justice in our legal system', and a 'basic mechanism of ensuring judicial accountability' (Spigelman 1999: 3, 9).[1] Open justice has been regarded for a number of centuries as one of the strengths of the English judicial process. In 1583 Sir Thomas Smith thought that one of the virtues of a criminal trial was that it was 'done openlie in the presence of the Judges, the Justices, the enquest, the prisoner, and so manie as can come so neare as to heare it' (Nettheim 1984: 27).

In England, and those countries whose laws are based upon those of England, the principle of open justice is enshrined in the 1913 English case *Scott v Scott,*[2] in which it was declared that 'there is no inherent power in a Court of justice to exclude the public inasmuch as one of the normal attributes of a Court is publicity, that is the admission to the public to attend proceedings' (Spigelman 1999: 5). In the United States the principle is reflected in the Sixth Amendment to the US Constitution, which provides for a 'a speedy and public trial', and also in the First Amendment, which is commonly regarded as supporting a public right of access to a criminal trial.[3] In Canada, Section 11(d) of the Charter of Rights and Freedoms provides that everyone is entitled to a 'fair and public hearing' (Linden 1986: 303).

---

[1] By allowing the communication of judicial decisions to the wider public, open justice is also said to serve other functions, including allowing the court to express and uphold the values embodied in various sources of law, and to deter other potential offenders (Jones 1974; Fiss 1984). For a different view, namely that judges are unaccountable, see John Griffith (1997).

[2] *Scott v Scott* [1913] AC 417

[3] *Richmond Newspapers Inc. v Virginia (Richmond Newspapers I)*, 448 US 555, 65 LEd 2d 973, 100, SCt 2814, 48 LW 5008 (1980), *Globe Newspapers v Superior Court* 102 SCt 2613 (1982). See also *Re Oliver* 333 US 257, 267–68 (1948): 'Today almost without exception every state by constitution, statute or judicial decision, requires that all criminal trials be open to the public.'

In international law, the principle of open justice is enshrined in the International Covenant on Civil and Political Rights (ICCPR) and the European Convention on Human Rights (ECHR). Article 14 of the ICCPR provides that 'All persons shall be equal before the courts and tribunals. In the determination of any criminal charge against him, or his rights and obligations in a suit at law, everyone shall be entitled to a fair and public hearing by a competent, independent and impartial tribunal established by law'. Article 6 of the ECHR reflects the principle of open justice in similar terms.

The value of open justice

Openness is thought to be a valuable check on the exercise of power, whatever the form of that power. Jeremy Bentham argued that 'without publicity, all other checks are insufficient: in comparison of publicity, all other checks are of small account' (quoted in Davis 1969: 112). In relation to the exercise of judicial power, openness is thought to encourage judicial impartiality and, in the process, build public confidence and respect in the judiciary (Stepniak 1995: 488). Judges have an incentive to do their best job when they know their failings will be widely visible.

The openness of restorative justice

Unlike the court, restorative justice is often held to be a form of private, or semi-private, justice. But in fact, it is far from closed; a wide range of observers attend restorative justice meetings: researchers, students, representatives of the media, policy makers, representatives of criminal justice agencies, members of community groups, fellow convenors (including trainee convenors[4]), and restorative justice programme managers. To answer the question of whether the attendance of these people itself constitutes a kind of accountability, we should look again at the essential elements.

Elements of accountability

Obligation

Accountability requires that decision-makers be *obliged* to account for their actions. On the question of whether or not participants in restorative justice programmes are obliged to allow people to

---

[4] A number of restorative justice practitioners consider that attending a meeting is the best way to learn how to convene a meeting.

observe them, programmes can be sorted into three broad groups (see Table 3.1). The first and largest group consists of programmes which only allow observers to attend if the participants in a meeting consent.[5] The justification for this policy is usually based in overlapping concerns about participants' privacy, and concerns that observers will disrupt the atmosphere of a restorative meeting. The strongest objections arise in relation to cases involving young offenders.

Within this first group there are some variations on the basic consensual approach to attendance. Two programmes, the Queensland Community Conferencing and the Zwelethemba Peacemaker Committee, adopt as a general rule the allowance of observers only when participants consent but at the same time the imposition of a blanket prohibition on media attendance. In Queensland, the ban is designed to protect young offenders from media scrutiny, whereas in Zwelethemba it is designed to protect the programme itself. John Cartwright, Programme Manager of the Community Peace Programme, says that the programme is too fragile to withstand negative media comment: 'It would be too easy for the press to seize on one juicy morsel, and ruin the good work of the programme.'

Instead of allowing participants to choose whether or not the meeting will be open, programmes in the other two groups have adopted a uniform rule: one group comprises those programmes generally closed to observers[6] while the other comprises pro-

---

[5] Conference programmes: New Zealand Family Group Conferencing; Australian Federal Police, Canberra; Woodbury Police, St Paul; Thames Valley Police Restorative Justice Programme; Community Conferencing, Central City Neighbourhoods Partnership, Minneapolis; Waitakere District Court Restorative Justice Pilot, Auckland; Queensland Schools Conferencing.

Circle programmes: Northside Community Justice Committee, Zwelethemba Mediation Committee.

Mediation: Victim/Offender Mediation/Dialogue Program, Texas.

Multi-form programmes: Spectrum Just Youth Restorative Justice Project, Burlington; Restorative Justice Program, Prince William County, Virginia; Connections Program, Redwing.

[6] Conference programmes: New Zealand Family Group Conferencing; Wagga Wagga Police, New South Wales; Youth Justice Conferencing, New South Wales.

Sentencing Panels: Toronto Community Council; Vancouver Restorative Justice Programme; Youth Offender Panels, England and Wales.

Multi-form programmes: Washington County Community Justice; Minneapolis.

grammes that are generally open.[7] In the former group three programmes, the Australian Wagga Wagga Police Programme, the Toronto Community Council, and the Vancouver Restorative Justice Programme, make an exception for researchers, who can attend with the permission of participants. The Toronto and Vancouver programmes—both of which deal exclusively with aboriginal offenders—also make an exception for aboriginal groups wishing to observe a meeting: they are welcome to observe provided all participants consent. In New South Wales Youth Justice conferences, researchers can attend provided they obtain the written permission of the New South Wales Attorney General[8] as well as the permission of conference participants.

Only a small number of programmes are completely open to observers. In the case of the Navajo peacemaking, the public is entitled to attend, but members of the media must obtain participants' permission. The openness of the Navajo Peacemaking and Carcross Circle Programs appears to be based on community norms that the resolution of conflict is public business. In the case of the Vermont Reparative Boards, openness can be linked to the long tradition of participatory government in the New England region of the United States.

It is programmes in the first two groups which have prompted concerns about the closed nature, or semi-closed nature of restorative justice programmes.[9] The more difficult it has been made for people to attend meetings, the more doubtful it becomes that their attendance will provide any accountability. The most extreme example of this is the Youth Justice Conferencing Programme in New South Wales, where a researcher who wishes to attend a conference must go through not just the rigmarole of obtaining the written approval of the State Attorney General, but also must obtain the permission of the convenor, the offender, and the victim.

---

[7] Conference programmes: Fredrick H. Tuttle Middle School, Burlington.

Circles: Navajo Peacemaking, Navajo Nation; Carcross Circle Program, Yukon Territory; South St Paul Restorative Justice Council, St Paul.

Sentencing panels: Reparative Boards, Vermont.

[8] See Section 47(3) *Young Offenders Act* (NSW) (1997). Chair of the Youth Justice Advisory Council, Patrick Power, says that in practice the Attorney General makes a decision based on the recommendation of the Director of Youth Justice Conferencing, and the Chair of the Youth Justice Advisory Council.

[9] These concerns were discussed in Chapter Two.

A practice which allows the government to decide carefully who can attend and who cannot is more akin to a public relations exercise—designed to promote restorative justice—than it is an accountability mechanism designed to scrutinize it.

Scrutiny of meetings

Accountability also depends on adequate scrutiny. If decision-makers provide accounts in the knowledge that those accounts will never be scrutinized, then we can be confident that accountability will collapse. In order to better understand the kind of scrutiny that observers provide, I spent a number of weeks in 1998 in the Canberra Magistrates' Court interviewing people who were there for guilty pleas in summary matters. I asked them all (other than court staff, police, and lawyers) why they were there. In one hundred guilty pleas, I found that 87 per cent of all people attending court were there because they were appearing, representing, or supporting someone appearing or giving evidence for the prosecution. This means that 87 per cent of those people had a connection with the case which meant that they would have been entitled to attend even if the court had been closed to the public. The remaining 13 per cent consisted of high-school students on excursion or work experience (6 per cent), law students (4 per cent), the media (1.5 per cent) and regular court watchers (1.5 per cent). These results confirm that in spite of all the rhetoric of open justice, justice is administered by professionals in empty courtrooms. As Paul Rock (1991: 267) put it, 'The public work of the Crown Court only infrequently attracts a public. It is composed of a sequence of formal, repeated—indeed, ritualised—processes, administered and serviced by familiars in a state of near privacy.'

My experience sitting there in court also confirmed that the attendance of a member of the public was something of a rarity. A number of times I was approached by court staff to ask me who I was, whether I was lost, what was I doing, whether I was before the court, and whether I needed any help. On at least one occasion, enquiries were clearly made on the magistrate's behalf. This experience echoes that of Doreen McBarnet (1981) in the 1970s in lower courts in the United Kingdom. Things are still as they were then, that is 'to go to these courts as a member of the public is to become an object of curiosity; to sit there taking notes is to invite paroxysms of paranoia' (McBarnet 1994: 195).

Notwithstanding the fact that it is in only a small fraction of all cases that people actually attend court, there are those who argue that it is the public's *right* to do so which holds judges accountable (Kirby 1995: 485). This seems plausible enough, given that the prospect of scrutiny can be sufficient in itself to hold someone accountable. For open justice to work in this way, though, it is fundamental that decision-makers know that they may be scrutinized and the public know that they are entitled to scrutinize. Unfortunately, many members of the public seem completely unaware of their rights. While I was conducting my research in the Canberra Magistrates' court, people frequently approached me to ask whether they were allowed to sit in court while they waited for their cases to be called.[10] It seems that the same lack of awareness may apply to restorative justice. While I did not specifically conduct research to find out the degree of public knowledge, in one programme it became apparent that not all participants were aware that observers were entitled to attend. In one meeting an experienced community volunteer told me that it was a 'special favour' that I was allowed to attend, as meetings were usually closed to the public.[11] If regular participants do not know the public can attend, it is quite unlikely that less frequent participants—such as victims and offenders—do.

Infrequent attendance by the public makes the media an important link between courts and the wider community, allowing the community to scrutinize judges' decisions and comments without having to attend court themselves. Media coverage can also promote debate about judgments, which in turn can inform judges about community standards.[12] This reciprocal process may make judges

---

[10] Presumably they approached me because dressed as I was in a suit, carrying a folder, and talking to people, I looked like someone who may have worked at the court.

[11] It was another volunteer and then a member of the programme staff who corrected him, pointing out that the meeting times were listed in the paper and open to the public.

[12] A notorious Australian example of this comes from *R v Johns*,[12] a criminal case in South Australia. In instructing the jury in a case involving charges of sexual assault, Justice Bollen stated that: 'There is, of course, nothing wrong with a husband, faced with his wife's initial refusal to engage in intercourse, in attempting, in an acceptable way, to persuade her to change her mind, and this may involve a measure of rougher than usual handling. It may be, in the end, that handling and persuasion will persuade the wife to agree.' These comments rightly attracted considerable attention and

accountable for any dated attitudes, but equally in some cases judges will be able to play a role in updating community standards.[13]

The Canberra conference in which a young offender agreed to wear the 'I am a thief' T-shirt clearly demonstrates that the media are able to prompt community debate about restorative justice procedures and outcomes. This conference was not open to the public, but the very public nature of the sanction meant that the conference outcome quickly came to wider attention, followed by intensive and widespread debate in the community about the outcome.[14] Although not everyone objected to the outcome, a widely held view emerged that it was inappropriate to humiliate young offenders (perhaps as an attempt to belatedly counteract this, 'I am a thief' T-shirts went on sale at the local university).[15]

Restorative justice as spectator sport

Some people watch court cases simply because they find them entertaining. Sitting in the public gallery in a recent civil case in Sydney one regular court watcher explained the attraction:

It's free, it's warm, it's true life ... [I] can't afford to go to the Opera House. This is my substitute. I follow a case all the way through ... I get a lot of amusement from it ... I'm a great reader. But this is even better than reading. It's got absolutely everything (Lawson 2000: 3).[16]

---

criticism (see e.g. Cass 1992; Pringle 1993; Thacker 1993), and together with comments by judges in other sexual offence cases, prompted a parliamentary inquiry into gender balance in the judiciary (SSCLCA 1994).

[13] The case usually offered as an example of this is the decision of the US Supreme Court in *Brown v Board of Education* 347 US 483 (1954) where the Court held unanimously that racial segregation in state schools violated the constitutional right to equal protection. (That it is cited so often arguably raises doubts about just how often judges do lead changes in community standards.)

[14] A series of newspaper articles and letters to the editor of the city's newspaper reflected this debate (e.g. Hepworth 1998a, b).

[15] In the conference case, the mother of the young offender, who had supported the outcome suggested a reconvening of the conference to atone for the inappropriate outcome. By this stage, however, the young boy had had enough of the saga and declined to participate.

[16] A regular court watcher in Melbourne, Australia described the attraction in these terms: 'It's just like a magnet to me for some reason. I have no intention of coming in, then I get up in the morning and think "Ah, might as well go in and see what's going on." It's better than being at the tote all day, and a lot cheaper' (Tippet 2001).

It seems some people observe, or even participate in, restorative justice meetings for the same reason. As one regular volunteer in a restorative justice programme told me: 'I've been to 150 of these things, and I just love them.'

Media coverage can be explained partly on the same basis.[17] The same Sydney trial being watched by the woman above also received sustained media coverage, with newspapers running numerous reports about the trial, sometimes multiple articles in one edition. And judging by the letters to the editor of the *Sydney Morning Herald* when the case was settled five weeks into the hearing, many readers had enjoyed following the unfolding drama. One reader complained: 'I have to say that I am bitterly disappointed at the sudden ending of the Moran saga . . . personally I feel like someone just ripped out the last half of my Barbara Taylor Bradford book just before it got really dirty' (MacGregor 2000).

In the United States, the television network 'Court TV' is devoted solely to televising real court cases. Its founder, Steve Brill, explains the success of the concept:

A trial, when televised live, he says, is . . . a cliffhanger. Nobody knows the end until the end. Not the judges, not the viewers, not the lawyers, not the defendants. That's the basis for Court TV's recent advertising campaign: 'Great Drama. No Scripts' (Lassiter 1996: 928).

Can people looking for something to keep them entertained or amused be relied upon to scrutinize what occurs in a restorative justice meeting? Some might argue that if people attend only to be entertained then accountability is seriously compromised. However, the fact that these same people come looking for entertainment does not preclude them from also providing a form of accountability about the cases they observe. Perhaps the more fundamental problem is that if a desire to be entertained is what draws people, only the most lurid and dramatic cases are likely to receive scrutiny. To the public, the typical cases in most restorative programmes (and most lower courts) such as theft, property damage, and assault do not offer the juicy appeal of more sensational ones.

Restricted access to meetings remains the biggest obstacle to public attendance providing a form of accountability in restorative justice. Meeting participants are not held to account in any

[17] Stuart Hall *et al.* (1978: 66) argue that crime is news because crime 'evokes threats to, but also reaffirms' society's underlying morality.

programme in which observers have to obtain the approval of various people, including the participants themselves, before they can
observe the process. It is only programmes which are open to the
public for which observers provide a form of accountability. There
remains, however, the problem of privacy.

Participants' privacy

A bundle of privacy-related arguments are used to justify placing
restrictions on access to restorative meetings. Practitioners argue
that these restrictions are justified, because meetings discuss
personal and sensitive aspects of participants' lives. It is also argued
that the presence of observers may disrupt the atmosphere in a
meeting, making already difficult communication between victims,
offenders, and their families even more so. Finally, it is argued
that it is necessary to protect participants' privacy to avoid any
negative media coverage which might result from the media
attending.

Because restorative justice is centrally concerned with the personal nature of crime, restorative justice meetings provide a forum
in which the personal effects of crime can be explored. Practitioners
frequently cite the intimate nature of meetings as the justification for
making them closed to observers. Jonathan Rudin reports that when
the Toronto Community Council was established it was originally
intended that hearings should be open to everyone, excluding the
media, except when the hearings dealt with sensitive information.
The council soon found, however, that 'virtually all hearings are
about things that are intensely personal'. Arguments about protecting participants' privacy do find some support in law: the legal
principle of open justice is qualified by the need to respect parties'
private lives. Both the International Covenant on Civil and Political
Rights and the European Convention on Human Rights recognize
that the press and the public may be excluded where their presence
interferes with the private lives of the parties.[18]

Against this, it could be argued that a person does to some extent
relinquish his or her privacy if he or she commits a crime. This
argument is consistent with the practice in adult courts, where
personal details of people's lives are routinely discussed. Some

---

[18] See Article 14 of the ICCPR, Article 6 of the ECHR.

restorative justice practitioners insist that conferences are a more personal process than courts are, but even a short visit to the public gallery of any local court, where mothers and fathers confess to life-wrecking gambling and alcohol addictions in pleas of mitigation, show that painfully private details are revealed there as well. Indeed, restorative justice meetings may much better provide a sympathetic forum in which to reveal and discuss such problems. To begin with, restorative justice meetings usually take longer than court hearings. (The average length of court hearings in Canberra, Australia, is between seven and twenty-seven minutes—depending on the type of offence—while diversionary conferences last on average between sixty and ninety-four minutes.[19]) This gives offenders and supporters a better opportunity to put an offence into context, revealing the personal background of an offence in their own words, and in their own time.

What about victims' loss of privacy? They have committed no offence, yet suffer a loss of privacy whether their case is dealt with by a court or in a restorative justice meeting. At least in a restorative justice meeting the loss may be more justifiable than it is in court on the basis that, in accepting a share of the responsibility for determining an offender's sanction, a victim must also accept that his or her privacy yields to the public interest in knowing how that responsibility is exercised: any person holding such a power, whether as a judge or a participant in a meeting, should be publicly accountable for its exercise.

A second and potentially more serious concern about opening meetings to the public is that observers' presence may disrupt meetings. Practitioners worry that participants will feel inhibited from participating by the presence of what Hawaiian restorative justice practitioner, Lorenn Walker, calls 'a peanut gallery'. The law, again, provides some support for this view. While the ICCPR and ECHR enshrine the principle of open justice, both instruments recognize that the press and public may be excluded for a variety of reasons, including and especially those times when their presence threatens

---

[19] In drink-driving offences, the average total duration is 7.3 minutes for court, 87.2 minutes for conference; in Juvenile Personal Property cases, 18.2 minutes for court, 85.3 minutes for conference; in Juvenile Property (Security), 10.5 minutes for court, 69.7 minutes for conference; in Youth Violence, 29.0 minutes for court, 93.4 minutes for conference (Strang et al. 1999: 52–53, tables 4.2, 4.4, 4.6).

the achievement of justice:[20] it might be argued that the presence of observers threatens the achievement of restorative justice in a meeting, particularly in the case of young offenders.

From an accountability perspective it is also important that participants in a restorative meeting do not feel intimidated, overwhelmed, or distracted. We have seen that the principle of non-domination is one of the essential preconditions for deliberative accountability. Just why exactly most practitioners appear more concerned about the effect on participants of observers rather than that of fellow participants is slightly perplexing. The commonly held assumption seems to be that participants have more noble and virtuous motives for attending meetings than do observers.

Thirdly and finally, often underlying anxieties about observers are worries about the manner in which the media report criminal cases. In western democracies the media are a crucial link between what happens in court and the general public. Practitioners consider that offenders should be spared the harmful effects of negative publicity, and certainly there are many examples of negative coverage of restorative justice meetings. Not unexpectedly perhaps, practitioners from two programmes reported that media representatives decided not to run stories after attending meetings because they were 'too positive'.[21] Most importantly, negative publicity hinders an offender's reintegration, which is one of the central elements of restorative justice.

Arguments for closing meetings also find some support in the practice in many jurisdictions of closing juvenile courts to the public. While the risk of public identification (and humiliation) is sometimes

---

[20] See Article 14 of the ICCPR, Article 6 of the ECHR.
In the case of *T v The United Kingdom*, App. No. 00024724/94, decision of 16 December 1999, the European Court of Human Rights held that a juvenile's right to a fair trial may be compromised where juveniles are tried in open court. In 1993 Robert Thompson and Jon Venables, both then aged 11, were tried and convicted in open adult court for the murder of British toddler Jamie Bulger (in England juveniles are tried in closed courts except for cases dealing with serious offences such as murder, which are tried in open court: see *Children and Young Persons Act* (1933)(UK)). The European Commission of Human Rights and the European Court of Human Rights held that the boys were subjected to a 'severely intimidating procedure' by the public trial with attendant publicity and this consequently seriously affected their ability to participate.
[21] Community Conferencing, Queensland, and Navajo Peacemaking, Navajo Nation.

regarded as an element of an offender's punishment (Jones 1974; FPTTFYJ 1996),[22] it is seen as unjust to expose young people to this additional informal form of punishment when their immaturity makes them less responsible for their actions. Moreover, because it is generally regarded as more important to promote the reintegration and rehabilitation of young people, juvenile courts in many countries are closed to the public. The United Nations Standard Minimum Rules for the Administration of Juvenile Justice (the Beijing Rules) also recognize the importance of protecting juveniles' privacy to avoid the harm caused by negative publicity.[23] Most programmes dealing with young offenders impose restrictions for the same reason.[24] For example, the Media Policy for Youth Justice conferencing in New South Wales states that 'It is a well-established principle of criminal law that young offenders are to be afforded special considerations not available to adult offenders due to their youth, immaturity, and vulnerability' (Power 1998: para. 1.4). Many programmes dealing with young offenders could rightly argue that they are more open than court, in the sense that at least they allow observers if participants consent. Where they are less open is in extending protection to adult offenders.

Reconciling privacy and accountability

While there is some basis for restricting observers' access to restorative justice meetings on privacy related grounds, we should be wary of accepting these privacy arguments too quickly. Feminists have long highlighted how the legal division between the private and the public plays an important role in concealing and legitimizing the subordination of groups within society (e.g. Graycar and Morgan 1990: 30–40). Just as respecting the privacy of the family has hidden problems such as domestic violence, respecting the privacy

---

[22] Under this view the risk of public exposure becomes part of the cost, or sanction, of committing the crime. Richard Pildes (1995: 2074) explains how some laws specifically try to 'piggyback onto the authority of social norms by invoking the sanction of public humiliation to enforce the legal prohibition'; state-mandated publication of the names of those who hire prostitutes, or drink-drive, for example.

[23] Rule 8.1 states that 'The juvenile's privacy shall be respected at all stages in order to avoid harm being caused to her or him by undue publicity or by the process of labelling'.

[24] New South Wales Youth Justice Conferencing; Wagga Wagga Police, New South Wales; and Tuttle Middle School, Burlington, but not the Reparative Boards in Vermont.

of restorative justice deliberations may also hide the abuses which can occur within the process itself. Due consideration should be given to the ways privacy needs can be reconciled with those of accountability.

One way would be to rely on other forms, such as the deliberative accountability between participants in meetings, or internal or external review, to provide the necessary accountability for what transpires in restorative meetings. However, rather than discarding open justice entirely, it may be possible to tailor it in such a way that it does not interfere with participants' privacy. People could be allowed to observe meetings, but in order to prevent them distracting participants, a limit could be placed on the number allowed to attend any one meeting. This could be a blanket limit on the number of people who can attend (for example, a programme may provide no more than three seats for observers in any conference), but perhaps more pertinent than limiting the number of observers is to control the ratio of observers to participants: two or three observers may disrupt a small meeting, yet go unnoticed in a larger one. The approach adopted by the Texas Victim/Offender Mediation/Dialogue Program, whereby observers cannot attend, but can later watch videotapes of them also helps ensure that observers do not disrupt meetings.

It may also be relevant to differentiate between types of crime. In some offences, such as sexual assault and offences involving young people, there may be a stronger argument to protect the privacy of participants than there is in cases dealing with more routine crimes such as property offences. It may be possible to open meetings to observers in these more routine cases and close them in the more sensitive cases, accepting the attendant loss of accountability. On the other hand, the label 'routine' may conceal the important and personal issues—such as a burglar's drug habit—at stake in many such cases.

People disagree about whether offenders should suffer negative publicity as a result of an offence. If it is thought that there is any possibility of this happening, the media could be excluded and everyone else allowed to attend.[25] Such an approach would allow

---

[25] A number of programmes have a ban on media attendance but none of them allow everyone else to attend. The Queensland Juvenile Justice Conferencing and the Zwelethemba Peacemaking Programme are closed to the media and are open to others on a consensual basis. A number of programmes are closed to everyone.

the presence of fellow convenors and of others, which can provide an important source of accountability.[26] However, if the experience of courts is anything to go by, open justice does largely rely upon the media. Therefore, a second option would be to do as many programmes do and allow the media to attend only with the permission of participants, but there are two weaknesses to this approach. First, requiring participants' consent weakens the very existence of accountability. Secondly, a conditional basis may not prevent the damaging effects of media coverage, as participants are asked for their consent in advance without knowing how the meeting will turn out or how the media will report what transpires.

Still another option is to allow the media to attend, but only on condition that they do not identify the names of participants (unless the participants consent). This would allow a level of scrutiny and debate in the media though not at the expense of individual participants in a meeting. There is some precedent for this sort of policy in the practice of some juvenile and family courts.

Yet another option is to provide a written record of meetings which could be examined by the public, the media, researchers, and others. Restorative justice advocate Martin Wright (1999: 202) has proposed that the 'outcome, but not the proceedings, should be reported in the press'. Arguably however, this proposal only provides a partial account. Without knowing the reasoning behind them, restorative justice decisions can seem idiosyncratic and outlandish, and may be difficult to scrutinize.

Canadian Judge Barry Stuart has a different sort of recommendation for balancing accountability and privacy concerns. Stuart (1997) recommends using closed pre-meeting hearings to air sensitive material before the public meeting. The idea is that pre-meeting hearings provide a safe and private forum in which to discuss sensitive material. However, for practical reasons there are difficulties with such an approach: it is difficult to imagine how participants might sort through the issues which could be canvassed in a meeting and separate out those that are sensitive from those that are not. As Jonathan Rudin from the Toronto Community Council points out, participants are often not able to predict all the issues that may be

---

[26] As Maury Peiperl (2001: 13) points out, 'peer appraisal begins with a simple premise: the people best suited to judge the performance of others are those who work most closely with them'.

discussed at a meeting and even if they can, almost inevitably these issues are intertwined. There is also the difficulty involved in organizing people to meet on separate occasions. However, in cases where sensitive issues can be disentangled from less sensitive ones, holding a pre-meeting may be an effective way of respecting participants' privacy and ensuring the accountability of the process. A useful variation might be to allow a short adjournment of the main meeting, so that a smaller group of participants might deliberate in private.

Any discussions of the part played by media coverage must consider the role of television in modern societies. Television has played an important role in improving the transparency of our social and government institutions, making 'bad decisions and shoddy practices' more visible than ever before (see Garland 2001: 86). The ubiquity of television cameras does not, for the most part, extend to the courtroom, but increasingly judges are coming under pressure to allow access to the medium on which the majority of people rely for their information (Stepniak 1995; Parker 1998: 90). Australian High Court Judge Michael Kirby (1995: 485) argues that if one of the purposes of open justice is to ensure that 'those who judge are themselves constantly subject to judgment':

then it is difficult to justify limiting the open court principle to straggling groups of partly interested schoolchildren or to the new brigade of pensioners and foreign visitors who are increasingly brought to sit in the back row to watch our courts until boredom or the incessant demands of the tour guides send them on their way. Nor is it easy to see how the technology can forever be limited to the ball-point pen of the observant news reporter when modern means of recording can do the job so much more accurately.

Such an argument could equally well be made about restorative justice programmes.[27] One problem is that televising meetings would enable the identification of participants. Television coverage may also be objectionable on the basis that it is likely to interfere with the process by distracting participants.[28] In addition, it may be

---

[27] The Reparative Board Programme run by the Department of Corrections in Vermont currently has plans to televise board hearings.

[28] On the other hand, the presence of multiple television cameras did not distract participants in a conference held in the aftermath of a murder, according to its

more costly to televise a restorative meeting than a court case be-cause, ideally, multiple cameras are needed to show the faces of each participant in the circle. Against this, videotaping technology is becoming increasingly more convenient and affordable.

Effectiveness of attendance as a form of accountability

While the effectiveness of observers as a form of accountability in itself is generally taken for granted, there is still a need to assess openness of proceedings against general accountability principles. It transpires that the effectiveness of open justice in the context of restorative justice depends on the manner in which the privacy of participants is accommodated. At first glance, the attendance of observers itself appears a very simple form of accountability. It does not necessarily require the establishment of any institutional struc-ture: it simply implies that programmes throw their doors open. On closer inspection, however, it is not so simple. The informal nature of the proceedings may make it difficult to allow the attendance of observers: members of the public wishing to observe a case cannot just turn up at the local courthouse. In many programmes, meetings are held in a venue and a time of the parties' choosing. The Vermont Reparative Boards deal with this problem by holding meetings at a regular time and at a regular venue, and by advertising meetings in the local newspaper. Such a degree of formalization might be neces-sary if it is to be easy for the general public and other observers to attend meetings. On the other hand, this routine may make it harder for the principal participants to attend, as they will be denied the opportunity to choose their own mutually convenient time and venue.[29] Other options designed to protect the privacy of partici-pants (such as videotaping meetings, holding private meetings before public ones, or imposing legislative or contractual restrictions on the way the media report meetings) also increase the complexity of this form of accountability.

Nonetheless, the attendance of observers is a timely form of accountability which occurs contemporaneously with the decision-

convenor, Terry O'Connell: 'They were not even aware of the cameras—once you get into the process you become completely focussed.'

[29] For example, in the Reparative Boards in Vermont the routine scheduling of meetings during working hours may partly explain the very low levels of victim attendance, as opposed to many other programmes where participants select a time in the evening or on weekends that is convenient for them.

making process. Timely accountability mechanisms are very effect-ive, because they provide an immediate incentive to lift one's performance and may allow—depending on the type of accountabil-ity—the prompt correction of mistakes. For the most part, open justice does not allow mistakes to be corrected: the attendance of observers is strictly a persuasive form of accountability, which works by using the prospect of scrutiny to inspire participants to do the right thing. When this does not work there is usually no provision for a silent observer to correct, or even request participants to correct the mistakes;[30] however, in a minority of programmes, ob-servers are invited to participate in the meeting. In this case, they become part of the deliberative accountability described in the previous chapter.

The degree of inclusiveness of this form of accountability will depend on who attends. The most inclusive form of accountability includes the media, but the media's presence raises concerns about invading victims' and offenders' privacy and disrupting meetings. One way to juggle inclusiveness and any anticipated problems of this nature may be to allow everyone (including the media) to attend while preventing the media from identifying participants and limiting the number of observers who can attend any single meeting.

It is a matter of speculation whether participants will resent the presence of observers. At first glance it seems less motivationally sensitive than deliberative accountability in which participants are not simply checking up on each other, but making decisions together. However, from my own experience and interviews with restorative justice practitioners, I can say that it is very uncommon for a partici-pant to refuse to allow an observer to attend a meeting,[31] which suggests that participants do not take observers' presence as a sign of distrust. No doubt this is partly because observers' requests to attend are usually phrased as requests to learn about the process rather than to monitor participants. If it becomes clear that an observer is monitoring proceedings, there is a real likelihood that the attendance will be misunderstood as a lack of trust in participants, and there may not be any way of mitigating this impression. For fellow con-

---

[30] Unless this works in conjunction with other types of accountability described later in this chapter.

[31] Except in the case of the media, to whom some participants deny access.

venors or programme managers sitting in on cases it could be made clear that this was part of ongoing training and mutual education. For the media, journalists could be allowed in not to monitor a particular case but to observe a number of cases in order to write an evaluative piece on a programme. Any publicity arising from such a process will depend on who is permitted to attend meetings. Obviously the more limited the range of people allowed to attend, the less publicity will be provided by this form of accountability. The attendance of observers does reflect the principle of independence, particularly where people apart from programme staff (such as researchers) are allowed to observe meetings. However, this form of accountability often lacks the quality of iterative accountability: in many cases observers are not themselves accountable. This may be defensible, though, on the grounds that they are not participants in the decision-making process.[32]

External review

Along with worries about closed meetings, a perceived lack of judicial oversight troubles critics of restorative justice. In fact, not all programmes lack judicial or other kinds of external review: many restorative justice programmes are obliged to submit reports about meetings to external agencies responsible for scrutinizing those reports. The process for activating such review processes varies. In most cases, reports are submitted as a matter of routine.[33] However, in one programme—the Carcross Circle Program—external review is only activated when one of the parties appeals a meeting's

[32] In programmes where observers become participants and thus have more power, they also become accountable to other participants through the deliberative accountability described in Chapter Four.

[33] Principally, courts undertake this form of review. The following programmes are required to submit reports to court for all cases referred by court:

Conference programmes: New Zealand Family Group Conferencing; New South Wales Juvenile Justice Conferencing; Queensland Community Conferencing; Central City Neighborhoods Partnership Community Conferencing, Minneapolis; Waitakere District Court Restorative Justice Pilot, Auckland;

Circle programmes: Navajo Peacemaking, Navajo Nation; Northside Community Justice Committee, Minneapolis; South St Paul Restorative Justice Council, St Paul;

Sentencing Panels: Young Offender Panels, England and Wales;

Multi-form programmes: Washington County Community Justice, Minneapolis.

decision.[34] Like the process activating a review, the powers of external review bodies also vary. When the review is undertaken by police or an advocacy group, the model of accountability is more persuasive than directive. However, when the review is done by a court, whether as a routine form of monitoring or on appeal, accountability is more akin to a directive model of accountability, as the court can vary—or even ignore—the outcome of a meeting.

Judicial review

Assessing judicial review against the seven accountability principles is easier for some of these than it is for others. We can confidently make some general observations about the quality of accountability it provides in terms of timeliness, motivational sensitivity, publicity, independence, and iterative accountability. Like any *ex post* review, judicial review is necessarily less timely than deliberative accountability, in which the process of explanation and justification is part of the very decision-making process; it can nevertheless influence what occurs in meetings, provided that participants consider that there is a possibility that an external review may occur. The deliberative form of accountability in a restorative meeting is also more motivationally sensitive because it is built into the decision-making process. By contrast, judicial review is more vulnerable to the risk that it may well convey the impression that participants are not trusted to make the right decisions.

Traditionally the accepted strengths in accountability of formal courts have been their publicity and their independence. It is also generally accepted (although this is slightly more controversial) that courts reflect the need for iterative accountability through their accountability to superior courts, the general public, and the media, and ultimately other branches of government (Gleeson 1995; cf. Griffith 1997).

More complicated is the inclusiveness of judicial oversight, and to a lesser extent, its simplicity.

Inclusiveness

Where deliberative accountability fails, it can be quite futile to hope that external review will take into account any interests neglected in

---

[34] The significance of the distinction between routine review and review by appeal is explored below.

the original decision-making process, whether these interests are those of offenders, victims, or of the wider community. Christine Parker (1999: 74) expands this point: 'while recourse to formal legal processes might help solve the tyranny of majority in community, it exposes citizens to the risk of tyranny by formalistic and professional procedures.'

This is particularly so in programmes in use in indigenous communities, which have experienced long and painful histories of discrimination and exclusion by the state. Here the debate about the proper relationship between indigenous restorative justice programmes and the formal justice system is one instance of a larger debate about whether and how indigenous institutions should be accountable to the state (e.g. Rowse 2000: 1517; O'Malley 1996). To some indigenous people, the idea that the state can be relied upon to represent their interests is profoundly offensive. Moreover, it is widely believed that the principle of self-determination requires that the state not interfere with indigenous forms of government (see e.g. Palys 1999). Other writers, however, stress that it is important that everyone—including members of indigenous communities— should have access to the state at such times when their own communities seek to impose unwarranted or unjustifiable restrictions or obligations on them (Shachar 1999). John Braithwaite (1999: 86), for example, argues that:

Liberal justice regimes that turn a blind eye to violent indigenous justice succumb to a dangerous kind of cultural relativism. It is one thing to accept the legitimacy of traditional forms of social control in a unicultural society. In a multicultural society where all people learn to count on the state for protection of their rights, without state oversight of respect for fundamental human rights there is no way of being sure that those punished really are members of the traditional society, or even if they are, that they are not cultural dissidents who wish to call on the protections afforded to all citizens by the state regardless of race. Without state oversight, there is no way of assuring that the rights of a victim from a different cultural group than the offender will be protected.[35]

It seems that the degree of conflict between collective and individual rights is easily overdrawn. Indeed, debates about customary law

[35] Also see, for example, the United Nations Declaration on the Elimination of Violence Against Women, which sets out that 'States should condemn violence against women and should not invoke any custom, tradition or religious consideration to avoid their obligations with respect to its elimination' (Article 4).

tend to become fixated with its more controversial forms, ignoring the fact that traditional or customary justice takes numerous forms, most of which are consistent with human rights standards (Bronitt and McSherry 2001: 136–7). Also often lost is the point that indigenous cultures are themselves fluid, and subject to change as the result of internal debate (Webber 1993: 137; Krygier 1999: 97). Indeed, a restorative meeting attentive to the principle of non-domination can provide an appropriate forum in which communities can debate and revise their laws and customs. Notwithstanding this, some tension may remain on the question of collective versus individual rights. Some practices may be consistent with the cultural traditions of that community, yet be utterly unacceptable to those championing modern liberal conceptions of human rights.

In Navajo Peacemaking, such problems are addressed by a Navajo Court responsible for monitoring peacemaking; however, it remains rare for indigenous communities to establish successfully their own formal court. In many communities to replicate this form of modern liberal rule would be unworkable, and in communities where it has been attempted, the result has been a second-class form of justice, poorly funded and poorly run (ALRC 1986: 13, 18, 24).[36] It may be more realistic to appoint to existing courts people from a more diverse range of backgrounds, including people from indigenous communities, but the suggestion to 'indigenize' existing state institutions does not go far enough for some people's liking.

Another way to reconcile the requirements of indigenous self-government on the one hand and state accountability on the other, is to conceive of the state more broadly than just a nation-state: that is, rather than subjecting 'individuals to the vulnerabilities of having only one jurisdiction within which to appeal to redress injustice' (Young 2000: 13), individuals should have access to 'multiple, overlapping sovereignties' (Goodin 1996: 362). On this question, Will Kymlicka (1995: 169) argues that while national minority groups may not accept the involvement of the state, they may accept the

---

[36] The Australian Law Reform Commission details some of the failings of attempts to establish Aboriginal courts modelled on English courts. This is one of the reasons the ALRC (1986: 52) recommended against the establishment of Aboriginal courts. There is a relevant difference however: these failed courts were used as a forum of first instance, whereas in restorative justice programmes courts play a smaller role, only stepping in as a back-up to the restorative meeting, the forum used in the first instance.

legitimacy of an international tribunal responsible for enforcing declarations of human rights:

Many Indian tribes have expressed a willingness to abide by international declarations of human rights, and to answer to international tribunals for complaints of rights violations within their community. Indeed, they have shown greater willingness to accept this kind of international review than many majority nations, which jealously guard their sovereignty in domestic affairs. Most Indian tribes do not oppose all forms of external review. What they object to is being subject to the constitution of their conquerors, which they had no role in drafting, and being answerable to federal courts, composed solely of non-Indian justices.

Such a suggestion may enhance the inclusiveness of external review, although of course it would also be an infinitely more complex and less timely form of accountability. In addition, while the thought of the European Court of Human Rights reviewing an agreement made in a member country is just conceivable, in many other countries it seems hopelessly unrealistic to imagine national governments handing authority to a supra-national body. In Australia, for example, the Federal government revoked access to UN human rights monitoring bodies after receiving critical findings about their treatment of Aborigines and asylum seekers (AAP 2000). It is equally unrealistic to imagine disempowered indigenous community members exercising such a right of appeal, particularly in remote communities such as in the north of Canada or the middle of Australia. It also goes without saying that many developing countries do not have the legal institutions necessary to support such an appeal mechanism. In some of these countries, such as Papua New Guinea, international organizations working in local communities (such as NGOs), could well play a role in this matter, but these organizations may lack the requisite legitimacy in the eyes of the local community.

Whichever type of state institution comes to be used, a degree of flexibility is required. One major problem in using formal justice to oversee informal justice is that in some situations at least, the local offence and the punishment for that offence will not translate into recognizable legal categories. Many local offences (such as insults, breaches of ceremonial rituals, omission of kinship duties, and acts of infidelity or witchcraft) do not have direct counterpart offences in state criminal offences. Indeed, in most indigenous communities, the very distinction between criminal and other types of legal wrongdoing does not exist.

Formal law reshaped by informal justice

Some writers think that the 'tyranny of formalistic and professional procedures' is mitigated by the ability of informal justice to reshape formal justice (Merry 1993: 5). Christine Parker (1999: 75) argues that 'Integrating formal and informal justice means not only that formal justice can be an alternative and regulator of informal justice, but that informal justice can be used persistently to critique professional models of justice and challenge it to become more collaborative, personal, and based in community norms and power'. John Braithwaite and Christine Parker (1999: 116) describe the implications of this for restorative justice:

the prevalence of restorative justice conferences that institutionalize community concerns with restoration and healing institutionalize a critique of and alternative to traditional trial processes, which helps make the whole criminal justice system more responsive. Citizens' concerns have an avenue for bubbling up the pyramid into legal discourses and procedures through legal supervision of conferences, just as the discourse of law has a way of percolating down.

Such a model of justice in which the formal and the informal act as a check on each other is attractive, but to change formal law requires more than the 'bubbling up' of informal justice. While there are several examples of judges reviewing the outcomes of meetings, there is little evidence that these meetings by themselves do change the formal law. It is only when these cases 'bubbling up' are also accompanied by top-down legislative reform that the formal law will change to accommodate restorative values. What specific individual cases can do is to provide an occasion for courts to consider the implications of top-down changes in the law. Take for example the *Clotworthy*[37] case in New Zealand.

Twenty-seven-year-old Patrick Clotworthy pleaded guilty to a charge of assault with intent to cause grievous bodily harm, after stabbing Wayne Cowan in a vicious and unprovoked attack. As a result, the victim underwent emergency surgery to repair a collapsed lung and diaphragm which required blood transfusions; then spent two days in intensive care, and was left with an 'embarrassing scar' and serious epilepsy. In sentencing the offender, Judge Thorburn

---

[37] *Clotworthy*, 24 April 1998, District Court, Auckland, unreported decision, T.971545, Judge Thorburn.

considered a probation report, an emotional harm report, and a report of a conference between the prisoner, the victim, and their respective supporters convened by Justice Alternatives. At that conference, the victim had said that he did not see any benefit for society, himself, or the prisoner in a sentence of imprisonment, and instead sought $15,000 to pay for plastic surgery to fix his scar. Clotworthy agreed to pay some of the money immediately, and the rest over the following twelve months. Judge Thorburn noted that the starting point for such an offence was a three-and-a-half to four-year term of imprisonment, but on the basis of the conference report sentenced the offender to a two-year suspended sentence. The Crown appealed to the New Zealand Court of Appeal,[38] arguing that the sentence was too lenient. The Court of Appeal commended the victim 'for having forgiven Mr. Clotworthy and for the sympathetic way he has approached the matter', but went on to say: 'a wider dimension must come into the sentencing exercise than simply the position as between victim and offender. The public interest in consistency, integrity of the criminal justice system and deterrence of others are factors of major importance.'

The Court overruled the original sentence and instead sentenced Clotworthy to three years' imprisonment and ordered him to pay $5,000 in reparation to the victim.[39] On first glance, the formal acknowledgment of restorative justice appears to resemble the 'bubbling up' of informal justice. Restorative justice advocates, disappointed with the final outcome, were nevertheless heartened at the Court's acknowledgement of the legitimate role of restorative justice in less serious cases (e.g. Boyack 1999).[40] However, the driver of this change was statutory sentencing principles, as this passage from the joint judgment shows:

---

[38] *Clotworthy* 29 June 1998, Court of Appeal of New Zealand, unreported decision, CA114/98.

[39] The Court held that the trial judge's starting point of three and a half to four years jail was too low. The Court held the appropriate starting point should have been five to six years' imprisonment.

[40] The New Zealand Court of Appeal's decision was subsequently interpreted by one District Court judge as giving 'support to the view that a successful restorative justice meeting can be a factor and be given considerable weight in assessing a penalty' (*Police v Seong Woo Choi*, 31 July 1998, District Court, Auckland, Cr No. 8004042362, Hubble J).

We would not wish this judgment to be seen as expressing any general opposition to the concept of restorative justice (essentially the policies behind ss11 and 12 of the Criminal Justice Act). Those policies must, however, be balanced against other sentencing policies, particularly in this case those inherent in s5, dealing with cases of serious violence. Which aspect should predominate will depend on an assessment of where the balance should lie in the individual case. Even if the balance is found, as in this case, to lie in favour of s5 policies, the restorative aspects can have, as here, a significant impact on the length of the term of imprisonment which the Court is directed to impose. They find their place in the ultimate outcome in that way (p. 14).

In *R v Gladue*[41] the Canadian Supreme Court decision also recognized the principle of restorative justice. Again, however, recognition only came through a process of statutory interpretation, with the Court holding that 'Parliament has provided new restorative principles for sentencing that respond to the needs of offenders, victims, and communities' (Roach and Rudin 2000: 383). While meetings provide the opportunity for courts to consider restorative justice, the real instrument of change of formal law is formal law itself; to believe that the law changes simply because of judges' exposure to restorative justice agreements is to completely misunderstand the nature of formal legal systems. The law works as a self-referential system of communication, that deals with outside events by classifying them as either legal or illegal (Teubner 1993). Agreements reached in restorative justice meetings will quite likely be regarded as illegal unless legislation is passed allowing judges to regard them as legal.

Interviews for this book suggested that whereas internal review is more concerned with ensuring agreements are not too onerous for offenders,[42] external review by courts is more interested in ensuring that outcomes are not too lenient. Practitioners reported that in most cases judges endorsed the outcomes of restorative justice programmes, but where they did not, they invariably increased the severity of a punishment. On this point, Carolyn McLeod, co-ordinator of the Washington County Community Justice Program in Minneapolis, says that:

No judge has ever lessened an agreement and only one time did a Judge add. It was for an attempted murder case and the victim asked (in addition

---

[41] *Gladue* (1999) 133 CCC (3d) 385 (SCC).
[42] See Chapter Six.

to several other stipulations) that the 58 year old offender be put on probation for fifteen years. The judge put him on probation for twenty years and kept the rest of the victim's wishes as well.

This pattern is also reflected in two separate quantitative evaluations of how judges review the outcomes of restorative justice programmes. In New Zealand, in cases where a young person has been arrested and does not deny committing the offence, the court must refer him or her to a family group conference and afterwards review the recommendations of the conference. Gabrielle Maxwell and Allison Morris' (1993: 156) study of New Zealand family group conferencing shows that in most cases (81 per cent), the judge followed the conference's recommendation, but in cases where the recommendations were not followed, the order was much more likely to be higher than that recommended by the family (17 per cent), than lower (2 per cent).

This New Zealand finding is replicated in an evaluation of a Canadian restorative justice project. The John Howard Society's Restorative Resolutions Programme in Winnipeg, Manitoba diverts offenders from court with the aim of providing a community-based alternative to incarceration. An evaluation of the programme by James Bonta, Jennifer Rooney, and Suzanne Wallace-Capretta (1998) reveals that in nearly 19 per cent of cases (eighteen of ninety-nine) the judge increased the punishment by imposing a custodial sentence in addition to the proposed agreement. There were no occasions on which the judge varied the outcome to reduce the punishment.

The same pattern is discernible from the available decisions at an appeal court level. There are a growing number of reported appeal decisions in Canada, New Zealand, and the United States, dealing with restorative meetings. In a number of these, Appeal Courts have upheld the sentencing judge's endorsement of the outcome of a restorative meeting.[43] However, in those cases where courts have allowed the appeal, it has been to increase, rather than decrease, the severity of punishment. I have already discussed one such case—*R v Clotworthy*—where the Court of Appeal overruled the sentencing judge's orders endorsing the outcome of a conference, instead

---

[43] See for example: *R v BJK* (2000) ABPC 125 (Provincial Court of Alberta, Youth Division); *R v Rope* [1995] 4 CNLR 98 (Saskatchewan Court of Queen's Bench).

ruling that Mr Clotworthy should be sent to prison for three years, as well as paying $5,000 reparation to the victim.

The Canadian case of *R v Morin*[44] is another such example. In this case the Saskatchewan Court of Appeal increased the punishment negotiated in a sentencing circle, convened after Mr Morin (a Métis man), was charged with robbery and assault. A sentencing circle attended by the defendant, the victims, police, corrections officials, and Aboriginal elders recommended a period of incarceration of approximately eighteen months, and a follow-up treatment programme. The judge followed these recommendations, noting that without the circle's recommendations he would have imposed a longer custodial sentence. On appeal, however, a majority of the court held that it was not appropriate to depart from the usual range of sentencing for such an offence, and imposed an additional eighteen months imprisonment.[45]

It thus appears that internal review mechanisms generally intervene to prevent overly harsh outcomes, while external mechanisms generally intervene to prevent too lenient ones: internal review mechanisms tend to enforce upper limits, while external mechanisms enforce lower ones.

A procedural approach to external review

Readers concerned that restorative justice meetings do not consider the interests of the wider community in ensuring that offenders receive consistent, proportionate punishment, can take some comfort from the finding that judges are able to, and do intervene when they consider an agreement deviates too far below the penalty a court would impose. Others will read this empirical finding in a less optimistic light. In particular, advocates of restorative justice will argue that agreements should not be assessed by traditional sentencing principles of proportionality and consistency. However, if restorative justice is to reject these long-standing principles, it must suggest some alternative basis on which to review restorative

[44] *R v Morin* (1995), 101 CCC (3d) 124, appeal from *R v Morin* (1994), 114 Sask R 2 (Saskatchewan Court of Queen's Bench). For further discussions of the case see (RCAP 1996; Quigley 1999).

[45] The court, however, said that it made this decision based on the facts of the case—in particular the lack of remorse shown by the offender (based on the transcript of the sentencing circle), and the poor prospects for rehabilitation. In different circumstances, a judge may be justified in departing from the starting point sentence on the basis of the recommendations of a sentencing circle.

agreements. It is interesting to contrast what judicial review might look like if it were done according to restorative justice principles.

The fundamental difference is that a restorative justice approach would firstly, and primarily, be concerned with reviewing the decision-making process. According to restorative justice, responses to crime should concentrate on repairing the harm suffered by victims and reintegrating offenders; moreover that victims, offenders, and supporters are themselves the best judge of how to do this. A victim may decide that what makes her feel better is to show her offender mercy; equally, offering to do more than he is required to do is one way for an offender to show his sincere remorse and desired to be reaccepted by his community. For victims and offenders alike, the right to make such choices is vital to regaining lost feelings of personal dignity and autonomy. The role of review should not be to deny them this freedom but to preserve it; judges' proper role should be to ensure that when parties depart from traditional tariffs they do so as a result of choice rather than coercion. Thus, under a procedural approach to review, an agreement's acceptability depends not on its severity or leniency but on the quality of the deliberative negotiations.[46]

There is some limited evidence that judges are already looking at the decision-making process before making decisions. In New South Wales, Australia, Bernadette O'Reilly, Principal Solicitor with the Children's Legal Service, says that magistrates are much more likely to approve an agreement if they are given a fuller report from convenors about the conference. O'Reilly says that a magistrate may look at an outcome and initially consider it too lenient; however, if the outcome is accompanied by a report saying that the victim attended the meeting and supports the end result, then a magistrate is much more likely to endorse that outcome. In other words, the legitimacy of the substantive decisions is gauged by the quality of accountability in the original meeting. This returns us to

---

[46] In administrative law terms, a restorative approach would rely on a court's review (or supervisory), as opposed to appellate, jurisdiction. Whereas an appellate court has power to decide whether a decision under appeal was right or wrong, a court exercising review or supervisory powers may only decide whether the decision was lawfully made. The distinction is also relevant to the power of the court. An appellate court can substitute its decision for that of the body appealed from, whereas in review proceedings a court's basic power is to hold a decision to be invalid (Cane 1996: 8,9).

Clotworthy, where it was the victim's expressed wishes which swayed the sentencing judge to impose a suspended sentence. While the decision-making process is thus meeting with approval in some quarters, legislative reform will be required for this procedural approach to judicial review to be fully adopted.[47] Up to now, legislation has taken the form of specifying reparation as one of the factors judges should consider in deciding upon sentence,[48] an approach which does not restrict judges' discretion: reparation is simply added to the mix of principles to which judges may refer in selecting and justifying a sentence. Under a procedural approach to judicial review, legislation would limit a judge's powers to making a determination about the adequacy of the deliberative decision-making process. This sort of legislative reform would help ensure that judges do not replace the decision of a properly constituted and well-run restorative process with their own.

Legislation could require judges to enquire about procedural matters (such as who was present at the meeting, whether they agreed to the meeting—and if not, why not—and whether participants had an opportunity to consult a lawyer before or during the deliberations). The remedy in those cases in which judges detect a defect in the decision-making process should also be faithful to this procedural approach; only as the last resort should judges impose a penalty in place of a defective restorative agreement. In the first place, judges should offer the parties concerned the chance to attend a reconvened meeting, with the judge taking appropriate steps to correct the defect in the original meeting; when a victim was not invited to the original meeting, or the meeting was at an inconvenient time, the judge could instruct the convenor to make contact with the victim in person to discuss matters. Whenever a judge considers

---

[47] *Police v Seong Woo Choi*, 31 July 1998, District Court, Auckland, Cr No. 8004012362, Hubble J.

[48] e.g. s 11 *Criminal Justice Act* (1985)(NZ):
In every case where an offender is convicted of an offence for which a sentence to make reparation may be imposed, the court shall impose such a sentence (whether by itself or in conjunction with any other sentence or order) unless it is satisfied that it would be inappropriate to do so.
See also s 718 of the *Criminal Code* (Canada):
(e) to provide reparations for harm done to victims or to the community; and
(f) to promote a sense of responsibility in offenders, and acknowledgment of the harm done to victims and to the community.

that a young offender has agreed to an outcome under duress, that judge could require the convenor to find more supporters for the offender or (in more serious cases) to perhaps order a youth advocate to attend the reconvened meeting. Where the judge considers that the public interest in a case has not been considered, it could be possible to send a public prosecutor to represent the wider community. Only when a deliberative remedy is not possible—because, for example, the main participants decline the invitation to attend another meeting—would a judge be entitled to hand down a traditional formal sentence.

The approach outlined above would require a significant change in judicial roles and may be resisted, but a number of things could be done to facilitate the transition. At the very least, practitioners would need to provide judges with full reports of the decision-making process. In cases where doubts exist about the decision-making process, judges would also be assisted by seeing a videotape of the original meeting, and by questioning participants. A visual record of the meeting would provide a better guide than a written report about whether the agreement before the judge is the product of genuine deliberation between the affected parties. At a more general level, a useful innovation is that of the Navajo nation who have appointed a liaison officer who explains the work of peacemakers to judges (and vice versa). Inviting judges to observe meetings might also create a pathway for formal law to learn about restorative justice.

The role of limits
This procedural approach would be heavily slanted towards reviewing the decision-making process itself, rather than the decision. Agreements would be allowed to deviate significantly from those which a court would otherwise impose. Under this approach, however, traditional legal tariffs would still play an important role. In particular, it is only the existence of these tariffs which allows parties to be merciful or generous. People show their mercy or generosity by deviating from that to which they are strictly entitled (Kymlicka 2002: 174); moreover, people may only realize that they are the beneficiaries of these acts of kindness when they know the penalty or compensation they would otherwise have received. Information about the sort of penalty a court would impose could be communicated by convenors to participants in the preparation phase prior to

the meeting. This is the sort of information a legal aid hotline could also give.

Moreover, although agreements may deviate from the outcomes a court would impose, they should still be required to conform to some more general, wider standards based on human rights. For example, the human right against cruel, inhuman, or degrading punishment would justify a judge overruling an agreement that an offender should undergo some form of penalty such as wearing an 'I am a thief' T-shirt.[49] In such cases, a judge's role would be to explain to the parties in which ways the agreement infringed the human right, and give the parties an opportunity to revise the agreement.

Some restorative justice advocates argue that there should be upper limits about what offenders can agree to, but no lower ones (e.g. Braithwaite 1994: 204). Arguably, however, there are those cases where it might also be appropriate to constrain the discretion of restorative justice meetings by imposing lower limits on them. An evaluation of conferencing in Canberra found that drink-drivers who attended a conference are more likely to re-offend than offenders sentenced in court (Sherman *et al.* 2000). One possible reason for this is that court penalties almost always included the suspension of a driving licence, while restorative agreements did not. It could be argued, on public interest grounds, that restorative agreements should include, as a minimum, that offenders forfeit their licences for, say, a period of three months. Before or during a meeting, the convenor could explain this constraint on participants' decision-making discretion. Further, when a requirement was not met, judges should first give participants the option of reconvening. Only where the parties declined would the judge be entitled to unilaterally vary the agreement to include the suspension. Threats to public safety may equally justify the imposition of lower limits in other types of cases.

Agreements infringing upper limits based on human rights or lower limits based on public safety will usually raise questions about the original decision-making process (e.g. such as whether the offender properly participated or whether other affected parties

---

[49] In *Keenan v the United Kingdom*, App. No. 00027229/95, decision of 3 April 2001 (para 108) the European Court of Human Rights held that 'In considering whether a punishment or treatment is degrading within the meaning of Article 3, the Court will also have regard to whether its object is to humiliate and debase the person concerned...'.

contributed to the agreement), but even when the decision-making process seems sound, legislation should not prevent judges from taking remedial action. Legislation should tie judges' hands, but not too tightly: a balance must be struck between allowing room for the variation and creativity of democratic deliberation in restorative justice meetings on the one hand, and protecting human rights and public safety on the other.[50]

Simplicity

External review is not a simple form of accountability. It is expensive and time-consuming, and thus may undo some of the benefits of informal justice, one of which has been that it 'promises to be cheaper and quicker by abandoning technicalities, cumbersome procedures, and expensive professionals' (Parker 1999: 60). Any formal external review threatens to undermine this advantage. However, it is important that external review remain available, if only to help prevent the tyranny of the majority in a restorative meeting.

There is a way to minimize the cost and complexity of this type of accountability: not to make external review automatic or routine, but instead to reserve it for cases in which one of the parties requests it,[51] or perhaps whenever the seriousness of the offence demands it. Under this approach, institutions of formal justice can concentrate their energies on a smaller number of cases, which would be preferable to stretching their resources to review all cases, and running the risk that reviews would become perfunctory. Such a strategy is consistent with Ian Ayres' and John Braithwaite's pyramid of regulatory strategies, which places the most informal approaches to regulation at the base of the pyramid, and the most formal at the peak. Christine Parker (1999: 67) shows what the pyramid looks like in the context of access to justice (see Fig. 7.1 on p. 222).

Behind this pyramid lie both empirical and normative claims. Empirically, the pyramid claims to describe how regulation generally works, the wide base of the pyramid representing the bulk of matters that are handled informally, with the narrowing towards the top illustrating the increasingly smaller number of cases handled by progressively more formal means. Provided that people are free to

---

[50] This task is similar to that endorsed by Michael Dorf and Charles Sabel (1998: 283–4) in their concept of democratic experimentalism.

[51] This is the approach of Carcross Circle Program in the Yukon Territory.

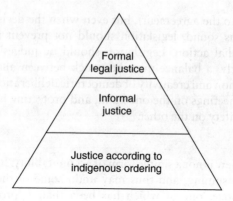

Fig. 7.1.   Pyramid showing access to justice options

move up and down the pyramid, the model also provides a normative ideal. Parker (1999: 68) explains that 'the pyramid is a preference ordering against rushing to formal legal justice before testing the presumption that indigenous ordering and informal justice are best tried first, maximizing access without compromising justice'. In the context of the external review of restorative justice programmes, this implies that it would be unnecessarily demanding for a court to review all cases as a matter of routine.

While review triggered by appeal may be simpler, it runs the risk of being less inclusive. For the pyramid to describe a normative ideal, parties must be able to access the appropriate level of justice necessary. A system of review which relies on parties to lodge an appeal is unlikely to be exercised by those victims and offenders whose need is greatest but whose very disempowerment and vulnerability ensures their silence. Advocacy groups can reduce this problem by proactively advising parties of appeal rights (Braithwaite 1998: 96; Braithwaite and Parker 1999: 111–13).[52]

Additional forms of external review

External review of agreements is undertaken not just by judges but also by a number of other bodies including police, prosecutors,

---

[52] Three of the programmes surveyed mentioned the regular involvement of victim advocacy groups: New Zealand Family Group Conferencing (Victim Support), Waitakere District Court Restorative Justice Pilot, Auckland (Victim Support), and Washington County Community Justice, Minneapolis (Victim Witness).

and advocacy groups. In most cases, these bodies appear to work as a persuasive form of accountability in conducting reviews on a co-operative basis with programmes. Unlike courts, they do not unilaterally vary an outcome, but instead contact the people working in the restorative programme whenever they consider there is a problem. Although these forms of review may be simpler, more timely, and more motivationally sensitive than judicial oversight, they rate much more poorly in terms of publicity, iterative accountability, and inclusiveness. While some may question the inclusiveness of courts, most would probably concede that the law requires judges to consider a broader range of interests than those considered by victims' advocacy groups. Given the more limited viewpoints represented by non-judicial forms of review, it is appropriate that they do not have the power to unilaterally vary or ignore an outcome.

While no programme surveyed has established its own appeal body, there have been some examples of this occurring. The REAL Justice Training Manual (O'Connell *et al.* 1999: 119)[53] describes a restorative justice programme in Hawke's Bay, New Zealand, which has established a complaints committee to deal with cases where parties are unhappy with some aspect of a meeting. While this may provide a source of accountability more independent than is a programme manager, it comes at a financial and administrative cost more than most programmes can bear. A discussion paper by the South African Law Commission (1999) recommended the country-wide adoption of models similar to the Zwelethemba Peacemaking Programme, as well as the establishment of a Community Forum as a second tier above the peace committee. One of the functions of such a forum would be to resolve complaints about the peacemaking process. The South African Law Commission envisages that the forums, like the peace committees, would remain independent of the formal legal system.

From the point of view of simplicity it may be simpler to use existing formal justice mechanisms (principally courts) rather than

---

Lucia Zedner (2002:433) reviews research showing that victims are much more likely to avail themselves of services when service providers are proactive about contacting victims.

[53] REAL Justice is the NGO that provided training to a number of the programmes surveyed.

to establish new institutions.[54] Failing to connect up restorative justice programmes to formal institutions of justice consigns restorative justice to a marginal role in the administration of criminal justice.

Conclusion

Questions about two modes of accountability feature prominently in accountability critiques of restorative and other kinds of informal justice—openness and judicial review. These questions reflect a more general fixation in accountability literatures with external, formal modes of accountability. Certainly there are grounds for the criticism that restorative justice programmes are not sufficiently open to the public: the majority of programmes only allow observers where all the participants consent, and some programmes allow no observers at all. Only a small number of programmes make themselves accountable through the simple strategy of allowing any member of the public to attend. That said, there are sensible, defensible reasons underlying restrictions on anyone's right to attend meetings, reasons concerned with protecting participants, particularly young offenders, and creating conditions conducive to communication about private matters. Rather than just accept the loss of accountability as fixed, I have suggested a number of ways in which these considerations can be reconciled with the demands of accountability:

- limiting the number of people who can attend any one meeting;
- limiting the way people can report what goes on in a meeting (for example, by prohibiting people from identifying participants);
- videotaping meetings, and afterwards allowing interested parties to view tapes of the event, under the same condition that they not reveal participants' identities.

External review, unlike internal review which is concerned to ensure that offenders are not overburdened, focuses on making sure punishment is sufficiently severe. Instead of guarding lower limits, judges should instead be concerned with safeguarding the conditions necessary for restorative deliberation.

[54] There is also a risk that these new institutions—like the advisory boards discussed in Chapter Six—will be later abandoned due to a lack of time and other resources.

A number of strategies were suggested for establishing such a system of judicial review:

- legislative reform, which sets out broad standards for judges to use to assess restorative agreements. These broad standards should allow some deviation from the usual sentences a judge would otherwise impose, and should be primarily concerned with the quality of the decision-making process within limits consistent with human rights and public safety;
- traditional judicial sentencing only to be used as a last resort. In the first instance when the decision-making process is defective, judges should offer parties the opportunity to attend a reconvened meeting, with the judge responsible for taking steps to correct the defects of the original process;
- full reports from practitioners provided to judges to aid them in making judgments about the adequacy of deliberative processes;
- review only to be undertaken when absolutely necessary, and only where it is sought by one of the affected parties; this should prevent unnecessary state intrusion;
- monitoring of agreements by advocacy groups who are responsible for assisting parties to bring appeals in appropriate cases.

This sort of approach builds up deliberative democracy at the level of restorative justice by making it a criterion for judicial review, and at the formal level, by restricting judges' ability to substitute any agreements reached in restorative justice meetings with their own sentences.

8
Semi-Formal Justice: Combining Informal and Formal Justice

Fears about restorative justice

Modern criminal justice is characterized by a rapid rate of change and innovation in penal philosophy, policy, and practice (Zedner 2002). Prominent among these changes is the emergence of restorative justice, a practice-led theory of justice concerned with the personal consequences of crime which gives citizens, rather than professionals, primary responsibility for determining how best to repair victims' harm and secure offenders' reintegration into law-abiding communities. New Zealand, Australia, Canada, England, and the United States have led many other countries in adopting different kinds of restorative justice programmes. In these, meetings between victims, offenders, and their supporters provide victims with opportunities they are otherwise denied in court: to meet offenders, express their feelings, describe their hurt, ask questions, and seek compensation. Meetings bring offenders—supported by their family and friends—face-to-face with the consequences of their actions, and give them an opportunity to make amends. The effects of these meetings can be so profound that proponents speak about the reconciliation, reparation, and reintegration that occur in them with an enthusiasm that is almost evangelical.

Given these heady expectations, it has become increasingly important not to look at what can be accomplished in restorative justice meetings, but at what can go wrong. A historical perspective on informal justice is critical to understanding concerns about its modern manifestation. References to ancient methods of conflict resolution feature prominently in writing about restorative justice, but in proponents' nostalgic and selective accounts of history nearly every form of informal justice becomes a fine example of restorative justice, while cruel and severe forms of punishment exist solely as the creation of the modern state.

By looking at some of the periods omitted by these selective constructions of history, we start to better understand the serious risk posed by informal justice. Many of its modes are cruel, oppressive, and sometimes violent. The vigilante movement in colonial America (Brown 1963; Walker 1980), the forms of charivari, or rough music, once practised throughout Europe (Thompson 1988), the history of street committees and people's courts in South African townships (Burman and Scharf 1990), and the harsh physical punishments administered by some forms of indigenous justice all provide vivid illustrations of the excesses of informal justice. Much restorative justice writing puts a benign gloss on a community's impulses when dealing with crime, but the history of informal justice contains innumerable examples of how, even with the best of intentions, communities can become as violent and oppressive as the misconduct they seek to control.

Restorative justice should also be viewed in the context of current penal developments. Its rapid growth and widening acceptance can be partly explained by its compatibility with other recent developments, including the growth of the victim's movement, the privatization of traditional state criminal justice functions, and the enlistment of civil society in crime control. At the same time, however, restorative justice is at odds with the prevailing trends in policy and practice. In particular, the humane ideals of restorative justice run contrary to the exclusionary, punitive ethos of prominent trends such as the adoption of zero-tolerance policing, mandatory sentencing, and shaming penalties, as well as the massive growth in the use of prison (changes summarized by Garland 2001: 6–20).

This antithesis should sound a note of caution for restorative justice proponents for it would be most surprising if restorative justice programmes were completely immune from these wider trends and the impulses which sustain them. Indeed, the examples at the beginning of this book, in which restorative justice meetings become opportunities for 'payback', to 'rub offenders' noses in it' and to make a child wear an 'I am a thief' T-shirt, suggest that restorative justice is not divorced from the attitudes popularizing more overtly punitive policies. The progressive ideals which characterize restorative justice can easily (if they have not already) become corrupted by the punitive impulses dominating current criminal justice policy and practice. According to restorative justice scholar Howard Zehr (1990:146), the Old Testament phrase 'an eye for an eye, a tooth for a tooth', 'commonly taken to summarize the retributive "tit-for-tat" natures of the biblical law', was in fact 'a law of proportion intended to limit rather than encourage revenge . . . that laid the basis for restitution'. To Zehr this illustrates the long history of restorative justice, but if Zehr is correct, it perhaps better illustrates how comprehensively benevolence can be corrupted.

Both the chequered history of informal justice and the contemporary criminal justice environment help frame critics' concerns about restorative justice. Critics fear that restorative justice dispenses with the formal rules and rights which otherwise restrain people's worst impulses, while retaining—or even exacerbating—the disadvantages of formal justice, most notably, the individualistic construction of responsibility for crime. Its critics worry that restorative justice utilizes programmes designed around the hope that people will be compassionate, when from a humanitarian perspective, they should be designed around the fear that they will not be. The most obvious problem is that the agreements negotiated in restorative justice meetings are—as even advocates of restorative justice are fond of saying themselves—limited only by the 'imagination of the parties' (Maxwell and Morris 1993: 10). This freedom may be used for reparative and reintegrative ends but, just as easily, for stigmatizing and oppressive ones. There is a real risk that participants in restorative justice meetings may have unfettered discretion to bully, hector, harass, and traumatize one another.

Public accountability is one of the procedural safeguards critics most fear restorative justice programmes lack. One of the oldest and most important principles of institutional design, accountability is designed to prevent the abuse and misuse of power. When decision-makers are required to explain their actions—or proposed actions—and have those explanations scrutinized, they are more likely to make better decisions, and their eventual decisions are more likely to be regarded as fair and legitimate. Many long-established and familiar institutional practices—from parliamentary elections to auditing—reflect this principle. Accountability is also evident in the design of formal systems of justice. For all their well-documented faults, courts are open institutions which can monitor other parts of the criminal justice system, and can themselves be monitored. For numerous writers (e.g. Warner 1993; Brown 1994; Young 2001), one of the most troubling aspects of informal justice generally, and restorative justice specifically, is the loss of this institutional accountability. Notwithstanding all these concerns, things may not be bad as critics fear. Drawing on research in twenty-five programmes in six countries leading the resurgence of restorative justice (Australia, Canada, England, New Zealand, South Africa, and the United States), I have identified important forms of accountability very largely overlooked in the copious critiques of restorative justice. In concentrating on forms of accountability prominent in formal justice—such as open justice and appeal rights—critics have neglected the emergence of some new modes of accountability in restorative justice programmes, in particular, a form of informal accountability (which I have termed 'deliberative accountability') occurring between citizens in restorative justice meetings. This finding echoes those from research into other areas of governance: early critiques expressing concern about the accountability deficit produced by privatization made the mistake of judging new forms of governance against traditional forms of accountability, neglecting 'the complex webs of extended accountability which spring up in practice' (Scott 2000: 60).

Even so, in many cases, meetings do not provide this deliberative accountability, and much of this book has been devoted to developing recommendations for its strengthening. Contrary to the general direction of restorative justice literature and the arguments of many critics of informal justice, I have argued that there can be a mutually beneficial relationship between informal justice and the formal criminal justice system, between community justice on the one hand, and state justice on the other.

Deliberative accountability

The participation of citizens is a fundamental element of restorative justice. In a contemporary context, the attempt to involve citizens in a central function of the criminal justice system is unusual, as it comes at a time when the dominant trend is in the reverse direction. The other practices of participatory democracy at the heart of criminal justice—the jury system, and in the UK, the lay magistracy—are under greater threat than ever before (Crawford and Newburn 2002: 492), and recent efforts to enlist civil society in crime control, such as Neighbourhood Watch, confine citizens to preventive roles on the margins of the criminal justice system.

When victims, offenders, and their supporters deliberate in a restorative justice meeting, they can hold each other accountable. Even when an offender is quite uninterested in making amends, he can still be held to account by his family and his victim. When a victim makes a demand for compensation, she cannot make arbitrary demands: when an offender agrees to take on an excessive amount of community service, he may be questioned by the convenor, or his mother, who in turn may be held to account by the victim. This process of negotiation contains its own in-built form of mutual accountability.

Any accountability mechanism runs the risk that the very act of reviewing people's actions may threaten to extinguish the goodwill which may otherwise be a powerful motivation for decision-makers to do the right thing. One of the advantages of deliberative accountability is that the accountability resides within the decision-making itself, and not after it, so that the requirement of explaining oneself and attracting scrutiny is less likely to be perceived as expressing a lack of trust. The ongoing nature of deliberative accountability also makes it more timely than retrospective forms and allows immediate adjustments to be made to an unsuitable restorative agreement. Communicative processes invariably favour some styles of communication over others, yet deliberative accountability is potentially less discriminatory than more formal modes, allowing people to use greetings, story-telling, and rhetoric in the process of explaining themselves (Young 2000). The practice of restorative justice programmes is also to encourage people to perform meaningful rituals, such as beginning meetings with a traditional prayer or blessing.

A further advantage of deliberative accountability is its potentially wide scope. Deliberative accountability between participants can be used to hold them accountable to one another for the decisions they make about dealing with the aftermath of a crime, and the same deliberative accountability can also be used to hold participants accountable for their conduct outside meetings. In particular, deliberative accountability can hold the police accountable for their handling of a case (albeit informally), providing a forum for police to explain and, if appropriate, apologize: in many cases, this is all complainants want (Bayley 1995: 107). One advantage of this form of accountability is that it provides an opportunity for offenders and victims to see their complaints in context: when a victim's mother complained that she was not kept informed about a case, a police officer was able to explain why this had happened.

Deliberative accountability can also be used to hold offenders accountable for completing agreements made in restorative justice meetings. In some programmes, offenders are required to report to one of the individual participants from the original meeting to confirm they have complied with the agreement. In other programmes, multiple meetings are held to monitor compliance. This is a time-consuming form of accountability and in many cases is unnecessary to generate compliance with an outcome. However, repeated meetings do offer at least two distinct benefits: the first is that they enable restorative justice to move away from an individualized conception of responsibility. In a subsequent meeting, not only can an offender's progress be monitored, but compliance with other agreements can be checked: a social worker can also be asked to report on her progress in placing an offender in a drug treatment programme, and an uncle can be asked whether he managed to help his niece, as he had volunteered to do. The second benefit is that meetings offer a wonderful opportunity to congratulate an offender on successfully completing an agreement. Praise can be as powerful a motivator as punishment, but for many offenders the opportunities to receive praise are few and far between. Two of the programmes surveyed—the Northside Community Justice Committee in Minneapolis, and the Connections Program in Red Wing—explicitly attempt to create new opportunities, by scheduling a 'celebration circle' for offenders who successfully complete their commitments. The practice of the Northside Community Justice Committee of scheduling multiple meetings, with participants assisting offenders in between meetings, is an exciting variation on the traditional one-off restorative justice meeting because it seeks to combine the benefits of a restorative justice meeting with the demonstrated benefits of mentoring schemes (Sherman *et al.* 1998: Chapter 3).

Fears about deliberative accountability

It would be a gross exaggeration to conclude that all meetings in all programmes demonstrated deliberative accountability. There were many cases that did so, but too often programmes are run—and meetings convened—in a way which leads to accountability collapsing. Because it depends on participants being able to hold each other accountable, deliberative accountability should make it necessary that people who wish to participate in meetings should feel required to explain and justify their various comments and demands. At the same time, however, it is vital that some participants not be able to bully or browbeat others: deliberative accountability only works when no one participant dominates the process; it requires that participants be empowered, rather than oppressed. From an accountability point of view, it is absolutely essential to guard against domination.

If meetings are to provide any sort of deliberative accountability, not only should attendance be voluntary, both for victims and offenders, but also, participants should be advised of the availability of an alternative forum for deciding the matter. Convenors should ensure that meetings comprise several participants: too often, deliberative accountability collapses because a young offender or a victim does not have any one to speak up on their behalf. Equally importantly, participants should be a diverse group: there is little to be gained, and much to be lost, by allowing an offender to invite six of his closest beer-drinking mates. Siblings and grandparents, aunts and uncles, employers and teachers, the whole gamut of contacts, all have an important role to play in restorative justice meetings, and identifying just who may be suitable is a key task for the convenor and the immediate parties during preparation for a meeting.

Further to this variety, a prominent view among restorative proponents is that there is no such thing as too big a conference. John Braithwaite and Heather Strang (2000: 205), for example, contend that 'If there is one thing our empirical experience of conferences and circles has taught us it is that allowing a large number of people into the circle does not produce chaos'.

However, just as meetings can be too small, they can also be too big, and allowed to run too long. If agreements are to be justified on the basis that they represent the negotiations of affected parties, meetings must be structured in such way as to in fact allow free negotiation. It is highly doubtful that a meeting involving one hundred people (as is the case in some American programmes) allows the immediately affected participants to participate properly, especially when they are young people. Thinking further about the need to prevent parties feeling intimidated, meetings should be held in genuinely neutral venues, chosen by the parties, and begun and concluded in ways which are meaningful and unthreatening to everybody.

The state's role in restorative justice meetings

The role the state should be allowed to play in restorative justice meetings is one of the most contentious issues in restorative justice. In practice, the state often plays a key role, with many programmes run by the state, and many meetings convened by state professionals. Many restorative justice advocates object to the state's involvement, continuing a long tradition of suspicion—and outright hostility—towards state involvement in informal justice. In the 1970s, prior to the emergence of the restorative justice, many criminologists and legal writers were critical of the role played by the state in informal justice, arguing that informal processes, contrary to their emancipatory rhetoric, are created and sustained by the state apparatus for its own ends. By treating conflicts as matters of individual dispute settlement, critics argued that informal justice perpetuates, rather than challenges, the liberal, governmental power formations responsible for the social inequality which nurtures particular conflicts in the first place (Abel 1982; Cohen 1984; Pavlich 1996: 729).

The role of the state in deliberative accountability provides greater possibilities for optimism. Deliberative accountability envisages an important role for the state in acting to minimize domination and enhance accountability in restorative justice meetings (while avoiding becoming a source of domination itself). To prevent the possibility of domination, police officers and judges should not convene restorative justice meetings. When they do, they wield—whether they like it or not—an authority which has little to do with the ideal role of a convenor, or with the participatory aspirations of restorative justice, and everything to do with their professional role and authority.[1] Police simply cannot be held accountable themselves if they convene meetings. Most police-run programmes at least recognize the inappropriateness of the investigating officer convening the meeting and pass the responsibility on to a colleague, but this practice does not go far enough, especially when solidarity is one of

---

[1] An observation Simon Roberts (1983: 555) also makes about judges mediating family disputes.

the key characteristics of police culture (Reiner 1997: 1016). Richard Young (2001: 214) notes that whenever an offender made criticisms of the investigating officer in the Thames Valley Conferencing Programme, 'however faintly or implicitly, the typical reaction of the facilitator was defensive'. As he observes, 'Such defensive comments achieve little other than conveying to offenders that criticisms of the police will not be welcomed'. One solution is the approach of the Woodbury Program, where community volunteers act as convenors. However, not even this solution is ideal, as the police retain power over the choice of the convenor.

The state does have, however, other appropriate roles to play. It is important that offenders make an informed decision about their participation, and in New South Wales the government funds a toll-free telephone legal advice service which offenders are encouraged to access before, and if necessary, during a restorative justice meeting. In New Zealand, offenders and victims have the option of inviting government-funded advocates to attend meetings with them. In both programmes, the government plays a large role in helping to empower participants. There is also a good argument that in some cases prosecutors should be able to attend meetings to represent a public interest which is not otherwise represented by victims.

Formal modes of accountability

Courts clearly have an important role to play in restorative justice. Ideally, they ensure that cases are referred to restorative justice programmes, screening cases prosecuted before them, and diverting those which are appropriate for restorative justice. Ideally, they also play an important role in supporting the deliberative accountability inherent in restorative justice meetings. Deliberative accountability does not work if offenders and victims are coerced, either into attending a meeting or agreeing to terms of an outcome. Offenders must retain the right to decline to attend a meeting and have their case dealt with by an alternative forum, without prejudice. If this choice is not available, that subsequent meeting is not an accountable form of justice. For the same reason, meetings must be run on a consensual basis, with participants informed of the availability of an alternative forum for dealing with the matter: if they do not have an exit option, then meetings are not accountable. Courts also should provide a forum for scrutinizing agreements reached in meetings, and monitoring offenders' compliance whenever deliberative accountability fails.

When it comes to the review of restorative justice agreements, I discovered that, regardless of the form of review, agreements are most often left undisturbed. In such cases as those when agreements are overruled, practitioners and judges take different approaches: when practitioners overrule it is to decrease their severity, when judges intervene it is to increase it; internal review tends to enforce upper limits, and external review lower ones. Restorative justice proponents object to the tendency to review outcomes against traditional sentencing principles such as proportionality and consistency, but if restorative justice is to reject them, it becomes incumbent upon it to suggest some alternative basis for review.

There is a possible alternative approach: it might be possible for a restorative justice approach to restrict judges to a role similar to their role in administrative law. In administrative law, when judges supervise the decisions of government, they are said to be concerned not with the substantive merits of the decision, but the legality of the decision-making process. When a defect is detected, a court cannot substitute its decision on the matters in issue for that of the body appealed from, but it can quash the decision and request that the original decision-maker remake it (Cane 1996: 8). Judges' expertise does not qualify them to gainsay restorative agreements, if only because restorative justice agreements do not involve the technical application of rules, but rather, highly contextualized, personal, and often emotional negotiation. What judges can do is ensure restorative practice comports with ideals of restorative justice, ensuring that all the affected parties are indeed present, or at least represented, and that agreements are the result of their consensus. Ultimately, the acceptability of a restorative agreement depends not on its severity or leniency but on that very decision-making quality.

For this procedural approach to judicial oversight to be fully adopted, legislative reform is required. We have seen how legislation in some jurisdictions has led to some recognition by the formal legal system of restorative justice. However, legislation to date has taken the form of specifying reparation as one of the factors judges should consider in deciding upon sentence. Such an approach does not restrict judges' discretion; reparation is simply added to the mix of sentencing principles. Furthermore, under a procedural approach to judicial review, legislation would limit a judge's powers to making a determination about the adequacy of the deliberative decision-making process: this reform should help ensure that judges do not replace the decision made by a properly constituted and well-run restorative process with their own.

Legislation should direct judges to enquire about procedural matters such as who was present at the meeting, whether they agreed to it (and if not, why not), and whether participants had an opportunity to consult a lawyer before or during the deliberations. Remedies for those cases where judges detect a defect in the decision-making process should also be faithful to the procedural approach to review: only as a last resort should judges impose a penalty in place of the defective restorative agreement. In the first instance, judges should offer the parties a chance to attend a reconvened meeting, with the judge taking appropriate steps to correct any defect found. Only when all else fails—because, for example, the main participants decline the invitation to attend another meeting—would a judge be entitled to hand down a traditional sentence.

The only role of traditional sentencing tariffs would be to provide a non-binding guide to participants in restorative justice meetings. It is only common knowledge about these tariffs among participants that enable offenders to demonstrate their generosity and victims their mercy. While victims and offenders would be able to depart from traditional sentencing tariffs, agreements would nevertheless have to conform to new upper and lower limits, drawn much more widely than existing tariffs, and designed to catch only the most egregious cases. At the upper end, a prohibition on cruel, unusual, and degrading treatment would allow a judge to declare illegal any agreements which employed public shaming. At the other end, questions of public safety may justify lower limits for some types of crimes. In most of these cases, however, judges would not need to rely on these limits in order to act, as close examination will in all probability raise doubts about the decision-making process, such as whether the offender really agreed to the sanctions or whether the interest of the affected community was represented.

This approach would represent a significant change in the traditional role of a sentencing judge. A number of things may be done to facilitate the transition. As a minimum requirement, practitioners should provide full reports of the decision-making process. Meetings should be videotaped in order to assist judges, who after viewing it, could also, if they felt it necessary, question the participants. At a more general level, a useful innovation is exemplified by the Navajo nation which has appointed a liaison officer to explain the work of peacemakers to judges and vice versa. Inviting judges to observe meetings might also create a pathway for formal law to learn from restorative justice.

Judicial review of agreements is not the only role the formal legal system should play. To avoid the problem of police domination of meetings, one solution is to use community volunteers, but the risk remains that police will simply choose those volunteers whose values and approach to convening coincide with their own. The obvious remedy, taking administration out of police hands, addresses this problem but creates others. In particular, many programmes not run by police struggle to persuade police to refer cases to them. Police readily refer trivial cases which they know would be dismissed or dealt with leniently in court, but are more reluctant to do so with those more serious cases, cases where restorative justice appears to have the most to offer—both in terms of participant satisfaction and preventing re-offending. Finding customers is one of the perennial problems for informal justice initiatives, and one of the biggest problems facing restorative justice programmes. Perhaps the most effective solution is to adopt legislation, as New Zealand has done, to limit police discretion and mandate referrals. Many programmes do not, however, have the luxury of the sort of political commitment necessary to pass such a law. For these, the best alternative is to accept referrals from multiple points in the criminal justice process. When police prosecute in court cases they should have sent to a restorative justice programme, judges should correct the error. Indeed, in programmes such as the New South Wales Conferencing Programme, the judiciary has been an important source of referrals: in accountability terms, the judiciary acts as an important source of accountability for the disposition decision. Time and time again, interviews with practitioners emphasized the importance of using accountability mechanisms in tandem with other initiatives. In particular, convenors stressed the importance of spending time on judicial education. To this it could also be added that attention be given to ensure an information loop from the judiciary to investigative officers, so that police can be informed when making decisions on similar cases.

Open justice is one of the most controversial aspects of the accountability of restorative justice, and it is certainly true that many programmes are not sufficiently open to the public: the majority of programmes allow observers only when all participants consent, and some programmes allow no observers at all. Only in a small number of programmes are people able to observe meetings in much the same way they can court cases. Access to meetings is restricted because most personnel are worried that allowing spectators would interfere with participants' privacy and threaten to disrupt proceedings. Nevertheless it may, and should, be possible to accommodate all these concerns and still allow observers. Quite explicit and unambiguous restrictions can be placed on the number of people able to attend meetings, and on the way journalists report them. A good compromise and an imaginative strategy is that of the Texas Victim/ Offender Mediation/Dialogue Program, which brings together imprisoned offenders and their victims. To ensure that these meetings are not disrupted, but nonetheless to ensure that a record exists, meetings are videotaped, and the tapes later made available to observers.

Rethinking the relationship between formal and informal justice

The declining trust in liberal democratic governments, which is both widespread and long-standing, points to a crisis of legitimacy for modern governments (Sherman 2001: 42). By bringing participatory deliberative democracy back into the centre of the criminal justice system, restorative justice offers a possible route for restoring not just victims and offenders, but also for restoring citizens' faith in governments perceived to be unresponsive to their concerns. Critics, aware of the chequered history of informal justice, and with a nervous eye on the punitive impulses dominating contemporary criminal justice policy, express anxieties about the adequacy of procedural safeguards in restorative justice programmes, including first and foremost the adequacy of public accountability mechanisms. But used to the formal modes of accountability popular in modern representative democracies, critics have overlooked the presence of informal accountability in the deliberations of a restorative justice meeting. This particular form of accountability, termed deliberative accountability, is able to, and does, hold accountable victims, perpetrators of crime, supporters of both, members of the wider community, and agents of the state. In many respects, though, current practice departs from the ideal sketched here. Thorough and exhaustive preparation is required before a meeting can ultimately come to represent the range of affected interests. In addition, it is important that police should not convene meetings because of a possible conflict of interest; nor should judges overrule agreements on grounds of inconsistency or lack of proportionality. The state has a crucial role to play in informal justice, especially in minimizing domination which otherwise could threaten the deliberative accountability in restorative justice meetings; at the same time, every effort must be made to avoid its becoming itself a source of domination. The ideal is that restorative justice and state justice are mutually supportive: restorative justice programmes can gain benefit from state guardianship, while citizens' deliberations in restorative justice meetings offer the potential to reinvigorate the justice of the state.

Appendix A: Individual Overviews of Case Studies

Conference programmes

New Zealand Family Group Conferencing

The New Zealand Family Group Conferencing Programme for young offenders is the oldest, and most influential, conferencing programme. Conferencing was introduced in New Zealand in 1989, as part of a comprehensive reform of the juvenile justice system. Under the *Children, Young Persons and Their Families Act* (1989) the majority of juvenile offences are dealt with by police warning. These warnings are either administered on the spot, or in more serious cases, at some later time in the presence of an offender's parents. For the remaining serious offences, family group conferences are mandatory where an offender does not deny committing an offence.[1] The only exceptions to this are for very serious crimes. Cases involving homicide are automatically transferred from the Youth Court to the High Court, and other serious offences, such as arson and armed robbery can be transferred to the High Court at the discretion of the Youth Court judge. In the majority of cases referred to conference, the conference serves as an alternative to formal conviction and sentencing.[2]

A Youth Justice Co-ordinator (YJC) from the Department of Social Welfare is responsible for organizing a conference within statutory

[1] Prior to conference an offender is not required to enter a guilty plea, and instead is referred to a conference if he or she does not deny committing the offence. Asking offenders to only not deny committing the offence is designed to preserve their right to plead not guilty if they choose, and to have the matter tried in court (Bowen, *et al.* 2000: 46). This may encourage some guilty offenders to participate in a conference knowing that they are not waiving their right to require a prosecution to prove the offence beyond reasonable doubt. Once in the conference they may then decide to admit the offence.

[2] Except where conference participants agree the matter should be prosecuted, or if the offence was one for which the offender was originally arrested, in which case the Youth Court judge makes a formal court order confirming or varying the conference outcome.

deadlines. The YJC invites victims and their supporters to attend a conference with the offender and supporters. One of the distinctive features of the New Zealand model is that provision is made for a number of professionals to attend. Nearly all conferences are attended by a police officer, and in nearly two-thirds of all cases, a social worker. Offenders are entitled to invite government-employed youth advocates, an entitlement which is exercised in roughly half of all cases (Maxwell and Morris 1993: 75). Some victims also have access to a government-run victim advocacy service. Conferences are held at a venue of the parties' choosing, often a Department of Social Welfare office or the offender's home, or a Marae (a Maori meeting house) in some cases involving Maori offenders (Maxwell and Morris 1993: 73).

Conferences aim to reach unanimous agreement about what the offender should do to accept responsibility for his or her actions. Gabrielle Maxwell and Allison Morris (1993: 10) state that 'the exact details are limited only by the imagination of the parties' but also note that:

In practice in the FGC (Family Group Conference) this is most likely to mean that the young person apologizes, pays reparation or makes a donation to a charity, undertakes some type of work (in some cases for the victim) or accepts some form of restriction on their liberty such as a curfew, grounding or agreement not to drive (Maxwell and Morris 1993: 92).

A distinctive feature of the deliberative process is that a short break is taken during a conference to allow the offender's family to confer, and devise possible conference outcomes without state officials being present. These proposals are then presented to other participants for further discussion. Conferences can be observed by researchers with the consent of participants, but are closed to the media.

After attending a conference, an offender may be required to attend court, either if participants agree that the matter should be prosecuted, or if the offence was one for which the offender was originally arrested,[3] in which case the Youth Court judge is responsible for reviewing and, if necessary, varying the conference outcome. Any subsequent order made nominates the person or agency

---

[3] No arrest can be made unless it is necessary to prevent the young person from offending further, or absconding, or interfering with witnesses or evidence (McElrea 1996).

responsible for monitoring completion of the order, depending on its nature. Where an offender is not required to go to court, the Department of Social Welfare is responsible for monitoring the completion of any agreed outcome.

Wagga Wagga Police, New South Wales

In 1991, after learning about the New Zealand Programme, a small group of Australians established a conferencing programme for young offenders in the inland town of Wagga Wagga in New South Wales. The programme no longer exists, with conferencing in New South Wales now run on a state-wide legislative basis.[4] The programme differed from the New Zealand model in two significant ways: police ran it, and the approach adopted by convenors was influenced by John Braithwaite's (1989) theory of reintegrative shaming. Unlike that in New Zealand, the Wagga Wagga Programme had no express statutory basis, with police instead running conferences under the police power to administer cautions to young offenders.[5]

As support for the conferencing programme grew, it was decided to create a formal institutional mechanism for selecting cases. A sergeants' review panel was formed, comprising sergeants from a number of different squads such as traffic, general policing, and detective.[6] Meeting on a weekly basis, this panel was responsible for making the final decision about how to deal with each juvenile matter. Police officer Terry O'Connell, one of the instigators of the programme, says that the primary motivation for establishing the panel was to generate support for conferencing, to 'get cop buy-in', but that once it was established it became an important accountability mechanism for scrutinizing the actions of investigating officers. David Moore (another developer of the programme) and O'Connell (1993: 57) attribute a subsequent drop in the number of young people charged with minor offences partly to the effect of the sergeants' review:

---

[4] See description of New South Wales Youth Justice Conferencing below.

[5] Consequently conferencing acted as an alternative to formal conviction and sentencing.

[6] Terry O'Connell says that his original intention was to broaden the range of people involved in the panel to include others such as juvenile justice employees, and representatives of community groups, but for a variety of reasons this did not eventuate.

General duties police officers had to take account of the fact that a panel of sergeants would review any charge they might make and would not take kindly to trivialities that involved the wounded pride of an officer on the beat or on patrol.

Conferences were convened by a police officer and were attended on a voluntary basis by offenders and victims, together with their respective supporters. As with all the programmes surveyed, participants aimed to reach consensus about what offenders should do to repair the harm they had caused.[7] The investigating officer was not allowed to convene the conference and was usually not present.

Unlike the New Zealand model, the conference process drew heavily on John Braithwaite's (1989) theory of reintegrative shaming, with police asking questions designed to generate shame for an offender's actions, while at the same time eliciting support for the offender as a person. In order to protect the confidentiality and privacy of young offenders, conferences were generally closed to the public, including the media, although there were individual cases where the media attended with the consent of participants. Researchers could attend conferences with the consent of participants.

To monitor whether an offender completed the agreed outcome, victims were provided with a form which police asked them to complete and return (using the stamped, addressed envelope provided) once an offender had completed the agreement. If an offender failed to do so, the police officer who convened the conference would visit the offender to enquire why, and encourage completion. However, because conferences were held under the police power to caution, O'Connell says that police had no formal power to enforce the agreements made in conferences.

Australian Federal Police Diversionary Conferencing, Canberra

In Canberra, the Australian Federal Police have run conferences since 1994. Many of these conferences have been part of the Reintegrative

---

[7] There is one exception to this. The Youth Offender Panels in England are not intended to operate on a consensus basis, as a victim's consent is not required for an outcome. Victim consent is not strictly required in the Thames Valley model, but in practice, where a victim attends a conference, the conference convenor seeks to ensure the victim approves of any outcome. The Youth Offender Panels may end up operating in the same way.

Shaming Experiments (RISE), a large-scale research project conducted by the Australian National University comparing, by random assignment of offenders, the effects of conferencing and court treatments. Four kinds of cases are included within RISE: drink-driving, juvenile property offences with personal victims, juvenile shoplifting offences detected by store security officers, and violent crime committed by people under the age of 30 (Sherman *et al.* 1998). Outside RISE, police have run conferences for many other kinds of cases, including serious adult fraud, indecent exposure, and drug offences.

This programme is similar to the Wagga Wagga Programme on which it was based, with conferences convened by trained police officers.[8] One relevant difference is that the Canberra Programme does not have a panel responsible for scrutinizing all juvenile matters to decide which should have access to the programme. Instead, the programme relies on an investigating officer to send a case to the unit responsible for running conferences, where a trained officer decides whether to accept it. Jeff Knight, one of the members of that unit, says that approximately 90 per cent of cases are accepted. He says that conferencing is only meant to deal with cases that would otherwise be serious enough to go to court, and that he has rejected trivial cases on this basis.

Another novel feature of the Canberra Programme is the use of volunteers as community representatives in conferences. Originally it was intended to use such representatives for offences where there was no direct victim (for example drink-driving), but in practice, community representatives are also used where there is a direct victim, who in over 80 per cent of cases are also present at the conference. It was originally intended that police would be able to select a representative from a panel of trained volunteers from the same neighbourhood as an offender. In practice, however, there is often little training, and representatives are chosen more on the basis of their availability and perceived ability to contribute to the conference. Researchers can attend conferences with the permission of other participants, but the media is excluded. As is the case with most of the other programmes surveyed, if the participants cannot

---

[8] The conference is an alternative to formal conviction and sentencing.

reach agreement, the offender may be referred to court for formal prosecution for the original offence.[9]

In December 1997 an advisory committee was formed to oversee the practice and development of conferencing in Canberra (AFP undated). The committee, comprising representatives from police, the prosecutor's and public defender's offices, as well as other legal practitioners and community representatives, met a number of times during its first year but has not met again since.

Woodbury Police, St Paul

In 1995 Woodbury police officer Dave Hines started a conferencing programme for young offenders after undertaking training in conferencing conducted by REAL Justice, an American NGO.[10] All juvenile cases in the Woodbury police station are referred to Hines, who selects cases appropriate for conferencing. Typically these include theft, assault, and public-order offences such as possession of alcohol by an under-age person. As with many other programmes, conferencing acts as an alternative to formal conviction and sentencing by a court.

Once a case is selected, it is assigned to a convenor who contacts both victim and offender by telephone to ask them if they wish to participate in a conference. If either victim or offender declines, the matter is referred to court. All programmes surveyed give offenders this choice, but only a small number also give this power to victims.[11] The practice of the majority of programmes is to allow a victim to choose whether they wish to participate in the process, but not to choose whether the process goes ahead at all.

---

[9] The exceptions discussed below are the Zwelethemba Peacemaker Committee, the Toronto Community Council and the Vancouver Restorative Justice Programme. Also, in the two prison-based programmes, the Texas Victim/Offender Mediation Program and the Connections Program run by the Minnesota Correctional Facility in Red Wing, no further action is taken if parties cannot reach agreement. Where agreement cannot be reached in school-based programmes, offenders are referred not to court, but to an alternative forum such as a school disciplinary board.

[10] REAL Justice was started after one of its directors, Ted Wachtel heard Terry O'Connell, who now works for REAL Justice, speak about the Wagga Wagga Programme.

[11] In addition to Woodbury Police, the programmes that give victims this extra power are Queensland Community Conferencing, the Community Conferencing Program in Minneapolis run by Central City Neighbourhoods Partnership, and

Originally all convenors in the Woodbury Program were police officers, but now, due to a shortage of police officers, community volunteers are increasingly used as convenors. Victims and offenders are asked to bring supporters to conferences held in the police station. Hines also invites investigating officers, but duty rosters make it difficult for them to attend. In common with a number of American restorative justice programmes, co-convenors are often used. As Hines says, this practice allows convenors to 'keep an eye on each other'. Observers can attend with the consent of participants, and are invited to sit in the circle with them.

At the conclusion of a conference, convenors are required to report back to Hines about their own performance. Evaluation questionnaires are also sent to the victim and offender, and the offender's parents or guardians. Hines monitors the completion of conference outcomes, and a copy of the conference outcome is sent to the prosecutor's office, which prosecutes in cases where offenders fail to complete agreements.

As with all the programmes surveyed, Hines is required to file reports on a regular basis showing the number and types of meetings held; these are prepared for police management, as well as the City Council, who jointly fund the programme. Like many restorative justice programmes, the Woodbury programme relies heavily on the commitment of a single person, in this case Hines himself. To try to ensure the programme survives him, Hines plans to establish a Community Justice Council comprised of community volunteers, who would be responsible for screening cases and monitoring the completion of outcomes, two tasks he currently performs.

Thames Valley Police Restorative Justice Programme

Since 1998 the Thames Valley Police (TVP), using its power to caution offenders, have run conferences for juvenile and adult of-

---

the South St Paul Restorative Justice Council. This is also the effect of the Texas Victim/ Offender Mediation Program's policy of only offering offenders the opportunity to participate in mediation where a victim has requested it.

In two multi-form programmes, the Washington County Community Justice Program in Minneapolis, and the Restorative Justice Program in Prince William County, Virginia, victims are offered a range of options including a face-to-face meeting with an offender, indirect mediation, and financial reparation (see below under multi-form programmes). If none of these options is satisfactory to the victim the case is referred back to court.

fenders. TVP began conferencing after success with an earlier programme for juvenile shoplifters (where offenders attended presenta-
tions by store managers), and after inviting Australian police officer
Terry O'Connell to give a series of seminars to TVP (TVP 2000). In
2000, conferencing for juveniles was given a statutory basis as part
of a series of legislative reforms introduced under the *Crime and
Disorder Act* (1998) and the *Youth Justice and Criminal Evidence
Act* (1999).[12]

As with nearly all restorative justice programmes, conferences are
voluntary for offenders and victims.[13] Offenders are first asked if
they wish to attend a conference and, if so, whether they wish the
victim to attend. This is unusual: most programmes do not offer
the offender the option of a victimless conference.[14] Victims and
offenders are encouraged to bring supporters with them to a conference held in a police station. Observers including judges and
members of the media can attend conferences with participants'
consent. Thames Valley conferences have been filmed for television.
It is most common for a police officer to convene conferences, but
other people including teachers, community volunteers, and probation officers also convene conferences. The investigating officer in an
incident is not allowed to convene a conference about it. Simon
Beaton, a police constable in the TVP Restorative Justice Consult-
ancy, says that ordinarily investigating officers are also discouraged
from attending as participants, as it is thought that the presence of
multiple police officers may overwhelm and intimidate an offender.
The exception to this is in cases where the investigating officer is also
the victim—of an assault, for example.

Convenors are instructed to run conferences by closely following
scripted questions designed to encourage reintegrative shaming,
that is, combining social disapproval for an offender's action with
support for an offender as a person (Braithwaite 1989). As with all
other programmes surveyed, part of the meeting revolves around

---

[12] Perhaps most significantly these Acts establish Youth Offender Panels for young
offenders convicted in court. These are discussed below. Under the new legislation
conferences continue to act as an alternative to formal conviction and sentencing, just
as they did prior to the legislation.

[13] The only exceptions among the programmes surveyed are New Zealand Family
Group Conferencing and Youth Offender Panels in England and Wales.

[14] In practice victims frequently do not attend restorative justice meetings but this is
not because the offender requests that they do not.

negotiating an outcome that an offender will complete. While legally a victim's agreement is not required (as the conference has the legal status of a caution administered by police), convenors attempt to reach agreement between all the parties about what an offender will do to make amends. As was the case in the Wagga Wagga programme, police do not formally monitor completion of outcomes as an offender is under no legal obligation to do anything beyond attending the conference. In practice, however, Beaton says police sometimes ring offenders to urge them to complete agreements, appealing to their sense of moral obligation.

Youth Justice Conferencing, Department of Juvenile Justice, New South Wales

During the 1990s parliamentary inquiries were established in Western Australia, Queensland, New South Wales, and South Australia to address a perceived problem of increased juvenile offences and to consider more effective approaches to juvenile justice (Daly and Hayes 2001). Since then these jurisdictions have passed detailed legislation establishing conferencing, beginning with South Australia in 1993.[15] The conferencing programme established in New South Wales by the *Young Offenders Act* (1997) is an example of such an approach.

Conferencing is one of a hierarchy of interventions for dealing with young offenders. Juvenile matters can be dealt with—in ascending order of severity—by police warning, by formal caution administered by police in the presence of a person's parents or guardians, by conference, or by court. Police are meant to use the least severe form of intervention appropriate. Conferences can be held for a range of offences including assault, theft, property damage, disorderly conduct (Trimboli 2000: 6), and some drug offences.[16] Where a conference is held, it is as an alternative to formal conviction and sentencing. As with all but three of the programmes surveyed, an offender must admit to an offence before a conference can be held.[17]

---

[15] Kathy Daly and Hennessey Hayes observe (2001: 2) an opposite trend outside Australia, where conferences are run on a more local basis, often as a police caution (such as the Woodbury and Thames Valley Police models described above).

[16] See *Drug Summit Legislative Response Act* (1999) (NSW).

[17] The exceptions are New Zealand Family Group Conferencing, the Zwelethemba Peacemaker committee, and Navajo Peacemaking.

If a police officer decides that a warning or caution is not appropriate he or she must refer the matter to a specialist youth police officer (SYO) who can recommend a conference be held. This recommendation is then reviewed by a conference administrator (CA) from the Department of Juvenile Justice. Jenny Bargen, Director of the Youth Conferencing Directorate within the Department of Juvenile Justice, sees this review function as providing an important source of accountability for police disposition decisions. The CA also accepts conference referrals from the prosecutor's office and magistrates, who both screen cases referred to them (usually by police) for prosecution in court.[18] Where the CA and SYO are unable to reach agreement about how the matter should be dealt with, the CA can also refer a matter to the prosecutor's office.[19]

Community members employed on a casual basis convene conferences. CAs select an appropriate convenor for a conference from a panel. It is the convenor's responsibility to contact the victim and offender to see if they wish to participate in the conference. Offenders are encouraged to seek legal advice before agreeing to participate, and are given the phone number for a government-funded toll free legal advice hotline. Conference convenors and administrators are also encouraged to use this service.

Conferences are supposed to be held within twenty-one days of a convenor receiving a referral but research over a seventeen-month period (from June 1998 to November 1999) found that this deadline was not met in 91.9 per cent of cases (Trimboli 2000: 68).[20] As with all restorative programmes surveyed, victim attendance is voluntary. In NSW there is express provision for the victim to send a representative in their place where the victim does not wish to attend personally.[21] Where victims attend they are encouraged to bring supporters, as are offenders. Police officers and a lawyer responsible for advising the young offender are entitled to attend conferences, and the convenor can also invite other people such as social workers and respected members of the community (such as Aboriginal elders).[22] Conferences are closed to the public, including the media

---

[18] Section 40.

[19] Section 41.

[20] Sixty per cent are held within twice the statutory time period (Trimboli 2000: 68).

[21] Section 47(1)(i).

[22] Section 47.

(Power 1998), but researchers may attend a conference provided that they obtain the approval of the government minister responsible for conferencing, the Youth Conference Advisory Committee, and the participants in the conference.[23]

Conference outcomes must not be 'more severe than those that might have been imposed in court proceedings for the offence concerned', and where outcomes involve community service or the payment of money, they must not exceed the limits prescribed by regulations accompanying the *Young Offenders Act*.[24] When parties cannot reach agreement the matter is referred back to the body that referred it to conference, which then decides what further action, if any, should be taken. As is the case in other programmes, interviewees report that it is rare for parties not to reach agreement.

Where a magistrate has referred a matter to conference, the convenor must refer an outcome plan back to court for his or her approval.[25] While conference participants are encouraged to assist in the task of monitoring the completion of outcome plans (as is the case in most programmes surveyed), CAs bear final responsibility for supervising, and signing off on outcomes. This includes a responsibility to inform the young offender, any victims, and the referral body as to whether an outcome plan has been completed. If an outcome is not completed formal proceedings may be commenced or resumed. Conferences can be reconvened where a plan becomes unworkable or where other participants request an outcome be reconsidered.[26]

Meetings are held between CAs on a regular basis, and between conference convenors on an occasional basis, which provide, according to Bargen, an informal form of accountability. CAs also occasionally attend conferences to provide feedback to convenors on their performance. Every three months Bargen also visits each of the seventeen conferencing regions to monitor the Administrators' work. A number of government and non-government bodies are represented on an advisory committee, which provides another form of accountability. NSW is one of

---

[23] Section 47(3).
[24] Section 52. The New South Wales Programme is the only programme surveyed to set specific upper limits.
[25] Section 54.
[26] Section 55.

a small number of programmes surveyed that has such an advisory committee.[27]

Community Conferencing, Queensland

Conferencing was introduced in Queensland as a new diversionary response for dealing with young offenders, as part of the 1996 amendments to the *Juvenile Justice Act* (1992).[28] In early 1997 pilot programmes were established at three sites, and conferencing has now expanded modestly to include some other parts of Queensland. Like the programmes described above, the programme is designed as an alternative to conviction and sentencing by the criminal justice system. During the first thirteen months of the trial most referrals came from police (Hayes *et al.* 1998: 53). Conferences, however, can also be held at the request of a judge prior to formal judicial sentencing.[29] Gail Pollard, a project officer with the Queensland Programme, would prefer that conferences be run as an alternative to formal sentencing because she feels that offenders are effectively punished twice when expected to attend a conference and then a formal court sentencing (where the judge may disregard the conference outcome). Queensland judges prefer conferences be held as a pre-sentence intervention, as this allows them to retain ultimate control over proceedings. Pollard is also frustrated that judges and police are not legally required to consider referring a matter to conference. As a result the programme has had trouble attracting referrals. To assist in attracting more referrals, an evaluation of the pilot concluded that police, judges, and lawyers should be better educated about the benefits of conferencing.

---

[27] The other two programmes are the Community Conferencing Program in Minneapolis run by the Central City Neighbourhoods Partnership described below, and the Australian Federal Police Programme described above. The Spectrum Just Youth Restorative Justice Project in Burlington (described below) would like to establish a board.

[28] Before this, conferencing was introduced in Queensland in schools (see below).

[29] A number of the programmes surveyed run conferences as a pre-sentence intervention. One of these programmes (the Waitakere District Court Restorative Justice Pilot) runs all conferences as a pre-sentence diversion, whereas with three other programmes (South St Paul Restorative Justice Council, Washington County Community Justice Program, and the Virginia County Restorative Justice Program) meetings can be either an alternative to formal sentencing, or part of the formal sentencing process, as occurs in the Queensland Programme.

The Queensland Programme is unusual for allowing victims to veto a conference altogether.[30] Victims may also consent to a conference being held, but choose not to participate. If they choose to participate, they are legally entitled to invite supporters including a solicitor, as are offenders.[31] If a matter is referred to conference by police, a police officer is required to attend each conference, although there is no requirement that this be the investigating officer.[32] If the court refers a matter, a representative of the prosecutor's office is required to attend.[33] Unlike most of the programmes surveyed, the person who prepares conference participants does not also convene the conference, this task being performed by another employee from the Queensland Department of Justice. The media are not allowed to attend conferences, but other observers can attend with the permission of participants. Convenors are legally required to provide the referral body (whether police or court) with a copy of the conference outcome.[34] Like the New South Wales Programme, outcomes are meant to be no more severe than the penalty a court would impose, and there are also legal limits on the amount of compensation and community service an offender may agree to provide.[35] An evaluation of the pilot uncovered some concerns about conferencing producing 'higher tariffs'. The report suggested that state co-ordinators of the programme 'maintain a watching brief on outcomes and advise convenors if problems are identified' (Hayes et al. 1998: 155). As with all the programmes surveyed, Pollard said outcomes are also influenced by convenors, who are responsible for articulating restorative values, 'reality testing' proposed agreements (to ensure outcomes are appropriate and achievable) and ensuring that agreements do not exceed specified limits.

A case is referred back to the original referral body if the offender fails to attend a conference, or a conference fails to reach agreement, or an offender fails to complete an agreement.[36] The Department of Justice in Queensland monitors offenders' completion of outcomes. Unlike the New South Wales conferencing model, there is no express statutory power to reconvene conferences in Queensland. Pollard

---

[30] Section 18H *Juvenile Justice Act* (1992) (Qld).
[31] Section 18D.   [32] Ibid.   [33] Ibid.
[34] Section 18E.   [35] Section 18F.   [36] Section 18J.

argues that there should be such a power when problems arise with an outcome.

One of the pilot sites was an Aboriginal community on Palm Island, off the coast of Queensland. Conferencing on Palm Island took a different form from the other sites, and raises issues relevant to a discussion of accountability. The Palm Island Programme was less formal and regulated, and conferences produced different types of outcomes to conferences held elsewhere. These outcomes often reflected customary Aboriginal laws, such as the banishment of a young person from a community. The evaluators of the pilot argue that in such communities, programmes must strike a difficult balance between respecting the principle of Aboriginal self-government and ensuring adequate procedural protections, including accountability to the formal criminal justice system (Hayes *et al.* 1998: 107).

Community Conferencing, Central City Neighbourhoods Partnership, Minneapolis

The Community Conferencing Program was established after a number of inner-city neighbourhoods in Minneapolis formed a partnership in 1994 to consider ways to reduce street crime in their neighbourhoods. The programme targets adult offenders and mainly deals with public-order misdemeanour offences, such as soliciting prostitution, public consumption of alcohol, public urination, begging, and loitering with intent to buy or sell drugs. The programme also deals with some felony offences such as theft.

Cases are usually referred to the programme from court. Where the offence is a misdemeanour, the conference becomes an alternative to formal conviction,[37] whereas with felony offences the conference outcome is part of the sentence imposed by court. Where there are direct victims, they are asked whether they wish the offender to be offered the opportunity to participate in the programme. In most instances, however, there is no direct victim, and offenders are asked whether they wish to attend a conference with a number of volunteers from the community in which the offence was committed.

---

[37] More accurately, the offence is struck from an offender's record once he or she completes the agreement.

Typically three or four community members attend, in addition to a trained volunteer convenor who asks participants questions from a script. When participants come to negotiating an outcome, a talking piece (an object such as an eagle feather) is passed around the circle from participant to participant, entitling the holder to speak without interruption. Observers can attend with the permission of participants, and police do not participate or attend conferences.

While there are no formal limits on conference outcomes, programme co-ordinator Gena Gerard says facilitators are responsible for ensuring that a proposed outcome is achievable and reflects restorative values, and after each conference Gerard also checks the outcome to ensure that it reflects restorative values.[38] Gerard says that in questionnaires sent to all participants at the conclusion of each conference, community volunteers indicated they felt they were often spending too long on individual cases, as conferences typically last between one and two hours. This has led to two changes: a single conference now often deals with two or three offenders who have committed similar offences, and offenders are provided with a short list of suggested outcomes (based on outcomes from previous cases), from which they choose and construct their own outcomes.

Originally, programme staff were responsible for monitoring agreements. Now responsibility has been devolved to conference participants, whom Gerard argues are more likely to make enforceable agreements when they know they have to enforce them. When an outcome is completed, programme staff are notified, who then in turn inform the court as well as all other participants in the conference. If an outcome is not completed the matter is sent back to court.

The CCNP programme is one of the programmes with an advisory board. While it has not lapsed completely as has the Canberra conferencing advisory board, police and prosecutors have stopped attending meetings regularly. Gerard is not sure whether this is because they trust the programme to run without their frequent input, or have lost interest in it. Two private foundations fund the programme, and it is required to submit annual reports to these.

---

[38] Gerard says that the requirement that outcomes reflect restorative values was introduced after some early conferences proposed outcomes that were considered inappropriate, but where there was no basis on which to overrule the agreement.

Waitakere District Court Restorative Justice Pilot, Auckland
In 2000 a pilot conferencing programme was established in the Waitakere District in Auckland, New Zealand. It deals with adult offenders who have committed serious, often violent, offences. The primary inspiration for this programme came from two New Zealand defence lawyers, Jim Boyack and Helen Bowen, who for a number of years have organized restorative justice conferences for clients awaiting sentencing. A four-year trial of pre-sentencing conferencing for adult offenders, along similar lines to the Waitakere programme, began in 2001 in four sites across New Zealand.

Cases are referred to conference by a sentencing judge, either at the request of one of the counsel in the case or at the judge's own initiative, and the sentencing hearing is then adjourned to allow a conference to be held. If the pilot administrator considers the case to be prima facie suitable for conference, it is in turn referred to two convenors who meet with the offender to determine if the case is suitable for conference. The West Auckland Victim Support office is also informed that a case is being considered for conference: its victim support officers are government-funded employees who work within police departments to assist victims, both in the immediate aftermath of a crime, and while the case proceeds through the criminal justice system.

If a conference is held, both victims and offenders are encouraged to bring supporters to the conference. A victim support officer may attend at the victim's request, and the offender's lawyer at the offender's.[39] Convenors also invite an offender's probation officer and the investigating officer. Both convenors attend the conference, with one primarily responsible for convening the conference, and the other for taking notes. Observers, including the media, can attend with the permission of participants. Like the New Zealand Family Group Conferencing Programme described above, conferences involving Maori offenders often begin with a Maori blessing or a Christian prayer. As with all but one of the other programmes surveyed, conferences work towards reaching some agreement about how an offender will attempt to make amends to the victim.[40]

---

[39] Victim Support officers are also entitled to attend, at a victim's request, Family Group Conferences for juveniles in New Zealand (see above).

[40] The only programme surveyed where the outcome is not a focus of a restorative justice meeting is the Texas Victim/Offender Mediation/Dialogue Program (see

At a conference's conclusion an extensive report based on the convenor's notes is sent to the sentencing judge, describing both what took place, and the details of any agreement reached between the victim and the offender.

Queensland Schools Conferencing

In 1994 the Queensland Department of Education introduced conferencing on a trial basis as a disciplinary intervention in serious incidents of misconduct. Most commonly conferences dealt with various types of physical assault, and cases involving property damage and theft. Conferences were also used to address incidents involving verbal abuse, drugs, damaging the reputation of the school, persistent disruption in class and, in one instance, a bomb threat (Thorsborne 1999: 2).

Only students who admitted to an offence were eligible for a conference. Once a decision was made to hold one, parents were contacted by telephone and asked if they wished to participate. Co-manager of the trial, Lisa Cameron, says that, in hindsight, schools should have met face-to-face with parents to discuss whether they wished a conference to go ahead.

In addition to offenders and victims, their supporters, and a convenor who was a Department of Education employee, conferences were also attended by an observer and, where possible, the school principal. Co-manager of the trial, Marg Thorsborne, argues that attendance makes the principal accountable to the other participants, and vice versa. The observer's role was to take notes and provide feedback to the convenor at the conclusion. With the consent of the participants, any others wishing to attend, typically to learn about conferencing, sat with the observer outside the participants' circle. Department of Education officials were responsible for monitoring the completion of any outcome agreed to by an offender. For evaluation purposes participants were interviewed by Department of Education staff two to three weeks after a conference, and again four months later.

below). In that programme the primary focus is on providing the victim and the offender with an opportunity to meet and talk, with no expectation that they will negotiate an agreement as to what the offender will do after the meeting. This is because the offender is already in prison, often serving a life sentence, and in some cases awaiting execution.

Fredrick H. Tuttle Middle School, South Burlington, Vermont

The Fredrick H. Tuttle Middle School in South Burlington, Vermont, is a co-educational school for students between the ages of 10 and 14. Conferencing was introduced to the school in 1995 by a local police officer. Since then, the school has run approximately four conferences a year for what vice-principal Mike Simpson calls 'fairly serious offences' such as assaults. Under regional school policy, offences classified as more serious—such as weapons violations, sale of drugs and alcohol, assaults on teachers, and extreme acts of vandalism—result in automatic suspension, and a school board hearing to determine whether the offending student should be expelled. Simpson feels that many of these cases would also be suitable for conferencing.

As in the Queensland Schools Programme, the school principal is invited to conferences along with offenders, victims, and their supporters. Conferences are convened by a range of trained people, including guidance counsellors, police officers, and members of a local youth agency. In cases where a victim or offender does not have supporters, counsellors are asked to attend in their places. A trained observer provides feedback to the convenor after the conference. Conferences are open to anyone who wishes to attend, except the media, with observers seated in a second outer circle. Conference convenors contact victims to establish whether offenders have completed outcomes: if an offender fails to complete, the school considers taking alternative disciplinary action.

Circle programmes

Navajo Peacemaking, Navajo Nation

The Navajo Nation covers about 27,000 square miles of high desert and forest mainly in the corners of Arizona, New Mexico, and Utah, and is the largest Native American reservation in the United States. In 1982 the Navajo Nation established the Navajo Peacemaker Court as part of an attempt to revive traditional Native American customs (Bluehouse and Zion 1993: 327). Authority for the Navajo court system comes from the self-governing power of American Indian tribes, which in turn has its origins in the original Native American sovereignty, limited but not abolished by inclusion within the territorial bounds of the United States. Today self-government is recognized by a combination of legal instruments including the United States Constitution, legislation, treaties, judicial decisions, and administrative practice (ALRC 1986: 27). Peacemaking is inextricably linked to Navajo spirituality. Chief Peacemaker Philmer Bluehouse explains that in Navajo cosmology people are on a journey that begins with chaos, passes through trial and error, before ultimately moving towards wisdom and healing. Navajo peacemaking aims to assist those who have committed and suffered from crime to move towards wisdom and healing. The attainment of Hozho is a central theme in peacemaking, and more broadly, Navajo cosmology. Hozho is a term that can be approximated in English by combining words such as beauty, balance, and harmony (Zion and Yazzie 1997: 79; Coker 1999: 66).

A wide variety of problems are accepted for peacemaking, including both civil and criminal offences. According to Bluehouse, the three types of problems handled by peacemaking relate to people, business, and property. People problems range from poor communication skills and drug abuse through to serious interpersonal crimes such as sexual assault and domestic violence. Business problems include civil offences such as failure to repay loans, while property problems include theft and property damage (Bluehouse: 13). One of the distinctive characteristics of this programme is that an admission of guilt is not a prerequisite for access.

The peacemaker court accepts referrals from a wide range of sources including various parts of the criminal justice system, health and community services, and from any person affected by a problem (including the offender). In cases dealing with criminal conduct, peacemaking may be in addition to, or an alternative to, formal prosecution and sentencing. Once the programme receives a case, a peacemaker invites the victim and offender and other affected parties to attend. Bluehouse says that attorneys can attend provided that 'they are not attending in attorney mode'. According to Bluehouse, it is uncommon for judges to attend. Another distinctive feature of the programme is that in general, peacemaking circles are open to everyone in the community, provided that they are willing to participate.[41] The only exception is the media, who can

---

[41] The only other programmes that are generally open are the Fredrick H. Tuttle Middle School in Vermont, the Carcross Circle Program in the Yukon Territory, the South St Paul Restorative Justice Council, and the Vermont Reparative Boards.

attend only with the permission of other participants. Meetings can range in size from three to thirty people. Peacemakers are paid a small fee by participants to convene a circle (Zion and McCabe 1982: 117). Between one and four peacemakers convene a single circle, depending on a case's complexity and peacemakers' availability. They are Navajo elders—both male and female—recognized by their peers as wise leaders. Circles usually begin with a prayer that calls for spiritual assistance (Zion and Yazzie 1997: 78), and end with a prayer of thanks. These prayers typically reflect a peacemaker's beliefs, which may be Navajo, Christian, or a combination of these belief systems. As convenors, peacemakers are expected to play a more interventionist role than convenors in most restorative justice programmes. As Philmer Bluehouse and Jim Zion (1993: 334) explain:

There are lectures on how or why the parties have violated Navajo values, have breached solidarity, or are out of harmony. Lectures are not recitations or exhortations of abstract moral principles, but practical and pragmatic examinations of the particular problem in light of Navajo values.

Storytelling is one technique often used by peacemakers: for example, in cases involving domestic violence, they may tell stories with gender egalitarian themes (Coker 1999: 59).

Peacemakers assist parties to strike agreements, which are then recorded by court-employed liaison officers. If the police or court refer a case to a circle, they receive a copy of the resulting agreement, and are entitled to request modifications to any aspect of it. The consequences of a failure to complete an outcome (which are monitored by the peacemakers) depend on the source and nature of the referral. When referrals are received from outside the criminal justice system, parties retain the right to engage that system. When they come from the criminal justice system, offenders failing to complete an outcome are referred to court for formal prosecution and sentencing, or if that has already occurred, for the possible imposition of an alternative penalty.

Carcross Circle Program, Yukon Territory

Carcross is a town of 700 people in the Yukon Territory. With the encouragement of Judge Barry Stuart, in 1992 the Carcross community began to use circles on a regular basis for juvenile and adult offences. The programme is administered by a local Justice

Committee that comprises a number of community volunteers, representatives of the criminal justice system, and other government employees such as social workers. Typically, the programme accepts cases such as theft, trespass, probation offences, and assaults.

As with most of the circle programmes surveyed, this programme accepts referrals from police, prosecutors, and judges, and circles may be run as an alternative to formal conviction and sentencing or as part of the sentencing process (in which case they are called sentencing circles). Referrals are only made to the programme at an offender's request, and with the support of another community member. Once a member of the Justice Committee has interviewed the offender, the whole Committee reviews the offender's application to decide whether to accept it. If an offender is accepted into the programme, a circle is held after the offender has drafted a plan as to how he or she will make amends to the victim, and work to prevent future offences. Victims are invited to attend a circle meeting, which is often convened by two or more community members called circle keepers.

One of the distinctive features of this programme is that where circles are part of the sentencing process, defence and prosecution lawyers and the sentencing judge participate in the circle in addition to victims, offenders, and other community members. A number of other programmes surveyed make provision for police or defence lawyers to attend, but lawyers for both sides as well as a judge attend routinely in only one other programme.[42] Lawyers make recommendations that contribute to deliberations about the outcome. In deciding on an outcome, participants can confirm, vary, or ignore the offender's pre-circle plan, although usually it is reflected in the final outcome. In the event that participants cannot reach agreement, the hearing may be adjourned or the judge may impose a sentence. Circles are usually held in a community hall, and proceedings are usually recorded electronically.

The public, including the media, are welcome to attend provided they are prepared to participate rather than just observe. In cases where sensitive information may be discussed in the course of the circle hearing there is provision to hold an earlier circle closed to the public, where the sensitive information is discussed.

---

[42] i.e. the South St Paul Restorative Justice Council. In sentencing circles, the judge, defence, and prosecutor always attend (LaPrairie 1995: 84).

Where circles take place as part of the sentencing process, an offender retains a right to appeal the outcome, but Carsten Erbe, who worked with the Carcross Program, says that he does not know of any instance of an offender exercising this right. A second, follow-up circle attended by the same people who attended the original circle is held to monitor an offender's progress. If an offender fails to complete an outcome, the Justice Committee notifies the referral agency, which may take further action.

Northside Community Justice Committee, Minneapolis

The Northside Community Justice Committee is the product of a collaboration between the Minnesota Department of Corrections and the North Minneapolis African American community. In 1997 the Department of Corrections invited Judge Barry Stuart to conduct training for community leaders in the African American community.[43]

The programme accepts a range of referrals, though most are for property and assault offences. Referrals are accepted from police, prosecutors, and judges. In police and prosecutor referrals, as well as pre-conviction court referrals, the programme acts as an alternative to formal conviction and sentencing. In post-conviction court referrals, the programme acts as part of the formal sentencing process.

The most distinctive feature of this programme is the comprehensiveness and length of intervention. In the majority of programmes an intervention consists of a single meeting. In contrast, the Northside committee usually holds five or six meetings for a single offender, as well as providing mentoring to young offenders between meetings. The first circle is an introductory meeting attended by a

---

[43] Authorization for the programme is provided by Minnesota Statute 611A. 775 (1998) which states that: 'a community-based organization, in collaboration with a local government unit, may establish a restorative justice programme. A restorative justice programme is a programme that provides forums where certain individuals charged with or petitioned for having committed an offence meet with the victim, if appropriate; the victim's family members or other supportive persons, if appropriate; the offender's family members or other supportive persons, if appropriate; a law enforcement official or prosecutor when appropriate; other criminal justice system professionals when appropriate; and members of the community, in order to: i) discuss the impact of the offence on the victim and the community; ii) provide support to the victim and methods for reintegrating the victim into community life; iii) assign an appropriate sanction to the offender; and iv) provide methods for reintegrating the offender into community life.'

number of unpaid community volunteers (mainly young African Americans), as well as the offender and his or her supporters. The crime itself is not mentioned: instead, the young person's interests and needs are discussed, and individual members of the circle volunteer to act as mentors. In the circle that I attended, two volunteers said they would watch the young person play basketball, and another that she would help him with his maths homework. At the end of this meeting, both volunteers and offender decide whether they wish to proceed.

In a subsequent circle, the crime is discussed and the offender agrees to do a number of things, assisted by the volunteers. The victim does not attend this circle, instead attending a third circle, which is not attended by the offender. This provides support for victims even when they do not agree to meet offenders. If the victim does agree to meet the offender this happens in a fourth circle. A follow-up circle is then held (which victims may or may not attend) when the volunteers again meet with the offender to monitor progress. The final meeting is a celebration circle where the volunteers, the offender, and his or her family, and the victims (if they wish to attend) meet to celebrate the offender's completion of his commitments. The whole process can take over twelve months. Observers, including the media, can attend each of these meetings with the permission of other participants.

South St Paul Restorative Justice Council, St Paul

The South St Paul Restorative Justice Council (SSPRJC) was established in 1996, primarily through the efforts of a group of local community members, local judges, and the district superintendent of schools. The programme accepts cases from schools, police, the county attorney, and judges. In the vast majority of cases a circle is an alternative either to formal conviction and sentencing by the criminal justice system, or to traditional school disciplinary sanctions. In a minority of cases, circles are run as part of the formal sentencing process. The bulk of cases handled by the programme involve misdemeanour offences, although it also accepts some felony cases (such as assault), and some cases from schools dealing with conduct which is objectionable but not criminal (such as teasing). The programme is administered by two full-time staff who also convene circles.

The SSPRJC is one of the small number of programmes where both victim and offender consent is required before a meeting can be held. If either refuses, the case is sent back to the referral agency. If both consent, a circle keeper invites the victim, offender, and their supporters to attend a meeting. A second circle may assist convene the meeting. Circles are also attended by community volunteers and, in cases referred by the criminal justice system, a judge and a representative of the County Attorney's office. District Judge Leslie Metzen anticipates that as the programme becomes more established, judges will be content to receive reports at the conclusion of circles, rather than attending themselves. Assistant County Attorney, Mary Theisen, points out that it is very time-consuming for a representative of the County Attorney's office to attend every circle.

As with many other programmes, circles begin and end with prayers or readings. Most of the time during circle discussions a talking piece is passed around which allows the holder to speak without interruption. Meetings aim to reach an agreement an offender can complete, and the talking piece is passed around until participants reach consensus. Meetings can be lengthy, with an individual circle sometimes lasting up to five or six hours.[44] SSPRJC planner, Michael Stanefski, says that when it is not possible to reach consensus in one sitting, it is sometimes necessary to adjourn a meeting for some days. Circles are open to anyone who wishes to attend, on condition that they participate rather than sit outside the circle as an observer.

At the conclusion of the circle, the convenor gives a report to the referral body. Participants are also told that if they are unhappy with the circle outcome they can complain to the convenor, or another nominated person.

The common practice of the SSPRJC is to convene a second circle to monitor whether the agreement reached in the initial circle has been fulfilled (Coates *et al.* 2000: 26). In theory, the case is sent back to the referral agency for further action if an offender fails to complete an outcome, but an evaluation of the programme has found that, in practice, the programme is reluctant to send cases back and 'matters tend to drag on and on' (Coates *et al.* 2000: 57).

---

[44] Generally it appears that conferences, and sentencing panels sessions are shorter than circle meetings.

Zwelethemba Peacemaker Committee, Western Cape

With the support of the South African government, Clifford Shearing established the Community Peace Foundation (CPF) in 1992, in the period between the lifting of the ban on the ANC and other liberation movements in February 1990 and the first national democratic elections in April 1994. Its brief was to rethink policing, in the broadest sense, in post-apartheid South Africa. In 1997 the CPF was dissolved and succeeded by the Community Peacemaking Programme (CPP), a programme consistent with the community approach to policing advocated by the CPF, and funded by the South African and overseas governments (originally Sweden and then Finland).

The CPP began working with the local community in Zwelethemba, a township 120 kilometres outside Cape Town, to develop a community-based conflict resolution process using peace committees. Based on the model developed in Zwelethemba, a number of other South African townships have established their own peace committees, or are in the process of doing so.[45] In Cape Town, a small group of full-time staff assists in the establishment of new peace committees and oversees the maintenance of existing ones.

The peace committees comprise local township residents engaged in two separate activities: peacemaking and peace-building. In the peacemaking process, members attempt to help community members resolve specific conflicts, while the peace-building process aims to address the structural problems underlying conflicts, such as extreme poverty and the chronic lack of employment opportunities and basic amenities.[46]

Of the programmes surveyed, the Zwelethemba Peace Committee handles the widest range of conflicts. As well as a wide range of criminal cases (from minor assaults to serious violent crime including domestic violence and rape), the committee addresses other types

---

[45] In addition to Zwelethemba, the townships with functioning peace committees are Strand/Nomzamo, Paarl/Fairyland, Mbekweni (Blocks E, F, G, and H, and Thembani), Fransch Hoek, and Beaufort West. Peace Committees are also active in Thabong (Free State), Cala and Elliot (Eastern Cape) and Umlazi and Inanda (Durban, KwaZulu-Natal). A programme based on the Zwelethemba model has also recently been established in Rosario, Argentina.

[46] Among restorative justice programmes this peace-building feature is quite unique (Roche 2002).

of legal problems (relating to contract, property, family, and succession law) and 'non-legal' problems (such as infidelity, noise disturbances, and insults). The peace committee is also unusual in that it does not receive cases from the criminal justice system, instead relying on community members (usually victims) to come forward to request its assistance.[47] Another distinctive feature is that an offender is not required to admit an offence to gain access to the programme.[48]

Peace committee members—comprising township men and women of all ages—convene peacemaking gatherings. Between two and ten members usually convene a single meeting (Shearing 2001: 18), for which they receive a small stipend from the CPP. For each case the peace committee handles it receives a small amount of money from the CPP, which is used to finance peace-building activities and a loan fund for local micro-enterprises, as well as to pay the committee's administration expenses. Peace-building funds have been used to build a children's playground and refurbish an old-age home. Examples of loans include support for a small business selling cooked food, and for another selling knitted stockings (Shearing 2001: 11).

Peace gatherings begin in an unusual fashion for restorative justice programmes: committee members first separate the affected parties and take written statements from them, before bringing the parties together to read the statements to them. Shearing says that this process allows basic facts to be established without unnecessary disagreement and emotional stress, and provides an unintimidating environment in which victims can make allegations which peace committee members can then articulate to the group. That a fact-finding mechanism must be incorporated into the restorative process reflects the almost total absence of state police to conduct this sort of investigation.

---

[47] While this has been the case in Zwelethemba, CPP Manager John Cartwright says that in other townships, some magistrates and police are referring cases to peace committees. In these cases circles are an alternative to formal processing, and the committee is not required to seek the magistrate's or police's approval for an outcome, nor notify them of an offender's completion of that outcome.

[48] The only other programme surveyed that also imposes no such requirement is the Navajo Peacemaking Program.

Participants then work towards a consensus agreement about how to repair the harm that has been caused. Members of the public, except for the media, can attend with the permission of other participants.[49] Peace committee members encourage the participants to end the circle in some way that will show that they have made peace, for instance, by shaking hands, or saying a prayer (Shearing 2001: 11).

Peace committee members prepare a report on each meeting that is later collected by a CPP fieldworker (Cartwright undated). The criminal justice system does not receive reports of meetings, or copies of outcomes. There is no formal monitoring of the completion of outcomes: committees rely on the victim to come back to them if the offender does not complete the outcome, or indeed if the victim is dissatisfied for any reason. Nor does the criminal justice system intervene when an offender fails to complete an outcome. In this event, however, peace committee members may encourage a victim to go to the police and make a formal complaint about the original offence.

Under a code of good practice, peace committee members make a number of commitments: to respect the South African constitution, to not use force or take sides, and to aim to heal and not hurt. This code is an important source of authority and guidance for the peace committee. Flyers printed in Xhosa, Zulu, Afrikaan, and English are distributed around the townships to promote the peace committees and to advertise the code, as well as to provide names and addresses of peace committee members. The code is read aloud at the beginning of each peacemaking gathering, and is often again referred to by peace committee members during a gathering. When community members become peace committee members they are given six-month renewable licences, and failure to follow the code of good practice is a ground for not renewing a peacemaker's licence. Government proposals for the regulation of peace committees would also make a committee's registration and funding conditional upon the use of such a code.

---

[49] John Cartwright says that the media are not allowed to attend as it 'would be too easy for the press to seize on one juicy morsel' and ruin the good work of the programme. A similar justification underlies the restrictions placed on media attendance in the Navajo Peacemaking Program.

Sentencing panels

Reparative Boards, Department of Corrections, Vermont

The Department of Corrections in Vermont established reparative boards in 1996 after an earlier public survey that it commissioned showed strong support for community reparative boards for non-violent offences as a way of dealing with overcrowded prisons (Walther and Perry 1997). The state-wide programme deals with non-violent offences of both a misdemeanour and felony nature committed by juveniles and adults. These include property offences, such as theft and damage, and drink-driving offences.

Judges may refer offenders to the programme after they have been convicted as part of the formal sentencing process. Offenders may elect not to appear before a board, and instead receive their full sentence from the judge. Before attending a board hearing, an offender participates in an intake process run by the Court and Reparative Services Unit (Walther and Perry 1997: 29), where the offender's probation status, and the reparative programme and goals are explained.

Reparative board hearings are usually attended by the offender, between three to five board members, and where the offender is a juvenile, one or more of the offender's parents or guardians. Board members are drawn from a large panel of unpaid community workers. As with other sentencing panels, victims rarely attend hearings, although according to John Perry, the Director of Planning for the Vermont Department of Corrections, they now attend more frequently than when the programme was first established—partly because in the past they were seldom invited (VDC undated). As with other restorative justice programmes, meetings revolve around discussing the incident and negotiating an outcome that makes amends for the harm the offender has caused.

Offenders are not entitled to bring attorneys with them to a hearing. Perry says attorneys are contrary to the spirit of the programme, which is about providing speedy community justice. Lawyers would delay this process and 'justice delayed is justice denied'. Perry also says that as an offender's 'liberty is not at threat', legal representation is unnecessary. The public—including the media—are welcome to attend hearings, and do not require the permission of participants to do so. Perry says the Department of Corrections intends to cable-cast Reparative Board hearings in the future. Staff from the Department of Corrections attend meetings regularly as a form of internal review, while other board members are encouraged to attend to provide peer review as well as to learn from other board members.

Offenders are required to attend a follow-up meeting with board members (although not necessarily with the same members who attended the original meeting) to review the offender's completion of the outcome plan. When offenders complete their obligations, the Board reports this fact to the court and notifies the victim. If offenders do not complete outcomes, the Board notifies the relevant probation officer who in turn notifies the court that the offender has breached probation.

Toronto Community Council

Since 1992 the Toronto Community Council has run a restorative justice programme for adult Aboriginal offenders living in Toronto. The programme was established after a lengthy period of consultation between Aboriginal Legal Services of Toronto (ALST) (which administers the programme), the prosecutor's office, and the Aboriginal community, including Aboriginal elders (Moyer and Axon 1993: v; RCAP 1996: 149–51). It accepts a wide range of offences up to, and including, serious assaults, and is open to people regardless of their criminal record (RCAP 1996: 150).

Referrals are usually made before an offender is convicted, and the programme acts as an alternative to formal conviction. It relies upon a wide range of people working in the criminal justice system to identify cases that might be suitable including police, prosecutors, judges, defendant lawyers, court-workers employed by ALST, court chaplains, probation officers, bail programme staff, and offenders themselves (Moyer and Axon 1993: 53). The approval of the prosecutor's office is required in all cases. Project director, Jonathan Rudin, says that in serious cases victim approval is also sought.

If prosecutorial approval is forthcoming, offenders are then asked whether they accept responsibility for the offence and wish to participate in the programme. If the answer is 'yes' to both questions, the charges are withdrawn, and a hearing is scheduled. Three council members usually attend Council hearings, as well as the offender and his or her supporters. Council members are unpaid workers from local Aboriginal communities. Full-time Council staff try to select members with backgrounds that may be helpful to the particular offender, such as experience with overcoming alcohol addiction (ALST 1991). Victims are invited but rarely attend. If they do attend, they are asked whether they wish to meet offenders face-to-face, or meet with the Council separately and allow Council members to communicate their wishes to the offender.

While offenders are encouraged to bring a supporter to the meeting, the Council may ask the latter to sit outside the room during the hearing if it considers that the supporter is a source of the offender's problems.

Council meetings are not open to the public. Originally it was intended that meetings should be open except when hearings dealt with sensitive information, but Rudin says that the Council discovered that 'virtually all hearings are about things that are intensely personal' and so hearings were closed to the public. Researchers and Aboriginal groups can attend with participants' permission.

As with other restorative justice programmes, participants aim to reach some agreement about what an offender will do to put things right. The process for reaching this agreement is, however, slightly unusual. After discussing the offence, the Council asks the offender to leave the room while it considers an appropriate outcome. This outcome is then presented to the offender who can agree or disagree. If the offender disagrees, the participants keep deliberating until they reach agreement. A hearing can be reconvened if necessary.

The programme is also unusual in that it places very little emphasis on monitoring an offender's completion of an outcome plan; offenders are simply encouraged to ring the Council when they complete their plan. Nor is there any penalty for failing to complete an outcome (or for that matter, failing to attend a hearing), other than not being considered for referral to the programme for any future offences.

Restorative Justice Programme

The Vancouver Restorative Justice Programme (VRJP) established in 1999 is based on the Toronto Community Council, and with a few exceptions is identical. Differences relate to the criteria for eligibility to enter the programme, the role of Council members, and the monitoring of outcomes.

First, the programme does not cover the wide range of offences accepted by the Toronto Community Council: only first-time offenders who commit misdemeanour offences are eligible. The prosecutor's office insisted that the programme prove its competence in relation to less serious offences before being allowed to deal with more serious ones.

Other differences include expectations that every meeting will be attended by an elder, and that a council member will volunteer to act as mentor to the offender after the meeting. VRJP director, Barry Warhaft, says that ideally offenders would be matched with council members of the same ethnicity (for example, Cree Nation offenders with Cree Nation council members), but admits that often this is not logistically possible and that, in any event, many offenders do not have a strong connection with their culture.

The final difference is that there is more emphasis on monitoring completion of outcomes. If the prosecutor does not receive from the VRJP notification of an offender's completion within six months of a hearing date, offenders are formally prosecuted for the original offence.

Young Offender Panels, England and Wales

In England a series of juvenile justice legislative reforms have been introduced under the *Crime and Disorder Act* (1998) and the *Youth Justice and Criminal Evidence Act* (1999). Depending on the seriousness of an offence, an offender may be referred for a reprimand, a warning, or to court. Investigating police administer reprimands, while final warnings are administered either by police or youth offending teams (YOTs). YOTs are multi-agency teams charged with co-ordinating the provision of youth justice in their local areas. As a minimum requirement a YOT must consist of a probation officer, a local authority social worker, a police officer, a representative of the local health authority, and a person nominated by the chief education officer. Police and YOTs are encouraged to use conferences as a final warning.[50]

Most offenders convicted for the first time in court will be referred automatically to a Youth Offender Panel, unless the crime

---

[50] Home Office guidelines (HOYJB 2000) refer interchangeably to restorative warnings and restorative conferences. This is the basis on which the Thames Valley police continue to run conferences (see above).

is serious enough to warrant custody or the court orders an absolute discharge.[51] Referral to the panel is treated as the entire sentence.[52] Panels have recently been established nationally following the introduction of pilot panels in eleven areas across England and Wales.[53] While it is anticipated that panels will vary, they must consist of at least two community representatives, one of whom chairs the meeting, together with one YOT member. Volunteers can become community representatives after undertaking nearly seventy hours of training. The panels seek to involve offenders, their families,[54] victims and their supporters, and youth offending team members in drawing up an agreed 'contract'. Where there is no direct victim, the panel may wish to invite someone who can bring a victim's perspective to the meeting, for example 'a local business person or an individual who has suffered a similar offence'.[55] It is a matter for local YOTs to decide whether lawyers should also attend. Panel meetings are not open to the public, and are intended to be held in informal, non-institutional venues close to where the young offender lives, but not in an offender's home.[56]

The panels draw eclectically on a number of older programmes. From within the United Kingdom they explicitly draw on the Scottish Children's Hearing system, and implicitly on the history of victim/offender mediation and the development of restorative cautioning by the Thames Valley Police, while from outside they draw on the New Zealand Family Group Conferencing model (Crawford and Newburn 2002: 479).

Over a period of between three and twelve months (determined by the court in the original referral order[57]), a panel meets with an

---

[51] For future offences an offender cannot receive the same, or less serious intervention again. So, for example, an offender who has received a warning cannot receive another warning or reprimand for future offences, and an offender can only be referred once to a youth offender panel.

[52] Although a referral order to court can be accompanied by ancillary orders, such as orders for costs, compensation, forfeiture of items used in committing an offence, or exclusion from football matches (section 4(2) and (3) *Youth Justice and Criminal Evidence Act* (1999)).

[53] The pilots are in Blackburn with Darwen, Nottingham, Nottinghamshire, Suffolk, Cardiff, Oxfordshire, Swindon, Wiltshire, Hammersmith and Fulham, Kensington and Chelsea, and the City of Westminster.

[54] s 5(5) and (6) *Youth Justice and Criminal Evidence Act* (1999).

[55] Para 3.31 The Guidance.

[56] Para 3.38 The Guidance.

[57] Section 3(6) *Youth Justice and Criminal Evidence Act* (1999).

offender on a number of occasions (although it does not always consist of the same members for each meeting). The first meeting is expected to take place within fifteen working days of the court hearing at which the referral is made.[58] At this time the panel conducts a full examination of the reasons for the offending behaviour, and devises a programme of activity aimed at tackling the behaviour and preventing reoffending. This includes an element of reparation, either directly to the victim or to the community at large. Outcomes do not require a victim's approval. This is very unusual among programmes surveyed. If agreement cannot be reached, or the offender does not turn up to the meeting, the matter is referred back to court.

At subsequent meetings an offender's completion of the contract is monitored. If an offender successfully completes the obligations in a referral order period, the conviction will be considered 'spent'. However, if an offender fails to complete the agreement, the matter is referred back to court. When an offender is referred back to it for any reason, the court considers the circumstances of the referral before deciding whether to revoke the original order and resentence the young offender.

Mediation programmes

Victim/Offender Mediation/Dialogue Program, Texas

In December 1993 the Victim Services Division of the Texas Department of Criminal Justice established as one of its services the Victim/ Offender Mediation/Dialogue Program (VOM/D). This deals with a wide range of serious offences, including murder and attempted murder, aggravated sexual assault, and robbery. VOM/D Program co-ordinator David Doerfler says that over half the cases it deals with are murder cases. A large number of US states now run prison-based mediation programmes.

Unlike most programmes that receive referrals from some part of the criminal justice system, the VOM/D Program waits for victims, or in murder cases, the deceased's family, to request its

---

[58] The evaluation of the pilot found a low level of compliance with this deadline (31%), in light of which the deadline has been extended to 20 days (Newburn *et al.* 2002: 23–4).

assistance.[59] Victims learn about the programme from a variety of sources, including a victim's advocate employed by the District Attorney's office. Once a victim has approached the programme, the offender is then asked if he or she wishes to participate. To be accepted an offender must admit to the offence in question. Participation is not an alternative to formal conviction and sentencing. Most offenders are already serving long sentences in prison for the offence, and Doerfler (undated) stresses that 'participation by the offender cannot be expected to enhance any chances for commutation of sentence or for any kind of clemency action'.[60] In some cases offenders on death row have been executed after their participation in the programme (Umbreit and Vos 2000).[61] Although offenders do not receive any favourable treatment in return for participation, victims do retain the right to make submissions to the parole board, and some victims have chosen to make submissions in an offender's favour.

If the offender agrees to participate, the case is referred to a mediator, who begins a preparation phase that typically lasts between six months and two years. This is far longer than the preparation phase in any other programme surveyed. The programme has approximately forty unpaid community workers who undertake ninety-six hours of training to become mediators. The mediator is responsible for explaining the process to both the victim and offender, and assisting them in the completion of extensive workbooks designed to encourage critical thinking about the offence and its repercussions. During this preparation phase, victim services staff also work with offenders to identify reasons why they committed the offence, as well as ways in which they may begin to address their

[59] This is similar to the Zwelethemba Peacemaking Committee. The programme sometimes also receives requests from offenders but will not approach victims to ask if they wish to participate, instead waiting for victims to come to them. This is done to try and ensure victims are not further traumatized by pressure to participate.

[60] The Texas Department of Criminal Justice web-site (TDCJ 2000) also stresses that 'The VOM/D is a personal process between victim and offender and is not intended to have any bearing on the participating offender's status in the judicial, appellate or corrections systems.'

[61] Many readers may have difficulties with including such a programme in a survey of restorative justice programmes, but the programme is included on the basis that it reflects restorative processes and values within the limits set by the Department of Criminal Justice.

victims' needs. During the preparation phase the mediator may also conduct indirect, or shuttle mediation, between the parties, relaying a victim's questions to the offender. Also during this phase mediators meet with a group of approximately ten other mediators to discuss their progress, and provide other mediators with an opportunity to ask questions about their individual approach.

At the conclusion of the preparation phase, the mediator and the victim services division staff decide whether to proceed to a face-to-face meeting between the victim and the offender. They do not proceed if they think the victim or offender will be victimized by the process. If a face-to-face meeting is held, it takes place in prison, and is attended by the offender, the victim, and either one or two mediators. While offenders do not usually bring a supporter, a supporter accompanies the victim in approximately 50 per cent of cases. Unlike other restorative justice programmes, the supporter cannot participate, and is asked to sit at the back of the room or to wait outside.[62] The public cannot attend, but mediation sessions are recorded on audio and videotape. These tapes are made available for the victim and offender to review at the conclusion of the conference and, if they agree, are also made available for viewing by people training to become mediators, the media, researchers, and other members of the public.

Meetings between victims and offenders typically last for six to eight hours. In murder cases, family members often bring photo albums of the deceased person which they show to the offender, and refer to when discussing the impact of the crime. David Doerfler (1997) says that the mediation process is not settlement driven, but that parties may make some agreement if they wish. This may involve the offender agreeing to write to the victims, or to pay money to a charity in the victim's honour. At the conclusion of the mediation, the mediator speaks separately with the parties as part of a 'debriefing process'. Afterwards, victim services staff conduct follow-up work with the victim and offender in order to evaluate the mediation process as well as to determine whether either party requests additional mediation. As agreements are not enforceable there is no formal monitoring and enforcement, but programme staff do contact offenders to encourage them to fulfil their commitments.

---

[62] Doerfler says only people who have been through the extensive preparation phase are expected to speak.

Multi-form programmes

'Just Youth' Project, Spectrum Youth & Family Services, Burlington

In 1998 Spectrum, a private non-profit agency, established a restorative justice programme for juveniles between the ages of 10 and 17 in Chittenden County, Vermont. The programme accepts misdemeanours and some felonies, as well as offences committed within schools. Referrals come from police, prosecutors, schools, and in some instances directly from young people involved in conflict. Police are entitled to refer misdemeanour cases directly to the programme. Felony cases must be referred to the prosecutor's office which then decides whether to refer them.

After referral, programme staff contact offenders to ask whether they want to participate. If so, staff (who are trained social workers) talk with offenders to gather information about the offender's antecedents. Staff also contact victims to ask 'what would meet their needs'—they have no formal power to deny offenders access to a programme, but if they express a preference that a case go to court, programme staff pass those views on to police. Staff select an appropriate intervention, taking into account the wishes of the victim and the offender. This may be one or a combination of a number of interventions including victim impact panels, competency classes, various types of mediation, conferences, and referrals to appropriate services (for example, to a substance abuse programme).

Conferences are convened by two people, with one playing a lead role and the other mainly observing. As well as the victim and offender, conferences are usually attended by their supporters, and often a local police officer. Observers, including the media, can attend with the permission of all participants. At the conclusion of the conference, a summary report is sent to the referral agency, although the referral agency is not required to approve the outcome.

As with a number of the other programmes, at the conclusion of the conference all participants are asked to complete surveys in which they are asked to evaluate the conference process. If it appears an offender is likely not to complete the outcome from a conference, or to comply with other aspects of the intervention, co-ordinators keep the police informed. When it becomes apparent that offenders will not complete their commitments they are sent back to the referral agency.

Washington County Community Justice, Minneapolis

In 1995 Washington County Department of Court Services established a restorative justice programme for juvenile and adult offenders. A wide range of offences are eligible for the programme, from non-violent misdemeanours through to violent assaults including rape and murder (Roberts and Masters 1999: 65). All referrals come from court: most cases are referred post-sentence, but occasionally judges in consultation with the prosecutor will refer cases pre-sentence. Offenders must admit their guilt and be willing to participate.

At the outset, the victim is asked whether he or she would like to meet the offender. If not, he or she is offered the opportunity to communicate with the offender through a third party. Failing that, victims are asked whether they would like to be reimbursed for any financial costs associated with the crime. If a victim nominates an amount, this is taken to the probation officer who can impose an amount or ask for an evidentiary hearing. If a victim does not find any option acceptable the case is referred to a judge, but Community Justice Programme Co-ordinator, Carolyn McLeod, says this has never happened.

Each meeting is convened by two community volunteers, with more experienced facilitators paired with less experienced ones. McLeod says that co-facilitators form an important 'check and balance' on the process, which 'ensures the process keeps its integrity'. She says the practice of using co-facilitators is also some safeguard against the risk of vigilantism. Conferences vary enormously in size—the largest involving up to one hundred people. McLeod says these people participate because they are all affected by an incident, and meetings are closed to anyone not affected.

A contract is made between the parties. As with many of the programmes surveyed, McLeod as supervisor assesses every agreement, and will contact the parties if she thinks any unsuitable. For instance, in one case involving the theft of twenty dollars, the victim and offender agreed that the latter would complete one hundred hours of community service. McLeod called the victim, pointing out that the court might find this unacceptable, and suggested reducing the number of hours. The victim readily agreed, saying that the number of hours was never important. In pre-sentence cases, the agreement goes back to court for its approval or variation.

A copy of this contract is sent to the probation office and to members of Victim Witness, a victim's advocacy service within the Prosecutor's office. If they are dissatisfied with an outcome they discuss it with McLeod, and attempt to persuade her to encourage the parties to change their original agreement.

The programme monitors an offender's completion of the outcome plan, and if not completed, the matter is referred back to court.

Restorative Justice Program, Prince William County, Virginia

Since December 1998 the Virginia Office of Dispute Resolution has run a restorative justice programme for juvenile offenders between the ages of 9 and 18. The programme accepts a wide range of offences referred by police, Juvenile Court Services (JCS), prosecutors, and judges.

Once the programme receives referrals it approaches offenders to ask whether they want to participate. When the programme was first established, if the victim and offender did not want to participate in a conference, then the matter was sent back to court. However, with time the programme has changed to offer a range of options, from which offenders and victims can choose. For victims who do not want to participate in a conference with the offender, programme co-ordinator Phyllis Turner Lawrence offers shuttle mediation, surrogate victims, and a victim impact programme. In consultation with both victim and offender, Turner Lawrence decides upon an appropriate intervention.

The victim impact programme is designed for offenders, and modelled on programmes developed in Norfolk and Oregon. Run over five sessions, it offers the opportunity for offenders to learn about victimization and the legal system, as well as to meet representative victims. Offenders are given tasks to complete in between sessions, such as thinking about their own crime. The programme may be used as an intervention by itself or to prepare offenders before a conference, encouraging them to think about whom they may have hurt, and giving them an opportunity to practise describing what happened.

For those cases where a direct face-to-face conference is convened, there is still some flexibility as to its nature. Originally, convenors were trained by Real Justice and used a scripted approach to conferencing, but some facilitators complained that the script was inflexible. The guiding principle for the programme is to allow people to choose a process with which they are comfortable. Convenors are unpaid community workers. Most meetings have a single convenor, although if the programme can attract more volunteers Turner Lawrence would like to use co-convenors, to act both as a check on the process, and specifically as a check on each other's performance. Researchers and members of the public are allowed to observe conferences if participants consent.

At the end of the intervention a brief report is made to the referral body. Turner Lawrence checks with the participants that they do not object to such a report being made. At the conclusion, all participants are asked to complete a questionnaire about their participation.

Turner Lawrence monitors outcomes and when they are completed, notifies both the victim and referral service. The tailored, one-off nature of agreements can pose problems for monitoring compliance. An example of this was a 12-year-old boy who agreed to make amends for stealing the victim's car by writing a letter to the victim each year on the anniversary of the theft until he reached the age of 18.

Connections Program, Minnesota Correctional Facility, Red Wing

The state-run Minnesota Correctional Facility in Red Wing (MCF-RW) is for juvenile males between the ages of 12 and 20, and takes 'only serious, violent and chronic offenders'. Since 1998 it has run a restorative justice programme called 'Connections' for offenders approaching the end of their sentence.

There are a range of sources of referrals, says programme manager Kelly Pribyl, including 'caseworkers, cottage staff, teachers and other MCF-RW staff, probation officers and victims, but many referrals come from residents themselves'. The programme is completely voluntary. After a referral, staff work with a resident to identify those he has hurt.

Depending on a number of factors, an offender will participate in one to four or more community meetings. Kelly Pribyl explains that the form of meeting used is determined by participants, and may be family group conferencing, victim/offender mediation, community conferencing, or a circle process. 'We do not take a cookie cutter approach to the kids or the communities we work with', Pribyl says. Participants may include facility staff, community workers who will assist an offender upon his release, and victims of the offender's prior offences. Together, participants negotiate an agreement about what the youth will do upon leaving the correctional facility. The meeting does not have responsibility for negotiating release dates but conditions of probation may be determined. Victims are not entitled to ask for material reparation, but may seek assurances about their safety once an offender is released.

At a second meeting, which takes place approximately two months after the youth has left MCF-RW and while he is living at a community placement, the group discusses the youth's progress and his plans for returning to the community. Participants express 'their concerns and expectations for his return and they offer their assistance in helping him to adjust' (Pribyl 1999). At this meeting the agreement is reviewed and changes are made if necessary, to accommodate new needs arising from the young person's transition from community placement back into the community.

A third meeting is held two months after the youth has moved full time back into the community, by which time 'the youth has had the opportunity to see what is going well, to determine where his own weak spots are, and to decide where other outside obstacles to his success lie' (Pribyl 1999). At this meeting, the 'community group reviews the youth's progress and provides supportive direction and feedback'.

A fourth and usually final meeting occurs within two weeks of parole completion. This meeting is a celebration, and 'is an acknowledgment of the youth's successes and a celebration of his reintegration into the community'. Pribyl (1999: 2) explains the importance of this celebration: 'These boys have often seen little success in their lives and when they do succeed, it is rarely acknowledged.' There is no mechanism for monitoring completion of outcomes.

Appendix B: Observations of Restorative Justice Meetings

Type of process	Location of programme	Number of meetings observed
Conference	Australian Federal Police, Canberra, Australian Capital Territory	two
Conference	Woodbury Public Safety, Woodbury, Minnesota	two
Conference	Youth Justice Conferencing, Department of Juvenile Justice, New South Wales	eight
Conference	Connections Program, Minnesota Corrections Facility, Red Wing	one
Circle	Northside Community Justice Committee, Minneapolis, Minnesota	one
Circle	South St Paul Restorative Justice Council, St Paul, Minnesota	one
Circle	Zwelethemba Peacemaker Committee, Cape Town	four
Circle	Waseskun House Healing Lodge, Quebec	one
Sentencing Panel	Reparative Boards, Department of Corrections, Burlington, Vermont	two
Mediation	Victim/Offender Mediation/ Dialogue Program, Texas Department of Criminal Justice, Austin, Texas	three
Mediation	Restorative Justice Program, North Minneapolis	one

Appendix C: Interviewees

Conference programmes

Family Group Conferencing, New Zealand

Ms Helen Bowen, Barrister/Mediator, Restorative Justice Trust, Auckland

Police Conferencing, Wagga Wagga, NSW, Australia

Mr Terry O'Connell, formerly New South Wales Police Service, now REAL Justice Australia, Springwood, New South Wales

Australian Federal Police Conferencing, Canberra, ACT, Australia

Mr Jeff Knight, Diversionary Conferencing Unit, Australian Federal Police, Canberra

Mr Bob Sobey, Diversionary Conferencing Unit, Australian Federal Police, Canberra

Woodbury Police Conferencing, MN, United States

Mr Dave Hines, Woodbury Public Safety, Minnesota

Thames Valley Police Restorative Justice Programme

Dr Marie Hilder, Thames Valley Police, England

Sir Charles Pollard, former Chief Constable, Thames Valley Police, England

Youth Justice Conferencing, NSW, Australia

Ms Jenny Bargen, Director, Youth Justice Conferencing, Department of Juvenile Justice, Sydney, New South Wales

Mr Peter Brock, Conference Administrator, Youth Justice Conferencing, Department of Juvenile Justice, Blacktown, Sydney

Ms Marcia Ella Duncan, Chair Aboriginal Justice Advisory Council, New South Wales

Mr Richard Funston, Senior Solicitor, Children's Legal Service, New South Wales Legal Aid, Sydney

Mr James McDougall, Operations Co-ordinator, Youth Justice Conferencing, Department of Juvenile Justice, Sydney

Dr Patrick Power, Chair, New South Wales Youth Justice Conferencing Advisory Committee

Ms Michaela Wengert, Conference Administrator, Youth Justice Conferencing, Department of Juvenile Justice, Queanbeyan, New South Wales

Community Conferencing, QLD, Australia

Mr Jason Kidd, Case Worker, Community Conferencing, Families, Youth and Community Care, Queensland

Ms Gail Pollard, Project Officer, Community Conferencing, Youth Justice Program, Families, Youth and Community Care, Queensland

Community Conferencing, Central City Neighbourhoods Partnership, MN, United States

Ms Gena Gerard, Program Co-ordinator, Community Conferencing, Central City Neighbourhoods Partnership, Minnesota

Waitakere District Court Restorative Justice Pilot, Auckland, New Zealand

Mr Jim Boyack, Barrister/Mediator, Restorative Justice Trust, Auckland

Ms Kathryn Lawlor, Manager, West Auckland Victim Support, Waitakere Police Headquarters, Henderson, Auckland

Mrs Helen Marshall, Administrator, Restorative Justice Trust, Waitakere Restorative Justice Pilot, Auckland

School Conferencing, Sunshine Coast, QLD, Australia

Ms Lisa Cameron, Acting Manager, Queensland Education, Brisbane, Queensland

Ms Marg Thorsborne, formerly Queensland Education, now Transformative Justice Australia (Queensland), Buderim, Queensland

Fredrick H. Tuttle Middle School, South Burlington, VT, United States

Mr Mike Simpson, Assistant Principal, Fredrick H. Tuttle Middle School, South Burlington, Vermont

Circle programmes

Navajo Peacemaking, Navajo Nation, AZ, United States

Mr Philmer Bluehouse, Co-ordinator, Navajo Peacemaker Court, Navajo Nation Judicial Branch, Window Rock, Arizona

Carcross Circle Program, Yukon Territory, Canada

Mr Carsten Erbe, Formerly Carcross Circle Program, Yukon Territory, now Florida Atlantic University

Ms Anna McCormick, School of Criminology, Simon Fraser University, Vancouver, British Columbia

Northside Community Justice Committee, MN, United States

Ms Stephanie Erickson, Restorative Justice Planner, Legal Rights Center, Minneapolis, Minnesota

South St Paul Restorative Justice Council, St Paul, MN, United States

Judge Leslie Metzen, South St Paul District Court Judge, St Paul, Minnesota

Mr Michael Stanefski, Restorative Justice Planner, South St Paul Public Schools, Special School District No. 6

Ms Mary Theisen, South St Paul Assistant County Attorney, St Paul, Minnesota

Zwelethemba Peacemaker Committee, Western Cape, South Africa

Mr John Cartwright, Programme Manager, Community Peacemaking Programme, Cape Town

Mr Mbuyi Dyasi, Community Peace Programme, Cape Town Professor Clifford Shearing, Community Peacemaking Programme, also Research School of Social Sciences, Australian National University, Canberra

Sentencing panels

Reparative Boards, Vermont Department of Corrections, Burlington, VT, United States

Mr John Perry, Director of Planning, Department of Corrections, Vermont

Toronto Community Council, Ontario, Canada

Mr Jonathan Rudin, Project Director, Toronto Community Council, Aboriginal Legal Services, Toronto

Vancouver Restorative Justice Programme, BC, Canada

Mr Kent Patenaude, Manager, Legal Services Society of British Columbia

Mr Barry Warhaft, Director, Vancouver Restorative Justice Programme, Vancouver

Mediation programmes

Victim/Offender Mediation/Dialogue Program, TX, United States

Mr David Doerfler, State Co-ordinator, Victim/Offender Mediation/Dialogue, Texas Department of Criminal Justice Victim Services Division, Austin, Texas

Ms Luci Kelly, Volunteer Co-ordinator Victim/Offender Mediation/Dialogue, Texas Department of Criminal Justice, Victim Services Division, Austin, Texas

Mr Eddie Mendoza, Mediator/Trainer, Victim/Offender Mediation/Dialogue, Texas Department of Criminal Justice, Victim Services Division, Austin, Texas

Multi-form programmes

'Just Youth' Project, Spectrum Youth and Family Services, Burlington, VT, United States

Ms Hillary Kramer, Co-ordinator, 'Just Youth' Project, Spectrum Youth & Family Services, Burlington, Vermont

Ms Mariellen Woods, Co-ordinator, 'Just Youth' Project, Spectrum Youth & Family Services, Burlington, Vermont

Washington County Community Justice, MN, United States

Ms Carolyn McLeod, Co-ordinator, Washington County Community Justice, Minneapolis, Minnesota

Prince William County Restorative Justice Program, VA,
United States

Ms Phyllis Turner-Lawrence, Co-ordinator, Restorative Justice Program, Prince William County, Virginia

Connections Program, Minnesota Correctional Facility, MN,
United States

Ms Kelly Pribyl, Connections Program, Minnesota Correctional Facility, Red Wing, Minnesota

Additional interviewees

Mr Antoine Archer, Chief, Canim Lake Band, British Columbia

Mr Mike Archie, Program Facilitator, Canim Lake Family Violence Program, Canim Lake, British Columbia

Ms Peta Blood, Circle Speak, Sydney

Ms Janet Boyce, Canim Lake Family Violence Program, Canim Lake, British Columbia

Ms Wilma Boyce, Director, Canim Lake Family Violence Program, Canim Lake, British Columbia

Professor Gale Burford, University of Vermont, Burlington, Vermont, United States

Mr Charlie Commando, Firekeeper, Waseskun House, Quebec

Dr Paul McCold, Director of Research, International Institute for Restorative Practices, Bethlehem, Pennsylvania

Judge Fred McElrea, District Court Judge, Auckland District Court

Mr Malcolm Naea Chun, Cultural Specialist, The Queen Lili'uokalani Children's Center, Honolulu, Hawai'i

Ms Kay Pranis, Restorative Justice Planner, Minnesota Department of Corrections, St Paul, Minnesota

Mr Brian Pugh, Counsellor, Canim Lake Family Violence Program, Canim Lake, British Columbia

Mr Johnny Quinteros, Clinical Co-ordinator, Waseskun House, Quebec

Ms Dianne Reid, Elder, Waseskun House, Quebec

Ms Ann Warner Roberts, Center for Restorative Justice & Mediation, School of Social Work, University of Minnesota, St Paul, Minnesota

References

AAP (Australian Associated Press) (2000). 'Howard Likely to Continue Criticism of UN in New York', *The Sydney Morning Herald*. Sydney.

ABA (American Bar Association) (1994). Recommendations Concerning Victim–Offender Mediation/Dialogue Programs. American Bar Association.

ABC (Australian Broadcasting Corporation) (2002). 'Thousands Evacuated, Homes Destroyed in Terror Blaze'.

Abel, R. (1981). 'Conservative Conflict and the Reproduction of Capitalism: The Role of Informal Justice', *International Journal of the Sociology of Law*, 9: 245–67.

—— (1982a). 'The Contradictions of Informal Justice', in R. Abel (ed.), *The Politics of Informal Justice: Volume 1: The American Experience*, New York: Academic Press.

—— (1982b). 'Introduction', in R. Abel (ed.), *The Politics of Informal Justice: Volume 2: Comparative Studies*. New York: Academic Press, 1–13.

ACPU (Aboriginal Corrections Policy Unit) (2000). Paths to Wellness: A Gathering of Communities Addressing Sexual Offending Behaviour.

AFP (Australian Federal Police) (undated). 'Australian Federal Police: Diversionary Conference Information Kit, including article "Nipping Crime in the Bud". *Time Magazine* 28.8.95.'

Alder, C. (2000). 'Young Women Offenders and the Challenge for Restorative Justice', in H. Strang and J. Braithwaite (eds.), *Restorative Justice: Philosophy to Practice*. Aldershot: Ashgate Dartmouth, 105–19.

Allen, J. (1999). 'Balancing Justice and Social Utility: Political Theory and the Idea of a Truth and Reconciliation Commission', *University of Toronto Law Journal*, 49: 315.

ALRC (Australian Law Reform Commission) (1986). *Report No. 31: The Recognition of Aboriginal Customary Laws*. Canberra: Australian Government Publishing Service.

—— (1987). *Report No. 38: Evidence*. Canberra: Australian Government Publishing Service.

ALST (Aboriginal Legal Services of Toronto) (1991). 'Elders and Traditional Teachers Gathering.'

Anechiarico, F. and J. B. Jacobs (1996). *The Pursuit of Absolute Integrity*. Chicago: The University of Chicago Press.

Armstrong, J. (1998). 'Some Thoughts on Alternative Service Delivery', *Optimum, The Journal of Public Sector Management*, 28/1: 1–10.

Ashworth, A. (1998). 'Restorative Justice', in A. V. Hirsch and A. Ashworth (eds.), *Principled Sentencing: Readings on Theory and Policy.* Oxford: Hart Publishing, 300–11.

—— (1999). *Principles of Criminal Law.* Oxford: Oxford University Press.

Asmal, K. (2000). 'Truth, Reconciliation and Justice: The South African Experience in Perspective', *Modern Law Review*, 63/1: 1–24.

Auerbach, J. (1983). *Justice Without Law? Resolving Disputes Without Lawyers.* Oxford University Press.

Auld, Lord Justice (2001). *A Review of the Criminal Courts of England and Wales.* http://www.criminal-courts-review.org.uk/.

Ayres, I. and J. Braithwaite (1992). *Responsive Regulation: Transcending the Deregulation Debate.* Oxford: Oxford University Press.

Baldwin, R. and K. Hawkins (1984). 'Discretionary Justice: Davis Reconsidered', *Public Law*, Winter: 570–99.

Bandes, S. (1996). 'Empathy, Narrative and Victim Impact Statements', *University of Chicago Law Review*, 63: 361–412.

Bardach, E. and R. Kagan (1982). *Going by the Book: The Problem of Regulatory Unreasonableness.* Philadelphia: Temple University Press.

Bargen, J. (1995). 'Conferences: Set Up to Fail?' *Rights Now!* Newsletter of the National Children's and Youth Law Centre, 3/4: 1–3.

Barnett, R. (1977). 'Restitution: A New Paradigm of Criminal Justice', *Ethics*, 87/4: 279–301.

Barton, C. and K. V. D. Broek (1999). 'Restorative Justice Conferencing and the Ethic of Care', *Ethics and Justice*, 2/2: 55–64.

Bayley, D. (1984). 'Community Policing in Japan and Singapore', *Community Policing: AIC Seminar Proceedings*, No.4. Canberra: Australian Institute of Criminology.

—— (1985). *Patterns of Policing: A Comparative Perspective.* New Brunswick: Rutgers University Press.

—— (1994a). 'International Differences in Community Policing', in D. Rosenbaum (ed.), *The Challenge of Community Policing: Testing the Promises.* Thousand Oaks, CA: Sage Publications, 278–81.

—— (1994b). *Police for the Future.* New York: Oxford University Press.

—— (1995). 'Getting Serious about Police Brutality', in P. Stenning (ed.), *Accountability for Criminal Justice.* Toronto: University of Toronto Press, 93–109.

Bazemore, G. and M. Umbreit (1998). *Guide for Implementing the Balanced and Restorative Justice Model.* US Department of Justice, Office of Justice Programs, Office of Juvenile Justice and Delinquency Prevention.

—— and M. Schiff (2001). 'Understanding Restorative Justice: What and Why Now?' in G. Bazemore and M. Schiff (eds.), *Restorative Community Justice.* Cincinnati: Anderson Publishing, 21–46.

Bennett, T. (1990). *Evaluating Neighbourhood Watch*. Aldershot: Gower.

Beyer, L. (1993). *Community Policing: Lessons from Victoria*. Canberra: Australian Institute of Criminology.

Blagg, H. (1997). 'A Just Measure of Shame: Aboriginal Youth and Conferencing in Australia', *The British Journal of Criminology*, 37/4: 481–501.

—— (1998). 'Restorative Visions and Restorative Justice Practices: Conferencing, Ceremony and Reconciliation in Australia', *Current Issues in Criminal Justice*, 10/1: 5–14.

Bluehouse, P. (undated). 'The Philosophy of Peacemaking Based in K'e', unpublished paper.

—— and J. Zion (1993). 'Hozhooji Naat'aanii: The Navajo Justice and Harmony Ceremony', *Mediation Quarterly*, 10/4, Summer: 327–37.

Bohannan, P. (1957). *Justice and Judgment Among the Tiv*. International African Institute, London: Oxford University Press.

Bonta, J. J. Rooney and S. Wallace-Capretta (1998). *Restorative Justice: An Evaluation of the Restorative Resolutions Project*. Winnipeg: Ministry of the Solicitor General of Canada.

Bottomley, A. (1985). 'What is Happening to Family Law? A Feminist Critique of Conciliation', in J. Brophy and C. Smart (eds.), *Women in Law: Explorations in Law, Family and Sexuality*. London: Routledge and Kegan Paul, 162–87.

Bovens, M. (1998). *The Quest for Responsibility*. Cambridge: Cambridge University Press.

Bowen, H., J. Boyack and S. Hooper (2000). *New Zealand Restorative Justice Manual*. Auckland: Restorative Justice Trust.

Boyack, J. (1999). 'How Sayest the Court of Appeal?' in H. Bowen and J. Consedine (eds.), *Restorative Justice: Contemporary Themes and Practice*. Lyttelton, New Zealand: Ploughshares Publications.

Braithwaite, J. (1989). *Crime, Shame and Reintegration*: Cambridge University Press.

—— (1996). *Restorative Justice and a Better Future*. Dorothy J Killam Memorial Lecture, Dalhousie University, Halifax, Nova Scotia.

—— (1997a). 'Conferencing and Plurality: Reply to Blagg', *British Journal of Criminology*, 37/4: 502–6.

—— (1997b). 'On Speaking Softly and Carrying Big Sticks: Neglected Dimensions of a Republication Separation of Powers', *University of Toronto Law Journal*, 47: 305–61.

—— (1998a). 'Commentary: Law, Morality and Restorative Justice'. *European Journal on Criminal Policy and Research*, 5/1: 93–8.

—— (1998b). 'Institutionalizing Distrust, Enculturating Trust', in V. Braithwaite and M. Levi (eds.), *Trust and Governance*. New York: Russell Sage Foundation, 343–75.

—— (1999). 'Restorative Justice: Assessing Optimistic and Pessimistic Accounts', in M. Tonry (ed.), *Crime and Justice: A Review of Research*. University of Chicago Press, 1–125.

—— (2000). 'The New Regulatory State and the Transformation of Criminology', *British Journal of Criminology*, 40/2: 222–38.

—— (2001). *Restorative Justice and Responsive Regulation*. Oxford University Press.

—— and K. Daly (1994). 'Masculinities, Violence and Communitarian Control', in T. Newburn and E. Stanko (eds.), *Just Boys Doing Business*. London and New York: Routledge, 189–213.

—— and T. Makkai (1994). 'Trust and Compliance', *Policing and Society*, 4/1: 1–12.

—— and S. Mugford (1994). 'Conditions of Successful Reintegration Ceremonies: Dealing with Juvenile Offenders', *British Journal of Criminology*, 34/2: 139–71.

—— and C. Parker (1999). 'Restorative Justice is Republican Justice', in G. Bazemore and L. Walgrave (eds.), *Restorative Juvenile Justice: Repairing the Harm of Youth Crime*. Monsey: Willow Tree Press, 103–26.

—— and P. Pettit (1994). 'Republican Criminology and Victim Advocacy', *Law and Society Review*, 28/4: 765–76.

—— and D. Roche (2001). 'Responsibility and Restorative Justice', in G. Bazemore and M. Schiff (eds.), *Restorative Community Justice: Repairing Harm and Transforming Communities*. Cincinnati: Anderson Publishing, 203–20.

—— and H. Strang (2000). 'Connecting Philosophy and Practice', in H. Strang and J. Braithwaite (eds.), *Restorative Justice: Philosophy to Practice*. Aldershot: Ashgate Dartmouth, 203–20.

Brockie, J. (1991). *Cop it Sweet*. Sydney: Australian Broadcasting Corporation TV.

—— (1994). 'Police and Minority Groups', in D. Moore and R. Wettenhall (eds.), *Keeping the Peace: Police Accountability and Oversight*. Canberra: University of Canberra, 177–9.

Bronitt, S. and B. McSherry (2001). *Principles of Criminal Law*. Sydney: LBC.

Brown, J. G. (1994). 'The Use of Mediation to Resolve Criminal Cases: A Procedural Critique', *Emory Law Journal*, 43: 1247–1309.

Brown, R. M. (1963). *The South Carolina Regulators*. Cambridge: Harvard University Press.

Brundage, W. (1993). *Lynching in the New South: Georgia and Virginia, 1880–1930*. Urbana and Chicago: University of Illinois Press.

Burford, G. and J. Pennell (1994). 'Family Group Decision Making: An Innovation in Child and Family Welfare', final draft.

Burgess, R. (1982). 'Some Role Problems in Field Research', in R. Burgess (ed.), *Field Research: A Sourcebook and Field Manual*. London: George Allen and Unwin, 45–9.

Burman, S. and W. Scharf (1990). 'Creating People's Justice: Street Committees and People's Courts in a South African City', *Law and Society Review*, 24/3: 693–744.

Bush, R. B. and J. Folger (1994). *The Promise of Mediation: Responding to Conflict Through Empowerment and Recognition*. San Francisco: Jossey-Bass Publishers.

Cameron, N. and W. Young (1986). *Policing at the Crossroads*. New Zealand: Allen & Unwin.

Campbell, T. (1998). 'Legal Positivism and Deliberative Democracy', in M. Freeman (ed.), *Current Legal Problems 1998: Legal Theory at the End of the Millennium*. Oxford: Oxford University Press, 65–92.

Cane, P. (1996). *An Introduction to Administrative Law*. Oxford: Clarendon Press.

Cappelletti, M. (1983). 'Who Watches the Watchmen? A Comparative Study on Judicial Responsibility', *The American Journal of Comparative Law*, 31: 1–62.

Cartwright, J. (undated). 'Local Capacity Policing: Building a model of democratic governance.'

Cass, D. (1992). 'Case and Comment: Hakopian', *Criminal Law Journal*, 16: 200–4.

Chan, J. (1999). 'Governing Police Practice: Limits of the New Accountability', *British Journal of Sociology*, 50/2: 251–70.

Charlesworth, H. (1994). 'The Australian Reluctance About Rights', in P. Alston (ed.), *Towards an Australian Bill of Rights*. Canberra: CIPL and HREOC.

Christie, N. (1977). 'Conflicts as Property', *The British Journal of Criminology*, 17/1: 1–15.

Coates, R., M. Umbreit, and B. Vos (2000). 'Restorative Justice Circles in South St Paul, Minnesota', unpublished paper.

Cohen, J. and C. Sabel (1997). 'Directly-Deliberative Polyarchy', *European Law Journal*, 3/4: 313–42.

Cohen, S. (1984). 'The Deeper Structures of the Law or Beware the Rulers Bearing Justice: A Review Essay', *Contemporary Crises*, 8: 83–93.

—— (1985). *Visions of Social Control: Crime, Punishment and Classification*. Cambridge: Polity Press.

Coker, D. (1999). 'Enhancing Autonomy for Battered Women: Lessons from Navajo Peacemaking', *UCLA Law Review*, 47 /1: 1–111.

Consedine, J. (1999). *Restorative Justice: Healing the Effects of Crime*. Lytellton, New Zealand: Ploughshares Publications.

Crawford, A. (1997). *The Local Governance of Crime: Appeals to Community and Partnerships.* Oxford: Clarendon.

—— and T. Newburn (2002). 'Recent Developments in Restorative Justice for Young People in England and Wales', *British Journal of Criminology*, 42/3: 476–95.

Cunneen, C. (1997). 'Community Conferencing and the Fiction of Indigenous Control', *The Australian and New Zealand Journal of Criminology*, 30: 292–311.

—— (2000). 'Restorative Justice and the Politics of Decolonisation.' Paper presented to the Fourth International Conference on Restorative Justice for Juveniles.

Daly, K. (2000). 'Revisiting the Relationship between Retributive and Restorative Justice', in H. Strang and J. Braithwaite (eds.), *Restorative Justice: Philosophy to Practice.* Aldershot: Ashgate.

—— (2002). 'Restorative Justice: The Real Story', *Punishment and Society*, 4/1: 55–79.

—— and H. Hayes (2001). 'Restorative Justice and Conferencing in Australia', Australian Institute of Criminology, *Trends and Issues in Crime and Criminal Justice*, 186: 1–6.

—— and J. Kitcher (1998). 'The R(evolution) of Restorative Justice through Researcher–Practitioner Partnerships', *Ethics and Justice*: on line at *www.ethics–justice.org/v2n1*, 2/1: 14–20.

Davis, K. C. (1969). *Discretionary Justice: A Preliminary Inquiry.* Baton Rouge: Louisiana State University Press.

Day, P. and R. Klein (1987). *Accountabilities: Five Public Services.* London: Tavistock Publications.

Delgado, R. (2000). 'Goodbye to Hammurabi: Analyzing the Atavistic Appeal of Restorative Justice', *Stanford Law Review*, April: 751–75.

—— C. Dunn, P. Brown, H. Lee, and D. Hubbert (1985). 'Fairness and Formality: Minimizing the Risk of Prejudice in Alternative Dispute Resolution', *Wisconsin Law Review*, 6: 1359–1404.

Diamond, L., M. Plattner, and A. Schedler (1999). 'Introduction', in A. Schedler, L. Diamond, and M. Plattner (eds.), *The Self-Restraining State: Power and Accountability in New Democracies.* Boulder: Lynne Rienner, 1–10.

Dinnan, C. (undated). *High School Hazing Incident—A Conferencing Case Study.* Vermont Department of Corrections Website: Community and Restorative Services (http://www.doc.state.vt.us/Communit.htm).

Dinnen, S. (2002). 'Building Bridges—Directions for Law and Justice Reform in Papua New Guinea', in T. Newton and A. Jowett (eds.), *Law, Society and Change in the South Pacific.*

Dixon, D. (1997). *Law in Policing: Legal Regulation and Police Practices.* Oxford: Clarendon Press.

Dobry, J. (2001). *Restorative Justice and Police Complaints*. London: Police Complaints Authority.

Doerfler, D. (1997). 'Facing the Pain That Heals', *The Victim's Informer: TDCJ Crime Victim Clearinghouse*, 1/3: 1–3.

——(undated). *Victim/Offender Mediation/Dialogue Program Policies*. Texas Department of Criminal Justice, Victim Services Division.

Dordick, G. (1997). *Something Left to Lose: Personal Relations and Survival Among New York's Homeless*. Philadelphia: Temple University Press.

Dorf, M. and C. Sabel (1998). 'A Constitution of Democratic Experimentalism', *Columbia Law Review*, 98/2: 267–473.

Doyle, J. (1998). *Accountability: Parliament, the Executive and the Judiciary*. Australian Institute of Administrate Law Forum.

Dray, P. (2002). *At the Hands of Persons Unknown: The Lynching of Black America*. New York: Random House.

Dryzek, J. (2000). *Deliberative Democracy and Beyond: Liberals, Critics, Contestations*. Oxford: Oxford University Press.

Duff, R. (2001). *Punishment, Communication, and Community*. New York: Oxford University Press.

Eades, D. (1994). 'A Case of Communicative Clash: Aboriginal English and the Legal System', in J. Gibbons (ed.), *Language and the Law*. Longman: New York, 234–64.

Elias, O. (1956). *The Nature of African Customary Law*. Manchester: Manchester University Press.

Ellickson, R. (1991). *Order without Law: How Neighbors Settle Disputes*. Cambridge, Massachusetts: Harvard University Press.

Farrington, D. (1996). *Understanding and Preventing Youth Crime*. London: Joseph Rowntree Foundation.

Feeley, M. (1979). *The Process is the Punishment: Handling Cases in a Lower Criminal Court*. New York: Russell Sage Foundation.

Finnane, M. (2001). '"Payback", Customary Law and Criminal Law in Colonised Australia', *Journal of the Sociology of Law*, 29/4: 293–310.

Fishkin, J. (1995). *The Voice of the People*. Yale University Press.

Fiss, O. (1984). 'Against Settlement', *The Yale Law Journal*, 93: 1073–90.

Foucault, M. (1977). *Discipline and Punish: The Birth of the Prison*. London: Penguin Books.

FPTTFYJ (Federal/Provincial/Territorial Task Force on Youth Justice) (1996). *A Review of the Young Offenders Act and the Youth Justice System in Canada*.

Gans, H. (1982). 'The Participant Observer as a Human Being: Observations on the Personal Aspects of Fieldwork', in R. Burgess (ed.), *Field Research: A Sourcebook and Field Manual*. London: George Allen and Unwin, 53–61.

Garland, D. (1996). 'The Limits of the Sovereign State: Strategies of Crime Control in Contemporary Society', *The British Journal of Criminology*, 36/4: 445–71.

—— (2001). *The Culture of Control: Crime and Social Order in Contemporary Society*. Oxford: Oxford University Press.

Gerard, G. and K. Nelson (1998). 'Pioneering Restorative Justice: A New Response to Urban Crime', *Cura Reporter*, April: 6–11.

Gibbons, J. (1994). 'Language and Disadvantage Before the Law', in J. Gibbons (ed.), *Language and the Law*. New York: Longman, 195–8.

Gilligan, C. (1993). *In a Different Voice: Psychological Theory and Women's Development*. Cambridge, Massachusetts: Harvard University Press.

Glasser, C. and S. Roberts (1993). 'Dispute Resolution: Civil Justice and its Alternatives—Introduction', *The Modern Law Review*, 277–81.

Gleeson, M. (1995). 'Judicial Accountability', *The Judicial Review*, 2/2: 117–40.

Gluckman, M. (1965). *The Ideas in Barotse Jurisprudence*. New Haven: Yale University Press.

—— (1973). *The Judicial Process Among the Barotse of Northern Rhodesia*. Manchester: Manchester University Press.

Goldring, J. and P. Blazey (1994). 'Constitutional and Legal Mechanisms of Police Accountability in Australia', in D. Moore and R. Wettenhall (eds.), *Keeping the Peace: Police Accountability and Oversight*. Canberra: The Royal Institute of Public Administration Australia, 145–55.

Goldsmith, A. (1995). 'Public Complaints Procedures in Police Accountability', in P. Stenning (ed.), *Accountability for Criminal Justice*. Toronto: University of Toronto Press, 110–34.

Goodin, R. (1992). *Motivating Political Morality*. Oxford: Blackwell.

—— (1996). 'Inclusion and Exclusion', *Archives of European Sociology*, 2: 343–71.

—— (1996). 'Institutions and Their Design', in R. Goodin (ed.), *The Theory of Institutional Design*. Cambridge: Cambridge University Press, 1–53.

Gordon, A. and J. Heinz (1979). 'The Continuing Struggle Over Citizen Access to Government Information', in A. Gordon and J. Heinz (eds.), *Public Access to Information*. New Brunswick: Transaction Books, xiii–xxii.

Grabosky, P. (1995). 'Using Non-Governmental Resources to Foster Regulatory Compliance', *Governance: An International Journal of Policy and Administration*, 8/4: 527–50.

Graycar, R. and J. Morgan (1990). *The Hidden Gender of Law*. Sydney: The Federation Press.

Griffin, M. (1996). 'Beating the System', *Connexions*, 16/5: 3–5.

Grillo, T. (1991). 'The Mediation Alternative: Process Dangers for Women', *The Yale Law Journal*, 100: 1545–1610.

Gunningham, N. (1987). 'Negotiated Non-Compliance: A Case Strategy of Regulatory Failure', *Law and Policy*, 9/1: 69–97.

Gwyn, W. (1986). 'The Separation of Powers and Modern Forms of Democratic Government', in R. Goldwin and A. Kaufman (eds.), *Separation of Powers—Does it Still Work*. Washington: American Enterprise Institute Constitutional Studies, 65–89.

Hagan, J. and B. McCarthy (1997). *Mean Streets: Youth Crime and Homelessness*. Cambridge: Cambridge University Press.

Hall, S., C. Critcher, T. Jefferson, J. Clarke, and B. Roberts (1978). *Policing the Crisis, Mugging, the State, and Law and Order*. London: Macmillan.

Hammersley, M. and P. Atkinson (1995). *Ethnography: Principles in Practice*. London: Routledge.

Harmon, M. and R. Mayer (1986). *Organization Theory for Public Administration*. Boston: Little, Brown and Company.

Harris, N. (1999). 'Shame and Shaming: An Empirical Analysis.' Unpublished PhD Thesis, Law Program, Research School of Social Sciences. Canberra: Australian National University.

Hayes, H., T. Prenzler, and R. Wortley (1998). Making Amends: Final Evaluation of the Queensland Community Conferencing Pilot School of Criminology and Criminal Justice, Griffith University.

Heimer, C. (1998). 'Legislating Responsibility', *American Bar Foundation Working #9711*. Chicago.

Hennessy, N. (1999). Review of Gatekeeping Role in Young Offenders Act 1997 (NSW): Report to Youth Justice Advisory Committee. Sydney.

Hepworth, K. (1998). 'Shoplifter, 12, Shamed in Front of Shoppers in Busy Mall', *The Canberra Times*, 4 March. Canberra.

Herbert, I. (2002). 'Vigilantes to be Given Life for Killing Pensioner', *The Independent*, 21 March. London.

Hooper, S. and R. Busch (1996). 'Domestic Violence and the Restorative Justice Initiatives: The Risks of a New Panacea', *Waikato Law Review*, 4: 101–30.

Howley, P. (1999). Interim Evaluation Report on the Conflict Resolution Training Among the Toaripi of the Gulf Province.

Ignatieff, M. (1981). 'State, Civil Society, and Total Institutions: A Critique of Recent Social Histories of Punishment', in M. Tonry and N. Morris (eds.), *Crime and Justice, An Annual Review of Research*. Chicago and London: The University of Chicago Press, 153–92.

Jackson, M. (1992). 'The Treaty and the Word: The Colonization of Maori Philosophy', in G. Oddie and R. Perrett (eds.), *Justice, Ethics, and New Zealand Society*. Auckland: Oxford University Press, 1–10.

Jeffery, A. (1999). *The Truth About the Truth Commission: South Africa Institute of Race Relations.* Spotlight Series, Johannesburg: South African Institute of Race Relations.

Johnstone, G. (2002). *Restorative Justice: Ideas, Values, Debates.* Cullompton: Willan Publishing.

Jones, C. (1993). 'Auditing Criminal Justice', *British Journal of Criminology*, 33/2: 187–202.

Jones, M. (1974). *Justice and Journalism: A study of the Influence of Newspaper Reporting upon the Administration of Justice by Magistrates.* Chichester and London: Barry Rose Publishers.

JSC (Joint Select Committee on Certain Aspects of the Operation and Interpretation of the Family Law Act) (1992). The Family Law Act 1975: Aspects of its Operation and Interpretation: Report of the Joint Select Committee on Certain Aspects of the Operation and Interpretation of the Family Law Act. Canberra: Parliament of the Commonwealth of Australia.

Kahan, D. (1996). 'What Do Alternative Sanctions Mean?', *University of Chicago Law Review*, 63: 591–653.

Kant, I. (1795). 'Perpetual Peace', in H. Reiss (ed.), *Kant's Political Writings*. Cambridge: Cambridge University Press, 93–130.

Kirby, M. (1995). 'Forum: Televising Court Proceedings', *University of New South Wales Law Journal*, 18/2: 483–7.

Krog, A. (1999). *Country of My Skull*. London: Vintage.

Krygier, M. (1999). 'Institutional Optimism, Cultural Pessimism and the Rule of Law', in M. Krygier and A. Czarnota (eds.), *The Rule of Law after Communism: Problems and Prospects in East-Central Europe*. Aldershot: Ashgate Dartmouth, 77–105.

Kymlicka, W. (1995). *Multicultural Citizenship*. Oxford: Clarendon Press.

LaFree, G. (1998). *Losing Legitimacy: Street Crime and the Decline of Social Institutions in America*. Boulder, CO: Westview Press.

LaPrairie, C. (1992). Exploring the Boundaries of Justice: Aboriginal Justice in the Yukon: Report to Department of Justice, Yukon Territory, Canada.

——(1995). 'Altering Course: New Directions in Criminal Justice and Correctional Sentencing Circles and Family Group Conferences', *The Australian and New Zealand Journal of Criminology*, 28: 78–99.

——(1999). 'Some Reflections on New Criminal Justice Policies in Canada: Restorative Justice, Alternative Measures and Conditional Sentences', *The Australian and New Zealand Journal of Criminology*, 32/2: 139–52.

Lassiter, C. (1996). 'The Appearance of Justice: TV or not TV—That is the Question', *Journal of Criminal Law and Criminology*, 86: 928–1001.

Latimer, J., C. Dowden, and D. Muise (2001). *The Effectiveness of Restorative Justice Practices: A Meta-Analysis*. Ottawa: Department of Justice Canada.

Lawson, V. (2000). 'Trial Groupies at the Best Show in Town', *The Sydney Morning Herald*. 23 March. Sydney.

Lenman, B. and G. Parker (1980). 'The State, the Community and the Criminal Law in Early Modern Europe', in V. Gatrell, B. Lenman, and G. Parker (eds.), *Crime and the Law: The Social History of Crime in Western Europe Since 1500*. London: Europa, 11–48.

Lerman, L. (1984). 'Mediation of Wife Abuse Cases: The Adverse Impact of Informal Dispute Resolution on Women', *Harvard Women's Law Journal*, 7: 57–113.

Levrant, S., F. Cullen, B. Fulton, and J. Wozniak (1999). 'Reconsidering Restorative Justice: The Corruption of Benevolence Revisited?', *Crime & Delinquency*, 45/1: 3–27.

Levy, A. (1999). 'Why Children Under 14 Should Not be Tried as Adults', *The Sunday Times*, 23 March. London.

Lewis, C. and T. Prenzler (1999). 'Civilian Oversight of Police in Australia', *Trends and Issues in Crime and Criminal Justice*, No. 141. Canberra: Australian Institute of Criminology.

Liberman, K. (1981). 'Understanding Aborigines in Australian Courts of Law', *Human Organization*, 40: 247–55.

Linden, A. (1986). 'Limitations on Media Coverage of Legal Proceedings: A Critique and Some Proposals for Reform', in P. Anisman and A. Linden (eds.), *The Media, the Courts and the Charter*. Toronto: Calgary, 301–30.

Lister, D. (2002). 'Newspaper Campaign Led to Series of Attacks on Innocent People', *Independent*, 22 February. London.

Llewellyn, J. and R. Howse (1999). 'Institutions for Restorative Justice: The South African Truth and Reconciliation Commission', *University of Toronto Law Journal*, 49: 355–88.

Lloyd, D. (1998). *Judicial Accountability*. The Judicial Conference of Australia, Gold Coast.

Luban, D. (1996). 'The Publicity Principle', in R. Goodin (ed.), *The Theory of Institutional Design*. Cambridge: Cambridge University Press.

McBarnet, D. (1988). 'Victims in the Witness Box—Confronting Victimology's Stereotype', *Contemporary Crises*, 7: 279–303.

—— (1994). 'Two Tiers of Justice', in N. Lacey (ed.), *Criminal Justice*. Oxford: Oxford University Press, 177–205.

McCold, P. (1998). *Police-Facilitated Restorative Conferencing: What the Data Show*. Second Annual International Conference on Restorative Justice for Juveniles, Fort Lauderdale, Florida.

—— (2000). 'Toward a Mid-Range Theory of Restorative Criminal Justice: A Reply to the Maximalist Model', *Contemporary Justice Review*, 3/4: 357–414.

—— (2001). *Basic Evaluation Measures*. e-mail to Family Group Conference Interest.

—— and B. Wachtel (1998). 'Community is Not a Place: A New Look at Community Justice Initiatives', *Contemporary Justice Review*, 1: 71–85.

—— —— (1998). *Restorative Policing Experiment: The Bethlehem Pennsylvania Police Family Group Conferencing Project*. Pipersville, PA: Community Service Foundation.

McDonald, R. (1996). 'Face to Face Justice', *The Sydney Morning Herald: Good Weekend Magazine Supplement*, 18 May. Sydney.

McElrea, F. (1996). 'The New Zealand Youth Court: A Model for Use with Adults', in B. Galaway and J. Hudson (eds.), *Restorative Justice: International Perspectives*. Monsey, New York: Criminal Justice Press, 69–83.

McEvoy, K. and H. Mika (2002). 'Restorative Justice and the Critique of Informalism in Northern Ireland'. *British Journal of Criminology*, 42/3: 534–62.

McEwen, C. and R. Maiman (1981). 'Small Claims Mediation in Maine: An Empirical Assessment'. *Maine Law Review*, 33: 237–68.

McGarrell, E., K. Olivares, K. Crawford and N. Kroovand (2000). *Returning Justice to the Community: The Indianapolis Juvenile Restorative Justice Experiment*. Indianapolis: Hudson Institute Crime Control Policy Center.

MacGregor, T. (2000). 'Curtain Falls on Moran Matinee', *Sydney Morning Herald*, 30 March. Sydney.

McLaughlin, E. and A. Johansen (2002). 'The Prospects for Applying Restorative Justice to Citizen Complaints against the Police in England and Wales'. *British Journal of Criminology*, 42/3: 635–53.

Madison, J. (1961). 'No. 51: The Structure of the Government Must Furnish the Proper Checks and Balances Between the Different Departments', in C. Kesler and C. Rossiter (eds.), *The Federalist Papers* New York: Penguin Putnam, 288–93.

Makkai, T. and J. Braithwaite (1993). 'Praise, Pride and Corporate Compliance', *International Journal of the Sociology of Law*, 21: 73–91.

Mantziaris, C. and D. Martin (2000). *Native Title Corporations: A Legal and Anthropological Analysis*. Sydney: The Federation Press.

Marshall, G. (1978). 'Police Accountability Revisited', in D. Butler and A. H. Halsey (eds.), *Policy and Politics: Essays in Honour of Norman Chester: Warden of Nuffield College 1954–1978*. London: The Macmillan Press, 51–65.

Marshall, T. (1996). 'The Evolution of Restorative Justice in Britain', *European Journal on Criminal Policy and Research*, 4/4: 21–43.

——(1999). *Restorative Justice: An Overview*. London: Home Office Research Development and Statistics Directorate.

Masters, G. and D. Smith (1998). 'Portia and Persephone Revisited: Thinking about Feeling in Criminal Justice', *Theoretical Criminology*, 2/1: 5–27.

Maxwell, G. and A. Morris (1993). *Family, Victims and Culture: Youth Justice in New Zealand*. Wellington: Social Policy Agency and Institute of Criminology, Victoria University of Wellington.

—— —— and T. Anderson (1999). *Community Panel Adult Pre-Trial Diversion: Supplementary Evaluation*. Wellington: Institute of Criminology, Victoria University of Wellington.

Merry, S. E. (1993). 'Sorting Out Popular Justice', in S. E. Merry and N. Milner (eds.), *The Possibility of Popular Justice: A Case Study of Community Mediation in the United States*. Ann Arbor: The University of Michigan Press, 31–66.

——and N. Milner (1993). 'Introduction', in S. E. Merry and N. Milner (eds.), *The Possibility of Popular Justice: a Case Study of Community Mediation in the United States*. Ann Arbor: The University of Michigan Press, 3–30.

Mika, H. and K. McEvoy (2001). 'Restorative Justice in Conflict: Paramilitarism, Community, and the Construction of Legitimacy in Northern Ireland', *Contemporary Justice Review*, 4/3–4: 291–320.

Minow, M. (1998). *Between Vengeance and Forgiveness: Facing History after Genocide and Mass Violence*. Boston: Beacon Press.

Moore, D. (1994). 'Diversion? Reconciliation? Mediation? Confusion', *Socio-Legal Bulletin*, 14: 39.

——and T. O'Connell (1993). 'Family Conferencing in Wagga Wagga: A Communitarian Model of Justice', in C. Alder and J. Wundersitz (eds.), *Family Conferencing and Juvenile Justice: The Way Forward or Misplaced Optimism?* Canberra: Australian Institute of Criminology, 45–86.

Morgan, R. (2002). 'Imprisonment: A brief history, the contemporary scene, and likely prospects', in M. Maguire, R. Morgan, and R. Reiner (eds.), *The Oxford Handbook of Criminology*. Oxford: Oxford University Press, 1113–67.

Morris, A. and G. Maxwell (1993). 'Juvenile Justice in New Zealand: A New Paradigm', *Australian and New Zealand Journal of Criminology*, 26: 72–90.

Moyer, S. and L. Axon (1993). An Implementation Evaluation of the Native Community Council Project of the Aboriginal Legal Services of Toronto.

Mukherjee, S. and P. Wilson (1987). 'Neighbourhood Watch: Issues and Policy Implications', *Trends and Issues in Crime and Criminal Justice*, No. 8. Canberra: Australian Institute of Criminology

Mulgan, R. (1984). 'Who Should Have How Much Say About What? Some Problems in Pluralist Democracy', *Political Science*, 36/2: 112–24.

——(1989). *Maori, Pakeha and Democracy*. Auckland: Oxford University Press.

——(1997). 'Contracting Out and Accountability', *Australian Journal of Public Administration*, 56/4: 106–16.

——(2000). '"Accountability": An Ever-Expanding Concept?', *Public Administration*, 78/3: 555–73.

——and J. Uhr (2000). 'Accountability and Governance', in P. Weller (ed.), *The State and Citizens*. Sydney: Allen and Unwin.

Nettheim, G. (1984). 'The Principle of Open Justice', *University of Tasmania Law Review*, 8/1: 25–45.

Newburn, T., R. Earle, S. Goldie, A. Campbell, A. Crawford, K. Sharpe, G. Masters, C. Hale, R. Saunders, and S. Uglow (2002). *The Introduction of Referral Orders into the Youth Justice System. Final Report.* Home Office Research Study 242. London: Home Office.

Niebuhr, R. (1967). *Love and Justice: Selections of the Shorter Writings of Reinhold Niebuhr.* Cleveland: The World Publishing Company.

Norrie, A. (2001). *Crime, Reason and History: A Critical Introduction to Criminal Law.* London: Butterworths.

NSWDJJ (New South Wales Department of Juvenile Justice) (2000). *Youth Justice Conferencing: Procedures Manual.*

NSWLRC (New South Wales Law Reform Commission) (1996). *Sentencing: Discussion Paper 33.* Sydney: New South Wales Law Reform Commission.

NZMJ (New Zealand Ministry of Justice) (1995). *Restorative Justice: A Discussion Paper.* Ministry of Justice, New Zealand.

O'Connell, T., B. Wachtel, and T. Wachtel (1999). *Conferencing Handbook: The New Real Justice Training Manual.* Pipersville, Pennsylvania: The Piper's Press.

O'Malley, P. (1996). 'Indigenous Governance', *Economy and Society*, 25/3: 310–26.

O'Shea, F. (2001). 'Slap on the Wrist for $1.8m blaze', *Daily Telegraph*, 13 February. Sydney.

Palmer, M. and S. Roberts (1998). *Dispute Processes: ADR and the Primary Forms of Decision Making.* London: Butterworths.

Palys, T. (1999). 'Vancouver's Aboriginal Restorative Justice Program: The challenges ahead', *Aboriginal Justice Bulletin*, Summer 1999.

Parker, C. (1999). *Just Lawyers: Regulation and Access to Justice.* Oxford: Oxford University Press.

Pavlich, G. (1996). 'The Power of Community Mediation: Government and Formation of Self-Identity', *Law and Society Review*, 30/4: 707–33.

Peiperl, M. (2001). 'Peer Pressures', *Harvard Business Review*, reprinted in *Australian Financial Review* Boss Magazine, 48–51.

Pennell, J. and G. Burford (1997). Family Group Decision Making: *After the Conference—Progress in Resolving Violence and Promoting Well-Being. Outcome Report Summary.* St John's, Newfoundland, Canada: Memorial University of Newfoundland.

Perrett, R. (1999). 'Dual Justice: The Maori and the Criminal Justice System', *He Pukenga Korero: A Journal of Maori Studies*, 4/2: 17–26.

Pettit, P. (1990). 'Virtus Normativa: Rational Choice Perspectives', *Ethics*, 100/4: 725–55.

—— (1995). 'The Cunning of Trust', *Philosophy and Public Affairs*, 24/3: 202–25.

Philips, D. (1980). 'A New Engine of Power and Authority: The Institutionalization of Law-Enforcement in England 1780–1830', in V. Gatrell, B. Lenman, and G. Parker (eds.), *Crime and the Law: The Social History of Crime in Western Europe since 1500*. London: Europa, 155–89.

Phillips, A. (1994). 'Dealing with Difference: A Politics of Ideas or a Politics of Presence?', *Constellations*, 1/1: 74–91.

—— (1995). *Politics of Presence*. Oxford: Oxford University Press.

Pildes, R. (1995). 'The Destruction of Social Capital Through Law', *University of Pennsylvania Law Review*, 144: 2055–77.

Posner, E. (2000). *Law and Social Norms*. Cambridge, MA: Harvard University Press.

Power, M. (1997). *The Audit Society: Rituals of Verification*. Oxford: Oxford University Press.

Power, P. (1998). *Youth Justice Conferencing Media Policy*. Youth Justice Advisory Committee.

—— (2000). 'Restorative Conferences in Australia and New Zealand: Evaluated in terms of the Principles of Restorative Justice and the Preservation of the Procedural Rights of the Accused Juvenile.' Unpublished PhD Thesis, Law Faculty. Sydney: Sydney University.

Pranis, K. (1999). 'Restorative Justice, Social Justice, and the Empowerment of Marginalized Populations', in G. Bazemore and M. Schiff (eds.), *Restorative Community Justice: Repairing Harm and Transforming Communities*. Cincinnati: Anderson Publishing Co, 287–306.

Prenzler, T. and H. Hayes (1999). 'Victim/Offender Mediation and the Gatekeeping Role of Police', *International Journal of Police Science and Management*, 2/1: 17–32.

Pribyl, K. (1999). 'The Connections Program at the Minnesota Correctional Facility, Red Wing', *Hearts and Hands*: Minnesota's Restorative Justice Newsletter, Fall/Winter: 1–2.

Pringle, H. (1993). 'Acting Like a Man: Seduction and Rape in the Law', *Griffith Law Review*, 2/1: 64–74.

Putnam, R. (1993). *Making Democracy Work: Civic Tradition*. Princeton: Princeton University Press.

Quigley, T. (1999). 'Are We Doing Anything about the Disproportionate Jailing of Aboriginal People?', *The Criminal Law Quarterly*, 42: 129–60.

Rawls, J. (1972). *A Theory of Justice*. Oxford: Oxford University Press.

RCAP (Royal Commission on Aboriginal Peoples) (1996). Bridging the Cultural Divide: A Report on Aboriginal People and Criminal Justice in Canada. Ottawa.

Reiner, R. (1995). 'Counting the Coppers: Accountability in Policing', in P. Stenning (ed.), *Accountability for Criminal Justice*. Toronto: University of Toronto Press, 74–92.

——(1997). 'Policing and the Police', in M. Maguire, R. Morgan, and R. Reiner (eds.), *The Oxford Handbook of Criminology*. Oxford: Oxford University Press.

Retzinger, S. and T. Scheff (1996). 'Strategy for Community Conferences: Emotions and Social Bonds', in B. Galaway and J. Hudson (eds.), *Restorative Justice: International Perspectives*. Monsey, New York: Criminal Justice Press, 315–36.

Reynolds, H. (1995). *The Other Side of the Frontier: Aboriginal Resistance to the European Invasion of Australia*. Melbourne: Penguin Books.

Ritzer, G. (1996). *The McDonaldization of Society: An Investigation into the Changing Character of Contemporary Social Life*. Thousand Oaks, CA: Pine Forge Press.

Roach, K. and J. Rudin (2000). 'Gladue: The Judicial and Political Reception of a Promising Decision', *Canadian Journal of Criminology*, 42/3: 355–88.

Roberts, A. W. and G. Masters (1999). *Group Conferencing: Restorative Justice in Practice*. Minneapolis: Center for Restorative Justice and Mediation.

Roberts, J. and C. LaPrairie (1997). 'Sentencing Circles: Some Questions Unanswered', *Criminal Law Quarterly*, 39: 69–83.

Roberts, S. (1983). 'Mediation in Family Disputes', *Modern Law Review*, 46: 537.

Roche, D. (2002). 'Restorative Justice and the Regulatory State in South African Townships', *British Journal of Criminology*, 42/3: 514–33.

——(2003 forthcoming). 'Gluttons for Restorative Justice', *Economy and Society*.

Rock, P. (1991). 'Witnesses and Space in a Crown Court', *British Journal of Criminology*, 31/3: 266–79.

——(1993). *The Social World of an English Court: Witness and Professionals in the Crown Court Centre at Wood Green*. Oxford: Clarendon Press.

Rorty, R. (1998). *Truth and Progress: Philosophical Papers, Volume 3*. Cambridge: Cambridge University Press.

Rosenbaum, D. (1994). 'Preface', in D. Rosenbaum (ed.), *The Challenge of Community Policing: Testing the Promises*. Thousand Oaks, California: Sage Publications, xi–xvi.

Rowse, T. (2000). 'Culturally Appropriate Indigenous Accountability', *American Behavioral Scientist*, 43/9: 1514–32.

Sackville, R. (1994). *Access to Justice: an Action Plan*. Canberra: Commonwealth of Australia.

Said, E. (1995). *Orientalism: Western Conceptions of the Orient*. Harmondsworth: Penguin.

SALC (South African Law Commission) (1999). Discussion Paper 87, Project 94: Community Dispute Resolution Structures.

Sarre, R. (1994). 'The Family Conference as an Option in Dealing with Young Offenders.' Unpublished paper delivered to a seminar convened by the NSW Bureau of Crime Statistics and Research, Sydney.

SATRC (South African Truth and Reconciliation Commission) (1998). *Final Report*. http://www.truth.org.za/report/index.htm

Scarman, L. (1981). *The Brixton Disorders, 10–12 April 1981*. Report of an Inquiry by Lord Scarman, Cmnd 8427. London: HMSO.

Schedler, A. (1999). 'Conceptualizing Accountability', in A. Schedler, L. Diamond, and M. Plattner (eds.), *The Self-Restraining State: Power and Accountability in New Democracies*. Boulder: Lynne Rienner, 13–28.

Schiff, M., G. Bazemore, and C. Erbe (2001). Understanding Restorative Justice: A Study of Youth Conferencing Models in the United States. Updated Paper presented at the Annual Meeting of the American Society of Criminology, San Francisco, California.

Scholz, J. (1998). 'Trust, Taxes, and Compliance', in V. Braithwaite and M. Levi (eds.), *Trust and Governance*. New York: Russell Sage Foundation, 135–66.

Scott, C. (2000). 'Accountability in the Regulatory State', *Journal of Law and Society*, 27/1: 38–60.

Seymour, J. (1988). *Dealing with Young Offenders*. Sydney: Law Book Company.

Shachar, A. (1999). 'The Paradox of Multicultural Vulnerability: Individual Rights, Identity Groups, and the State', in C. Joppke and S. Lukes (eds.), *Multicultural Questions*. Oxford: Oxford University Press, 87–129.

Shapland, J., J. Willmore, and P. Duff (1985). *Victims in the Criminal Justice System*. Aldershot: Gower.

Sharpe, J. (1999). *Crime in Early Modern England, 1550–1750*. Harlow: Addison Wesley Longman.

Shearing, C. (2001). 'Transforming Security: A South African Experiment', in H. Strang and J. Braithwaite (eds.), *Restorative Justice and Civil Society*. Cambridge: Cambridge University Press, 14–34.

Sherman, L. (2001). 'Two Protestant Ethics and the Spirit of Restoration', in H. Strang and J. Braithwaite (eds.), *Restorative Justice and Civil Society*. Cambridge: Cambridge University Press, 35–55.

——J. Braithwaite, H. Strang, and G. Barnes (1997). *Experiments In Restorative Policing: Reintegrative Shaming of Violence, Drink Driving & Property Crime: A Randomised Controlled Trial*. Canberra: Australian National University and Australian Federal Police. http://www.aic.gov.au/rjustice/rise/progress/1997.html

——D. Gottfredson, D. MacKenzie, J. Eck, P. Reuter, and S. Bushway (1998). *Preventing Crime: What Works, What Doesn't, What's Promising: A Report to the United States Congress*. Washington, DC: National Institute of Justice. http://www.ncjrs.org/works/

——H. Strang, G. Barnes, J. Braithwaite, N. Inkpen, and M.-M. Teh (1998). *Experiments in Restorative Policing: A Progress Report on the Canberra Reintegrative Shaming Experiments (RISE)*. Canberra: Australian National University and Australian Federal Police. http://www.aic.gov.au/rjustice/rise/progress/1998.html

——————and D. Woods (2000). *Recidivism Patterns in the Canberra Reintegrative Shaming Experiments (RISE)*. Canberra: http://www.aic.gov.au/rjustice/rise/recidivism/index.html

Skolnick, J. (1994). 'Police Accountability in the United States', in D. Moore and R. Wettenhall (eds.), *Keeping the Peace: Police Accountability and Oversight*. Canberra: University of Canberra, 106–12.

——and J. Fyfe (1993). *Above the Law: Police and the Excessive Use of Force*. New York: The Free Press.

Smith, S. D. and R. Brazier (1998). *Constitutional and Administrative Law*. London: Penguin.

SMSRMS (SMS Research and Marketing Services) (1999). *Program Evaluation: Ohana Conferencing*. EPIC, Department of Human Services, State of Hawai'i.

Spigelman, J. (1999). *Seen to be Done: The Principle of Open Justice*. Keynote Address to the 31st Australian Legal Convention, Canberra.

——(2000). 'Seen to be Done: the Principle of Open Justice—Part I', *The Australian Law Journal*, 74: 290–7.

SSCLCA (Senate Standing Committee on Legal and Constitutional Affairs), (1994). *Gender Bias and the Judiciary*. Canberra: The Parliament of the Commonwealth of Australia.

Stenning, P. (1995). 'Accountability in the Ministry of the Solicitor General', in P. Stenning (ed.), *Accountability for Criminal Justice: Selected Essays*. Toronto: University of Toronto Press, 44–73.

——(1995). 'Introduction', in P. Stenning (ed.), *Accountability for Criminal Justice*. Toronto: University of Toronto, 3–14.

Stepniak, D. (1995). 'Forum: Televising Court Proceedings', *UNSWLJ*, 18/2: 488–92.

Stevenson, A. (2000). 'Take Me for What I Am', *The Sydney Morning Herald*, 25 May. Sydney.

Stone, L. (1977). *The Family, Sex and Marriage in England, 1500–1800*. London: Weidenfeld and Nicolson.

Strang, H. (2000). 'Victim Participation in a Restorative Justice Process: The Canberra Reintegrative Shaming Experiments.' Unpublished PhD Thesis, Research School of Social Sciences, Canberra: Australian National University.

——(2001). 'Justice for Victims of Young Offenders: The Centrality of Emotional Harm and Restoration', in A. Morris and G. Maxwell (eds.), *Restorative Justice for Juveniles: Conferencing, Mediation and Circles*. Oxford: Hart Publishing, 184–93.

——(2003). *Repair or Revenge*. Oxford: Oxford University Press.

——G. Barnes, J. Braithwaite, and L. Sherman (1999). 'Experiments in Restorative Policing: A Progress Report in the Canberra Reintegrative Shaming Experiments (RISE).' Canberra: Australian National University. http://www.aic.gov.au/rjustice/rise/progress/1999.html

Stuart, B. (1997). *Building Community Justice Partnerships: Community Peacemaking Circles*. Aboriginal Justice Directorate, Department of Justice of Canada.

Stubbs, J. (1995). '"Communitarian" Conferencing and Violence Against Women: A Cautionary Note', in M. Valverde, L. MacLeod, and K. Johnson (eds.), *Wife Assault and the Canadian Criminal Justice System*. Toronto: Centre of Criminology, University of Toronto, 260–89.

Sunstein, C. (2000). 'Deliberative Trouble? Why Groups Go to Extremes', *Yale Law Journal*, 110: 71–119.

Sykes, G. and D. Matza (1957). 'Techniques of Neutralization: A Theory of Delinquency', *American Sociological Review*, 22/6: 664–70.

Tavuchis, N. (1991). *Mea Culpa: A Sociology of Apology and Reconciliation*. California: Stanford University Press.

Taylor, I., P. Walton, and J. Young (1973). *The New Criminology: For a Social Theory of Deviance*. London: Routledge and Kegan Paul.

Thacker, A. (1993). 'Justice Bollen, Community Attitudes, the Power of Judges', *Alternative Law Journal*, 18: 90–1.

Thomas, P. (1998). 'The Changing Nature of Accountability', in G. Peters and D. Savoie (eds.), *Taking Stock: Assessing Public Sector Reforms*: McGill–Queen's University Press, 348–93.

Thompson, E. (1988). *Customs in Common*. London: Penguin Books.

Thompson, L. (1995). *A History of South Africa*. Revised Edition. New Haven: Yale University Press.

Thorsborne, M. (1999). School Violence and Community Conferencing: The Benefits of Restorative Justice. Transformative Justice Australia (Queensland).

Tippet, G. (2001). 'The Usual Suspects', *The Age*, 13 January. Melbourne.

Trimboli, L. (2000). *An Evaluation of the NSW Youth Justice Conferencing Scheme*. Sydney: New South Wales Bureau of Crime Statistics and Research.

Tronto, J. (1993). *Moral Boundaries: A Political Argument for an Ethic of Care*. New York: Routledge.

Tutu, D. (1999). *No Future Without Forgiveness*. London: Rider Books.

TVP (Thames Valley Police) (2000). The Development of Restorative Justice in the Thames Valley Police Area.

Tyler, T. (1990). *Why People Obey the Law*. London: Yale University Press.

Uhr, J. (2001). *Accountability, Scrutiny and Oversight: Background Paper*. The Commonwealth Secretariat, Canberra Workshop.

Umbreit, M. (1997). 'Restorative Justice: Interventions' Impact Varies; Manner of Implementation Critical', *The Crime Victims Report*, May/June: 22.

—— (1998). 'Restorative Justice Through Victim/Offender Mediation: A Multi-Site Assessment', *Western Criminology Review*, 1/1 [Online] http://wcr.sonoma.edu/v1n1/morris.html, 1–18.

—— (1999). 'Avoiding the Marginalization and "McDonaldization" of Victim/Offender Mediation: A Case Study in Moving Toward the Mainstream', in G. Bazemore and L. Walgrave (eds.), *Restorative Juvenile Justice: Repairing the Harm of Youth Crime*. Monsey, New York: Criminal Justice Press, 213–34.

—— R. Coates, and B. Vos (2001). 'Victim Impact of Meeting with Young Offenders: Two Decades of Victim Offender Mediation Practice and Research', in A. Morris and G. Maxwell (eds.), *Restorative Justice for Juveniles: Conferencing, Mediation and Circles*. Oxford: Hart Publishing, 121–43.

Van Ness, D. (1996). 'Restorative Justice and International Human Rights', in D. Galaway and J. Hudson (eds.), *Restorative Justice: International Perspectives*. Monsey, New York: Criminal Justice Press, 17–36.

—— (2002). 'UN Economic and Social Council endorses basic principles on restorative justice', http://www.restorativejustice.org/rj3/Feature/August02/ECOSOC%20Acts.htm

—— A. Morris, and G. Maxwell (2001). 'Introducing Restorative Justice', in A. Morris and G. Maxwell (eds.), *Restorative Justice for Juveniles: Conferencing, Mediation and Circles*. Oxford: Hart Publishing, 3–12.

VDC (Vermont Department of Corrections) (undated). *Program Summary*.

Volpe, M. (1991). 'Mediation in the Criminal Justice System: Process, Promises, Problems', in H. Pepinsky and R. Quinney (eds.), *Criminology as Peacemaking*. Bloomington: Indiana University Press, 194–206.

Walker, S. (1980). *Popular Justice: A History of American Criminal Justice*. New York: Oxford University Press.

——and B. Wright (1994). *Civilian Review of the Police: A National Survey*. Washington: Police Executive Research Forum.

Walmsley, R. (2002). *World Prison Population List (third edition)*. Home Office Findings 166. London: Communications Development Unit, Home Office.

Walsh, J. (2000). 'Restorative Justice Showing Results but Growth is Slow', *Star Tribune*, 16 February. Minneapolis.

Walther, L. and J. Perry (1997). 'The Vermont Reparative Probation Program', *The ICCA Journal on Community Corrections*, December: 26–34.

Warhaft, B., T. Palys, and W. Boyce (1999). ' "This is How We Did It": One Canadian First Nation Community's Efforts to Achieve Aboriginal Justice', *The Australian and New Zealand Journal of Criminology*, 32/2: 168–81.

Warner, K. (1993). 'Family Group Conferences and the Rights of the Offender', in C. Alder and J. Wundersitz (eds.), *Family Conferencing and Juvenile Justice: The Way Forward or Misplaced Optimism?* Australian Institute of Criminology, 141–52.

Webber, J. (1993). 'Individuality, Equality and Difference: Justification for a Parallel System of Aboriginal Justice', in *Aboriginal Peoples and the Justice System: Report of the National Round Table on Aboriginal Justice Issues*. Ottawa: Royal Commission on Aboriginal Peoples, 133–60.

Woolf, Lord (2001). Court of Appeal Criminal Division: Practice Direction (Crime Victims' Personal Statements). *The Times*. http://thetimes. co.uk/ article/ accessed 29 November 2001.

Wright, M. (1999). *Restoring Respect for Justice: A Symposium*. Winchester: Waterside Press.

——(2002). 'The Court as Last Resort: Victim-Sensitive, Community-Based Responses to Crime', *British Journal of Criminology*, 42/3: 654–67.

Yazzie, R. (1998). 'Navajo peacemaking: Implications for adjudication-based systems of justice'.*Contemporary Justice Review*, 1/1/:123–131.

Young, I. M. (1997). *Intersecting Voices: Dilemmas of Gender, Political Philosophy, and Policy*. Princeton: Princeton University Press.

——(2000). *Inclusion and Democracy*. Oxford: Oxford University Press.

Young, R. (2001). 'Just Cops Doing "Shameful" Business? Police-led Restorative Justice and the Lessons of Research', in A. Morris and

G. Maxwell (eds.), *Restorative Justice for Juveniles: Conferencing, Mediation and Circles*. Oxford: Hart Publishing, 195–226.

——and B. Goold (1999). 'Restorative Police Cautioning in Aylesbury—From Degrading to Reintegrative Shaming Ceremonies?', *Criminal Law Review*, 126–38.

Zedner, L. (1994). 'Reparation and Retribution: Are They Reconcilable?', *Modern Law Review*, 57/2: 228–50.

——(1997). 'Victims', in M. Maguire, R. Morgan, and R. Reiner (eds.), *The Oxford Handbook of Criminology*. Oxford: Oxford University Press, 577–608.

——(2002). 'Dangers of Dystopias in Penal Theory', *Oxford Journal of Legal Studies*, 22/2: 341–66.

——(2002). 'Victims', in M. Maguire, R. Morgan, and R. Reiner (eds.), *The Oxford Handbook of Criminology*. Oxford: Oxford University Press, 577–608.

Zehr, H. (1990). *Changing Lenses: A New Focus for Crime and Justice*. Scottsdale, PA: Herald Press.

Zion, J. (1998). 'The Use of Custom and Legal Tradition in the Modern Justice Setting', *Contemporary Justice Review*, 1/1: 133–48.

——and N. McCabe (1982). Navajo Peacemaker Court Manual: A Guide to the Use of the Navajo Peacemaker Court for Judges, Community Leaders and Court Personnel.

——and R. Yazzie (1997). 'Indigenous Law in North American in the Wake of Conquest', *Boston College International and Comparative Law Review*, xx/1: 55–84.

Index

Abel, Richard 9, 20, 143
Aborigines, see indigenous peoples
accountability 3–7, 19–24, 25,
    79–94, 101–19, 123–5,
    159–87, 189–225, 226–39
  classic sense of 42–3
  counterproductive nature of 26,
    50–7
  criticisms of restorative
    justice 19–20, 121, 123–5, 229
  definition of 3, 21, 41–2
  deliberative 79–88, 92–119,
    123–5, 170, 183, 202, 206,
    229–34
  directive 44–5, 106–9, 136, 151,
    162, 200, 208
  financial 43
  formal 43–4, 81–2, 142, 176,
    189–225, 234–9
  guiding principles of 50–7
  history of 43
  informal 43–4, 81, 134, 147, 229
  ongoing 45–6, 140, 162
  persuasive 44–5, 83, 136, 172,
    183, 206, 223
  practitioners' views on 76–7, 80
  purposes of 46–9, 228
  requirement to account 43, 80,
    191
  strengthening deliberative
    accountability 82–94, 101–6,
    189, 234–9
  timing of 45–6, 106–9, 140, 206
agreements 37–8
  compliance with 148–53, 174–7
  concerns about 37–8, 196
  enforcement
    mechanisms 148–59, 174–7

review of 172–7, 206–25
  see also limits on aggrements
alternative dispute resolution 7
apology 9, 15, 36, 87, 111, 140,
    149, 230
Ashworth, Andrew 18, 31, 164
Australia see, Australian Federal
    Police Diversionary
    Conferencing, Canberra, ACT;
    Community Conferencing,
    QLD; Police Conferencing,
    Wagga Wagga, NSW; School
    Conferencing, Sunshine Coast,
    QLD; Youth Justice
    Conferencing, NSW
Australian Federal Court
  experience with open justice 49
Australian Federal Police
    Diversionary Conferencing,
    Canberra, ACT 66, 69, 70, 117,
    133, 136, 147, 179, 192, 243–5
Ayres, Ian 175–7, 221

Bargen, Jenny 179
Barnett, Randy 65
Bayley, David 42, 127, 130, 135,
    139, 141, 146, 147
Blagg, Harry 33, 37, 39, 117–18,
    138
Braithwaite, John 7, 10, 11, 12, 83,
    88, 108, 111, 124, 164, 175–7,
    209, 212, 232
Brockie, Jenny 127
Brown, Jennifer 16, 19, 39
Bush, Robert 118

Canada
  Winnipeg, Manitoba 215

see also Canim Lake Family
Violence Program, BC;
Carcross Circle Program,
Yukon Territory; Toronto
Community Council, Ontario;
Vancouver Restorative Justice
Programme, BC
Cane, Peter 46
Canim Lake Family Violence
Program, BC 63
Carcross Circle Program, Yukon
Territory 67, 70, 103–4, 154,
193, 207, 221, 259–61
Carr, Bob 1
Cartwright, John 80, 192
Chan, Janet 127
charivari, *see* 'rough music'
*Children, Young Persons and Their
Families Act* (1989), NZ 91,
161
Christie, Nils 9, 31
circles 31, 66–7, 73, 100, 111, 154,
156–7, 193, 232
Clotworthy case 212–18
Cohen, Stan 163
Coker, Donna 110, 114, 116
communication 53
different modes of 109–18,
141–2
difficulties in 84
community
role in restorative justice 29–33,
95–106
volunteers 16, 96, 137, 154–8
Community Conferencing, Central
City Neighbourhoods
Partnership, MN 66, 70, 145,
153, 169, 173, 178–80, 192,
207, 253–4
Community Conferencing,
QLD 66, 70, 71, 103, 131,
169, 192, 201, 207, 251–3
community policing 146–7
conferences 19, 22, 66

breaks in 93
police-led conferencing 138
professional domination of 37
see also meetings
Connections Program, Minnesota
Correctional Facility, MN 68,
70, 151, 155, 156, 159, 174,
231, 278–9
consistency between outcomes 4–5,
38, 213, 216, 235, 239
convenors 9, 70, 118–21, 178
co-convenors 72, 156, 183
concerns about 36–7, 137, 182
ideal role of 118–21, 219, 220,
233–4
identity of 71, 137, 140
scrutiny of 183–4, 186
skilful convening 120, 177
Cop it Sweet 127
Crawford, Adam 95, 97, 155
Crime and Disorder Act (1998),
UK 247, 270
*Crime, Shame and
Reintegration* 10–12
Criminal Code, Canada 218
Criminal Justice Act (1985),
NZ 214, 218
criminal justice system
criticisms of 7, 26, 109, 209
Cunneen, Chris 33, 39, 128
customary law, *see* indigenous
justice

Daly, Kathleen 28, 33, 34, 38
Delgado, Richard 14, 40, 139
deliberative democracy 5, 238–9
reinvigorating representative
democracy 238–9
restorative justice as 5
transforming opinions 94
Doerfler, David 174, 179
domestic violence and restorative
justice 10, 20, 35, 37, 40, 86,
114

drink drivers 11, 41, 69, 89–90,
102, 105–6, 131, 199, 201,
220, 232
drug-related offences 31, 34, 41,
69, 79, 156–7, 202, 231
Dryzek, John 5, 113

Eades, Diana 84
Ella Duncan, Marcia 100
European Court of Human
Rights 211, 220
evaluation of restorative justice
programmes 10–12

Family Group Conferencing, New
Zealand 37, 70, 71, 74, 83,
117, 131, 137, 161, 192, 207,
215, 222, 241–2
Feeley, Malcolm 168
feminist perspectives
on informal justice 28
on privacy 201
Fishkin, James 95
Folger, Joseph 118
forgiveness 2, 9, 11, 12, 32, 36,
120, 213
formal justice 4–5, 23, 234–9
as check on restorative
justice 208–12, 216–21
ideal relationship with restorative
justice 4–5, 23–24, 234–9
influenced by restorative
justice 212–16
see also criminal justice system
Foucault, Michel 17
Fredrick H. Tuttle Middle School,
South Burlington, VT 67, 70,
92, 193, 257
Funston, Richard 93, 126–7
Fyfe, James 144

Gans, Herbert 62
Garland, David 6, 7, 18, 31, 125,
151

gatekeepers 11, 18, 40, 161–2, 165,
187
Gerard, Gena 145, 173
Gibbons, John 109
Goodin, Robert 47, 53, 210
Grabosky, Peter 185
Grillo, Tina 36

Hagan, John 88
Harris, Nathan 96
Hennessy, Nancy 163
Hines, Dave 166–7, 180
Hooper, Stephen 37
Howley, Pat 101
Hoyle, Carolyn 19, 125, 137
human rights 5, 210, 211, 220, 225
ECHR & ICCPR 191, 199
see also limits
humiliation, see stigmatization

I Am a Thief T-shirt 1, 12, 15, 18,
37, 89, 196, 220, 227
Ignatieff, Michael 17–18
indigenous justice 2, 14, 28–9, 31,
33, 39, 97–101, 104, 174,
209–10
changes in 210
role of elders 99–101
see also informal justice, Navajo
Nation
indigenous peoples 39, 85, 117,
127–8, 138, 211
informal justice 9, 226–7
tyranny of 13–17, 227

Johnstone, Gerry 10, 29, 35–6,
40
Jones, Carol 178
Joyi, Chief Anderson 112–13
judges 2, 4–5, 18, 23, 47–9, 162,
167–8, 212
accountability of 40, 44, 50, 56
as form of accountability 40,
167–8

role in reviewing agreements 23,
  208–22
juries 96, 107, 229
'Just Youth' Project, Spectrum
  Youth and Family Services,
  Burlington, VT 68, 70, 71,
  162, 179–80, 192, 275
juvenile justice 1, 6, 15, 39, 70,
  91
Juvenile Justice Act (1992), Qld,
  Australia 131, 152, 251

Keenan v the United Kingdom
  App No. 00027229/95
  (3 April 2001) 220
Kirby, Michael 195, 204
Kramer, Hillary 162, 180
Krog, Antjie 112–13
Kymlicka, Will 98, 210

La Prairie, Carol 39, 100,
law, *see* formal justice
legal aid advice
  to young offenders 92, 220
legislation *see*
  *Children, Young Persons and
    Their Families Act* (1989), NZ;
  Crime and Disorder Act (1998),
    UK; *Criminal Code*, Canada;
  Criminal Justice Act (1985),
    NZ; *Juvenile Justice Act* (1992),
    QLD, Australia; *Minnesota
    Statute* (1998); *Young
    Offenders Act* (1997), NSW,
    Australia; *Youth Justice and
    Criminal Evidence Act*
    (1999), UK
legitimacy
  as aim of accountability 25, 44,
    48–9
  of governments 208–9, 238–9
Lenman, Bruce 16
limits on agreements 23, 38, 173,
  216, 235

based on human rights and public
  safety 5, 216–21, 236
love 3

McBarnet, Doreen 8, 194
McCold, Paul 26, 95, 137
McDougall, James 179
McLeod, Carolyn 162, 214
Makkai, Toni 50, 144
Mantziaris, Christos 100
Marshall, Geoffrey 45
Marshall, Tony 30, 65, 68
Martin, David 100
Maxwell, Gabrielle 35, 37, 42, 91,
  113, 116, 118–19, 129, 131,
  181, 215, 228
media 191–207
  access to restorative justice 70,
    75, 191–2
  coverage of court cases 194–6
mediation sessions, *see* meetings
mediators, *see* convenors
meetings
  benefits of 7–12
  concerns about 12–21, 33–41,
    82–92
  decision-making in 79–122
  flexibility of 106–18, 123
mercy 217, 219, 236
Merry, Sally Engle 119, 212
Milner, Neal 119
Minnesota Statute (1998) 261
Minow, Martha 27, 36
Morris, Allison 34–5, 42, 68, 73–4,
  91, 113, 116, 118–19, 129,
  131, 181, 215, 228
Mugford, Stephen 26, 29, 102,
Mulgan, Richard 41–3, 45, 52, 55,
  100

Navajo Peacemaking, Navajo
  Nation, AZ 27, 67, 70, 73, 99,
  104, 115–16, 118, 193, 200,
  207, 210, 219, 237, 257–9

nets of social control,
  widening 39–40, 164
neutralization, techniques of 2, 144
New South Wales, *see* Police
  Conferencing, Wagga Wagga;
  Youth Justice Conferencing
New South Wales Children's Legal
  Service 93, 126, 217
New Zealand, *see* Family Group
  Conferencing; Waitakere
  District Court Restorative
  Justice Pilot, Auckland
non-domination 22, 82, 85–96,
  121–2, 132, 134, 210, 237–9
non-governmental
  organizations 211, 223
Northside Community Justice
  Committee, MN 67, 70, 116,
  156, 158–9, 192, 207, 231,
  261–2

O'Connell, Terry 80, 119–20, 141,
  166, 174, 204–5, 223
offences
  handled by restorative justice
  programmes 39–40, 164
offender(s)
  as a label 10
  in restorative justice
  meetings 79–95, 121
'Ohana conferences, Hawaii' 111,
  156
outcomes, *see* agreements

Palmer, Michael 13–14, 106, 118,
  152
panels 67
  see also meetings
Papua New Guinea 101
Parker, Christine 124, 204, 209,
  212, 221–2
Parker, Geoffrey 14, 16
participation
  as restorative justice ideal 30

personalism
  as restorative justice ideal 26
Pildes, Richard 201
plurality
  of deliberation 86, 91, 94–5,
  136, 156
police
  accountability 22, 124–47,
  158
  as convenors 136–8
  culture 127, 234
Police Conferencing, Wagga
  Wagga 70–1, 80, 111, 117,
  141–2, 151, 166, 174, 192–3,
  201, 242–3
Pollard, Gail 131
power
  accountability as a check on 3,
  34, 36, 42, 46, 191
  imbalances 20, 79–95, 123–40
Power, Michael 22
Power, Patrick 40, 193, 201
Pranis, Kay 97, 129
Pribyl, Kelly 175
Prince William County Restorative
  Justice Program, VA 69, 70,
  192, 277–8
prison 18
  based restorative justice
  programmes, *see* Connections
  Program, Minnesota
  Correctional Facility, MN;
  Victim/Offender Mediation/
  Dialogue Program, TX
procedural safeguards 19–21
  see also accountability and
  informal justice
proportionality 5, 28, 29, 38, 216,
  235, 239
public
  attendance in court 190–1,
  194
  attendance in restorative justice
  meetings 189, 193

attitudes towards
punishment 17–18, 33–4
punishment
definition of 34
punitiveness 17–18, 34
see also public; stigmatization
Putnam, Robert 50

Queensland, Australia, see School
Conferencing, Sunshine Coast,
QLD; Community
Conferencing, QLD

R v Gladue 214
R v Morin 216
Rawls, John 95
REAL Justice 74, 102, 110, 119,
120, 164, 224
recidivism, see reoffending
reconciliation 2, 3, 14, 26, 33, 36,
120, 226
Reiner, Robert 124, 234
reintegration 2, 16, 18, 21, 25,
28–9, 83, 95, 155, 200, 201,
217, 226, 228
religion 28, 116
reoffending 10, 11
reparation 27–8
Reparative Boards, Vermont
Department of Corrections,
Burlington, VT 67, 69, 70, 71,
80, 86, 102, 156, 183, 193,
201, 204, 205, 267–8
research methods 60–6
participant observation 61–6
restorative justice
accommodating cultural
difference 97–101
accommodating different
communicative styles 109–18
benefits of 7–12
coercive v voluntary 83–5,
121
criticisms of 12–20, 33–41

definition of 25–32
development of 6–7
ideal relationship with formal
justice 4–5, 23, 234–9
outcomes, see agreements and
limits
procedural concerns
about 19–20
relationship with criminal
proceedings 69
relationship with punishment 34
types of meetings 66–8
Retzinger, Suzanne 35
rights 32
individual versus collective 209
to fair trial 200
RISE (Re-Integrative Shaming
Experiments) experiment
11, 84, 89, 103, 131, 182,
244
Roberts, Simon 13–14, 106, 118,
152
Rock, Paul 8, 115, 194
Rorty, Richard 32
'rough music' 15, 18, 227

Scheff, Thomas 35
School Conferencing, Sunshine
Coast, Queensland,
Australia 66, 129, 133, 256
sentencing panels, see panels
Seymour, John 40
shame 10
modern resurgence of 15, 18
'name and shame' campaign 18
reintegrative shaming 10, 29; see
also Braithwaite, John;
reintegration
shaming practices 15
Shapland, Joanna 14
Shearing, Clifford 119, 175
Skolnick, Jerome 134–5, 144,
146
Sobey, Bob 133, 147

South Africa
community courts 17, 227
customary law 27, 33
Truth and Reconciliation
Commission 36, 65, 112, 115
see also Zwelethemba
Peacemaker Committee,
Western Cape
South St Paul Restorative Justice
Council, St Paul, MN 67, 70,
71, 103, 104, 116, 133, 148,
154, 169, 193, 207, 262–3
Stanefski, Michael 104, 148, 154
state
role in restorative justice 91–3,
233–9; *see also* formal justice
weak states 14–15, 212
Stenning, Philip 3, 20, 43, 80, 81
stigmatization 2, 3, 14–16, 35, 88,
196, 200, 220, 228
Stone, Lawrence 14–15
story-telling
in restorative justice meetings 10,
114–18, 141–2
Strang, Heather 9, 38, 90, 139,
232
Sunstein, Cass 94
supporters in meetings 86–92,
138–40
difficulties in finding 87–8
government funded 91–2

Tavuchis, Nicholas 9
teachers 129, 133, 135, 144, 160,
172, 173
as convenors 71, 72, 136
Thames Valley Police Restorative
Justice Programme, UK 66, 70,
74, 117, 132, 136, 137, 145,
151, 174, 192, 246–8
Thompson, E.P. 2, 15
Thorsborne, Marg 81, 129
Toronto Community Council,
Ontario 268–9

trust
importance to compliance 50,
53, 107–8, 144
truth
adversarial *v* restorative
conceptions of 115
Tutu, Archbishop Desmond 27
Tyler, Tom 48, 142

ubuntu 27
Uhr, John 43, 54
Umbreit, Mark 6, 42, 178
United Kingdom, *see* Thames Valley
Police Restorative Justice
Programme; Youth Offender
Panels, England and Wales
United Nations
principles on restorative justice 7
United States
number of restorative justice
programmes 6
see also Community
Conferencing, Central City
Neighbourhoods Partnership,
MN; Connections Program,
Minnesota Correctional
Facility, MN; Fredrick H.
Tuttle Middle School, South
Burlington, VT; 'Just Youth'
Project, Spectrum Youth and
Family Services, Burlington,
VT; Navajo Peacemaking,
Navajo Nation, AZ; Northside
Community Justice
Committee, MN; Prince
William County Restorative
Justice Program, VA;
Reparative Boards, Vermont
Department of Corrections,
Burlington, VT; South St Paul
Restorative Justice Council, St
Paul, MN; Victim/Offender
Mediation/Dialogue Program,
TX; Washington County

Community Justice, MN;
Woodbury Police
Conferencing, MN

Vancouver Restorative Justice
Programme, BC 67, 70, 97, 99,
192–3, 269–70
victim(s)
advocacy 91, 208, 223
as a label 10
blaming 108
and burdens imposed by
restorative justice 13–14, 154
exclusion from formal criminal
justice system 8–9
needs 27, 127
participation in restorative
justice 85–92
supporters 86–92
victim impact statements 8
victim–offender mediation 39, 42
development of 67–8
Victim Offender Mediation/
Dialogue Program, TX 70, 71,
72, 92, 102, 151, 169, 174,
179, 192, 202, 272–4
vigilantism 1, 14–16

Waitakere District Court
Restorative Justice Pilot,
Auckland, New Zealand 70,
74, 92, 137, 150, 192, 207,
255–6
Washington County Community
Justice, MN 68, 70, 74, 162,
192, 207, 214, 276–7
Wengert, Michaela 162, 168

Woodbury Police Conferencing,
MN 66, 69, 70, 71, 117, 136,
137, 163, 166, 169, 180, 192,
234, 245–6
Woods, Mariellen 162, 180

Young, Iris Marion 109, 114–17
Young, Richard 19, 125, 132, 137,
234
Young Offenders Act (1997), NSW,
Australia 62, 73, 93, 148, 165,
193, 248
Youth Justice and Criminal
Evidence Act (1999), UK
Youth Justice Conferencing,
NSW 1, 66, 69, 70, 76, 79, 80,
99, 123 162, 163, 179, 192,
193, 201, 248–51
see also New South Wales
Children's Legal Service; Young
Offenders Act (1997), NSW,
Australia
Youth Offender Panels, England
and Wales 67, 70, 73, 83, 97,
131, 154, 156, 171, 192, 207,
270–2

Zedner, Lucia 6, 7, 8, 29, 127, 189,
223, 226
Zehr, Howard 3, 26, 27, 28, 31
Zion, James 17
Zwelethemba Peacemaker
Committee, Western Cape,
South Africa 67, 69, 70, 82,
86 7, 97, 101, 108, 118 9,
143, 131, 134, 160, 175, 179,
189, 202, 223, 264–6